ADVANCED
GMAT QUANT

Math Strategy Guide

This supplemental guide provides in-depth and comprehensive explanations of the advanced math skills necessary for the highest-level performance on the GMAT.

Advanced GMAT Quant Strategy Guide

10-digit International Standard Book Number: 1-935707-22-6
13-digit Internaxtional Standard Book Number: 978-1-935707-15-8
eISBN: 978-0-974806-98-3

Note: *GMAT, Graduate Management Admission Test, Graduate Management Admission Council,*
and *GMAC* are all registered trademarks of Educational Testing Services, which neither
sponsors nor is affiliated in any way with this product.

This Advanced GMAT Quant Math Guide is a supplement to our

8 GUIDE INSTRUCTIONAL SERIES

Math GMAT Strategy Guides

Number Properties
(ISBN: 978-0-982423-84-4)

Fractions, Decimals, & Percents
(ISBN: 978-0-982423-82-0)

Equations, Inequalities, & VICs
(ISBN: 978-0-982423-81-3)

Word Translations
(ISBN: 978-0-982423-87-5)

Geometry
(ISBN: 978-0-982423-83-7)

Verbal GMAT Strategy Guides

Critical Reasoning
(ISBN: 978-0-982423-80-6)

Reading Comprehension
(ISBN: 978-0-982423-85-1)

Sentence Correction
(ISBN: 978-0-982423-86-8)

ManhattanGMAT
the new standard

May 31st, 2011

Dear Student,

Thank you for picking up a copy of *Advanced GMAT Math*. This book is aptly titled—it's designed to provide you with the most advanced knowledge and skills you'll need to perform at the highest level on the GMAT quantitative section. Be sure that you have mastered the content found in our core strategy guides before tackling these tougher math concepts. We hope it ends up being the most challenging and rewarding GMAT quant book you'll put your hands on.

As with most accomplishments, there were many people involved in the creation of the book you're holding. First and foremost is Zeke Vanderhoek, the founder of MG Prep and Manhattan GMAT. Zeke was a lone tutor in New York when he started the Company in 2000. Now, eleven years later, the Company has Instructors and offices nationwide and contributes to the studies and successes of thousands of students each year.

Our Manhattan GMAT Strategy Guides are based on the continuing experiences of our Instructors and students. For this *Advanced GMAT Math Guide*, we are particularly indebted to Tate Shafer and Emily Sledge who drove the development of this book over a long period of time and deserve kudos for the countless hours spent creating this book. Many other instructors, including Josh Braslow, Matt Cressy, Steven Jupiter, Jad Lee, and Dave Mahler, made valuable contributions. Dan McNaney and Cathy Huang provided their design expertise to make the books as user-friendly as possible, and Liz Krisher made sure all the moving pieces came together at just the right time. Finally, many thanks to Chris Ryan. Beyond providing content additions and edits for this book (and more than a few sleepless nights), Chris continues to be the driving force behind all of our curriculum and instruction efforts. His leadership is invaluable.

At Manhattan GMAT, we continually aspire to provide the best Instructors and resources possible. We hope that you'll find our commitment manifest in this book. If you have any questions or comments, please email me at dgonzalez@manhattangmat.com. I'll look forward to reading your comments, and I'll be sure to pass them along to our curriculum team.

Thanks again, and best of luck preparing for the GMAT!

Sincerely,

Dan Gonzalez
President
Manhattan GMAT

HOW TO ACCESS YOUR ONLINE RESOURCES

If you...

⊚ **are a registered Manhattan GMAT student**

and have received this book as part of your course materials, you have AUTOMATIC
access to ALL of our online resources. This includes all practice exams, question banks,
and online updates to this book. To access these resources, follow the instructions in
the Welcome Guide provided to you at the start of your program. Do NOT follow the
instructions below.

⊚ **purchased this book from the Manhattan GMAT Online store or**
at one of our Centers

1. Go to: http://www.manhattangmat.com/practicecenter.cfm

2. Log in using the username and password used when your account was set up.
Your one year of online access begins on the day that you purchase the book from the
Manhattan GMAT online store or at one of our centers.

⊚ **purchased this book at a retail location**

1. Create an account with Manhattan GMAT at the website: https://www.manhattangmat.com/createaccount.cfm

2. Go to: http://www.manhattangmat.com/access.cfm

3. Follow the instructions on the screen.

Your one year of online access begins on the day that you register your book at the above URL.

You only need to register your product ONCE at the above URL. To use your online resources any
time AFTER you have completed the registration process, login to the following URL:
http://www.manhattangmat.com/practicecenter.cfm

Please note that online access is non-transferable. This means that only NEW and UNREGISTERED copies of the book
will grant you online access. Previously used books will not provide any online resources.

⊚ **purchased an e-book version of this book**

1. Create an account with Manhattan GMAT at the website:
https://www.manhattangmat.com/createaccount.cfm

2. Email a copy of your purchase receipt to books@manhattangmat.com to activate
your resources. Please be sure to use the same email address to create an account
that you used to purchase the e-book.

For any technical issues, email books@manhattangmat.com or call 800-576-4628.

Please refer to the following page for a description of the online resources that come with this book.

YOUR ONLINE RESOURCES

Your purchase includes ONLINE ACCESS to the following:

 Advanced GMAT Quant Online Question Bank

The Bonus Online Drill Sets for ADVANCED GMAT QUANT consist of extra practice questions (with detailed explanations) that test the variety of Advanced Math concepts and skills covered in this book. These questions provide you with extra practice beyond the problem sets contained in this book. You may use our online timer to practice your pacing by setting time limits for each question in the banks.

Online Updates to the Contents in this Book

The content presented in this book is updated periodically to ensure that it reflects the GMAT's most current trends. You may view all updates, including any known errors or changes, upon registering for online access.

TABLE OF CONTENTS

g

Part III

9. WORKOUT SETS   229

TABLE OF CONTENTS

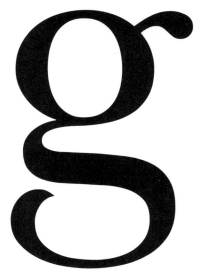

Chapter 0

of

ADVANCED GMAT QUANT

INTRODUCTION

In This Chapter . . .

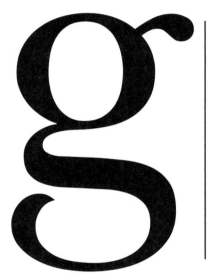

A Qualified Welcome

Welcome to Advanced GMAT Quant! In this venue, we decided to be a little nerdy and call the introduction "Chapter 0." After all, the point (0, 0) in the coordinate plane is called the *origin*, right? (That's the first and last math joke in this book.)

Unfortunately, we have to qualify our welcome right away, because **this book isn't for everyone**. At least, it's not for everyone *right away*.

Who Should Use This Book

You should use this book if you meet the following conditions:

- You have achieved at least 70th percentile math scores on GMAT practice exams.

- You have worked through the 5 math-focused Manhattan GMAT Strategy Guides, which are organized around broad topics:

    o   Number Properties
    o   Fractions, Decimals, & Percents
    o   Equations, Inequalities, & VICs (Algebra)
    o   Word Translations
    o   Geometry

- Or you have worked through similar material from another company.

- You are already comfortable with the core principles in these topics.

- You want to raise your performance to the 90th percentile or higher.

- You want to become a significantly smarter test-taker.

If you match this description, then please turn the page!

If you don't match this description, then please recognize that you will probably find this book too difficult at this stage of your preparation.

For now, you are better off working on topic-focused material, such as our Strategy Guides, and ensuring that you have mastered that material *before* you return to this book.

Try Them

Take a look at the following three problems, which are very difficult. They are at least as hard as any real GMAT problem—probably even harder.

Go ahead and give these problems a try. You should not expect to solve any of them in 2 minutes. In fact, you might find yourself completely stuck. If that's the case, switch gears. Do your best to eliminate some wrong choices and take an educated guess.

Try-It #0-1

A jar is filled with red, white, and blue tokens that are equivalent except for their color. The chance of randomly selecting a red token, replacing it, then randomly selecting a white token is the same as the chance of randomly selecting a blue token. If the number of tokens of every color is a multiple of 3, what is the smallest possible total number of tokens in the jar?

(A) 9   (B) 12   (C) 15   (D) 18   (E) 21

Try-It #0-2

Arrow $\overline{AB}$, which is a line segment exactly 5 units long with an arrowhead at A, is to be constructed in the xy-plane. The x- and y-coordinates of A and B are to be integers that satisfy the inequalities $0 \le x \le 9$ and $0 \le y \le 9$. How many different arrows with these properties can be constructed?

(A) 50   (B) 168   (C) 200   (D) 368   (E) 536

Try-It #0-3

In the diagram to the right, what is the value of x?

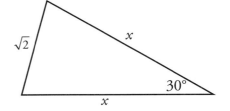

(A) $1+\sqrt{2}$ (B) $1+\sqrt{3}$ (C) $2\sqrt{2}$ (D) $\sqrt{2}+\sqrt{3}$ (E) $2\sqrt{3}$

(Note: this problem does not require any non-GMAT math, such as trigonometry.)

The Purpose of This Book

This book is designed to prepare you for the *most difficult* math problems on the GMAT.

So... what *is* a difficult math problem, from the point of view of the GMAT?

A difficult math problem is one that *most* GMAT test takers get wrong under exam conditions. In fact, this is essentially how the GMAT measures difficulty: by the percent of test takers who get the problem wrong.

So, what kinds of math questions do most test takers get wrong? What characterizes these problems? There are two kinds of features:

1) **Topical nuances or obscure principles**

   - Connected to a particular topic
   - Inherently hard to grasp, or simply unfamiliar
   - Easy to mix up

   These topical nuances are largely covered in the Advanced sections of the Manhattan GMAT Strategy Guides. The book you are holding includes many problems that involve topical nuances. However, the complete theory of Advanced Divisibility & Primes, for instance, is not repeated here.

2) **Complex structures**

   - Based only on simple principles but have non-obvious solution paths
   - May require multiple steps
   - May make you consider many cases
   - May combine more than one topic
   - May need a flash of real insight to complete
   - May make you change direction or switch strategies along the way

Complex structures are essentially *disguises* for simpler content. These disguises may be difficult to pierce. The path to the answer is twisted or clouded somehow.

To solve problems that have simple content but complex structures, **we need approaches that are both *more general* and *more creative*. This book concentrates on such approaches.**

The three problems on the previous page have complex structures. We will return to them shortly. In the meantime, let's look at another problem.

An Illustration

Give this problem a whirl. Don't go on until you have spent a few minutes on it—or until you have figured it out!

Try-It #0-4

What should the next number in this sequence be?

1   2   9   64   ___

Note: this problem is *not* exactly GMAT-like, because there is no mathematically definite rule. However, you'll know when you've solved the problem. The answer will be elegant.

This problem has very simple content but a complex structure. Researchers in cognitive science have used sequence-completion problems such as this one to develop realistic models of human thought. Here is one such model, simplified but practical.

Top-Down Brain and Bottom-Up Brain

To solve the sequence-completion problem above, we need two kinds of thinking:

We can even say that we need two types of brain.

The Top-Down brain is your conscious self. If you imagine the contents of your head as a big corporation, then your Top-Down brain is the CEO, responding to input, making decisions and issuing orders. In cognitive science, the Top-Down brain is called the "executive function." Top-Down thinking and planning is indispensible to any problem-solving process.

But the corporation in your head is a big place. For one thing, how does information get to the CEO? And how pre-processed is that information?

The Bottom-Up brain is your PRE-conscious processor. After raw sensory input arrives, your Bottom-Up brain processes that input extensively *before* it reaches your Top-Down brain.

For instance, to your optic nerve, every word on this page is simply a lot of black squiggles. Your Bottom-Up brain immediately turns these squiggles into letters, joins the letters into words, summons relevant images and concepts, and finally serves these images and concepts to your Top-Down brain. This all happens automatically and swiftly. In fact, it takes effort to *interrupt* this process. Also, unlike your Top-Down brain, which does things one at a time, your Bottom-Up brain can easily do many things at once.

How does all this relate to solving the sequence problem above?

Each of your brains needs the other one to solve difficult problems.

Your Top-Down brain needs your Bottom-Up brain to notice patterns, sniff out valuable leads, and make quick, intuitive leaps and connections.

But your Bottom-Up brain is inarticulate and distractible. Only your Top-Down brain can build plans, pose explicit questions, follow procedures, and state findings.

An analogy may clarify the ideal relationship between your Top-Down and your Bottom-Up brains. Imagine that you are trying to solve a tough murder case. To find all the clues in the woods, you need both a savvy detective and a sharp-nosed bloodhound.

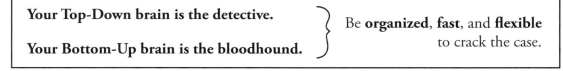

Your Top-Down brain is the detective.

Your Bottom-Up brain is the bloodhound.

Be **organized**, **fast**, and **flexible** to crack the case.

To solve difficult GMAT problems, try to harmonize the activity of your two brains by following an organized, fast, and flexible problem-solving process.

Organized

You need a general step-by-step approach to guide you. One such approach, inspired by the expert mathematician George Polya, is ***Understand, Plan, Solve***:

1) ***Understand*** the problem first.

2) ***Plan*** your attack by adapting known techniques in new ways.

3) ***Solve*** by executing your plan.

You may never have thought you needed steps 1 and 2 before. It may have been easy or even automatic for you to *Understand* easier problems and to *Plan* your approach to them. As a result, you may tend to dive right into the *Solve* stage. This is a bad strategy. Mathematicians know that the real math on hard problems is not *Solve*; the real math is *Understand* and *Plan*.

Fast

Speed is important for its own sake on the GMAT, of course. What you may not have thought as much about is that being fast can also lower your stress level and promote good process. If you know you can *Solve* quickly, then you can take more time to comprehend the question, consider the given information, and select a strategy. To this end, make sure that you can rapidly complete calculations and manipulate algebraic expressions.

At the same time, avoid focusing too much on speed, especially in the early *Understand* and *Plan* stages of your problem-solving process. A little extra time invested upfront can pay off handsomely later.

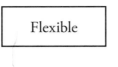

To succeed against difficult problems, you sometimes have to "unstick" yourself. Expect to run into brick walls and encounter dead ends. Returning to first principles and to the general process (e.g., making sure that you fully *Understand* the problem) can help you back up out of the mud.

Let's return to the sequence problem and play out a sample interaction between the two brains. The path is not linear; there are several dead ends, as you would expect. This dialogue will lead to the answer, so don't start reading until you've given the problem a final shot (if you haven't already solved it). The Top-Down brain is labeled TD; the Bottom-Up brain is labeled BU.

1	2	9	64	___	TD: "Okay, let's *Understand* this thing. They've given us some numbers, and they want us to find the number that 'should' go in the blank, whatever 'should' means. What's our *Plan*? Hmm. No idea. Stare at the numbers they gave us?" *BU notices that $9 = 3^2$ and $64 = 8^2$. Likes the two squares.*
1	2	3^2	8^2	___	TD: "Let's write in the two squares."
1	2	3^2	8^2	___	*BU notices that 1 is a square too.*
sq	no	sq	sq	___	TD: "Are they all perfect squares? No, since 2 isn't." *BU doesn't like this break in the pattern.*
					TD: "Let's back up. We could try primes, factoring all the way. $8 = 2^3$, and so $8^2 = (2^3)^2 = 2^6$."
1	2	3^2	2^6	___	*BU notices $6 = 2 \times 3$, but so what.*
					TD: "Let's write 2^6 as $(2^3)^2$. Anything there?"
1	2	3^2	$(2^3)^2$	___	*BU notices lots of 2's and 3's, but so what.*
					TD: "Let's keep looking at this. Are the 2's and 3's stacked somehow?"
1	2	3^2	$(2^3)^2$	___	*BU notices no real pattern. There's 2–3–2 twice as you go across, but so what. And the 1 is weird by itself.*
					TD: "No good leads there. Hmm... Let's go back to the original and try taking differences."
1	2	9	64	___	*BU notices no pattern. The numbers look even uglier.*
1	7	55			
					TD: "Hmm. No good. Go back to original numbers again. What's going on there?"
1	2	9	64	___	*BU notices that the numbers are growing quickly, like squares or exponentials.*
					TD: "Must have something to do with those squares. Let's look at those again."
1^2	2	3^2	8^2	___	*BU notices a gap on the left, among the powers.*

$1^?$	2^1	3^2	8^2	___	TD: "Let's look at 2. Write it with exponents... $2 = 2^1$. Actually, 1 doesn't have to be 1^2. 1 can be to any power and still be 1. The power is a question mark." *BU notices 2^1 then 3^2. Likes the counting numbers.* *BU really wants 1, 2, 3, 4 somehow.*
$1^?$	2^1	3^2	$4^{??}$	___	TD: "Let's try 4 in that last position. Could the last term be 4 somehow?" *BU likes the look of this. 8 and 4 are related.*
$1^?$	2^1	3^2	4^3	___	TD: "64 is 4 to the what... $4^2 = 16$, times another 4 equals 64, so it's 4 to the third power. That fits." *BU is thrilled. 1, 2, 3, 4 below and 1, 2, 3 up top.*
1^0	2^1	3^2	4^3	___	TD: "Extend left. It's 1^0. Confirmed. The bases are 1, 2, 3, 4, etc. and the powers are 0, 1, 2, 3, etc." *BU is content.*
1^0	2^1	3^2	4^3	$\underline{5^4}$	TD: "So the answer is 5^4, which is 25^2, or 625."

Your own process was almost certainly different in the details. Also, your internal dialogue was very rapid—parts of it probably only took fractions of a second to transpire. After all, you think at the speed of thought.

The important thing is to recognize how the Bottom-Up bloodhound and the Top-Down detective worked together in the case above. The TD detective set the overall agenda and then pointed the BU bloodhound at the clues. The bloodhound did practically all the "noticing," which in some sense is where all the magic happened. But sometimes the bloodhound got stuck, so the detective had to intervene, consciously trying a new path. For instance, 64 reads so strongly as 8^2 that the detective had to actively give up on that reading.

There are so many possible meaningful sequences that it wouldn't have made sense to apply a strict *recipe* from the outset: "Try X first, then Y, then Z..." Such an algorithm would require hundreds of possibilities. Should we always look for 1, 2, 3, 4? Should we *never* find differences or prime factors, because they weren't that useful here? Of course not! A computer can rapidly and easily apply a complicated algorithm with hundreds of steps, but humans can't. (If you are an engineer or programmer, maybe you *wish* you could program your own brain, but so far, that's not possible!)

What we *are* good at, though, is noticing patterns. Our Bottom-Up brain is extremely powerful—far more powerful than any computer yet built.

As we gather problem-solving tools, the task becomes **knowing when to apply which tool.** This task becomes harder as problem structures become more complex. But if we deploy our Bottom-Up bloodhound according to a general problem-solving process such as *Understand, Plan, Solve*, then we can count on the bloodhound to notice the relevant aspects of the problem—the aspects that tell us which tool to use.

Train your Top-Down brain to be:

- **Organized** in an overall approach to difficult problems,
- **Fast** at executing mechanical steps, and
- **Flexible** enough to abandon unpromising leads and try new paths.

This way, your Bottom-Up brain can do its best work. You will be able to solve problems that you might have given up on before. Speaking of which...

Giving Up Without Giving Up

This book is intended to make you smarter.

It is also intended to make you *scrappier*.

You might have failed to solve any of these Try-It problems, even with unlimited time.

The real question is this: what do you do when you run into a brick wall?

The problems in this book are designed to push you to the limit—and past. If you have traditionally been good at paper-based standardized tests, then you may be used to being able to solve practically every problem the *"textbook"* way. Problems that forced you to get down & dirty—to work backwards from the choices, to estimate and eliminate—may have annoyed you.

Well, you need to shift your thinking. As you know, the GMAT is an adaptive test. This means that if you keep getting questions right, the test will keep getting harder... and harder... and harder...

At some point, there will appear a monster problem, one that announces "I must break you." In your battle with this problem, you could lose the bigger war—whether or not you ultimately conquer this particular problem. Maybe it takes you 8 minutes, or it beats you up so badly that your head starts pounding. This will take its toll on your score.

A major purpose of this book is to help you learn to give up on the stereotypical "textbook" approach when necessary, without completely giving up on the problem. We will sometimes present a scrappy approach as a secondary method or even as the primary line of attack.

After all, the right way to deal with a monster problem can be to look for a scrappy approach right away. Or it can be to switch gears after you've looked for a "textbook" solution for a little while. Unfortunately, advanced test-takers are sometimes very stubborn. Sometimes they feel they *should* solve a problem according to some theoretical approach. Or they fail to move to Plan B or C rapidly enough, so they don't have enough gas in the tank to execute that plan. In the end, they might wind up guessing purely at random—and that's a shame.

GMAT problems often have **backdoors**—ways to solve them that don't involve crazy amounts of computation or genius-level insights. Remember that in theory, GMAT problems can all be solved in 2 minutes. Simply by searching for the backdoor, you might avoid all the bear traps that the problem writer set out by the front door!

Plan of This Book

The rest of this book has three parts:

Part I: Question Formats	Chapter 1 – Problem Solving: Advanced Principles Chapter 2 – Problem Solving: Advanced Strategies & Guessing Tactics Chapter 3 – Data Sufficiency: Advanced Principles Chapter 4 – Data Sufficiency: Advanced Strategies & Guessing Tactics
Part II: Cross-Topic Content	Chapter 5 – Pattern Recognition Chapter 6 – Common Terms & Quadratic Templates Chapter 7 – Visual Solutions Chapter 8 – Hybrid Problems
Part III: Workouts	Workouts 1–15—15 sets of 10 difficult problems

The four chapters in Part I focus on principles, strategies, and tactics related to the two types of GMAT math problems: Problem Solving and Data Sufficiency. The next four chapters, in Part II, focus on techniques that apply across several topics but are more specific than the approaches in Part I.

Each of the 8 chapters in Part I and Part II contains

> **Try-It Problems**, embedded throughout the text, and
> **In-Action Problems** at the end of the chapter.

Many of these problems will be GMAT-like in format, but many will not.

Part III contains sets of GMAT-like **Workout Problems**, designed to exercise your skills as if you were taking the GMAT and seeing its hardest problems. Several of these sets contain clusters of problems relating to the chapters in Parts I and II, although the problems within each set do not all resemble each other in obvious ways. Other Workout Problem sets are mixed by both approach and topic.

Note that these problems are *not* arranged in order of difficulty! Also,x you should know that some of these problems draw on advanced content covered in the 5 Manhattan GMAT Strategy Guides devoted to math.

Solutions to Try-It Problems

If you haven't tried to solve the first three *Try-It* problems on page 14, then go back and try them now. Think about how to get your Top-Down brain and your Bottom-Up brain to work together like a detective and a bloodhound. Come back when you've tackled the problems, or at least you've tried to. Get scrappy if necessary. Be sure to take a stab at the answer and write it down.

In these solutions, we'll outline sample dialogues between the Top-Down detective and the Bottom-Up bloodhound.

Try-It #0-1

> An jar is filled with red, white, and blue tokens that are equivalent except for their color. The chance of randomly selecting a red token, replacing it, then randomly selecting a white token is the same as the chance of randomly selecting a blue token. If the number of tokens of every color is a multiple of 3, what is the smallest possible total number of tokens in the jar?

> (A) 9   (B) 12   (C) 15   (D) 18   (E) 21

Solution to Try-It #0-1

…**jar** is filled with **red, white, and blue tokens**… **chance** of **randomly** selecting…	TD: "Let's *Understand* this problem first. There's a jar, and it's got red, white, and blue 'tokens' in it." *BU notices "chance" and "randomly." That's probability.* TD: "All right, this is a probability problem. Now, what's the situation?" *BU notices that there are two situations.*
…**chance of** randomly selecting **a red token**, replacing it, **then** randomly selecting **a white token** is the **same** as the **chance of** randomly selecting **a blue token**.	TD: "Let's rephrase. In simpler words, if I pick a red, then a white, that's the same chance as if I pick a blue. Okay, what else?" *BU doesn't want to deal with this "multiple of 3" thing yet.*
…**number of tokens of every color is a multiple of 3**…	TD: "Okay, what are they asking us?" *BU notices "smallest possible total number." Glances at answer choices. They're small, but not tiny. Hmm.*
…**smallest possible total number** of tokens in the jar? $$\frac{R}{R+W+B} \times \frac{W}{R+W+B} = \frac{B}{R+W+B}$$ $$\frac{RW}{\left(R+W+B\right)^2} = \frac{B}{R+W+B}$$ $$RW = B\left(R+W+B\right)$$ $$RW = BR + BW + B^2$$	TD: "Let's *Plan* for a moment. How can we approach this? How about algebra—if we name the number of each color, then we can represent each fact and also what we're looking for. Okay, let's use R, W, and B. Make probability fractions. Multiply red and white fractions. Simplify algebraically." *BU is now unsure. No obvious path forward.*
…The chance of randomly selecting a red token, replacing it, then randomly selecting a white token is the same as the chance of randomly selecting a blue token…	TD: "Let's start over conceptually. Reread the problem. Can we learn anything interesting?" *BU notices that blues are different.* TD: "How are blues different? Hmm. Picking a red, then a white is as likely as picking a blue. What does that mean?" *BU notices that it's unlikely to pick a blue. So there aren't many blues, compared to reds or whites.*

Fewer blues than reds or whites.

$B < R$ and $B < W$

In the very first equation above, each fraction on the left is less than 1, so their product is even smaller.

The denominators of the three fractions are all the same.

So the numerator of the product (B) must be smaller than either of the other numerators (R and W).

… If the number of tokens of every color is a multiple of 3, what is the smallest possible total number of tokens in the jar?

$$B = 3$$
$$RW = 3R + 3W + 9$$
$$1 = \frac{3}{W} + \frac{3}{R} + \frac{9}{RW}$$

Neither R nor W can equal 3 (since B is smaller than either).

Let $R = W = 6$.

(A) and (B) are out now. The smallest possible total is now 15.

$$\text{Is } 1 = \frac{3}{6} + \frac{3}{6} + \frac{9}{36}? \text{ No}$$

Let $R = 6$ and $W = 9$.

$$\text{Is } 1 = \frac{3}{6} + \frac{3}{9} + \frac{9}{54}?$$
$$\text{Is } 1 = \frac{1}{2} + \frac{1}{3} + \frac{1}{6}? \text{ Yes}$$

TD: "Are there fewer blues? Yes. Let's justify this. Focus on the algebraic setup."

BU notices fractions less than 1. All positive.

TD: "Two positive fractions less than 1, multiplied together, give you an even smaller number."

TD: "Yes, there are fewer blues."

BU is quiet.

TD: "Let's go back and reread the rest of the problem."

BU again notices "multiple of 3," also in answer choices. Small multiples.

TD: "Change of *Plan*: algebra by itself isn't getting us there. Let's plug a number in. Try the most constrained variable: *B*. Since it's the smallest quantity, but still positive, let's pretend *B* is 3. Execute this algebraically. Divide by *RW*."

BU likes just having 2 variables.

TD: "Let's test other numbers. Apply constraints we know—*B* is the smallest number. Rule out answer choices as we go."

TD: "6 and 6 don't work, because the right side adds up to larger than 1. (C) is out too. Try the next possibility."

BU doesn't like breaking the symmetry between R and W. They seem to be alike.

TD: "Does it matter whether we do *R* = 6 and *W* = 9 or the other way around? No, it doesn't. One is 6, the other is 9. Plug in and go."

TD: "This works. The answer is 3 + 6 + 9 = 18."

The correct answer is D.

Let's look at a scrappier pathway—one that moves more quickly to the backdoors.

Alternative Solution to Try-It #0-1

… chance of randomly selecting…	*BU notices "chance." BU doesn't like probability.* TD: "Oh man, probability. Okay, let's make sense of this and see whether there are any backdoors. That's the *Plan*."
… the number of tokens of every color is a multiple of 3…	*BU notices that there are only limited possibilities for each number.* TD: "Okay, every quantity is a multiple of 3. That simplifies things. We have 3, 6, 9, etc. of each color."
A jar is filled with red, white, and blue tokens…	*BU is alert—what about 0?* TD: "What about 0? Hmm… The wording at the beginning assumes that there actually are tokens of each color. So we can't have 0 tokens of any kind."
(A) 9 (B) 12 (C) 15 (D) 18 (E) 21	TD: "Now let's look at the answer choices." *BU notices that they're small.*
(A) 9	TD: "Well, we can try plugging in the choices. Let's start at the easy end—in this case, the smallest number." *BU notices 9 = 3 + 3 + 3.*
Select a red: 3/9 = 1/3 Select a white: 3/9 = 1/3 1/3 × 1/3 = 1/9, which is not "select a blue" (3/9)	TD: "The only possible way to have 9 total tokens is to have 3 reds, 3 whites, and 3 blues. So… does that work? Plug into probability formula."
~~(A) 9~~ (B) 12 (C) 15 (D) 18 (E) 21 (B) 12	TD: "No, that doesn't work. This is good. Knock out A. Let's keep going. Try B." *BU notices 12 = 3 + 3 + 6.*
Select a red: 3/12 = 1/4 Select a white: 6/12 = 1/2 1/4 × 1/2 = 1/8, which is not "select a blue" (3/12)	TD: "Only way to have 12 total is 3, 3, and 6. Which one's which… we probably want blue to be one of the 3's, to make it small. Let's say red is 3 and white is 6. Let's try it."
~~(A) 9~~ ~~(B) 12~~ (C) 15 (D) 18 (E) 21 (C) 15	TD: "That doesn't work either. Knock out B. Keep going." *BU notices 15 has a few options.*

Select a red: 6/15 = 2/5 Select a white: 6/15 = 2/5 2/5 × 2/5 = 4/25, which is not "select a blue" (3/15)	TD: "We can either make 15 by 3, 6, and 6 or by 3, 3, and 9. Let's try 3–6–6; make blue the 3."
3/15 × 9/15 = 3/25, which is not "select a blue" (3/15)	TD: "Nope. Let's try 3–3–9."
(A) 9 (B) 12 (C) 15 (D) 18 (E) 21 (D) 18	TD: "Knock out C. Try D." TD: "Let's try 3-6-9 first. Make blue the 3."
6/18 × 9/18 = 1/3 × 1/2 = 1/6 = 3/18, which IS "select a blue"	TD: "Thank goodness! Answer's D."

In hindsight, this second approach turned out to be less stressful and more efficient than the textbook approach. That's because in the end, there is no way to find the right answer by pure algebra. Ultimately, you have to test suitable numbers.

Try-It #0-2

Arrow $\overline{AB}$, which is a line segment exactly 5 units long with an arrowhead at A, is to be constructed in the xy-plane. The x- and y-coordinates of A and B are to be integers that satisfy the inequalities $0 \leq x \leq 9$ and $0 \leq y \leq 9$. How many different arrows with these properties can be constructed?

(A) 50 (B) 168 (C) 200 (D) 368 (E) 536

Solution to Try-It #0-2

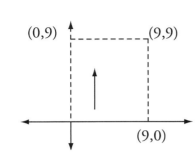

BU notices "xy-plane."

TD: "Let's *Understand* first. This is a coordinate-plane problem. Draw a quick general picture. Put in boundaries as necessary."

BU wonders where we're going.

How many different arrows with these properties can be constructed?

…exactly 5 units long with an arrowhead at *A*… the *x*- and *y*-coordinates of *A* and *B* are to be integers that satisfy the inequalities $0 \leq x \leq 9$. and $0 \leq x \leq 9$.

TD: "What are we asked for again? Reread the question."

BU wonders which properties.

TD: "What are the properties of the arrows supposed to be again? Each arrow is 5 units long."

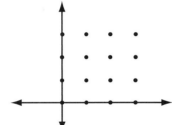

BU notices "integers" and "coordinates" and pictures a pegboard.

TD: "Both the tip and the end of the arrow have to touch holes in the pegboard exactly. Okay. The *Plan* is to start counting."

BU imagines many possible arrows. Brute force can't be the right way forward. The arrows can point in all sorts of different ways.

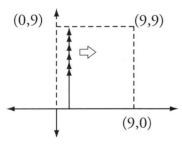

TD: "Let's simplify the *Plan*. Let's *focus* on just one orientation of arrows—pointing straight up. Draw this situation. How many places can the arrow be?"

BU wants to go up & down, then right & left.

In one column, there are 5 positions for the arrowhead: *y* = 5, 6, 7, 8, or 9. That's the same as 9 − 5 + 1, by the way.

There are 10 identical columns: *x* = 0 through *x* = 9. 5 × 10 = 50 possible positions for the arrow pointing straight up.

TD: "Keep simplifying the *Plan*. Count the positions in *one* column, then multiply by the number of columns. Be careful to count endpoints."

TD: "Great. We've *Solved* one part. Other possibilities?"

$50 \times 2 = 100$ possible positions for the arrow if it points straight up or to the right.

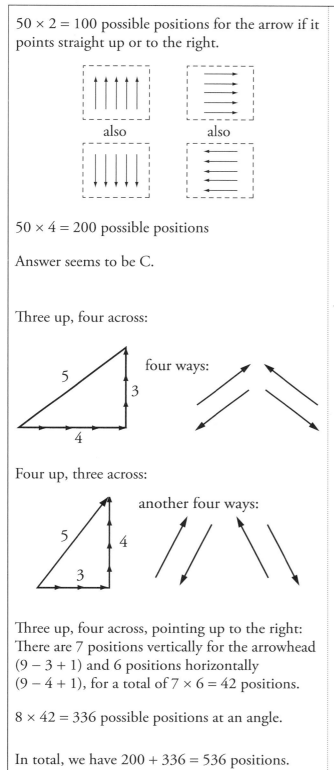

$50 \times 4 = 200$ possible positions

Answer seems to be C.

Three up, four across:

four ways:

Four up, three across:

another four ways:

Three up, four across, pointing up to the right: There are 7 positions vertically for the arrowhead $(9 - 3 + 1)$ and 6 positions horizontally $(9 - 4 + 1)$, for a total of $7 \times 6 = 42$ positions.

$8 \times 42 = 336$ possible positions at an angle.

In total, we have $200 + 336 = 536$ positions.

BU notices the square is the same vertically as horizontally. Go right.
TD: "We get the same result for arrows pointing right. 50 more positions. Is that it? Are we done?"

BU feels "up" and "right" are incomplete. What about "down" and "left"?
TD: "These arrows can point straight *down* or straight *left*, too. We'll get the same results. So we have 50 positions in each of the four directions. Calculate at this point and evaluate answers. Eliminate A and B."

BU is suspicious: somehow too easy.
TD: "Tentative answer is C, but we're not done."
BU wonders about still other ways for the arrows to point.
TD: "Could the arrows be at an angle?"
BU notices that the arrow is 5 units long, associated with 3–4–5 triangles.
TD: "3–4–5 triangles. Yes. We can put the arrow as the hypotenuse of a 3–4–5 triangle. How can this be done? Try to place the arrow. Remember the reversal. Looks like there are four ways if we go 3 up and 4 across: up right, up left, down right, down left."

BU is happy. This is the trick.

TD: "Likewise, there must be four ways if we go 4 up and 3 across: again, up right, up left, down right, and down left. By the way, the answer must be D or E."

TD: "Now count just one of these ways. Same ideas as before. Be sure to include endpoints."
BU notices the symmetry. The 3 up, 4 across is the same as the 4 up, 3 across, if you turn the square.

TD: "Each of these angled ways will be the same. There are 8 ways to point the arrow at an angle. Finish the calculation and confirm the answer."

The correct answer is E. There isn't much of an alternative to the approach above. With counting problems, it can often be very difficult to estimate the answer or work backwards from the answer choices.

Try-It #0-3.

In the diagram to the right, what is the value of *x*?

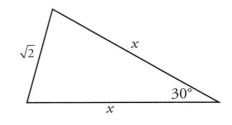

(A) $1+\sqrt{2}$ (B) $1+\sqrt{3}$ (C) $2\sqrt{2}$ (D) $\sqrt{2}+\sqrt{3}$ (E) $2\sqrt{3}$

Solution to Try-It #0-3

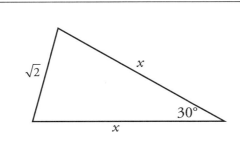

$180° - 30° = 150°$.
Divide 150° equally across the two missing angles. So each angle is 75°.

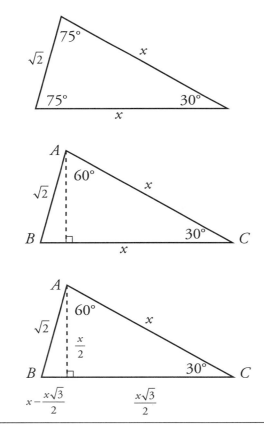

TD: "Okay, let's *Understand* this. Redraw the figure. We're looking for *x*. Now… how about a *Plan*?"
BU notices this is an isosceles triangle, because there are two sides labeled x. How about the two equal angles?
TD: "Figure out the two missing angles. Use the 180° rule."

BU doesn't recognize this triangle.

TD: "Hmm... Here's a *Plan*: add a perpendicular line to make right triangles. Drop the line from the top point. Let's label corners while we're at it. Now fill in angles."

BU notices 30–60–90 and is happy.

TD: "Use the 30–60–90 to write expressions for its sides. Then side $\overline{BC}$ can be split up into 2 pieces, and we can set up the Pythagorean Theorem."

BU feels that this process is kind of ugly.

TD: "Let's push through. Write the Pythagorean Theorem for the small triangle on the left, using the $\sqrt{2}$ as the hypotenuse."

$$\left(\frac{x}{2}\right)^2 + \left(x - \frac{x\sqrt{3}}{2}\right)^2 = \left(\sqrt{2}\right)^2$$

$$\frac{x^2}{4} + x^2 - x^2\sqrt{3} + \frac{3x^2}{4} = 2$$

$$\left(2 - \sqrt{3}\right)x^2 = 2$$

$$x^2 = \frac{2}{2-\sqrt{3}}\left(\frac{2+\sqrt{3}}{2+\sqrt{3}}\right)$$

$$= \frac{4+2\sqrt{3}}{4-3} = 4 + 2\sqrt{3}$$

Skip choice A, because it doesn't contain $\sqrt{3}$.

Square choice B.

$$\left(1 + \sqrt{3}\right)\left(1 + \sqrt{3}\right) = 1 + 2\sqrt{3} + 3 = 4 + 2\sqrt{3}$$

BU thinks this equation is really ugly.

TD: "Push through. Execute the algebra quickly. Expand the quadratic & simplify."

TD: "Rationalize the denominator to get x^2 equal to a simpler expression."

BU has no idea how to take the square root of this expression.

TD: "Almost there. Change of *Plan*. Let's just test answer choices by squaring them. Focus only on the ones involving $\sqrt{3}$."

TD: "This is it. Done."

The answer is B.

The method we just saw is algebraically intensive, and so our Bottom-Up bloodhound might have kicked up a fuss along the way. Sometimes, your Top-Down brain needs to ignore the Bottom-Up brain. Remember, when you're actually taking the GMAT, you have to solve problems quickly—and you don't need to publish your solutions in a mathematics journal. What you want is to get the right answer as quickly and as easily as possible. In this regard, the solution above works perfectly well.

As an alternative method, we can estimate lengths. Draw the triangle *carefully* and start with the same perpendicular line as before. This line is a little shorter than the side of length $\sqrt{2}$ (which is about 1.4). So we can estimate the length of the perpendicular to be 1.2 or 1.3. Since this length is the "30" side of the 30-60-90 triangle, it's half of the hypotenuse. Thus, we can estimate x to be 2.4 to 2.6.

Now we can examine the answer choices. Approximate them using 1.4 for $\sqrt{2}$ and 1.7 for $\sqrt{3}$.

    A) 2.4   B) 2.7   C) 2.8   D) 3.1   E) 3.4

They're all close, but we can pretty confidently eliminate D and E, and probably C for that matter. Now we're guessing between A and B. Unfortunately, we might guess wrong at this point! But the odds are much better than they were at the outset.

A third method involves drawing different interior lines. It's a good instinct to drop a perpendicular from the top point, but are there other possibilities?

Once we find that the two equal angles are 75°, we could try to split up one of the 75° angles in other ways. 75 = 30 + 45, both "friendly" angles (they show up in triangles we know). So let's split 75° two ways: 30° and 45°, and 45° and 30°.

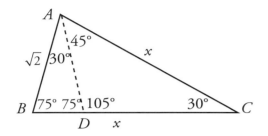

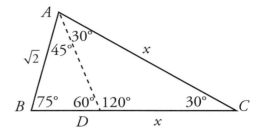

△*ABD* is similar to △*CAB*, but otherwise, we don't have a whole lot to go on.

△*ADC* is isosceles (and it's made up of two 30–60–90 triangles). △*ABD* now has a 60° angle.

The case on the right seems more promising. Maybe if we add one more line? We may also be inspired by the $\sqrt{2}$ together with the 45°. This might remind us of a 45–45–90 triangle. So let's try to make one.

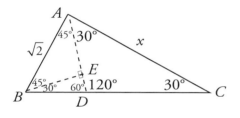

Now △*ABE* is a 45–45–90 triangle, △*BED* is a 30–60–90 triangle, and △*ADC* is still an isosceles triangle that, in the worst case, we can cut in half to make two 30–60–90 triangles.

We now have the problem cracked. From here, we just need to fill in side lengths.

The two short legs of △*ABE* each have length 1. Side $\overline{BE}$ is also part of the 30–60–90 triangle, so we can find the other two sides of that triangle. Now we find the length of side $\overline{AD}$, which also gives us side $\overline{DC}$. Finally, we get side $\overline{BC}$, which is *x*. Again, the answer is B, $1+\sqrt{3}$.

This third pathway is *extremely* difficult! It requires significant experimentation and at least a couple of flashes of insight. Thus, it is unlikely that the GMAT would *require* you to take such a path, even at the highest levels of difficulty.

However, it is still worthwhile to look for these sorts of solutions as you practice. Your Top-Down brain will become faster, more organized, and more flexible, enabling your Bottom-Up brain to have more flashes of insight.

That was a substantial introduction. Now, on to Chapter 1!

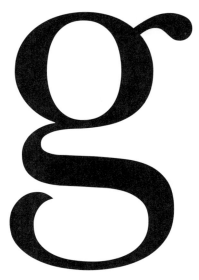

Chapter 1
of
ADVANCED GMAT QUANT

PROBLEM SOLVING
PRINCIPLES

In This Chapter . . .

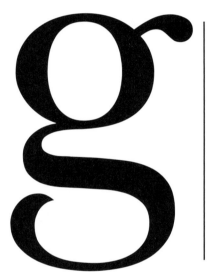

PROBLEM SOLVING: ADVANCED PRINCIPLES

Chapters 1 and 2 of this book focus on the more fundamental of the two types of GMAT math questions: Problem Solving (PS). Some of the content applies to any kind of math problem, including Data Sufficiency (DS). However, Chapters 3 and 4 deal specifically with Data Sufficiency issues.

This chapter outlines broad principles for solving advanced PS problems. We've already seen very basic versions of the first three principles in the Introduction, in the dialogues between the Top-Down and the Bottom-Up brain.

As we mentioned before, these principles draw on the work of George Polya, who was a brilliant mathematician and teacher of mathematics. Polya was teaching future mathematicians, not GMAT test-takers, but what he says still applies. His little book *How To Solve It* has never been out of print since 1945—it's worth getting a copy.

In the meantime, keep reading!

Principle #1: Understand the Basics

Slow down on difficult problems. Make sure that you truly *get* the problem.

Polya recommended that you ask yourself a few simple questions as you attack a problem. We whole-heartedly agree. Here are some great Polya-style questions that can help you *Understand:*

- **What exactly is the problem asking for?**

- **What are the quantities I care about?** These are often the *unknowns.*

- **What do I know?** This could be about certain quantities or about the situation more generally.

- **What *don't* I know?**

    o   Sometimes you care about something you don't know. This could be an intermediate unknown quantity that you didn't think of earlier.

    o   Other times, you don't know something, and you don't care. For instance, if a problem includes the quantity 11! (11 factorial), you will practically never need to know the exact number, with all its digits, that equals that quantity.

- **What is this problem testing me on?** In other words, why is this problem on the GMAT? What aspect of math are they testing? What kind of reasoning do they want me to demonstrate?

Think about what the answers mean. Rephrase the answers as well. Simply by expressing our findings in another way, we can often unlock a problem.

The *Understand the Basics* principle applies later on as well. If you get stuck, go back to basics. Re-read the problem and ask yourself these questions again.

Start the following problem by asking yourself the Polya questions.

Try-It #1-1

$x = 9^{10} - 3^{17}$ and x/n is an integer. If n is a positive integer that has exactly two factors, how many different values for n are possible?

(A) One   (B) Two   (C) Three   (D) Four   (E) Five

Now let's look at answers you might give to the Polya questions:

What exactly is the problem asking for?	The number of possible values for n. This means that n might have multiple possible values. In fact, it probably can take on more than one value. I may not need these actual values. I just need to count them.
What are the quantities I care about?	I'm given x and n as variables. These are the quantities I care about.
What do I know?	$x = 9^{10} - 3^{17}$ That is, x = a specific large integer, expressed in terms of powers of 9 and 3. x/n is an integer. That is, x is divisible by n, or n is a factor of x. n is a positive integer that has exactly two factors. This should make me think of prime numbers. Primes have exactly two factors. So I can rephrase the information: n is a positive prime number.
What *don't* I know?	Here's something I don't know: I don't know the value of x as a series of digits. Using a calculator or Excel, I could find out that x equals 3,357,644,238. But I don't know this number at the outset. Moreover, because this calculation is far too cumbersome, I must not *need* to find this number.
What is this problem testing me on?	From the foregoing, I can infer that this problem is testing us on divisibility and primes. We also need to manipulate exponents, since we see them in the expression for x.

You can ask these questions in whatever order is most helpful for the problem. For instance, you might not look at what the problem is asking for until you've understood the given information.

Principle #2: Build a Plan

Now you should think about *how* you will solve the problem. Ask yourself a few more Polya questions to build your *Plan*:

Is a good approach already obvious?	From your answers above, you may already see a way to reach the answer. Don't try to work out all the details in your head ahead of time. If you can envision the rough outlines of the right path, then go ahead and get started.
If not, what in the problem can help me figure out a good approach?	If you are stuck, look for particular *clues* to tell you what to do next. Revisit your answers to the basic questions. What do those answers mean? Can you rephrase or reword them? Can you combine two pieces of information in any way, or can you rephrase the question, given everything you know?
Can I remember a similar problem?	Try relating the problem to other problems you've faced. This can help you categorize the problem or recall a solution process.

For the Try-It problem, we have already rephrased some of the given information. We should go further now, combining information and simplifying the question.

Given: n is a prime number   AND n is a factor of x
Combined: **n is a prime factor of x**
Question: How many different values for n are possible?
Combined: How many different values for n, **a prime factor of x**, are possible?
Rephrased: **How many different prime factors does x have?**

Thus, we need to find the prime factorization of x. Notice that n is not even in the question any more. The variable n just gave us a way to ask this underlying question.

Now, we look at the other given fact: $x = 9^{10} - 3^{17}$. Earlier, we did not try to do very much with this piece of information. We just recognized that we were given a particular value for x, one involving powers. It can be helpful initially to put certain complicated facts to the side. Try to understand the kind of information you are given, but do not necessarily try to interpret it all of it right away.

At this stage, however, we know that we need the prime factors of x. So now we know what we need to do with $9^{10} - 3^{17}$. We have to factor this expression into primes.

This goal should motivate us to replace 9 (which is not prime) with 3^2 (which displays the prime factors of 9). We can now rewrite the equation for x:

$$x = (3^2)^{10} - 3^{17} = 3^{20} - 3^{17}$$

Now, we still have not expressed x as a product of prime numbers. We need to pull out a common factor from both terms. The largest common factor is 3^{17}, so we write

$$x = 3^{20} - 3^{17} = 3^{17}(3^3 - 1) = 3^{17}(27 - 1) = 3^{17}(26) = 3^{17}(13)(2)$$

Now we have what we need: the prime factorization of x. We can see that x has three different prime factors: 2, 3, and 13. The correct answer is C.

Principle #3: Solve—and Put Pen to Paper

The third step is to *Solve*. You'll want to execute that solution in an error-free way—it would be terrible to get all the thinking right, then make a careless computational error. That's why we say you should *Put Pen to Paper*.

This idea also applies when you get stuck *anywhere* along the way on a monster problem.

Think back to those killer Try-It problems in the introduction. Those are not the kinds of problems you can figure out just by looking at them.

When you get stuck on a tough problem, take action. Do not just stare, hoping that you suddenly "get" it.

Instead, ask yourself the Polya questions again and write down whatever you can:

- Reinterpretations of given information or of the question
- Intermediate results, whether specific or general
- Avenues or approaches that *didn't* work

This way, your Top-Down brain can help your Bottom-Up brain find the right leads. In particular, it's almost impossible to abandon an unpromising line of thinking without writing something down.

Think back to the sequence problem in the introduction. You'll keep seeing 64 as 8^2 unless you try *writing* it in another way.

Do not try to juggle everything in your head. Your working memory has limited capacity, and your Bottom-Up brain needs that space to work. A multi-step problem simply cannot be solved in your brain as quickly, easily, and accurately as it can be on paper.

As you put pen to paper, keep the following themes in mind:

1. Look for Patterns

Every GMAT problem has a reasonable solution path, which may depend upon a pattern that you'll need to extrapolate. Write down a set of easy cases in a natural sequence, and examine the pattern of your results. In many cases, you will see right away how to extend the pattern.

Try-It #1-2

$S_n = \dfrac{-1}{S_{n-1}+1}$ for all integer values of n greater than 1. If $S_1 = 1$, what is the sum of the first 61 terms in the sequence?

(A) −48   (B) −31   (C) −29   (D) 1   (E) 30

The recursive definition of S_n doesn't yield any secrets upon first glance. So let's write out the easy cases in the sequence, starting at $n = 1$ and going up until we notice a pattern:

$S_1 = 1$

$S_2 = \dfrac{-1}{1+1} = -\dfrac{1}{2}$

$S_3 = \dfrac{-1}{-\dfrac{1}{2}+1} = \dfrac{-1}{\dfrac{1}{2}} = (-1)(2) = -2$

$S_4 = \dfrac{-1}{-2+1} = \dfrac{-1}{-1} = 1$

$S_5 = \dfrac{-1}{1+1} = -\dfrac{1}{2}$

$S_6 = \dfrac{-1}{-\dfrac{1}{2}+1} = -2$

etc.

The terms of the sequence are 1, −1/2 , −2, 1, −1/2, −2... Three terms repeat in this cyclical pattern forever; every third term is the same.

Now, the sum of each group of three consecutive terms is 1 + (−1/2) + (−2) = −3/2. There are 20 groups in the first 61 terms, with one term left over. So, the sum of the first 61 terms is:

(Number of groups)(Sum of one group) + (Leftover term) = (20)(−3/2) + 1 = −29

The correct answer is C.

It is almost impossible to stare at the recursive definition of this sequence and discern the resulting pattern.

The best way to identify the pattern is simply to calculate a few simple values of the sequence. We will discuss Pattern Recognition in more detail in Chapter 5.

2. Draw Pictures

Some problems are much easier to solve if you draw pictures. For instance, if a problem involves motion, you can draw snapshots representing the problem at different points in time.

Try-It #1-3

Truck A is on a straight highway heading due south at the same time Truck B is on a different straight highway heading due east. At 1:00PM, Truck A is exactly 14 miles north of Truck B. If both trucks are traveling at a constant speed of 30 miles per hour, at which of the following times will they be exactly 10 miles apart?

(A) 1:10PM   (B) 1:12PM   (C) 1:14PM   (D) 1:15PM   (E) 1:20PM

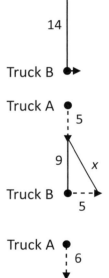

Don't try to *Solve* without drawing a diagram. Remember, you want to *Understand* and *Plan* first! Represent Truck A and Truck B as of 1:00PM. Next, you should ask, "how does the distance between Truck A and Truck B change as time goes by?"

Try another point in time. Since the answers are all a matter of minutes after 1:00PM, try a convenient increment of a few minutes. After 10 minutes, each truck will have traveled 5 miles (30 miles per hour = 1 mile in 2 minutes). How far apart will the trucks be then? Looking at the diagram to the right, we can see that the distance is represented by x.

Because Truck A is traveling south and Truck B is traveling east, the triangle must be a right triangle.

Therefore, $x^2 = 9^2 + 5^2$.

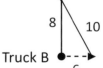

At this point, we could solve the problem in one of two ways. The first is to notice that once both trucks travel 6 miles, the diagram will contain a 6:8:10 triangle. Therefore, 6/30 = 1/5 of an hour later, at 1:12PM, the trucks will be exactly 10 miles apart.

Alternatively, we could set up an algebraic equation and solve for the unknown number of miles traveled, such that the distance between the trucks is 10. Let's call that distance y:

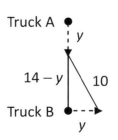

$$10^2 = y^2 + (14 - y)^2 \qquad 0 = y^2 - 14y + 48$$

$$100 = 2y^2 - 28y + 196 \qquad 0 = (y - 6)(y - 8)$$

$$50 = y^2 - 14y + 98$$

Therefore, y could equal 6 or 8 miles. In other words, the trucks will be exactly 10 miles apart at 1:12PM and at 1:16PM. Either way, the correct answer is B.

Notice how instrumental these diagrams were for our solution process. You may already accept that geometry problems require diagrams. However, many other kinds of problems can benefit from visual thinking. We will discuss advanced visualization techniques in more detail in Chapter 7.

3. Solve an Easier Problem

A problem may include many constraints: for example, some quantity must be positive, it must be an integer, it must be less than 15, etc.

One approach to problems with many constraints is to pretend that some of the constraints aren't there. Solve this hypothetical, easier, more relaxed problem. Then reintroduce the constraints you left out. You may be able to find the solution to the harder problem. Of course, you should do all of this on paper!

Try-It #1-4

> At an amusement park, Tom bought a number of red tokens and green tokens. Each red token costs $0.09, and each green token costs $0.14. If Tom spent a total of exactly $2.06, how many tokens in total did Tom buy?
>
> (A) 16   (B) 17   (C) 18   (D) 19   (E) 20

For ease of calculation, let's convert all prices to cents, so that the price of a red token is 9 cents, the price of a green token is 14 cents, and the total amount Tom spent is 206 cents.

Make up variables to represent the number of each kind of token. Let R be the number of red tokens, and let G be the number of green tokens. These quantities are subject to several constraints. Make sure that you *Understand* all of these constraints, in particular where we got them from in the problem:

R is positive (we can't have a negative number of tokens—this is an *implied* constraint).

R is an integer (we can't have fractional tokens—another implied constraint).

G is positive.

G is an integer.

$9R + 14G = 206$ (to avoid decimals, we write the equation in terms of cents, not dollars)

We might not realize this at first, but the prices of the tokens had to have been chosen so that there would be only one solution to the problem. Specifically, the prices do not share any prime factors (9 and 14 have no prime factors in common). Under these conditions, the tokens are not easily interchangeable. Fourteen 9-cent tokens are worth exactly the same as nine 14-cent tokens, but there are no smaller equivalencies.

Unless we can magically guess the right solution immediately, we ought to start by finding solutions that are *partially* right. That is, they meet some but not all of the constraints. Then we can adjust our partial solution until we find one that is completely right.

Let's ignore the constraint that R must be an integer. We can solve the equation for R:

$$9R + 14G = 206$$

$$R = \frac{206 - 14G}{9}$$

Now create a table to represent the partial solutions. Start with a large value of G, so that the value of the red tokens is close to 206 cents, but not so large that the value of the red tokens would be over 206. This way, R is still positive.

G = 14 gets us to 196, whereas G = 15 goes too high, to 210.

G	14G	206 − 14G	$R = \dfrac{206 - 14G}{9}$	R = integer?
14	196	10	10/9	No

This partial solution satisfies all the constraints except the one that R must be an integer. We can now use this partial solution as a starting point for generating other partial solutions. We decrease G by 1, examine the result, and keep going until we find the real solution. If necessary, we can look for a pattern to extrapolate.

G	14G	206 − 14G	$R = \dfrac{206 - 14G}{9}$	R = integer?
14	196	10	10/9	No
13	182	24	24/9	No
12	168	38	38/9	No
11	154	52	52/9	No

At this point, we should realize that what we really care about is the third column (206 − 14G). Specifically, what number in the third column is divisible by 9? We should also notice that the numbers in the third column are going up by 14, so we quickly list that column (adding 14 to each number) and look for divisibility by 9. That is, we are looking for numbers whose digits sum to a multiple of 9.

52	No
66	No
80	No
94	No
108	Yes

Counting, we find that the right value corresponds to $G = 7$ and $R = 108/9 = 12$. Thus, the total number of tokens Tom bought is $12 + 7 = 19$. The correct answer is D.

We can generalize this approach. If a problem has many complexities, we can attack it by ignoring some of the complexities at first. Solve a simpler problem. Then see whether you can adjust the solution to the simpler problem in order to solve the original problem.

To recap, you should put your work on paper. Don't try to solve hard problems in your head.

- To find a pattern, you need to see the first few cases on paper.
- To visualize a scene, you should draw a picture.
- If you solve an easier problem, you should write down your partial solutions.

In general, jot down intermediate results as you go. This way, you can often see them in a new light and consider how they fit into the solution.

Also, try to be organized. For instance, make tables to keep track of cases. The more organized you are, the more insights you can have into difficult problems.

Principle #4: Review Your Work

During a test, whether real or practice, you should generally move on once you've found an answer that you're happy with. After all, the GMAT is a timed test, and you can't go backward. So you should click "Next" and "Confirm" and then focus on the next problem, forgetting about the one you just answered.

But when you are doing a set of practice problems, you should not just check to see whether you got the answer right. You should leave a *good deal of time* for thorough review. Ask yourself these questions:

- What is the best pathway to the answer?
- What is the easiest and fastest way to complete each step?
- What are the alternate pathways? Could I have guessed effectively? If so, how?
- What traps or tricks are built into this problem?
- Where could I have made a mistake? If I did make a mistake, how can I avoid doing so next time?
- What are the key takeaways? What can I learn from this problem?
- What other problems are similar to this problem? What does this problem remind me of?

Over time, this discipline will make you a better problem-solver.

For each of the 5 problems on the next page, apply the principles from this chapter in the following order. Don't worry if your answers for each step don't match our explanations precisely—the point of this exercise is to get you to think *explicitly* about each step in the problem solving process:

a. Apply *Principle #1 (Understand the Basics).*

Ask yourself these questions (in any order that you find convenient):

- What exactly is the problem asking for?
- What are the quantities I care about?
- What do I know (about these quantities or the situation more generally)?
- What don't I know?
- What is this problem testing me on?

b. Apply *Principle #2 (Build a Plan).*

Ask yourself these questions:

- Is a good approach already obvious? If so, outline the steps (but do not carry them out yet).
- If not, what in the problem can help me figure out a good approach?
- Can I remember a similar problem?

c. Apply *Principle #3 (Solve—and Put Pen to Paper).*

Solve each problem, and then think about how you used your scratch paper. Ask yourself these questions:

- Did I look for patterns?
- Did I draw pictures?
- Did I solve an easier problem?

d. Apply *Principle #4 (Review Your Work).*

Ask yourself these questions:

- What is the best pathway to the answer?
- What is the easiest and fastest way to complete each step?
- What are the alternate pathways? Could I have guessed effectively? If so, how?
- What traps or tricks are built into this problem?
- Where could I have made a mistake? If I did make a mistake, how can I avoid doing so next time?
- What are the key takeaways? What can I learn from this problem?
- What other problems are similar to this problem? What does this problem remind me of?

In-Action Problem Set

1. Each factor of 210 is inscribed on its own plastic ball, and all of the balls are placed in a jar. If a ball is randomly selected from the jar, what is the probability that the ball is inscribed with a multiple of 42?

    (A) $\dfrac{1}{16}$ (B) $\dfrac{5}{42}$ (C) $\dfrac{1}{8}$ (D) $\dfrac{3}{16}$ (E) $\dfrac{1}{4}$

2. If x is a positive integer, what is the units digit of $(24)^{5+2x}(36)^6(17)^3$?

    (A) 2 (B) 3 (C) 4 (D) 6 (E) 8

3. A baker makes a combination of chocolate chip cookies and peanut butter cookies for a school bake sale. His recipes only allow him to make chocolate chip cookies in batches of 7, and peanut butter cookies in batches of 6. If he makes exactly 95 cookies for the bake sale, what is the minimum number of chocolate chip cookies that he makes?

    (A) 7 (B) 14 (C) 21 (D) 28 (E) 35

4. A rectangular solid is changed such that the width and length are increased by 1 inch apiece and the height is decreased by 9 inches. Despite these changes, the new rectangular solid has the same volume as the original rectangular solid. If the width and length of the original rectangular solid are equal and the height of the new rectangular solid is 4 times the width of the original rectangular solid, what is the volume of the rectangular solid?

    (A) 18 (B) 50 (C) 100 (D) 200 (E) 400

5. The sum of all solutions for x in the equation $x^2 - 8x + 21 = |x - 4| + 5$ is equal to:

    (A) −7 (B) 7 (C) 10 (D) 12 (E) 14

In-Action Problem Set (Solutions)

1. a. Problem is asking for: Probability that the selected ball is multiple of 42

    Quantities we care about: Factors of 210

    What we know: Many balls, each with a different factor of 210. Each factor of 210 is represented. 1 ball is selected randomly. Some balls have a multiple of 42 (e.g. 42 itself); some do not (e.g. 1).

    What don't we know: How many factors of 210 there are
                           How many of these factors are multiples of 42

    What the problem is testing us on: Probability; divisibility & primes

    We can rephrase the question at this point:

$$\text{Probability (multiple of 42)} = \frac{\text{\# of factors of 210 that are multiples of 42}}{\text{\# of factors of 210}} = ?$$

  b. Factor 210 to primes → Build full list of factors from prime components → Distinguish between multiples of 42 and non-multiples → Count factors → Compute probability.

    Alternatively, you might simply list all the factors of 210 using factor pairs.

  c. Let's first try listing factor pairs.

1	**210**
2	105
3	70
5	**42**
6	35
7	30
10	21
14	15

    Counting, we find that there are 16 factors of 210, and two of them (42 and 210) are multiples of 42.

    Alternatively, we could count the factors by studying 210's prime factorization $= (2)(3)(5)(7) = (2^1)(3^1)(5^1)(7^1)$.

    Here's a shortcut to determine the number of distinct factors of 210. Add 1 to the power of each prime factor and multiply:

        2^1: $1 + 1 = 2$
        3^1: $1 + 1 = 2$
        5^1: $1 + 1 = 2$
        7^1: $1 + 1 = 2$

Multiplying, we get $2 \times 2 \times 2 \times 2 = 16$. There are 16 different factors of 210.

How many of these 16 factors are multiples of 42? We can look at the "left-over" factors when we divide 210 by 42, of which there is only one prime (5), and of course, 1. Any combination of these "left-over" factors could be multiplied with 42 to create a factor of 210 that is divisible by 42. The only two possibilities are 42×1 and 42×5, so the probability is $2/16 = 1/8$. The answer is C.

   d. Listing all the factors is not so bad. It may be slightly faster to use the factor-counting shortcut, but only if you can quickly figure out how to deal with the multiples of 42.

2. a. Unknowns: Units digits of $(24)^{5+2x}$, $(36)^6$, and $(17)^3$.

      Given: We only need the units digit of the product, not the value.

               x is a positive integer.

      Constraints: If x is a positive integer, $2x$ is even, and $5 + 2x$ must be odd. Units digit of a product depends only on the units digit of multiplied numbers.

      Question: What is the units digit of the product $(24)^{5+2x}(36)^6(17)^3$?

   b. Find/Recall the pattern for units digits → use the Unit Digit Shortcut

   c. Units digit of $(24)^{5+2x}$ = units digit of $(4)^{odd}$. The pattern for the units digit of $4^{integer}$ = [4, 6]. Thus, the units digit is 4.

      Units digit of $(36)^6$ must be 6, as every power of 6 ends in 6.

      Units digit of $(17)^3$ = units digit of $(7)^3$. The pattern for the units digit of $7^{integer}$ = [7, 9, 3, 1]. Thus, the units digit is 3.

      The product of the units digits is $(4)(6)(3) = 72$, which has a units digit of 2. The answer is A.

   d. Patterns were very important on this one! If we had forgotten any of the patterns, we could just list at least the first four powers of 4, 6, and 7 to recreate them.

3. a. Unknowns: C = # of chocolate chip cookie batches, P = # of peanut butter cookie batches

      Given: Baker only makes chocolate or peanut butter cookies. He can only make chocolate in batches of 7, peanut butter in batches of 6. He makes exactly 95 cookies total.

      Constraints: He cannot make partial batches, i.e. C and P must be integers.
           $95 = 7C + 6P$.

      Question: What is the minimum number of chocolate chip cookies? Or, What is the minimum value of $7C$?

   b. Minimize $7C$ → Maximize $6P$ → Check both C and P against constraints.

c. Make a chart:

$7C$	$6P = 95 - 7C$	$6P$ a multiple of 6? (i.e. is P an integer?)
7	88	N
14	81	N
21	74	N
28	67	N
35	60	Y

The answer is E.

While constructing the chart, we relax the constraint that $6P$ has to be an integer to make it easier to meet the constraint that the total # of cookies is 95. We reintroduce the integer batch constraint as a final Y/N check.

While solving, we should notice the Pattern in the answer choices: they're all multiples of 7.

d. The two competing constraints made testing choices the most efficient method.

4. a. Unknowns: w, l, h (width, length, height of the original box)

Given: Width and length increase by 1.
Height decreases by 9.
The resulting volume is the same.
Width and length were equal originally.
The new height is 4 times the original width.

Constraints: $w = l$
$h - 9 = 4w$
$w \times l \times h = (w + 1)(l + 1)(h - 9)$
Question: What is the volume? What is wlh?

b. Write equations → Solve (substitution) → Check solution against the trickiest constraint → Answer the question.

c. w appears in all 3 constraint equations, so solve for the other variables *in terms of w* and substitute into the longest constraint:

$l = w$
$h = 4w + 9$

Substitute:

$w \times l \times h = (w + 1)(l + 1)(h - 9)$
$w(w)(4w + 9) = (w + 1)(w + 1)(4w)$ Since w can't be zero, we can divide it out safely.
$w(4w + 9) = 4(w + 1)(w + 1)$

*Manhattan*GMAT*Prep

$$4w^2 + 9w = 4(w^2 + 2w + 1)$$
$$4w^2 + 9w = 4w^2 + 8w + 4$$
$$w = 4$$

Solve for all variables:

$$l = w = 4$$
$$h = 4w + 9 = 4(4) + 9 = 25$$

Original Volume $= w \times l \times h = (4)(4)(25) = 400$
New Volume $= (w + 1)(l + 1)(h - 9) = (5)(5)(16) = 400$

The answer is E.

d. Checking the answer made a lot of sense: we had to compute volume anyway to answer the question, and the complexity of the volume constraint equation gave us plenty of chances to make computation errors.

Your Bottom-Up brain may have noticed along the way that the equal width and length implied a perfect square embedded in the calculation of the volume (assuming the box dimensions are integers—which is not stated, but likely on the GMAT). Your Bottom-Up brain may have also noticed that 9 (the height reduction) is a perfect square; this could suggest testing numbers such as 4, 5, 16 and 25.

5. a. Unknowns: x

Given: $x^2 - 8x + 21 = |x - 4| + 5$.

Constraints: The question implies that there may be multiple solutions, as does the non-linear given equation.

Question: What is the sum of all possible solutions for x?

b. Break into 2 equations (i.e. non-negative and negative inside absolute value sign) → Group all variables on one side of the equation, with 0 on the other → Factorable quadratic? → Factor → Solve → Answer.

c.

Scenario 1:	**Scenario 2:**
$x - 4 \geq 0$	$x - 4 \leq 0$
	$x^2 - 8x + 21 = |x - 4| + 5$
$x^2 - 8x + 21 = |x - 4| + 5$	$x^2 - 8x + 21 = -(x - 4) + 5$
$x^2 - 8x + 21 = x - 4 + 5$	$x^2 - 8x + 21 = -x + 4 + 5$
$x^2 - 9x + 20 = 0$	$x^2 - 7x + 12 = 0$
$(x - 5)(x - 4) = 0$	$(x - 4)(x - 3) = 0$
$x = 5 \ or \ 4$	$x = 4 \ or \ 3$

*Manhattan*GMAT*Prep

the new standard

Sum of the different solutions: $5 + 4 + 3 = 12$. The answer is D.

Alternatively, we could focus on the left side of the equation, which looks like a manageable quadratic, isolating the absolute value on the right:

$x^2 - 8x + 21 = |x - 4| + 5$
$x^2 - 8x + 16 = |x - 4|$
$(x - 4)(x - 4) = |x - 4|$
$(x - 4)^2 = |x - 4|$

"Something squared equals its absolute value. 1 squared equals 1, 0 squared equals 0...hmm, -1 squared equals 1..."

$x - 4 = -1, 0,$ or 1
$x = 3, 4,$ or 5

Sum of the different solutions: $5 + 4 + 3 = 12$.

d. On absolute value problems, some of the solutions might be duplicates. Just cross these off at the end. Additionally, we could check to make sure the results for each solutions satisfy the initial assumptions. For example, in Scenario 1 we assumed $x - 4 \geq 0$. Both solutions, 5 and 4, satisfy this inequality. Similarly, the solutions 4 and 3 satisfy Scenario 2's assumption, that $x - 4 \leq 0$. Thus all the solutions were valid. For complex absolute value equations such as this one, this need not always be the case.

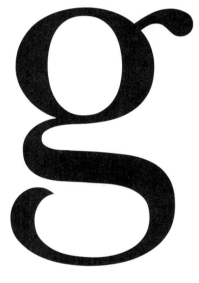

Chapter 2
of
ADVANCED GMAT QUANT

PROBLEM SOLVING: STRATEGIES & TACTICS

In This Chapter . . .

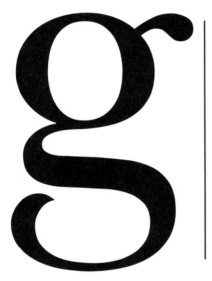

- Advanced Strategies
- Advanced Guessing Tactics

PROBLEM SOLVING: ADVANCED STRATEGIES & GUESSING TACTICS

Sometimes you will encounter a Problem Solving problem that you can't answer—either because its content is difficult or obscure, or because you don't have enough time to solve completely in 2 minutes.

This chapter describes a series of different methods you might try in these circumstances. Here, we make the distinction between **strategies** and **tactics**.

Strategies are broad: they apply to a wide variety of problems, they provide a complete approach, and they can be used safely in most circumstances.

In contrast, *tactics* can help you eliminate a few answer choices, but often leave a fair amount of uncertainty. Moreover, a particular tactic may only be useful in special situations or to parts of a problem.

The first section of this chapter outlines three Problem Solving strategies:

PS Strategy 1. **Plug In Numbers**

One of the most productive "Plan B" strategies on the GMAT is to pick good numbers and plug them into unknowns. Try this when the concepts are especially complex or when conditions are placed on key inputs that are otherwise unspecified (e.g., *n* is a prime number).

PS Strategy 2. **Test Answer Choices**

Another common "Plan B" approach is to work backwards from the answer choices, testing to see which one fits. Doing so can often help you avoid demanding calculations or the need to set up and solve complicated algebraic expressions.

PS Strategy 3. **Avoid Needless Computation**

The GMAT rarely requires you to carry out intensive calculations to arrive at an answer. Look for opportunities to avoid tedious computation by factoring, simplifying, or estimating.

The rest of the chapter is devoted to specialized tactics that can knock out answer choices or provide clues about how to approach the problem more effectively:

PS Tactic 1. **Look For Answer Pairs**

Some Problem Solving questions have answer choices that pair with each other in some way. The right answer may be part of one of these pairs.

PS Tactic 2. **Apply Cutoffs**

Sometimes a back-of-the-envelope estimation can help you eliminate any answer choice above or below a certain cutoff.

PS Tactic 3. **Look At Positive-Negative**

Some Problem Solving questions include both positive and negative answer choices. In such cases, look for clues as to the correct sign of the right answer.

PS Tactic 4. **Draw to Scale**

Many Geometry problems allow you to eliminate some answer choices using visual estimation, as long as you draw the diagram accurately enough.

Advanced Strategies

1. Plug In Numbers

Two common categories of problems almost always allow you to pick numbers:

- VICs problems (Variables In the answer Choices, discussed in Manhattan GMAT's *Equations, Inequalities, and VICs* Strategy Guide)

- Fractions and Percents problems without specified amounts (discussed in Manhattan GMAT's *Fractions, Decimals, and Percents* Strategy Guide)

Other problem types allow this strategy as well. For instance, a problem may put *specific conditions* on the inputs but not give you exact numbers. In this case, you can go ahead and simply pick inputs that fit the conditions. If a problem specifies that "*x* must be a positive even integer" but does not specify the value of *x*, simply picking 2 for *x* will probably get you to a solution quickly and easily.

The Official Guides contain many problems that are *theoretically* difficult but simple to solve with plugged-in numbers. For instance, Problem Solving #23 in the 12th edition asks about the remainder, after division by 12, of the square of any prime number greater than 3. Proving that there is a unique remainder in all cases is extremely tough. But the GMAT did the work for you: problem #23 couldn't exist unless there existed just one remainder. All you have to do is plug in a prime number greater than 3.

Now, this particular problem is considered relatively easy, as demonstrated by its low number in the Official Guide. That's because almost everyone just goes ahead and plugs in a number. However, as an advanced test-taker, you might consider it a point of pride *not* to plug in a number. You might want to prove a "theoretically correct" answer. Overcome your pride! Get scrappy and "plug and chug."

Try-It #2-1

The integer *k* is positive but less than 400. If 21*k* is a multiple of 180, how many unique prime factors does *k* have?

(A) One   (B) Two   (C) Three   (D) Four   (E) Five

A laborious way to solve this problem would be to determine *all* the possible values for *k* and take a prime factorization of each value, counting the number of different prime factors that each value has. Ugh!

An easier technique is to pick just *one* value of k that satisfies the constraints. Any value of k that fits the constraints must have the same number of different prime factors as any other legal value of k. Otherwise, the problem could not exist as written! There would be more than one right answer.

We know that $21k$ is a multiple of 180, so $\dfrac{21k}{180} = \dfrac{7k}{60}$ must be an integer. In other words, k must be divisible by 60. The easiest number to choose is $k = 60$.

The prime factorization of 60 is $2 \times 2 \times 3 \times 5$, so 60 has the unique prime factors 2, 3, and 5. Thus, k has three unique prime factors. The correct answer is C.

Incidentally, the other values for k that would work are 120, 180, 240, 300, and 360 (multiples of 60 that are less than 400). All of them have the unique prime factors 2, 3, and 5:

$120 = 2 \times 2 \times 2 \times 3 \times 5$ (unique prime factors = 2, 3, and 5)
$180 = 3 \times 2 \times 2 \times 3 \times 5$ (unique prime factors = 2, 3, and 5)
$240 = 2 \times 2 \times 2 \times 2 \times 3 \times 5$ (unique prime factors = 2, 3, and 5)
$300 = 5 \times 2 \times 2 \times 3 \times 5$ (unique prime factors = 2, 3, and 5)
$360 = 2 \times 3 \times 2 \times 2 \times 3 \times 5$ (unique prime factors = 2, 3, and 5)

We want to emphasize again that you should *not* figure out all these values! Plug in 60 and be done with it.

2. Test Answer Choices

In a number of cases, the easiest way to solve a GMAT problem is just to work backwards from the choices. Don't be too proud to try this technique either. Of course, we want you to know theory and be able to apply it. You wouldn't be reading this book if you didn't know how to set up and solve algebraic equations, for instance. But you should be open to switching gears and testing the choices.

Try-It #2-2

> A certain college party is attended by both male and female students. The ratio of male to female students is 3 to 5. If 5 of the male students were to leave the party, the ratio would change to 1 to 2. How many total students are at the party?
>
> (A) 24   (B) 30   (C) 48   (D) 64   (E) 80

Of course, we could set up equations for the unknowns in the problem and solve them algebraically. However, it may be easier just to test the answer choices. Give this approach a try:

(A) 24 students implies 9 male and 15 female students. If 5 male students left the party, the remaining ratio would be 4/14 = 2/7. INCORRECT.

(B) 30 students implies 11.25 male and 18.75 female students. These numbers must be integers. INCORRECT.

(C) 48 students implies 18 male and 30 female students. If 5 male students left the party, the remaining ratio would be 13/30. INCORRECT.

(D) 64 students implies 24 male and 40 female students. If 5 male students left the party, the remaining ratio would be 19/40. INCORRECT.

(E) 80 students implies 30 male and 50 female students. If 5 male students left the party, the remaining ratio would be 25/50 = 1/2. CORRECT.

We proved that the correct answer must be (E) without doing any algebra at all. A nice thing about Testing Answer Choices is that it doesn't require any fundamental knowledge or theory. You don't need to know a special formula. Instead, it forces you to concentrate on the *available* answer options. It also steadily reduces your uncertainty, since you eliminate wrong answer choices one by one.

A question might contain a phrase such as "Which of the following…" This is a great time to test choices.

Try-It #2-3

If $\dfrac{2}{z} = \dfrac{2}{z+1} + \dfrac{2}{z+9}$, which of these integers could be the value of z?

(A) 0   (B) 1   (C) 2   (D) 3   (E) 4

Solving for z algebraically in this problem would not be easy. Instead, we can follow the hint in the question ("which of these integers…") and test each answer choice:

(A) $\dfrac{2}{0} = \dfrac{2}{1} + \dfrac{2}{9}$ INCORRECT (Division by zero)

(B) $\dfrac{2}{1} = \dfrac{2}{2} + \dfrac{2}{10}$ INCORRECT

(C) $\dfrac{2}{2} = \dfrac{2}{3} + \dfrac{2}{11}$ INCORRECT

(D) $\dfrac{2}{3} = \dfrac{2}{4} + \dfrac{2}{12}$ CORRECT

(E) $\dfrac{2}{4} = \dfrac{2}{5} + \dfrac{2}{13}$ INCORRECT

The correct answer is D, because it contains the only value that makes the equation work. Notice how quickly this strategy worked in this case.

3. Avoid Needless Computation

You won't see many GMAT questions that require substantial calculation to arrive at a precise answer. Rather, correct answers on difficult problems will generally be relatively easy to compute *once the difficult concept or trick in the problem has been correctly identified and addressed.*

On several types of GMAT problems, a significant amount of computation can be avoided. A simple rule of thumb is this: *if it seems that calculating the answer is going to take a lot of work, there's a good chance that a shortcut exists.* Look for the backdoor!

Estimation

Intelligent estimation can save you much time and effort on many problems. Round to nearby benchmarks. Be ready to switch a fraction to a decimal or percent, and vice versa.

Try-It #2-4

What is 35% of 4/13 of 520?

(A) 56   (B) 84   (C) 160   (D) 182   (E) 250

This problem can be solved easily if we just use approximation: 35% is a little over 1/3, while 4/13 is a little less than 4/12, which is 1/3. Thus, the answer is about 1/3 of 1/3 of 520, or 1/9 of 520. Since the first 1/3 is a slight underestimate and the second 1/3 is a slight overestimate, the errors will partially cancel each other out. Our estimate will be relatively accurate.

Even the last step in this problem can be approximated. Pick a convenient number nearby, such as 540, which is 9×60. Thus, 1/9 of 520 is about 60. The correct answer must be A.

Actually, since 520 is less than 540, 1/9 of 520 must be slightly less than 60. Keeping track not only of your current estimate, but also of *the degree to which you have overestimated or underestimated*, can help you pinpoint the correct answer more confidently.

In a problem such as this one, *making a logical error* or *omitting a step* in the computation is the trap. For example, if you computed 4/13 of 520 but didn't take 35% of the result, you would get 160 and select answer choice C incorrectly. If instead you computed 35% of 520 but didn't take 4/13 of the result, you would get 182 and select answer choice D—again, incorrectly. On every problem, follow good process to avoid needless mistakes.

The wording of the question can sometimes provide a strong clue that estimation should be used. Look for phrases such as these:

- "…the number is approximately equal to:"
- "…this result is closest to:"
- "Which of the following is most nearly equal to…?"

Heavy Multiplication

Try-It #2-5

Simplify:
$$\dfrac{\dfrac{5 \times 4^2}{4 \times 6 \times 6^2}}{\dfrac{5 \times 4}{4 \times 3 \times 2^2}}$$

Without thinking, you may dive directly into multiplying the numbers all the way through:

$$\dfrac{\dfrac{5 \times 4^2}{4 \times 6 \times 6^2}}{\dfrac{5 \times 4}{4 \times 3 \times 2^2}} = \dfrac{\dfrac{5 \times 16}{4 \times 6 \times 36}}{\dfrac{5 \times 4}{4 \times 3 \times 4}} = \dfrac{\dfrac{80}{864}}{\dfrac{20}{48}}$$

$$\dfrac{\dfrac{80}{864}}{\dfrac{20}{48}} = \dfrac{80 \times 48}{864 \times 20} = \dfrac{3,840}{17,280}$$

This is already too much computation, and you still need to reduce the fraction!

You might not have fallen into this trap. If you didn't, great. If you did, recall our rule of thumb: *if it seems that calculating the answer is going to take a lot of work, there's a good chance that a shortcut exists.* The GMAT can't expect you to do all of this computation accurately in 2 minutes, so don't try it.

Instead, be "lazy"! Just eliminate common terms as you go:

$$\dfrac{\dfrac{5 \times 4^{\cancel{2}}}{4 \times 6 \times 6^2}}{\dfrac{5 \times 4}{4 \times 3 \times 2^2}} = \dfrac{\dfrac{5 \times 4}{6 \times 36}}{\dfrac{5}{3 \times 4}} = \left(\dfrac{\cancel{5} \times 4}{6 \times 36}\right) \times \left(\dfrac{3 \times 4}{\cancel{5}}\right) = \left(\dfrac{4 \times \cancel{3} \times 4}{6 \times \cancel{36}}_{3}\right) = \dfrac{4^2}{6 \times 3}_{3} = \dfrac{2}{9}.$$

Notice also that very little actual multiplication was done. By the end of the process, the fraction was already fully reduced. Practice being "lazy" in this way.

Heavy Long Division

Very few problems on the GMAT truly require long division, even though it might appear otherwise. You can almost always approximate the answer or reduce the division by taking out common factors.

Try-It #2-6

$$\frac{3.507}{10.02} =$$

(A) 0.35   (B) 0.3505   (C) 0.3509   (D) 0.351   (E) 0.3527

At first glance, it appears that precise long division is necessary. The answer choices are very close together, making estimation difficult. However, with some manipulation and factoring, the solution is straightforward.

The key to factoring this fraction is to move the decimals of both the numerator and denominator three places to the right, so that we're dealing with integers. Then, we might notice that 3,507 is divisible by 7 (35 and 7 are both divisible by 7, providing a clue that we may be able to factor out 7). Moreover, 10,020 is divisible by 10 and by 2 (10,020 ends in a 0, and 1,002 is even):

$$\frac{3.507}{10.02} = \frac{3,507}{10,020} = \frac{7(501)}{10(1,002)} = \frac{7(501)}{(10)(2)(501)} = \frac{7}{20} = 0.35.$$

Alternatively, we could observe that 10.02 is very slightly larger than 10. Therefore, the correct answer will be slightly lower than $\frac{3.507}{10} = 0.3507$. However, we are left guessing between choices A and B.

Try-It #2-7

What is the value of $\dfrac{81,918}{(10^5 - 10^2)}$?

(A) 8.19   (B) 8.02   (C) 0.89   (D) 0.82   (E) 0.81

10^2 is extremely small compared to 10^5, and the choices are somewhat spread out, so we can estimate:

$$\frac{81,918}{(10^5 - 10^2)} \approx \frac{81,918}{100,000} = 0.81918$$

Notice that by ignoring the 10^2 term, we made the denominator slightly larger than it originally was. Therefore 0.81918 is slightly *lower* than the correct answer. The correct answer is (D) 0.82.

Quadratic Expressions In Word Problems

Some word problems result in a quadratic equation. You are probably pretty good at solving quadratic equations, so your natural bias would be to set up and solve the equation. However, if the coefficients are huge, the equation may be very difficult to solve. In these cases, try testing the answer choices in the original problem (*not* in the translated and manipulated quadratic). You'll probably arrive at the answer much more quickly and easily.

Try-It #2-8

> A shoe cobbler charges n dollars to repair a single pair of loafers. Tomorrow, he intends
> to earn 240 dollars repairing loafers. If he were to reduce his fee per pair by 20 dollars,
> he would have to repair an additional pair of the loafers to earn the same amount of
> revenue. How many pair of loafers does he intend to repair tomorrow?
>
> (A) 1   (B) 2   (C) 3   (D) 4   (E) 5

The problem seems relatively straightforward, until we try solving it algebraically. Let's assign x to represent the number of pair of loafers he intends to repair tomorrow. Using the equation for revenue:

$$nx = 240$$

Furthermore, reducing his fee by $20 would result in the need to repair an additional pair of shoes for the same amount of revenue:

$$(n-20)(x+1) = 240$$

Even though the problem is relatively simple to understand, the algebra gets complicated very quickly.

Let's switch to a different approach—testing the answer choices:

	x	n	$x \times n$	$x+1$	$n-20$	$(x+1) \times (n-20)$
(A)	1	$240	$240	2	$220	$440
(B)	2	$120	$240	3	$100	$300
(C)	**3**	**$80**	**$240**	**4**	**$60**	**$240**
(D)	4	$60	$240	5	$40	$200
(E)	5	$48	$240	6	$28	$168

We're done! Only answer choice C results in the correct amount of revenue. In fact, with practice, you wouldn't have to fill out the whole table.

Notice how painful this can be to solve algebraically:

$$nx = 240$$
$$(n-20)(x+1) = 240$$
$$x = \frac{240}{n}$$
$$(n-20)\left(\frac{240}{n} + 1\right) = 240$$
$$240 + n - \frac{4,800}{n} - 20 = 240$$
$$n - \frac{4,800}{n} = 20$$

$$n^2 - 4,800 = 20n$$
$$n^2 - 20n - 4,800 = 0$$
$$(n+60)(n-80) = 0$$
$$n = -60 \text{ or } 80 \,(\text{price cannot be negative})$$
$$80x = 240$$
$$x = 3$$

Advanced Guessing Tactics

To repeat, the tactics below are less universally useful than the strategies we just covered. However, when all else fails, "break the glass" and try one or more of these tactics. They're almost always better than guessing completely randomly. If you're way behind on time and you have to sacrifice a couple of problems, apply one or more of these tactics as you guess and move on.

The examples below will not be too difficult, in order to illustrate the tactic clearly and not distract you with other issues. Of course, if you can solve the problem directly, do so! But also study the tactic, so you're ready to use it when the time comes.

1. Look for Answer Pairs   *Certainty:* Moderate

GMAT answer choices are sometimes paired in a mathematically relevant way. Pairs of answers may:

- Add up to 1 on a probability or fraction question.
- Add up to 100% on questions involving percents.
- Add up to 0 (be opposites of each other).
- Multiply to 1 (be reciprocals of each other.

The right answer is sometimes part of such a pair. Why? The GMAT likes to put in a final obstacle. Say you do everything right, except you solve for the wrong unknown or forget to subtract from 1. Under the pressure of the exam, people make this sort of *penultimate error* all the time (*penultimate* means "next to last").

In order to catch folks in this trap, the GMAT has to make an answer choice that's paired to the right answer—it's right *except* for that one last step.

This means that you can often eliminate *unpaired* answer choices. Also, the way in which the answers are paired may provide clues about the correct solution method and/or traps in the problem.

Try-It #2-9

> At a certain high school, the junior class is twice the size of the senior class. If 1/3 of the seniors and 1/4 of the juniors study Japanese, what fraction of the students in both classes do not study Japanese?
>
> (A) 1/6   (B) 5/18   (C) 5/12   (D) 7/12   (E) 13/18

Note that two pairs of answers each add up to one: 5/12 + 7/12, and 5/18 + 13/18. Thus we could conclude that (A) 1/6 is not likely to be correct, because it is not part of an answer pair. The fact that these pairs sum to one also provides a clue to double-check the wording of the question: *do* vs. *do not* study Japanese (the sum of the fractions of the students that *do* study Japanese and those who *do not* will equal 1).

By the way, to solve this problem, we can use a Double-Set Matrix that shows juniors vs. seniors and Japanese-studiers vs. non-Japanese-studiers. However, let's go back to the first strategy in this chapter and Plug In Numbers. Pick a smart number that is a multiple of the denominators in the problem: $3 \times 4 = 12$.

Let's say the junior class has 12 people. The senior class thus has 6. If 1/3 of the seniors study Japanese, that is $1/3 \times 6 = 2$ students. If 1/4 of the juniors study Japanese, that is $1/4 \times 12 = 3$ students. There are $12 + 6 = 18$ students total, and $2 + 3 = 5$ of them study Japanese. Thus 5/18 of the students *do* study Japanese, so the fraction of the students that *do not* study Japanese is 13/18. The correct answer is E.

Notice that 5/18 is a *trap answer* in this problem—it is the proportion of students who *do* study Japanese. The correct answer (13/18) was paired with 5/18, so our guessing tactic of eliminating the non-paired answer choice was good, in retrospect.

2. Apply Cutoffs   *Certainty:* High

You may be able to eliminate answers above or below some easily calculated threshold value. You have to imagine that the problem is slightly different (and easier) to come up with that threshold value, but once you do, you can often get rid of two or three answer choices.

This strategy can sometimes be used in combination with an Answer Pairs Strategy, as pairs of answers are often composed of a high and a low value.

In the previous problem, for example, 1/3 of the seniors and 1/4 of the juniors study Japanese. Therefore, somewhere between 1/3 and 1/4 of the students overall must study Japanese. This implies that the fraction of students who *do not* study Japanese must be between 2/3 and 3/4. We could thus eliminate answer choices A, B, and C, because each of these answer choices is smaller than 1/2.

Try-It #2-10

> Trains A and B start simultaneously from stations 300 miles apart, and travel the same route toward each other on adjacent parallel tracks. If Train A and Train B travel at a constant rate of 50 miles per hour and 40 miles per hour, respectively, how many miles will Train A have traveled when the trains pass each other, to the nearest mile?
>
> (A) 112   (B) 133   (C) 150   (D) 167   (E) 188

If the trains were going the same speed, it is easy to see that they would pass each other in the middle. Each train would have gone 150 miles. This is our simple hypothetical threshold.

In reality, train A goes faster than B, so the distance traveled by A has to be greater than 150 miles. So we can rapidly eliminate answer choices A, B, and C.

By the way, the quickest way to solve this problem precisely is to add the rates. The trains cover 300 miles of tracks at a combined rate of 90 miles per hour; thus, the total time will be 300/90, or 10/3 hours. Train A travels at a rate of 50 miles per hour for 10/3 hours, so it goes 500/3 miles. The closest approximation is 167 miles. The correct answer is D.

3. Look at Positive-Negative   *Certainty:* High

A special case of the Cutoff Strategy occurs when some of the answer choices are positive and others are negative. In this case, focus on figuring out the sign of the correct answer, then eliminate any answer choices of the opposite sign. (Again, this is something to do when you have run out of direct approaches or you are short on time!)

Try-It #2-11

If $x \square y$ is defined to equal x^2/y for all x and y, then $(-1 \square 2) \square 3 =$

(A) 4/3   (B) 1/3   (C) 1/12   (D) −1/12   (E) −4/3

By looking at the problem quickly, we can see that the negative sign in the term −1 will be extinguished, because the term before the $\square$ symbol is squared when this function is calculated. Therefore, the correct answer will be positive. You can eliminate D and E.

4. Draw to Scale   *Certainty:* Moderate

As we saw in the last section, many GMAT problems can be simplified by approximating an answer. This idea can be extended to some Geometry problems.

We can approximate the length of a line segment, size of an angle, or area of an object by drawing it as accurately as possible on our scrap paper. When you take the GMAT, the laminated scratch booklet is printed with a light grid. This grid can help you draw very accurate scale pictures, and often the picture alone is enough to answer the question.

Try-It #2-12

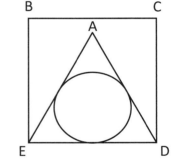

In the diagram to the right, equilateral triangle *ADE* is drawn inside square *BCDE*. A circle is then inscribed inside triangle *ADE*. What is the ratio of the area of the circle to the area of the square?

(A) $\dfrac{\pi}{12}$ (B) $\dfrac{\pi}{8}$ (C) $\dfrac{\pi}{6}$ (D) $\dfrac{\pi}{4}$ (E) $\dfrac{\pi}{2}$

If we redraw the diagram correctly, we can see that the circle is about 1/2 the height of the square, and about 1/2 the width. Therefore, the area of the circle should be approximately 1/4 of the area of the square. We can eliminate any answer choices that are far away from that estimate:

(A) $\dfrac{\pi}{12} \approx \dfrac{3.1}{12} \approx \dfrac{1}{4}$ OK

(B) $\dfrac{\pi}{8} \approx \dfrac{3.1}{8} \approx \dfrac{3}{8}$ TOO HIGH

(C) $\dfrac{\pi}{6} \approx \dfrac{3.1}{6} \approx \dfrac{1}{2}$ TOO HIGH

(D) $\dfrac{\pi}{4} \approx \dfrac{3.1}{4} \approx \dfrac{3}{4}$ TOO HIGH

(E) $\dfrac{\pi}{2} \approx \dfrac{3.1}{2} \approx 1\dfrac{1}{2}$ WAY TOO HIGH

As you can see, only answer choice A is close to our estimate, so it must be the right answer.

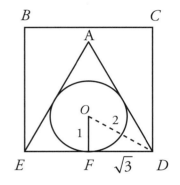

The easiest way to solve this problem fully is to assign a radius of 1 to the circle. This way, the circle has an area of π. Now work outwards.

If we call the center of the circle O, then $OF = 1$. Because ADE is an equilateral triangle, angle $ADE = 60°$. OD bisects angle ADE, so angle $ODE = 30°$. Therefore, triangle OFD is a 30:60:90 triangle, and OD must be twice the length of OF. Therefore, $OD = 2$, and $DF = \sqrt{3}$. DE must be twice the length of DF, meaning that $DE = 2\sqrt{3}$, and the area of square $BCDE = \left(2\sqrt{3}\right)^2 = 12$.

So the ratio of the area of the circle to the area of the square is $\dfrac{\pi}{12}$.

Notice how much easier the Draw to Scale tactic was! Will it work every time? No. But it's handy nonetheless.

In-Action Problem Set

Solve problems #1 through #10. In each case, identify whether you could use advanced strategies (*Plug In Numbers*, *Test Answer Choices*, or *Avoid Needless Computation*) and guessing tactics (*Look for Answer Pairs, Apply Cutoffs, Look at Positive-Negative,* or *Draw to Scale*) in any beneficial way. Of course, there are textbook ways to solve these problems directly; focus on applying the strategies and tactics described in this chapter.

1. To become a certified lifeguard, lifeguard trainees must take and pass a test. If 1/3 of lifeguard trainees do not take the test, and 1/4 of those who take the test fail, what fraction of the trainees will become certified lifeguards? (*Compute an answer.*)

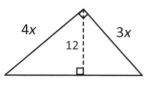

2. If the perimeter of the right triangle above is 60, what is the area of the triangle?

3. If $(x + 3)^2 = 225$, which of the following could be the value of $x - 1$?

    (A) 13   (B) 12   (C) -12 (D) -16 (E) -19

4. If $\left| x^2 - 6 \right| = x$, which of the following could be the value of x?

    (A) -2 (B) 0   (C) 1   (D) 3   (E) 5

5. $\sqrt{\dfrac{64.59}{13.04} \times \dfrac{15.04}{2.98}}$ is approximately equal to

    (A) 4   (B) 5   (C) 6   (D) 7   (E) 8

6. $\dfrac{1.206}{2.010} =$

    (A) 0.6   (B) 0.603   (C) 0.606   (D) 0.615   (E) 0.66

7. Last year, a magazine charged a $50 subscription fee. This year, the price will be increased by $10. If the magazine could lose 4 subscribers this year and still collect the same revenue as it did last year, how many subscribers did the magazine have last year?

    (A) 20   (B) 21   (C) 22   (D) 23   (E) 24

8. If $\dfrac{3}{\dfrac{m+1}{m}+1}=1$, then m must equal

   (A) −2   (B) −1   (C) 0   (D) 1   (E) 2

9. Simplify $\dfrac{\dfrac{35^3}{72}}{\left(\dfrac{7!}{3!4!}\right)^3}$

10. If $3^x + 3^x + 3^x = 1$, what is x?

   (A) −1   (B) −1/3   (C) 0   (D) 1/3   (E) 1

Without solving questions #11 through #14, which answers could you confidently eliminate and why?

11. $\dfrac{69,300}{10^5 - 10^3} =$

   (A) 0.693   (B) 0.7   (C) 0.71   (D) 6.93   (E) 7.1

12. $\dfrac{-(9.0)(0.25)-(1.5)(1.5)}{25} =$

   (A) −1.8   (B) −0.18   (C) 0   (D) 0.18   (E) 1.8

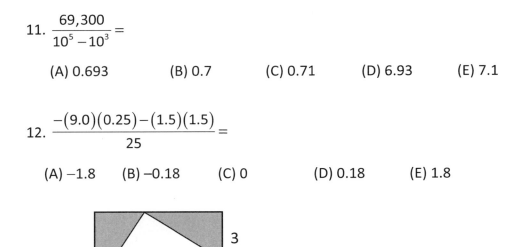

13. In the 7 inch square above, another square is inscribed. What fraction of the larger square is shaded?

   (A) 3/12   (B) 24/49   (C) 1/2   (D) 25/49   (E) 7/12

14. If Mason is now twice as old as Gunther was 10 years ago, and G is Gunther's current age in years, which of the following represents the sum of Mason and Gunther's ages 4 years from now?

   (A) $\dfrac{3G}{2}+3$ (B) $3G + 28$ (C) $3G - 12$ (D) $8 - G$ (E) $14 - \dfrac{3G}{2}$

In-Action Problem Set (Solutions)

1. **1/2:** (*Plug In Numbers*) Choose a smart number for the number of trainees. The common denominator of all fractions given is $(3)(4) = 12$. One third of trainees do not take the test, so we get rid of $(1/3)(12)$, or 4 trainees, leaving 8 who take the test. One quarter (2) of these people fail, leaving 6 who pass.

$6/12 = 1/2$ of trainees pass the test and become certified lifeguards.

2. **150:** (*Plug In Numbers*) We could solve algebraically, calling the hypotenuse b because it is the base.

$$Perimeter = 3x + 4x + b = 60$$
$$b = 60 - 7x$$

$$(3x)^2 + (4x)^2 = (60 - 7x)^2$$
$$9x^2 + 16x^2 = 3600 - 840x + 49x^2$$
$$0 = 3600 - 840x + 24x^2$$
$$0 = 150 - 35x + x^2$$
$$0 = (x - 5)(x - 30)$$
$$x = 5 \ or \ 30$$

Not only must we solve a quadratic, but we must then check the solutions. With $x = 30$, individual sides would exceed the given perimeter of 60, so the only valid solution is $x = 5$. And we are still not done:

$$b = 60 - 7x$$
$$b = 60 - 7(5)$$
$$b = 60 - 35 = 25$$

$$Area = \frac{1}{2}bh$$
$$= \frac{1}{2}(25)(12)$$
$$= 150$$

Picking and plugging numbers is a much more elegant approach. x is probably an integer. Also, 3–4–5 is the most common Pythagorean triple, so we might suspect multiples (e.g., 6–8–10, 9–12–15, etc.)

$$Perimeter = 9 + 12 + 15 = 36 \ (too \ low)$$
$$= 12 + 16 + 20 = 48 \ (too \ low)$$
$$= 15 + 20 + 25 = 60 \ ✔$$

Thus, the side that corresponds to $3x$ has a length of 15, $4x$ has a length of 20, and the hypotenuse has a length of 25. Use the hypotenuse as the base of the triangle.

$$Area = \frac{1}{2}bh$$
$$= \frac{1}{2}(25)(12)$$
$$= 150$$

3. **E) −19:** (*Test Answer Choices*)

	$x-1$	$x+3$	$(x+3)^2$
(A)	13	17	289
(B)	12	16	256
(C)	−12	−8	64
(D)	−16	−12	144
(E)	**−19**	**−15**	**225**

The correct answer must be E.

4. **D) 3:** (*Test Answer Choices*)

	x	x^2-6	$\lvert x^2-6 \rvert$
(A)	−2	$(-2)^2 - 6 = 4 - 6 = -2$	2
(B)	0	$(0)^2 - 6 = 0 - 6 = -6$	6
(C)	1	$(1)^2 - 6 = 1 - 6 = 5$	5
(D)	**3**	$\mathbf{(3)^2 - 6 = 9 - 6 = 3}$	**3**
(E)	5	$(5)^2 - 6 = 25 - 6 = 19$	19

The correct answer is D.

5. **B) 5:** (*Avoid Needless Computation by Estimation*) $\sqrt{\dfrac{64.59}{13.04} \times \dfrac{15.04}{2.98}} \approx \sqrt{\dfrac{65}{13} \times \dfrac{15}{3}} = \sqrt{5 \times 5} = 5.$

6. **A) 0.6:** (*Avoid Needless Computation by Heavy Long Division*) $\dfrac{1.206}{2.010} = \dfrac{1,206}{2,010} = \dfrac{3(402)}{5(402)} = \dfrac{3}{5} = 0.6.$

Alternatively, we could note that 2.010 is very slightly larger than 2. Therefore the fraction is very slightly

smaller than $\dfrac{1.206}{2} = 0.603.$ Only (A) is smaller than 0.603.

7. **E) 24:** (*Avoid Needless Computation by Testing Choices in Word Problems involving Quadratics*)

	Subscribers Last Year	Subscribers This Year (−4)	Revenue Last Year ($50 each)	Revenue This Year ($60 each)
(A)	20	16	$1,000	$960
(B)	21	17	$1,050	$1,020
(C)	22	18	$1,100	$1,080
(D)	23	19	$1,150	$1,140
(E)	**24**	**20**	**$1,200**	**$1,200**

The correct answer is E.

8. **D) 1:** (*Avoid Needless Computation by Testing Choices*)

We can quickly surmise that *m* has to be positive. In order for the fraction on the left hand side to equal 1,

the denominator must equal 3. Thus, $\dfrac{m+1}{m}$ must equal 2. By inspection, we can see that only $m = 1$ works.

9. $\dfrac{1}{72}$: (*Avoid Needless Computation by Heavy Multiplication*)

$$\frac{\dfrac{35^3}{72}}{\left(\dfrac{7!}{3!4!}\right)^3} = \frac{\dfrac{5^3 7^3}{2^3 3^2}}{\left(\dfrac{(7)(6)(5)}{(3)(2)}\right)^3} = \frac{\dfrac{5^3 7^3}{2^3 3^2}}{7^3 5^3} = \frac{1}{2^3 3^2} = \frac{1}{72}$$

10. **A) −1:** (*Test Answer Choices*) You might solve this one by inspection: three identical "somethings" sum to

1, so one of those "somethings" equals 1/3, or $3^x = \dfrac{1}{3} = 3^{-1}$.

Testing choices is fast, too.

	x	$3^x + 3^x + 3^x$
(A)	−1	1/3 + 1/3 + 1/3 = 1
(B)	−1/3	non-integer
(C)	0	1 + 1 + 1 = 3
(D)	1/3	non-integer
(E)	1	3 + 3 + 3 = 9

11. **A, D, and E can be eliminated:** If you ignore the 10^3 in the denominator, the division is $\dfrac{69,300}{10^5} = 0.693$.

This is an approximation of the answer, not an exact computation of it, so we can eliminate A. We have slightly overstated the denominator, thus slightly understated the result. B and C are possibilities, but D and E are both clearly too large. The correct answer turns out to be B.

12. **A, C, D, and E can be eliminated:** The numerator is negative, so eliminate C, D, and E. The numbers in the numerator are small (in absolute value) relative to 25, so eliminate A.

The correct answer must be B.

13. **A, C, D, and E can be eliminated:** Ignoring the dimensions 3 and 4 for a moment, think about the types of squares that might be inscribed in the larger square:

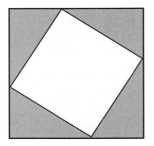 

The shaded area can be at most 1/2 of the larger square, which occurs when the smallest possible square is inscribed in the larger square. This gives us a great *Cutoff*.

The larger the inscribed square, the smaller the shaded area, and the more the inscribed square must be rotated from the vertical orientation of the minimum inscribed square.

Eliminate D and E, since they are larger than 1/2. Eliminate C, since the labeled lengths of 3 and 4 are not equal, indicating that the inscribed square is rotated from the minimum square position. B is paired with D to sum to 1. A is unpaired, so between A and B, the more likely answer is B. B is in fact the correct answer.

There is an easier way to arrive at the exact answer: simply compute the relevant areas and take the ratio. The point of this exercise, though, is to practice guessing tactics.

14. **D and E can be eliminated:** Gunther must be at least 10 years old, in order for him to have had a non-negative age "10 years ago" and in order for Mason to have a non-negative age now. We can therefore eliminate D and E, as both choices will give a negative result when $G > 10$. The correct answer is in fact C.

Chapter 3
of
ADVANCED GMAT QUANT

DATA
SUFFICIENCY:
PRINCIPLES

In This Chapter . . .

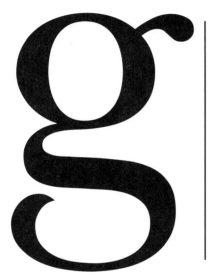

- Principle #1: Follow a Consistent Process
- Principle #2: Never Rephrase Yes/No as Value
- Principle #3: Work from Facts to Question
- Principle #4: Be a Contrarian
- Principle #5: Assume Nothing

DATA SUFFICIENCY: ADVANCED PRINCIPLES

The goal of every Data Sufficiency problem is the same: determine what information will let you answer the given question. This gives you a significant advantage. Once you know whether a piece of information lets you answer the given question, *you can stop calculating*. So you do not have to waste time finishing that calculation.

However, this type of problem presents its own challenges. Data Sufficiency answer choices are never numbers, so you can't plug them back into the question. Also, answer choice E—that the two statements combined are NOT sufficient—leaves open the possibility that the embedded math question is not solvable even with *all* the information given. That is, unlike Problem Solving, Data Sufficiency may contain math problems that *cannot* be solved! This aspect of Data Sufficiency is simply unsettling.

On Data Sufficiency problems, the issue being tested is *"answer-ability" itself*—can the given question be answered, and if so, with what information? So the GMAT disguises "answer-ability" as best it can. The given facts and the question itself are generally presented in ways that make this determination difficult.

For instance, information that *seems* to be sufficient may actually be insufficient, if it permits an alternate scenario that leads to a different answer. Likewise, information that seems to be *insufficient* may actually be sufficient, if all the possible scenarios lead to the same answer for the question.

Advanced Data Sufficiency problems require you to step up your game. You will have to get really good at elimination and number testing, which are even more important for advanced Data Sufficiency than for advanced Problem Solving.

You will also have to get really good at simplifying the given facts and the given question. The GMAT increases the trickiness of the *phrasing* of the question and/or statements even more than the complexity of the *underlying concepts*.

So how do you approach advanced Data Sufficiency problems? Unfortunately, there is no "one size fits all" approach for advanced Data Sufficiency:

- The best approach may involve precise application of theory, *or* it may involve a "quick and dirty" method that is not theoretically elegant.

- The statements may be easy *or* difficult to interpret.

- The question may require no rephrasing *or* elaborate rephrasing. In fact, the crux of the problem may rest entirely on a careful rephrasing of the question.

All that said, there are a few guiding principles you can follow.

Principle #1: Follow a Consistent Process

This is the most important principle. Consistent process will prevent most common errors. It will focus your efforts at any stage of the problem. Perhaps most importantly, it will reduce your stress level, because you will have confidence in the approach that you've practiced. No matter how difficult a problem seems, you will have a starting point and a "next step" to take.

You have to develop a process that suits your way of thinking. But observe these rules of the road:

- **Do your work on paper, not in your head.** This fits with the *Put Pen to Paper* concept discussed in Chapter 1. Writing down each thought as it occurs helps you keep track of the work you've done. Your mind is also freed up to think ahead. Many Data Sufficiency questions are *explicitly designed* to confuse you if you do all the work in your head.

- **Label everything and separate everything physically on your paper.** If you mix up the elements of the problem, you will often mess up the problem itself. Keep these 4 elements straight:

  - **Facts given in the question stem.** You can leave them unlabeled, or you can put them with each statement.

  - **Question.** Label the question with a question mark. Obvious, right? Amazingly, many people fail to take this simple step. Without a question mark, you might think the question is a fact—and you *will* get the problem wrong. Keep the question mark as you rephrase. It's also helpful to keep the helping verb in a yes/no question:

    - Original question: Is $x = 2$?
    - You write down: Is $x = 2$?
    - You could just write down: $x = 2$?
    - DO NOT just write down: $x = 2$ ✗

  - **Statement (1).** Label this with a (1).

  - **Statement (2).** Label this with a (2).

  It may be worth rewriting the facts from the question stem alongside each statement. Although this may seem redundant, the time is well spent if it prevents you from forgetting to use those facts.

- **Rephrase the question and statements whenever possible.** Any successful rephrasing will make the work you do later in the problem easier. In particular, try to rephrase the question *before* you dive into the statements. This habit will not only save you time and effort; occasionally, it will make all the difference between getting the problem right and getting it wrong.

- **Evaluate the easier statement first.** This facilitates quick elimination, which conserves time and reduces stress.

- **Physically separate the work that you do on the individual statements.** Doing so can help reduce the risk of *statement carryover*—unintentionally letting one statement influence you as you evaluate the other statement.

Here is one sample schema for setting up your work on a Data Sufficiency question:

Scrapwork for Rephrasing: ~~~~		
Constraints: ~~~~	(1)	(2)
AD BCE	FACT from question stem: ~~~~ FACT from (1): ~~~~ ...*and any work you do to combine these facts*	FACT from question stem: ~~~~ FACT from (2): ~~~~ ...*and any work you do to combine these facts*
QUESTION: ...?	ANSWER	ANSWER

Notice the *physical separation* between Statement (1) and Statement (2). You might even consider going so far as to cover up the Statement (1) work when evaluating Statement (2). Also observe in this schema that we explicitly parse out the facts given in the question stem, and evaluate those facts *alongside* each statement.

Let's explore an example problem, and then take a look at what our work on paper would look like according to this schema.

Try-It #3-1

If x and y are integers and $4xy = x^2y + 4y$, what is the value of xy?

(1) $y - x = 2$
(2) $x^3 < 0$

Because the question stem contains an equation, we should evaluate it before considering the statements:

$x^2y - 4xy + 4y = 0$
$y(x^2 - 4x + 4) = 0$
$y(x - 2)^2 = 0$

Therefore, either $x = 2$ or $y = 0$, or both. One of the following scenarios must be true:

x	y	$xy = ?$
2	Not 0	$2y$
Not 2	0	0
2	0	0

The question can thus be rephrased as "What is the value of y?" If $y = 0$, we would know that $xy = 0$. Otherwise, we would know that x must equal 2, in which case the value of xy depends on y.

(1) INSUFFICIENT: Rather than trying to combine this algebraically with the equation in the question stem, let's try a couple of the possible scenarios that fit this statement. Construct scenarios using the earlier table as inspiration.

- If $x = 2$, then $y = 2 + x = 4$, so $xy = (2)(4) = 8$.

- If $y = 0$, then $x = y - 2 = -2$, so $xy = (-2)(0) = 0$.

Since there are two possible answers, we have *proven* that this statement is not sufficient.

(2) SUFFICIENT: If $x^3 < 0$, then $x < 0$. If x does not equal 2, then y must equal 0, according to the fact from the question stem. Therefore, $xy = 0$.

Notice that we evaluated the fact in the question stem first, and used it to rephrase the question. We then considered each statement individually, alongside the given fact in the question stem. Here is approximately how your paper could look:

Scrapwork for Rephrasing:	$4xy = x^2y + 4y$ $x^2y - 4xy + 4y = 0$ $y(x^2 - 4x + 4) = 0$ $y(x - 2)^2 = 0$	<u>Does $x = 2$ or does $y = 0$?</u>
Constraints:	x and y <u>integers</u>	
~~AD~~ ⒷCE	**(1)** $x = 2$ or $y = 0$ or BOTH $y - x = 2$ $y = 2 + x$ (If $x = 2$, $y = 4$, so $xy = 8$) (If $y = 0$, $x = -2$, so $xy = 0$)	**(2)** $x = 2$ or $y = 0$ or BOTH $x^3 < 0$ $x < 0$ (If x is negative, y must equal 0)
QUESTION: Does $y = 0$?	Either Possible (INSUFFICIENT)	$y = 0$ (SUFFICIENT)

The correct answer is B.

If we didn't rephrase the question by manipulating the fact given in the question stem, we could have easily failed to see the sufficiency of Statement (2) alone and incorrectly answered C or E.

You can lay your paper out in many other ways. For instance, you might go with this simple version:

*Manhattan*GMAT Prep
the new standard

```
┌──────────────────────────────────────────────────────────────┐
│ Stem:                          Q:    ...?                      │
│                                                                │
│                                                                │
│ 1)                                                             │
│                                                                │
│                                                                │
│ 2)                                                             │
│                                                                │
└──────────────────────────────────────────────────────────────┘
```

In this second layout, facts go on the left, while the question and any rephrasing go on the right. Then the process is always to see whether you can bridge the gap, going from left to right.

The important thing is that you have a system that you always use. Don't give away points on Data Sufficiency because your work is sloppy or you mix up the logic.

Principle #2: Never Rephrase Yes/No as Value

All Data Sufficiency questions can be divided into two types: **Value** questions (such as "What is a?") and **Yes/No** questions (such as "Is x an integer?"). Value questions and Yes/No questions are fundamentally different: they require different levels of information to answer the question. Therefore you should *never* rephrase a Yes/No question as a value question. Value questions usually require more information than Yes/No questions.

Try-It #3-2

> Is the integer n odd?
>
> (1) $n^2 - 2n$ is not a multiple of 4.
> (2) n is a multiple of 3.

We don't need to know *which* value n might be, just *whether n is odd*. Therefore, do not rephrase this question to "What is integer n?" Doing so unnecessarily increases the amount of information we need to answer the question. Of course, if you happen to know what n is, then great, you can answer any Yes/No question about n. But you generally don't *need* to know the value of n to answer Yes/No questions about n, and the GMAT loves to exploit that truth at our expense.

(1) SUFFICIENT: $n^2 - 2n = n(n - 2)$. If n is even, both terms in this product will be even, and the product will be divisible by 4. Since $n^2 - 2n$ is not a multiple of 4, we know that the integer n cannot be even—it must be odd.

(2) INSUFFICIENT: Multiples of 3 can be either odd or even.

The correct answer is A.

Rephrasing a Yes/No Question into a value question makes the question *unnecessarily picky*. We would be making the assumption that we need a single value for sufficiency, when Yes/No questions can often be sufficiently answered despite having many value answers. If we rephrased this Question to "What is *n*?" we would *incorrectly* conclude that the answer is E.

Note that the converse of this principle is *not* always true. Occasionally it's okay to rephrase a value question as a Yes/No question—specifically, when it turns out that there are only two possible values.

Try-It #3-3

If x is a positive integer, what is the remainder of $\dfrac{x^2 - 1}{4}$?

Some quick analysis will show that $x^2 - 1$ can be factored into $(x + 1)(x - 1)$. If x is odd, then both of these terms will be even and the product will be divisible by 4 (yielding a remainder of 0 when divided by 4). If x is even, then x^2 will be divisible by 4, so the remainder of $x^2 - 1$ will be 3.

There are only two possible values of the remainder: 0 and 3. So this value question can be rephrased to the Yes/No question "Is x odd?" or similarly, "Is x even?" Although this value question seemed at first to have several different potential outcomes, we have determined that only two are possible, so we are able to *change* the question to a Yes/No format by suitable rephrasing.

Principle #3: Work from Facts to Question

Especially for simple Yes/No questions, people often think "*Could* the answer be yes?" or "Does the question fit the information in the statements?" They assume a "Yes" for the question, then look at the statements.

This line of thinking is backwards—and tempting, because of the order in which things are presented.

Instead you should ask "If I start with the applicable facts and consider *all* possibilities, do I get a *definitive* answer to the question?"

Always work from the given facts to the question—never the reverse! This is why you have to keep the facts separated from the question, and why you should always clearly mark the question on your paper.

Try-It #3-4

Is $x = 1$?

(1) $x^2 = 1/x^2$
(2) $x^2 = 1/x$

If you are doing this *wrong*, you would assume a "Yes" for the question, then plug into the statements. For instance, you would plug $x = 1$ into each statement. You would see that the value fits the equations in both statements, and you would pick D *incorrectly*. That's especially easy to do in this case, because this particular question is much simpler to think about than the statements (which are nasty little equations).

Don't do this wrong! No matter what, when you are judging sufficiency, you should always proceed from the *facts* to the *question*. It doesn't matter how easy or hard the question is at that point. After you've rephrased, put the question on hold and work *from* the statements and any other given facts *to* the question:

	(1)	(2)
	$x^2 = 1/x^2$ $x^4 = 1$ $x = 1$ or -1	$x^2 = 1/x$ $x^3 = 1$ $x = 1$
QUESTION: Is $x = 1$?	MAYBE	YES

The correct answer is B.

> **!**
>
> In a Yes/No question, when evaluating the statements, always try to determine whether the question can be answered the same way under *any possibility* that is consistent with those facts. Simply checking to see whether the question *might* be true given the facts from the statements is sloppy, and will often lead to an incorrect answer.

Principle #4: Be a Contrarian

To avoid statement carryover and to gain insight into the nature of a problem, you should *deliberately* try to violate one statement as you evaluate the other statement. This will make it much harder for you to make a faulty assumption that leads to the wrong answer. Think outside the first statement's box.

Try-It #3-5

If $x \neq 0$, is $xy > 0$?

(1) $x > 0$

(2) $\dfrac{1}{x} < y$

(1) INSUFFICIENT: This tells us nothing about the sign of y.

In evaluating Statement (2), you might be tempted to assume that x must be positive. After all, we just read information in Statement (1) that tells us that x is positive. Besides, it is natural to assume that a given variable will have a positive value, because positive numbers are much more intuitive than negative numbers.

Instead, if we follow Principle #4, we will *actively* try to violate Statement (1), helping us expose the trick in this question.

(2) INSUFFICIENT: If we contradict Statement (1) to consider the possibility that x is negative, we would realize that it is necessary to flip the sign of the inequality when we cross multiply. That is, if $x < 0$, then $\frac{1}{x} < y$ means that $1 > xy$, and the answer to the question is MAYBE.

(1) & (2) SUFFICIENT: If x is positive, then statement (2) says that $1 < xy$ (we do not flip the sign when cross multiplying). Thus, $xy > 0$.

The correct answer is C.

> When evaluating individual statements, *deliberately* trying to violate the other statement can help you see the full pattern or trick in the problem. You will be less likely to fall victim to *statement carryover*.

Principle #5: Assume Nothing

This principle is a corollary of the previous principle. You must avoid assuming constraints that aren't actually given in the problem—particularly assumptions that seem natural to make.

Try-It #3-6

> Is z an even integer?
>
> (1) $z/2$ is an even integer.
> (2) $3z$ is an even integer.

The wording of this question has a tendency to bias people towards integers. After all, the "opposite" of even is odd, and odd numbers are integers, too. However, the question does not state that z must be an integer in the first place, so *do not assume* that it is.

(1) SUFFICIENT: The fact that $z/2$ is an even integer implies that $z = 2 \times$ (an even integer), which much be an even integer. (In fact, according to statement (1), z must be divisible by 4).

(2) INSUFFICENT: The fact that $3z$ is an even integer implies that $z =$ (an even integer)/3, which might not be an integer at all. For example, z could equal 2/3.

One way to avoid assuming is to invoke Principle #3: Work from Facts to Question. Statement (2) tells us that $3z =$ even integer $= -2, 0, 2, 4, 6, 8, 10$, etc. No even integers have been skipped over, nor have we allowed the question to suggest z values. That is how assumptions sneak in.

Next, we divide $3z$ by 3 to get z, so we divide the numbers on our list by 3: $z = -2/3, 0, 2/3, 4/3, 2, 8/3, 10/3$, etc. Only then do we check this list against our question and see that the answer is *Maybe*.

The correct answer is A.

> **!**
>
> If we had assumed that z must be an integer, we might have evaluated statement (2) with two cases:
>
> - $3 \times$ even = even, so z could be even.
> - $3 \times$ odd = odd, so z is definitely not odd.
>
> We would have *incorrectly* concluded that Statement (2) was sufficient and therefore *incorrectly* selected answer (D).

Another common assumption is that a variable must be positive. Do not assume that any unknown is positive *unless it is stated as such* in the information given (or if the unknown counts physical things or measures some other positive-only quantity).

In-Action Problem Set

For questions 1–3, apply *Principle #1 (Follow a Consistent Process)* from this chapter to arrive at a solution to each question. Note that the solutions presented later in this chapter for problems 1–3 are specific examples. Your process may be different.

1. There are 19 batters on a baseball team. Every batter bats either right-handed only, left-handed only, or both right-handed and left-handed. How many of the 19 batters bat left-handed?

    (1) 7 of the batters bat right-handed but do not bat left-handed.
    (2) 4 of the batters bat both right-handed and left-handed.

2. If a is a positive integer and 81 divided by a results in a remainder of 1, what is the value of a?

    (1) The remainder when a is divided by 40 is 0.
    (2) The remainder when 40 is divided by a is 40.

3. If a, b, c, d, and e are positive integers such that $\dfrac{a \times 10^d}{b \times 10^e} = c \times 10^4$, is $\dfrac{bc}{a}$ an integer?

    (1) $d - e \geq 4$
    (2) $d - e > 4$

Solve questions 4–5. Applying *Principle #2*, describe why these Yes/No questions cannot be rephrased as value questions.

4. If n is a positive integer, is $n - 1$ divisible by 3?

    (1) $n^2 + n$ is not divisible by 6.
    (2) $3n = k + 3$, where k is a positive multiple of 3.

5. If a, b, and c are each integers greater than 1, is the product abc divisible by 6?

    (1) The product ab is even.
    (2) The product bc is divisible by 3.

6. Revisit questions 4 and 5 above, this time deliberately violating Principle #3 (*Work from Facts to Question*). Determine the incorrect answer you might have selected if you had reversed the process and worked from the *question* to the *facts*.

First, attempt to solve question 7 by evaluating Statement (1), and then evaluating Statement (2) *without violating the information* in Statement (1). Then, re-solve the problems by applying Principle #4 (*Be a Contrarian*). Do you get the same answer? Verify that applying Principle #4 leads to the correct answer, whereas not following the Principle could lead to an incorrect answer.

7. Is $m \neq 0$, is $m^3 > m^2$?

    (1) $m > 0$
    (2) $m^2 > m$

For questions 8–9, apply Principle #5 (*Assume Nothing*) by identifying the explicit constraints given in the problem. What values are still permissible? Next, solve using these constraints. Verify that different (incorrect) answers are attainable if incorrect assumptions about the variables in the problem are made, and identify examples of such incorrect assumptions.

8. If $yz \neq 0$, is $0 < y < 1$?

   (1) $y < \dfrac{1}{y}$

   (2) $y = z^2$

9. If x and y are positive integers, is y odd?

   (1) $\dfrac{(y+2)!}{x!}$ is an odd integer.

   (2) $\dfrac{(y+2)!}{x!}$ is greater than 2.

*Manhattan*GMAT*Prep
the new standard

In-Action Problem Set (Solutions)

(Note that the solutions presented for problems 1–3 are specific examples. Your process may be different.)

1.

<u>Rephrasing:</u>
19 batters total→ integers only!
some R only
some L only
some R & L
(none that are neither R nor L)

How many left-handed batters?

	L	not L	Total
R			
not R		0	
Total	x		19

What is the integer x?

	(1)	(2)
Ⓐ D ~~BCE~~		

(1)	L	not L	Total
R		7	
not R		0	
Total	x	7	19

(2)	L	not L	Total
R	4		
not R		0	
Total	x		19

QUESTION: **Integer x = ?**	$x = 19 - 7 = 12$ (SUFFICIENT)	can't set up equation for x. (INSUFFICIENT)

2.

<u>Rephrasing:</u> 81 divided by a → remainder of 1
        a goes evenly into 80, but $a \neq 1$
        a is one of the factors of 80 other than 1.
        a = 2, 4, 5, 8, 10, 16, 20, 40, or 80
Which of the numbers listed above is the value of a?

	(1) $a/40$ → remainder of 0 40 goes evenly into a a is a multiple of 40	(2) $40/a$ → remainder of 40 a must be larger than 40
~~AD~~ Ⓑ CE		
QUESTION: **Which of the listed numbers is a?**	a could be 40 or 80 (INSUFFICIENT)	a must be 80 (SUFFICIENT)

3.

Rephrasing:	
$\dfrac{a \times 10^d}{b \times 10^e} = c \times 10^4$	Is $\dfrac{bc}{a}$ an integer?
$\dfrac{a}{b} \times 10^{d-e} = c \times 10^4$	Is 10^{d-e-4} an integer? Is $d - e - 4 \geq 0$? **Is $d - e \geq 4$?**
$10^{d-e-4} = \dfrac{bc}{a}$	

(A)D ~~BCE~~	(1) $d - e \geq 4$	(2) $d - e > 4$
QUESTION: **Is $d - e \geq 4$?**	YES (SUFFICIENT)	YES (SUFFICIENT)

4. An accurate yes/no rephrase is the following:

- Is $\dfrac{n-1}{3}$ = integer ?

- Is $n - 1 = 3 \times$ integer?

- Is $n = 3 \times$ integer + 1?

- Is the positive integer n one greater than a multiple of 3?

This narrows down our values of interest to a certain type of number, which follows a pattern: 1, 4, 7, 10, etc.

A value question such as "What is n?" would be unnecessarily picky. We don't need to know the exact value, just whether n is a certain type of number.

(1) SUFFICIENT: If $n^2 + n = n(n + 1)$ is not divisible by 6, we can rule out certain values for n.

n	$n + 1$	$n(n + 1)$ not divisible by 6
1	2	✓
2	3	✗
3	4	✗
4	5	✓
5	6	✗
6	7	✗
7	8	✓

The correct yes/no rephrasing directs us to look for a certain pattern. We see that pattern here: n can only be 1, 4, 7, 10, etc., all integers that are one greater than a multiple of 3.

(2) INSUFFICIENT: If $3n = 3 \times$ *pos integer* + 3, then $n = $ *pos integer* + 1. Therefore, n is an integer such that $n \geq 2$. This does not resolve whether n is definitely one greater than a multiple of 3.

The correct answer is A.

5. An accurate yes/no rephrase is the following:

    - Is $\dfrac{abc}{6}$ = integer ?

    - Is abc = 6, 12, 18, 24, 30, 36, 42, 48, etc.?

    (OR)

    - Is abc divisible by 2 *and* by 3?

Alternatively, we could ask "Is there an even integer and a multiple of 3 among a, b, and c?"

A value question such as "What is abc?" would be unnecessarily picky. We don't need to know the exact value, just whether abc is a certain type of number.

An even worse value rephrase would be "What are the values of a, b, and c?" Even if we did need the exact value of the product abc, we would not necessarily need the value of each variable.

(1) INSUFFICIENT: ab is divisible by 2, but we don't know whether it is divisible by 3 (or whether c is divisible by 3).

(2) INSUFFICIENT: bc is divisible by 3, but we don't know whether it is divisible by 2 (or whether a is divisible by 2).

(1) AND (2) SUFFICIENT: Statement (1) tells us that a or b is even, and Statement (2) tells us that b or c is divisible by 3. Therefore abc is divisible by both 2 and 3.

The correct answer is C.

6. **Revisiting #4, working incorrectly from the *Question* to the *Facts*:**

We might try multiples of 3 for $n - 1$, to see whether they "work" with the statements:

(1) SUFFICIENT:

$n - 1$	n	$n + 1$	$n^2 + n = n(n + 1)$	not divis by 6
3	4	5	20	✓
6	7	8	56	✓
9	10	11	110	✓

(2) SEEMS SUFFICIENT (*incorrectly*): If $3n = k + 3$, then $k = 3n - 3 = 3(n - 1)$.

$n - 1$	$k = 3n - 3 = 3(n - 1)$	pos mult of 3
3	9	✓
6	18	✓
9	27	✓

*Manhattan*GMAT*Prep
the new standard

The *incorrect* answer we might get is D. Be sure to revisit how to do this problem correctly, so you are certain how to do so for the future!

Revisiting #5, working incorrectly from the *Question* to the *Facts*:

Manipulating the question to $abc = 6 \times integer$ (and losing track of the question mark), we might tempted to check whether it is *possible* for abc to be a multiple of 6, instead of whether abc is *in fact* definitely a multiple of 6:

   (1) $abc = 6 \times integer$, so ab is even. ✓
   (2) $abc = 6 \times integer$, so bc is divisible by 3. ✓

The incorrect answer we might get is D. Be sure to revisit how to do this problem correctly!

7.

Non-Contrarian Approach	**Contrarian Approach**
(1) INSUFFICIENT: $m > 0$ or $m = $ pos, so "Is $pos^3 > pos^2$?" • Yes if $m > 1$ • No if m is a small fraction or 1. $(0 < m \leq 1)$.	(1) INSUFFICIENT: $m > 0$ or $m = $ pos, so "Is $pos^3 > pos^2$?" • Yes if $m > 1$ • No if m is a small fraction or 1. $(0 < m \leq 1)$.
(2) SEEMS SUFFICIENT: $m^2 > m$ implies that m is <u>not</u> a fraction or 1, therefore $m^3 > m^2$. Or, if we *assume* that $m > 0$, carrying over from (1), we might do the following: $m^2 > m$ $m > 1$ (dividing by m) Therefore, $m^3 > m^2$.	(2) INSUFFICIENT: $m^2 > m$ implies that m is <u>not</u> a fraction or 1, so if $m > 1$ then the answer is Yes. BUT, contradicting (1), **what if m is negative?** That is possible according to (2), since $neg^2 > neg$. Is $m^3 > m^2$? → Is $neg^3 > neg^2$? No!
	(1) AND (2) SUFFICIENT: Combined, the statements eliminate negative, zero, positive proper fractions, and 1 for the value of m. If $m > 1$, then $m^3 > m^2$. Definite Yes answer.
The (incorrect) answer is B.	The correct answer is C.

Note that both solutions were hampered by inadequate rephrasing. Ideally, we would have first rephrased as follows:

   • Is $m^3 > m^2$?
   • Is $m > 1$? (it's okay to divide by m^2, which must be positive: it is never negative and is not zero according to either statement here)

Take-away: With proper rephrasing, other errors are less likely. But even with inadequate rephrasing, taking a Contrarian approach can save us from a wrong answer.

8. The explicit constraint is $yz \neq 0$, which implies that $y \neq 0$ and $z \neq 0$. Both y and z could be any non-zero value, including positive integer, negative integer, positive fraction, negative fraction, etc.

Making Assumptions:

For (1), we would like to cross multiply, so a *likely* assumption is that y is positive:

$$y < \frac{1}{y}$$
$$y^2 < 1$$
$$0 < y^2 < 1$$
$$\sqrt{0} < \sqrt{y^2} < \sqrt{1}$$
$$0 < y < 1$$

Conclusion: SEEMS SUFFICIENT (incorrect)

For (2), the fact that y equals a squared value, and is thus positive, reinforces the assumption made in (1). Furthermore, another assumption could be made by those who plug in values for z.

For example, if you plug $z = -2, -1, 1, 2, 3, 4$, etc., you would get $y = 1, 4, 9, 16$, etc. That would yield a definite No answer to the question, as all the y values are at least as great as 1. The (unverbalized) assumption is that z is an integer, but that's not necessarily so.

Assumptions lead to the *incorrect* answers A and D.

Correct solution:

(1) INSUFFICIENT:

	If $y < 0$:	If $y < 0$:
	$y < \dfrac{1}{y}$	$y < \dfrac{1}{y}$
	$y^2 < 1$	$y^2 > 1$
	$0 < y^2 < 1$	$\sqrt{y^2} > \sqrt{1}$
	$\sqrt{0} < \sqrt{y^2} < \sqrt{1}$	$|y| > 1$
	$0 < y < 1$	$y > 1$ or $y < -1$
		$y < -1$
		Since we're assuming $y < 0$,
		we get $y < -1$.
Is $0 < y < 1$?	YES	NO

*Manhattan*GMAT*Prep

(2) INSUFFICIENT: y must be positive, but is it a fraction or integer?

If $z = 2$, then $y = 4$ and the answer is No.
If $z = 1/2$, then $y = 1/4$ and the answer is Yes.

(1) AND (2) SUFFICIENT: If y is positive, then (1) indicates that $0 < y < 1$.

The correct answer is C.

9. Both statements give number properties of the expression $\dfrac{(y+2)!}{x!}$, so we might glance ahead and then rephrase the question with this in mind:

- Is y odd?
- Is $(y + 2)$ odd?

A typical division of one factorial by another will involve canceling of terms, so we might try several numbers to see what the statements are really saying.

Making Assumptions:

(1) If $\dfrac{(y+2)!}{x!}$ = odd, all of the terms in the denominator cancel out, only one term can remain in the numerator, and that remaining term must be odd. For example:

$$\frac{3!}{2!} = 3 = odd \quad (okay)$$

$$\frac{5!}{4!} = 5 = odd \quad (okay)$$

$$\frac{6!}{4!} = (6)(5) = even \quad (not\ OK)$$

We might incorrectly conclude that $(y + 2)$ must be odd, that $x = (y + 2) - 1$, and that the answer is definitely Yes.

(2) INSUFFICIENT: If $\dfrac{(y+2)!}{x!}$ = 3, 4, 5, 6, 7, etc. then $(y + 2)$ might be 3, 4, 5, 6, 7, etc., according to our test cases in which $x = (y + 2) - 1$. (This particular analysis is correct.)

Making assumptions might lead us to choose answer choice A incorrectly. However, we assumed that it could not be the case that $x = y + 2$. That assumption is unjustified.

Correct Solution:

If $x = y + 2$, then:

(1) INSUFFICIENT:

$$\frac{2!}{2!} = 1 = odd \quad (okay)$$

$$\frac{3!}{3!} = 1 = odd \quad (okay)$$

Therefore, $(y + 2)$ might be either odd *or* even.

(2) INSUFFICIENT: If $\dfrac{(y+2)!}{x!} = 3, 4, 5, 6, 7,$ etc. then $(y + 2)$ might be 3, 4, 5, 6, 7, etc., according to our test cases in which $x = (y + 2) - 1$.

(1) AND (2) SUFFICIENT: If $\dfrac{(y+2)!}{x!} > 2$, then $\dfrac{(y+2)!}{x!} \neq 1$. The only way for $\dfrac{(y+2)!}{x!}$ to be odd is if $x = (y + 2) - 1$ and $(y + 2)$ is odd.

The correct answer is C.

Chapter 4
of
ADVANCED GMAT QUANT

DATA SUFFICIENCY: STRATEGIES & TACTICS

In This Chapter . . .

- Advanced Strategies
- Advanced Guessing Tactics

DATA SUFFICIENCY: ADVANCED STRATEGIES & GUESSING TACTICS

Sometimes you will encounter a Data Sufficiency problem that you can't answer—either because its content is difficult or obscure, or because you don't have enough time to solve completely in 2 minutes.

Like Chapter 2, this chapter describes a series of different methods you might try in these circumstances. Again, we make the distinction between **strategies** and **tactics**.

Strategies are broad: they apply to a wide variety of problems, they provide a complete approach, and they can be used safely in most circumstances.

In contrast, *tactics* can help you eliminate a few answer choices, but often leave a fair amount of uncertainty. Moreover, a particular tactic may only be useful in special situations or to parts of a problem.

The first section of this chapter outlines six Data Sufficiency strategies:

DS Strategy 1. **Compute to Completion**
For some problems, we won't necessarily be able to tell whether the answer can be calculated until we follow through on the calculations *all the way*.

DS Strategy 2. **Extract the Equation**
For many Word Translations problems, we need to represent the problem with algebraic equations to avoid embedded tricks that can be difficult to spot otherwise.

DS Strategy 3. **Use the Constraints**
Many Data Sufficiency problems provide explicit constraints on the variables. In other problems, these constraints will be implicit (for example, "number of people" must be both positive and an integer). In either case, these constraints frequently determine the correct answer, so we *must* identify and use them.

DS Strategy 4. **Beware of Inequalities**
Whenever a Data Sufficiency problem involves inequality symbols, you should be especially careful—the GMAT loves to trick people with inequalities.

DS Strategy 5. **Use a Scenario Chart**
The given facts may suggest that only a handful of possible scenarios exist. In those cases, we should enumerate and test these scenarios in a systematic way. The Scenario Chart can help us organize our approach to these problems.

DS Strategy 6. **Test Numbers Systematically**
For some one-variable Data Sufficiency problems, many possible values of a variable may exist, but underlying those values is some sort of pattern. We can often discover that pattern by intelligently picking numbers that cover a wide range of potential patterns.

The rest of the chapter is devoted to tactics that can knock out answer choices or provide clues as to how to approach the problem more effectively. We'll wait to list these tactics. As with Problem Solving tactics, some of these Data Sufficiency tactics work wonders when used correctly. Others only slightly improve your guessing odds.

Advanced Strategies

1. Compute to Completion

A general principle of Data Sufficiency is that once we have determined whether we can answer the question with a given set of information, we can stop calculating. For some problems, however, we cannot determine whether a single answer can be obtained until we've calculated the problem *all the way through*. This is particularly common in the following situations:

- Multiple equations are involved—particularly if they are non-linear
- A complicated inequality expression is present
- Variables hidden within a Geometry problem are related

Try-It #4-1

What is the value of ab?

(1) $a = b + 1$
(2) $a^2 = b + 1$

(1) INSUFFICIENT: Statement (1) clearly does not answer the question. For example, if $a = 1$ and $b = 2$, then $ab = 2$, and if $a = 2$ and $b = 3$, then $ab = 6$.

(2) INSUFFICIENT: Statement (2) clearly does not answer the question. For example, if $a = 1$ and $b = 2$, then $ab = 2$, and if $a = 2$ and $b = 5$, then $ab = 10$.

(1) & (2): Evaluating both statements together is trickier, however.

$$b = a - 1$$
$$a^2 = (a-1)+1$$
$$a^2 - a = 0$$

$$a(a-1) = 0$$
$$a = 0 \text{ or } 1$$

Based on this work, we can determine that either $a = 0$ or $a = 1$. It would be tempting at this stage to decide that since a can have 2 different values, Statements (1) & (2) together are insufficient. However, this is *incorrect*.

Let's look at the values b can hold in these two scenarios:

a	b	ab
1	$= a - 1 = 0$	0
0	$= a - 1 = -1$	0

*Manhattan*GMAT*Prep
the new standard

While it is true that *a* can take on different values, *ab* is equal to zero in *either case*. When $a = 1$, $b = 0$, and $ab = 0$. When $a = 0$, $b = -1$ and $ab = 0$. Therefore (1) & (2) combined are SUFFICIENT to answer this *specific* question: what is the value of *ab*?

The correct answer is C.

!	If we hadn't bothered to **Compute to Completion**, we might have thought that Statements (1) & (2) together were insufficient. While we get multiple values for *a* and *b* in this problem, we ultimately get a *single value* for the quantity asked about (that is, *ab*).
	In a multiple scenario problem, be sure to compute each scenario all the way through to determine whether the end result for each scenario is *actually different*.

2. Extract the Equation

For word problems, setting up an algebraic representation of the question is *essential*. It is very easy to get lazy intellectually and miss an embedded trick in the problem. These tricks are usually much easier to spot if you are looking at the underlying algebra behind the problem.

Try-It #4-2

> A store sells two types of birdfeeder: Alphas and Bravos. Alphas feed one bird at a time, whereas Bravos feed two birds at a time. The total number of birds that can be fed at one time by birdfeeders sold last month is 50. What is the total revenue generated by birdfeeders sold last month?
>
> (1) Last month, the price of each Alpha was $15, and the price of each Bravo was $30.
> (2) 40 Alphas were sold last month.

From the words in the question stem, we must **Extract the Equation**. Specifically, we are told that Alphas can feed one bird at a time, and Bravos two. We are also told that last month 50 birds could be fed at a time, so we have this:

Total number of birds fed $= A + 2B = 50$, where *A* and *B* represent the number of birdfeeders of each type that have been sold.

To calculate the revenue, it seems we will need the prices of the birdfeeders and the number of birdfeeders, *A* and *B*.

(1) SUFFICIENT: Again we must **Extract the Equation** from the wording of the question:

Total revenue = $15A + $30B = $15(A + 2B)

It turns out that we don't need to know A and B individually, since the question stem equation told us that $A + 2B = 50$. Therefore total revenue equals $15(A + 2B) = $15(50) = $750.

It's true that there are many possible values of A and B that satisfy the condition that $A + 2B = 50$. However, mathematically *every possible combination* that satisfies this equation would lead to the same revenue of $750. The number of each type of birdfeeder sold is irrelevant. In this sense, Extract the Equation can be similar to the Compute to Completion strategy, because once the equation has been extracted, you may find that the multiple possibilities for the variables might converge to a single answer to the specific question that's been asked.

(2) INSUFFICIENT: If there were 40 Alphas sold, there were 10 Bravos sold. But we still don't know the prices, so we can't compute revenue.

The correct answer is A.

> ! Relying on our intuition, which indicated that we needed the prices and number of the two birdfeeder types, we might have ultimately chosen C *incorrectly*. Be sure to translate all word problems into algebra so they can be properly evaluated. These issues are sensitive to the exact numbers given.

3. Use the Constraints

Often, a Data Sufficiency question will provide relevant constraints on the variables in the problem—for example, that the variables must be integers or must be positive, or must be between 0 and 1. When this information is given, it is usually *essential* to the problem. If you don't use the constraints, you could easily end up choosing the wrong answer choice.

Try-It #4-3

If $8x > 3x + 4x$, what is the value of the integer x?

(1) $6 - 4x > -2$
(2) $3 - 2x \leq 4 - x \leq 5 - 2x$

There is an obvious fact given in the question stem:

$8x > 3x + 4x$
$8x > 7x$
$x > 0$

However, observe that on top of that, there is also a **Constraint** given: x must be an integer. This limits the scope of the potential values of x. *You should make note of this type of constraint in your work on paper.* Write

*Manhattan*GMAT*Prep

"$x =$ int" or something similar. You could also incorporate this information by rephrasing the question to include the constraint: "If the integer x is greater than 0, what is the value of x?"

(1) SUFFICIENT: Let's solve this inequality for x:

$$6 - 4x > -2$$
$$-4x > -8$$
$$x < 2$$

Since we know from the question stem that $x > 0$, we can conclude that $0 < x < 2$. The *only integer* between 0 and 2 is 1. Therefore, $x = 1$.

(2) SUFFICIENT: We can manipulate this compound inequality as follows:

$$
\begin{array}{c}
3 - 2x \le\ 4 - x \le 5 - 2x \\
\underline{+2x \qquad +2x \qquad +2x} \\
3 \quad\ \le\ 4 + x \le 5 \\
\underline{-4 \qquad -4 \qquad -4} \\
-1 \quad \le \quad\ x \le 1
\end{array}
$$

Note that it's fine to manipulate all the parts of the compound inequality at the same time as long as we perform each manipulation to *all three* parts of the inequality.

We find that $-1 \le x \le 1$. Since we know from the question stem that $x > 0$, we can conclude that $0 < x \le 1$. The only integer that fits this criteria is 1. Therefore, $x = 1$.

If we had simply overlooked the fact that x is an integer, we would have determined that there are many values between 0 and 1 or between 0 and 2. We might have chosen answer E, incorrectly.

The correct answer is D.

> **!**
>
> Make a note of any additional information given to you in the question stem (for example, "x is positive" or "x is an integer"). You often will have to use this information properly to get the correct answer.
>
> Integer constraints in particular are very potent: they often limit the possible solutions for a problem to a small set. Sometimes this set is so small that it contains *only one item*.

Constraints will not always be explicitly given. The ones the GMAT doesn't explicitly give you can be called **stealth constraints**. Stealth constraints are most prevalent in Word Translations and Geometry problems. Here are some examples of stealth constraints that you should train yourself to take note of:

a) The number of *countable* items must be a *non-negative integer*. Note that zero is only a possibility if it is possible for the items not to exist at all—if the problem clearly assumes that the items exist, then the number of items must be *positive*. Examples:

- Number of people.
- Number of yachts.
- Number of books.

b) Many *non-countable* quantities must be *non-negative numbers*, though not necessarily integers. Again, zero is only an option if the underlying object might not exist. If the problem clearly assumes the existence and typical definition of an object, then these quantities must be *positive*. Examples:

- The side of a triangle must have a positive length. (All geometric quantities shown in a diagram, such as lengths, areas, volumes, and angles, must be positive. The only exception is negative coordinates in a coordinate plane problem.)
- The weight of a shipment of products must be positive in any unit.
- The height of a person must be positive in any unit.

c) Many other *non-countable* quantities are allowed to take on *negative* values. Examples:

- The profit of a company.
- The growth rate of a population.
- The change in the value of essentially any variable.

We ran across these sorts of constraints in Problem Solving, but they are even more important and dangerous on Data Sufficiency. If these constraints are important in a Problem Solving problem, then in some cases you will be unable to solve the problem. That will alert you to the existence of the constraints, since every Problem Solving problem must be solvable. In contrast, you will get no such signal on a Data Sufficiency problem. After all, solvability is the very issue that Data Sufficiency tests!

4. Beware of Inequalities

Whenever a Data Sufficiency question involves inequality symbols, you should be especially careful. The GMAT can employ a variety of different inequality-specific tricks. Here are a few examples:

1) One inequality can imply another seemingly unrelated inequality, depending on the situation. For example, if we need to know whether $x > 0$, then knowing that $x > 5$ is sufficient. If x is larger than 5 it must be positive, thus $x > 0$. However the opposite is *not* the case. If we knew that $x < 5$, we would *not* be able to determine whether $x > 0$. After all, x could be positive but less than 5, or x could be negative.

2) As we saw in the previous section, inequalities can combine with integer constraints to produce a single value. For example, if $0 < x < 2$ and x is an integer, then x *must* equal 1. That's subtle.

3) Some word problems can create a stealth constraint involving inequalities. These inequalities may come into play in determining the correct answer. For example, a problem might read "The oldest student in the class….the next oldest student in the class…the youngest student in the class…" This can be translated to the following inequality: *Youngest < Middle < Oldest.*

4) Inequalities involving a variable in a denominator often involve two possibilities: a positive and a negative one. For example, if we know that $1/y < x$, you might be tempted to multiply by y and arrive at $1 < xy$. However, this may not be correct. It depends on whether y is a positive or negative number. If $y > 0$, then it is correct to infer that $1 < xy$. However, if $y < 0$, then $1 > xy$. Therefore, you'll need to set up two cases (positive and negative) in this situation.

5) At the same time, stealth constraints may allow you to manipulate inequalities more easily. For instance, if a quantity must be positive, then you can multiply both sides of an inequality by that quantity without having to set up two cases.

6) Many questions involving inequalities are actually disguised positive/negative questions. For example, if we know that $xy > 0$, the fact that xy is greater than 0 is not in and of itself very interesting. What is interesting is that the product is positive, meaning both x and y are positive, or both x and y are negative. Thus x and y have the *same sign*. Here, the inequality symbol is used to disguise the fact that x and y have the same sign.

Let's look at some examples to illustrate these concepts.

Try-It #4-4

If the three-digit integer $x =$ "abc", where a, b, and c represent nonzero digits of x, what is the value of x?

(1) $a \geq 3b$
(2) $b \geq 3c$

(1) INSUFFICIENT. The value of a depends on b. For example, if $b = 1$, then a could equal anything from 3 to 9. If $b = 3$, then a must equal exactly 9. Note that b cannot be larger than 3, because that would force a to be larger than 9 and therefore not a single digit value.

(2) INSUFFICIENT. The value of b depends on c. For example, if $c = 1$, then b could equal anything from 3 to 9. If $c = 3$, then b must equal exactly 9. Note that c cannot be larger than 3, because that would force b to be larger than 9 and therefore not a single digit value.

(1) & (2) SUFFICIENT: Since $b \geq 3c$, b must be at least 3. But since $a \geq 3b$, b can be at most 3 (anything larger would force a to be multiple digits). Therefore b equals exactly 3, a equals exactly 9, and c equals exactly 1. This makes $x = 931$.

The correct answer is C. Notice that digits are highly constrained (there are only 10 possible digits). A couple of clever inequalities can often pin down the value of a digit variable, as in this case.

Try-It #4-5

Is $m > n$?

(1) $n/m < 1$
(2) $n > 0$

(1) INSUFFICIENT. It is tempting to cross multiply to get $n < m$. However, we don't know whether m is positive, so we don't know whether to flip the sign.

(2) INSUFFICIENT. This statement tells us nothing about m.

(1) & (2) INSUFFICIENT. The fact that n is positive does not tell us whether m is positive. For example, it is possible than $n = 2$ and $m = -1$. It is also possible that $n = 2$ and $m = 3$. Either of these scenarios would fit Statements (1) and (2) but yield different answers to the question.

The correct answer is E.

5. Use a Scenario Chart

In many Data Sufficiency problems, the available information suggests that only a *handful* of possible scenarios exist. In other words, the possibilities *branch* into more than one possible outcome, but the number of total possible outcomes is limited. Thus, you can list them all out:

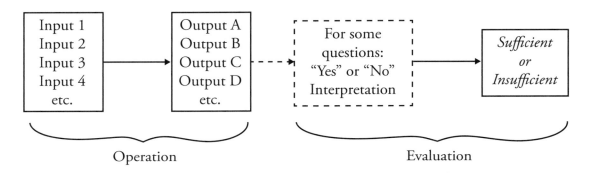

While it is always important to be organized when performing calculations on the GMAT, multiple scenario problems require a *very* organized approach in your work on paper: **The Scenario Chart**. We suggest creating the following elements in your Scenario Charts, though you should be flexible in your implementation.

1. **ORGANIZE YOUR WORK** in a table.	**WHY?**
Each variable gets its own <u>column</u>. Each scenario gets it own <u>row</u>.	• We must consider *every possible combination* of inputs to determine the *possible outputs*.
Example: if the question involves Odds/Evens, you would create a column for each variable, and populate the rows with applicable *Odd* and *Even* scenarios *for each variable*.	• There may be too many variables to track mentally. • Each variable individually may have too many possible values to track mentally. • Putting the inputs on paper makes it easier to evaluate the question for each scenario.

2. Consider **FACT CHECK COLUMNS.**

    Easy facts/constraints such as "*x* is an integer" can be addressed by listing only integer scenarios for *x*—no separate fact check column is necessary. However, you might want to add a fact check column for *complicated* or *algebraic* constraints.

WHY?

*   Ensures that you consider all the applicable constraints as you evaluate each statement.
*   Forces a check that the scenarios comply with more complicated constraints.
*   Minimizes the burden of implementing simple constraints, such as "*x* is positive."

3. Create a **QUESTION & ANSWER COLUMN.**

    Clearly label the question with a question mark. For each scenario (row), check to see what the answer to the question is. For more complicated questions, you may want to create extra columns to act as subtotals.

WHY?

*   Forces the generation of an answer for every allowable scenario.
*   Prevents confusion between the question and the facts.
*   Reduces the risk of becoming biased by the question (making unwarranted assumptions).

4. **MAKE SEPARATE CHARTS** for each Statement.

    You may also need to create a third chart for the combined Statements. Or, you could circle the scenarios in one Statement's chart that also exist in the other Statement's chart.

WHY?

*   To avoid *statement carryover*
*   One big chart with (1), (2) and possibly (1) & (2) combined could be unwieldy and/or confusing.

Scenario charts trade off *exhaustiveness* and *efficiency*. You will have to find your own balance, but we recommend that you work towards *efficiency* (e.g., evaluating only the scenarios that fit the given information) rather than *exhaustiveness* (e.g., evaluating all possible scenarios and then crossing out the scenarios that violate the given information). This helps keep you focused on the scenarios that remain possible, rather than wasting time on scenarios that are irrelevant.

Try-It #4-6

> If *a*, *b*, and *c* are integers, is $abc > 0$?
>
> (1) $ab > 0$
> (...)

In this partial problem, there are three variables, each of which might be positive or negative. Therefore there are a total of $2^3 = 8$ possible positive/negative scenarios to evaluate. However, based on the information available in Statement (1), you may realize early on that only 4 of the scenarios are possible (*a* and *b* have the same sign, so any combination involving *a* and *b* having different signs does not fit the statement). In an *exhaustive* scenario chart, you would write down 8 rows corresponding to each possible positive/negative combination, and cross out the 4 that violate this constraint. In an *efficient* scenario chart, you would only write the 4 scenarios that fit the constraint. Clearly, the efficient scenario chart will take less time to complete. For example, here are two examples of the chart you might set up for (1):

EXHAUSTIVE CHART   **EFFICIENT CHART**

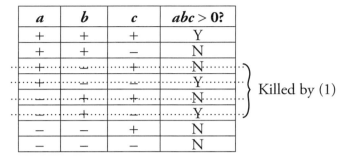

That said, sometimes a problem might be so complex that you decide you'd be more comfortable evaluating all possible scenarios. Or perhaps at first you can't determine which scenarios fit the facts in the problem (and you would therefore need to use the Scenario Chart to determine which scenarios fit the problem). In these cases, an exhaustive approach is perfectly acceptable, as long as you are mindful of the amount of time it will take to complete.

Also, be sure to *cross out* or mark as invalid any scenarios that do not fit your facts, as soon as you know that! You can't use these scenarios as "No" cases—they don't count at all.

Try-It #4-7

If *a*, *b*, and *c* are integers, is *abc* divisible by 4?

(1) $a + b + 2c$ is even.
(2) $a + 2b + c$ is odd.

Let's evaluate all possible Odd/Even combinations of *a*, *b*, and *c* using Scenario Charts to determine the answer to the question.

(1) INSUFFICIENT: $2c$ must be even because *c* is an integer. This statement implies that $a + b =$ Even, which occurs when *a* and *b* have the same Odd/Even parity. (There is no constraint on *c*.) An efficient Scenario Chart might look like:

a	*b*	*c*	$a + b + 2c =$ **Even**	**Is *abc* divisible by 4?**
E	E	E	✓	Y
E	E	O	✓	Y
O	O	E	✓	Maybe (only if *c* is divis by 4)
O	O	O	✓	N

You could stop here! MAYBE indicates insufficient.

(2) INSUFFICIENT: $2b$ must be even because b is an integer. Thus, this statement implies that $a + c =$ Odd, which occurs when a and c have opposite Odd/Even parity. (There is no constraint on b.)

a	b	c	$a + 2b + c =$ **Odd**	**Is abc divisible by 4?**
E	E	O	✓	Y
E	O	O	✓	Maybe ←
O	E	E	✓	Y
O	O	E	✓	Maybe

You could stop here! MAYBE indicates insufficient.

(1) AND (2) INSUFFICIENT: From (1) we know that a and b have the same Odd/Even parity, while from (2) we know that a and c have opposite Odd/Even parity.

a	b	c	**(1):** $a + b + 2c =$ **Even**	**(2):** $a + 2b + c =$ **Odd**	**Is abc divisible by 4?**
E	E	O	✓	✓	Y
O	O	E	✓	✓	Maybe

Even though we have constraints on all the variables, we do not have a definitive answer to the question. The correct answer is E.

Notice that in evaluating Statements (1) and (2) together, we would not need to write a complete new Scenario Chart. We could reuse the work from Statement (1) and Statement (2) to determine the answer (for instance, by circling the scenarios in one chart that also appear in the other chart). Just be careful as you do this! Know what case you're considering.

Try-It #4-8

If $|x| = |2y|$, what is the value of $x - 2y$?

(1) $x + 2y = 6$
(2) $xy > 0$

If $|x| = |2y|$, we have either $x = 2y$ or $x = -2y$, depending on the signs of x and y. To be on the safe side, we can list out cases and also consider the given question:

x	$2y$	$x - 2y = ?$
0	0	0
+	+	0
+	−	$2x$ (which is +)
−	+	$2x$ (which is −)
−	−	0

The answer is 0 when x and y have the same sign (or are both zero). The answer is $2x$ when x and y have opposite signs. Also, notice that the sign of $x - 2y$ will be the same sign as x whenever x and y have opposite signs.

(1) SUFFICIENT: You might realize that a positive sum indicates that both x and $2y$ must be positive, but if you didn't you could use a chart to check:

x	$2y$	$x + 2y$ (COMPUTATION)	$x + 2y = 6$ (FACT CHECK)	$x - 2y = ?$ (QUESTION)
0	0	0	Invalid	0
+	+	$2x$ (which is +)	Valid when $x = 3$	0
+	−	0	Invalid	$2x$ (which is +)
−	+	0	Invalid	$2x$ (which is −)
−	−	$2x$ (which is −)	Invalid	0

Only the second scenario in our chart is possible. We conclude that x and y must both be positive, so the value of $x - 2y$ is 0.

(2) SUFFICIENT: x and y must have the same sign, so only the second and fifth scenarios in our original chart are possible. Either way, the value of $x - 2y$ must be 0.

The correct answer is D.

Another way of devising this scenario chart is as follows:

x and $2y$	Constraint	$x - 2y = ?$
Same sign	$x = 2y$	$x - 2y = 0$
	OR	
Opposite sign	$x = -2y$	$x - 2y = (-2y) - 2y = -4y$

(1) SUFFICIENT. If x and $2y$ have the same sign, then $x = 2y$, so $(2y) + 2y = 6$. Thus $y = 3/2$ and $x = 3$. If x and $2y$ have the opposite sign, then $x = -2y$, so $(-2y) + 2y = 6$. Thus $0 = 6$, which is impossible. x and $2y$ must have the same sign, so $x - 2y = 0$.

(2) SUFFICIENT. This statement tells us that x and y have the same sign, so x and $2y$ have the same sign. Therefore $x = 2y$, and $x - 2y = 0$.

Another concept related to scenario charts is **Flow Charts**. Flow charts are a visual way to track scenarios. They are most useful when there are *question* scenarios—i.e., the exact question being asked is dependent upon certain conditions. A flow chart allows us to divide the different question scenarios and evaluate them separately.

Try-It #4-9

If $a \neq 0$, is $\dfrac{1}{a} > \dfrac{a}{b^4 + 3}$?

(1) $a^2 = b^2$
(2) $a^2 = b^4$

This problem would be easier to evaluate if we could cross-multiply the inequality to eliminate the fractions. But *watch out*! We can multiply by $(b^4 + 3)$, which is definitely positive because of the even exponent. But we will also multiply by a, which could be either positive or negative—and depending on the sign of a, we may need to flip the inequality symbol. That is, the rephrasing of the question depends on the sign of a.

Flow charts can help us with this dilemma. We can represent the scenarios this way:

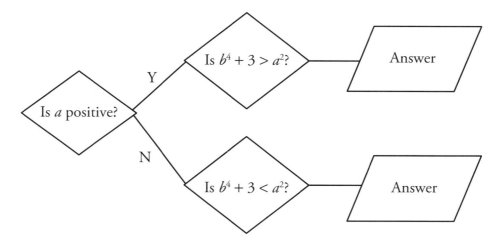

(1) SUFFICIENT: b^2 must be positive, so a is positive. Therefore we only have to evaluate the top branch of the flow chart:

Is $b^4 + 3 > a^2$?   Is $b^4 + 3 > b^4$?
Is $b^4 + 3 > (b^2)^2$?   Is $3 > 0$?

The answer to the ultimate question is a definite Yes.

(2) INSUFFICIENT: $a^2 = b^4$ can be true with positive or negative values for a. We don't know the sign of a, so we must answer both questions that follow in the flow chart:

If a is positive:	If a is negative:
Is $b^4 + 3 > a^2$?	Is $b^4 + 3 < a^2$?
Is $b^4 + 3 > b^4$?	Is $b^4 + 3 < b^4$?
Is $3 > 0$?	Is $3 < 0$?
The answer to this question is Yes.	The answer to this question is No.

Alternatively, you might simply observe that the two questions are exact opposites, so even if we get a definite answer to either one, we will get the opposite answer to the other, for a net result of Maybe. The correct answer is A.

For an in-depth list of situations in which you might consider using Scenario Charts, please see the Appendix at the end of this chapter entitled "Selected Applications of Scenario Charts."

6. Test Numbers Systematically

Scenario Charts can be both versatile and effective. For many problems, a full chart is not necessary, but we still need to consider a handful of possible values for the unknowns to identify an underlying pattern. In this case, you can test numbers systematically.

Again, as an advanced test-taker, you might be biased against number testing: it might somehow seem less advanced than theoretical approaches. However, the theory required to answer a question may be cumbersome to figure out in 2 minutes. If implemented correctly, systematic number testing can be fast, easy and accurate, so it should be part of your toolbox.

Plugging random numbers as they come to mind is the most common approach to number testing, and while this strategy can be successful, it is inherently ad hoc and therefore not the most reliable process. It's easy to overlook a salient scenario, for example. The key is to have a *systematic approach* to number testing. This relies on two approaches: The *Standard Number Set for Testing* and *Discrete Number Listing*.

Of course if you are completely at a loss as to how to approach a problem, picking a few random numbers to help think through the problem is still an option. In fact, it can be very helpful for a solid majority of the Data Sufficiency questions you'll encounter. However, that is a different type of number testing from what we are discussing in this section.

Standard Number Set for Testing

The GMAT often tests odd/even rules, positive/negative rules, fraction/integer rules, proper vs. improper fractions, etc. On any given problem, you may have trouble identifying which rule is relevant, and in fact the GMAT may test more than one rule within a given question. Therefore, if you must pick and test numbers, consider a set of numbers that covers every possible combination of properties:

	Odd	Even	Proper Fraction	Improper Fraction
Negative	−1	−2	−1/2	−3/2
Zero		0		
Positive	1	2	1/2	3/2

This set includes integers, non-integers, positive and negative numbers, and numbers greater than and less than 1. Thus a comprehensive set of test numbers (to memorize and apply) would be as follows:

$$\{-2, -3/2, -1, -1/2, 0, 1/2, 1, 3/2, 2\}$$

Remember this list as "every integer and half-integer between −2 and 2."

Not all of these numbers will be relevant or possible on every problem. For example, if the variable has to be positive, 5 of the 9 values presented above can be ignored. The question itself may suggest certain values to test, but always keep in mind the *potential* need to test a value of each relevant type.

Try-It #4-10

Is $a < 0$?

(1) $a^3 < a^2 + 2a$
(2) $a^2 > a^3$

This problem presents inequalities with non-linear terms, and the question asks whether a is negative. Therefore, we should test different values of a and see which values fit the statements.

But which values should we test? If we just test integers, we will get the wrong answer. Let's try testing {−2, −1, 0, 1, 2}. It'll be easier if we rephrase the statements as inequalities relative to zero:

(1) $a^3 - a^2 - 2a < 0$
(2) $a^2 - a^3 > 0$

Statement (1): This statement is insufficient, as both $a = -2$ and $a = 1$ fit the criteria. Let's cross out invalid cases that don't fit the statement. In those invalid cases, it's good to avoid answering the question. Only answer the question for valid cases, if you can help it.

a	(1): $a^3 - a^2 - 2a < 0$	$a < 0$?
−2	$(-2)^3 - (-2)^2 - 2(-2) = -8$ (valid)	YES
−1	$(-1)^3 - (-1)^2 - 2(-1) = 0$ (invalid)	
0	$(0)^3 - (0)^2 - 2(0) = 0$ (invalid)	
1	$(1)^3 - (1)^2 - 2(1) = -2$ (valid)	NO
2	$(2)^3 - (2)^2 - 2(2) = 0$ (invalid)	

Statement (2): This appears to be sufficient, as only $a = -2$ and $a = -1$ fit the criteria.

a	(2): $a^2 - a^3 > 0$	$a < 0$?
−2	$(-2)^2 - (-2)^3 = 12$ (valid)	YES
−1	$(-1)^2 - (-1)^3 = 2$ (valid)	YES
0	$(0)^2 - (0)^3 = 0$ (invalid)	
1	$(1)^2 - (1)^3 = 0$ (invalid)	
2	$(2)^2 - (2)^3 = -4$ (invalid)	

Thus, we might conclude based on this analysis that Statement (2) is sufficient. However, this conclusion is incorrect—it turns out that *neither statement is sufficient*. We could have seen this if we had used a complete set of numbers for testing.

Let's try analyzing the possibilities using the full recommended set of numbers: {−2, −3/2, −1, −1/2, 0, 1/2, 1, 3/2, 2}:

a	$a^3 - a^2 - 2a < 0$	$a < 0$?
-2	$(-2)^3 - (-2)^2 - 2(-2) = -8$ (valid)	YES
$-3/2$	$(-3/2)^3 - (-3/2)^2 - 2(-3/2) = -21/8$ (valid)	YES
-1	$(-1)^3 - (-1)^2 - 2(-1) = 0$ (invalid)	
$-1/2$	$(-1/2)^3 - (-1/2)^2 - 2(-1/2) = 5/8$ (invalid)	
0	$(0)^3 - (0)^2 - 2(0) = 0$ (invalid)	
$1/2$	$(1/2)^3 - (1/2)^2 - 2(1/2) = -9/8$ (valid)	NO
1	$(1)^3 - (1)^2 - 2(1) = -2$ (valid)	NO
$3/2$	$(3/2)^3 - (3/2)^2 - 2(3/2) = -15/8$ (valid)	NO
2	$(2)^3 - (2)^2 - 2(2) = 0$ (invalid)	

You could stop here! We have a case where $a > 0$ and another where $a < 0$.

Again, we find Statement (1) to be insufficient.

a	$a^2 - a^3 > 0$	$a < 0$?
-2	$(-2)^2 - (-2)^3 = 12$ (valid)	YES
$-3/2$	$(-3/2)^2 - (-3/2)^3 = 45/8$ (valid)	YES
-1	$(-1)^2 - (-1)^3 = 2$ (valid)	YES
$-1/2$	$(-1/2)^2 - (-1/2)^3 = 3/8$ (valid)	YES
0	$(0)^2 - (0)^3 = 0$ (invalid)	
$1/2$	$(1/2)^2 - (1/2)^3 = 1/8$ (valid)	NO
1	$(1)^2 - (1)^3 = 0$ (invalid)	
$3/2$	$(3/2)^2 - (3/2)^3 = -9/8$ (invalid)	
2	$(2)^2 - (2)^3 = -4$ (invalid)	

You could stop here! We have a case where $a > 0$ and another where $a < 0$.

This time, however, we find Statement (2) to be *insufficient*. When $a = 1/2$, the constraint is fulfilled, but a is not positive. We missed that case in the initial assessment using only integers.

Combining Statements (1) and (2), we see that whenever $a = -2$, $-3/2$, or $1/2$, both conditions are fulfilled. a could thus be positive or negative. The correct answer is E.

Notice that we did not need to test every possible value for a. For example, when $a = -2$, both conditions are easily satisfied. That means that testing $-3/2$ was unlikely to be necessary, since that value is not much different from -2. Furthermore, once we evaluated $a = 1/2$, we could stop testing. For a Yes/No question, all we need to do is find *one* valid Yes and *one* valid No to prove insufficiency.

This problem can also be solved algebraically, but it takes more conceptual work. A number line would help keep track of signs.

(1) $a^3 - a^2 - 2a < 0$
$a(a^2 - a - 2) < 0$
$a(a - 2)(a + 1) < 0$
$a < 2$, 0, or -1.

	-1		0		2	
a	$-$		$-$	$+$		$+$
$a - 2$	$-$		$-$	$-$		$+$
$a + 1$	$-$		$+$	$+$		$+$
Product:	$\ominus$		$+$	$\ominus$		$+$

This chart demonstrates that either $a < -1$ OR $0 < a < 2$. INSUFFICIENT.

(2) $a^2 - a^3 > 0$
   $a^2(1 - a) > 0$
   $1 - a > 0$
   $a < 1$. INSUFFICIENT.

(1) AND (2): Overlapping the possible ranges, either $a < -1$ OR $0 < a < 1$. This is still INSUFFICIENT. The correct answer is E.

In some cases, the *standard number testing* list may not quite suffice.

Try-It #4-11

> If x is positive, is $x \leq 1$?
>
> (1) $x^2 \leq 1.3$
>
> ...

If we used the standard number testing list of {1/2, 1, 3/2, 2} (ignoring the non-positive values in the set), all of the values for x above 1 would *fail* to fit Statement (1) and all of the values for x equal to or below 1 would *fit* Statement (1). Therefore, the standard number testing list would indicate that Statement (1) is sufficient. However, x could be 1.1, in which case $x^2 = 1.21$, which is less than 1.3. So Statement (1) is actually insufficient

Clearly, we could figure out that x *could* be greater than 1 upon a quick inspection of this problem. We would simply try a number slightly larger than 1. However, if the problem were more complicated, it might not be so obvious. In cases like these, use the **boundary principle**: test values that are *close to boundaries* given in the problem. In this case, the boundary value is 1, so you should add 0.9 and 1.1 to your list of numbers to test. You might even try 0.99 or 1.01. You should know that −1, 0, and 1 are natural boundaries, because numbers behave differently on either side of them (that's why our standard list contains numbers in the ranges defined by −1, 0, and 1).

Discrete Number Listing

In the previous problems, the variables a and x were not constrained, so we had to test a series of different numbers to solve the problem. By contrast, many questions suggest specific constraints: x must be odd, for example, or x must be a positive integer. In these cases, just *list* a series of consecutive numbers that fit these criteria and test them all. For example, if x must be even, we should test $x = 2, 4, 6, 8, 10$, etc.

Discrete number listing can be used whenever a problem specifies a sequence of discrete (separate) values that a variable or an expression can take on:

- Integers (the classic case): ...−3, −2, −1, 0, 1, 2, 3...
- Odd/even integers: ...−3, −1, 1, 3... or ...−4, −2, 0, 2, 4...
- Positive perfect squares: 1, 4, 9, 16, 25...
- Positive multiples of 5: 5, 10, 15, 20...
- Any set that is "integer-like," with well-defined, separated values

By contrast, some problems describe a *smooth range* of potential values for a variable or expression (for example, $0 < x < 1$ or x must be negative). In these cases, we cannot begin listing consecutive values to test, because the set of possible values is *not* discrete. If the variable can take on any real number in a range, then we must rely on the *standard number testing* list, potentially with some modifications, as described in the previous section.

A key to the discrete number listing process is **test consecutive values** that fit the criteria—it would be too easy to leave out the one exception that proves insufficiency. Never skip numbers that fit the constraint. This is especially important if you are listing discrete numbers to equal an expression, not just a variable. By the way, remember to work from the facts to the question, not the other way around! Don't assume that the question should be answered Yes and only test values that make it so.

Try-It #4-12

> Is x a multiple of 12?
>
> (1) $\sqrt{x-3}$ is odd.
> (2) x is a multiple of 3.

Since Statement (1) tells us that $\sqrt{x-3}$ is odd, we should list 1, 3, 5, 7, 9, etc.

Notice that we're picking values for $\sqrt{x-3}$, *not* x. It would be far too much work to test different values for x to make $\sqrt{x-3}$ odd, and we could potentially miss some values that fit the statement. Do not plug in numbers for x here! Instead, list consecutive odd values for $\sqrt{x-3}$, a quick and easy process. Then solve for x in each case.

For this problem, your work on paper should look something like this:

> (1): $\sqrt{x-3}$ = odds = 1, 3, 5, 7, 9, etc.
> $x - 3 = 1, 9, 25, 49, 81$, etc.
> $x = 4, 12, 28, 52, 84$, etc.
>   Is x divisible by 12? Maybe. For example, 12 is, while 28 is not.
>   INSUFFICIENT.

> (2): x = multiples of 3 = 3, 6, 9, 12, 15, etc.
>   Is x divisible by 12? Maybe. For example, 12 is, while 15 is not.
>   INSUFFICIENT.

(1) AND (2):   We can combine these statements by selecting only the values for x that are in both lists. On your paper, you would circle the following values: $x = 12$ and $x = 84$. These are the values calculated in Statement (1) that fit the criteria in Statement (2). This seems to be SUFFICIENT—the values for x that fit both statements are multiples of 12. At this point, if you wanted to check another value, you could, or you could go with the trend, which is almost always going to be right at this point.

*Manhattan*GMAT*Prep*
the new standard

The correct answer is C.

> ! In retrospect, it may seem obvious that (1) tells us x is a multiple of 4. But if you tried to evaluate (1) with algebra, you might reason that $\sqrt{x-3}$ is odd , so $(x-3)$ is odd^2, or an odd perfect square. Thus, x is an odd perfect square plus 3. One might conclude that x is even, which is a true but incomplete description! Listing Numbers is an easy way to see that these numbers are all multiples of 4.

As in the previous example, trying to solve Statement (1) algebraically is tricky. Yes, it's worth knowing how to do this algebra. The point is that a discrete number testing process is quick and simple, so it's also worth knowing how to do.

(1): $\sqrt{x-3} = 2k+1$, where k is an integer.
$x - 3 = (2k + 1)^2 = 4k^2 + 4k + 1$
$x = 4k^2 + 4k + 4 = 4(k^2 + k + 1)$
x must be divisible by 4.
INSUFFICIENT.

(2): x is a multiple of 3, so x must be divisible by 3. INSUFFICIENT.

(1) AND (2): x is divisible by 3 and by 4, so x is divisible by 12. SUFFICIENT.

Advanced Guessing Tactics

The rest of this chapter is devoted to scrappy tactics that can raise your odds of success. There will be fewer opportunities to apply these tactics than the strategies mentioned previously. However, when all else fails, these tactics may be your only friend. We've listed the tactics according to their reliability: the earlier tactics nearly always work, while the later tactics provide only a modest improvement over random guessing.

1. Spot Identical Statements   *Certainty:* Very High

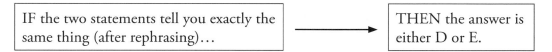

| IF the two statements tell you exactly the same thing (after rephrasing)… | $\longrightarrow$ | THEN the answer is either D or E. |

(...)

(1) $3y - 6 = 2x$

(2) $y = \dfrac{2}{3}x + 2$

By adding 6 to both sides of Statement (1) and multiplying Statement (2) by 3, you can see that both statements tell us that $3y = 2x + 6$. Depending on the question, either each Statement will be sufficient, or each will not—and because they are identical, there cannot be any benefit from looking at the Statements together. The answer must be D or E.

2. Spot Clear Sufficiency   *Certainty:* Very High

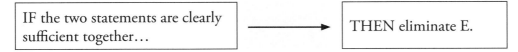

| IF the two statements are clearly sufficient together… | → | THEN eliminate E. |

Try-It #4-13

If $Z = \dfrac{m + \dfrac{m}{3}}{n + \dfrac{2}{n^{-1}}}$ and $mn \neq 0$, what is the value of Z?

(1) $m = \dfrac{15}{n^{-1}}$

(2) $m = 5$

It is obvious that you could plug $m = 5$ into Statement (1) to get a value for n, then plug values for m and n into the expression for Z. So you can knock out E for sure.

Note that this tactic does *not* imply that you should assume, or even *lean towards*, choosing answer choice C. Many of these types of problems are trying to trap you into choosing C because it's so obvious that the two combined statements are sufficient. Quite often, some algebraic work will reveal that one or both of the statements will be sufficient on their own. Indeed, in the example problem given above, Statement (1) alone is sufficient to answer the question, so the correct answer is A.

3. Spot One Statement Inside The Other   *Certainty:* Very High

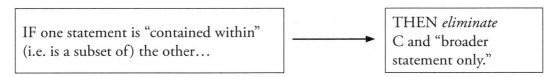

| IF one statement is "contained within" (i.e. is a subset of) the other… | → | THEN *eliminate* C and "broader statement only." |

(Some question involving *x*)

(1) $x > 50!$
(2) $x > 10!$

This trick only shows up occasionally, but when it does, it's useful. Notice that narrow Statement (1) is completely contained within broad Statement (2). In other words, any value that satisfies Statement (1) *also* satisfies Statement (2). Therefore, if Statement (2) is sufficient, Statement (1) *must* be sufficient also. However, the reverse is not true. If (2) is insufficient, (1) could still possibly be sufficient on its own.

Either way, it is impossible for both of the Statements to be required together to answer the question. It is also impossible for Statement (2) to be sufficient without Statement (1) being sufficient also. So we can definitively eliminate B, as it corresponds to the broader statement, as well as C (the together option).

This situation can occur with inequalities, as we've seen. Whenever one statement defines a range that is completely encompassed by the other statement's range, we can eliminate C, as well as the statement corresponding to the broader statement alone.

We must be careful with this tactic, though. It can be easy to think—incorrectly—that one statement is a subset of the other.

(Some question involving *x*)

(1) *x* is an odd number
(2) *x* is a prime number

At first, it might seem that Statement (2) is a subset of Statement (1), but upon further inspection, you should realize that 2 is a prime number that is not odd. *Almost* every prime number is odd, but *not all*. Therefore Statement (2) is *not* a subset of Statement (1). Even if just one value escapes, you cannot use this tactic.

4. Spot One Statement Adding Nothing   *Certainty*: High

(Some question involving *x, y,* and *z*)

(1) $y^x + (-y)^x = z$
(2) $y < 0$

This tactic may seem identical to the previous one, but it is not. Notice in this example that Statement (1) does not determine whether *y* is positive or negative, and Statement (2) does not even include *z*. Therefore, neither statement is a subset of the other.

That said, the fact that *y* is negative *does not change anything* in Statement (1), because regardless the value of *y, z* will be equal to the same value if we swap *y* and –*y*. If *y* = 4, then we get $4^x + (-4)^x = z$. If *y* = –4, then we get $(-4)^x + 4^x = z$. Those equations are the same! The sign of the value of *y* doesn't matter, because *y* and –*y* are in symmetrical positions. So knowing the sign of *y* adds no information to Statement (1).

Note that in this example, A, B, D, and E are all still possible answers, depending upon the question. Only C can be eliminated.

5. Spot a C Trap   *Certainty:* Moderate

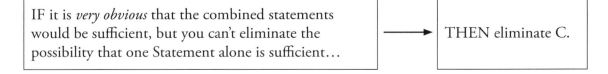

This situation can occur when one statement is particularly tricky or when you didn't rephrase the question fully. The GMAT may be trying to trap you into concluding that both statements are needed to answer the question.

Try-It #4-14

If $K = \dfrac{\dfrac{1}{3a} + \dfrac{1}{b}}{\dfrac{5}{ab}}$ and $ab \neq 0$, what is the value of K?

(1) $a = 3$
(2) $b - 3(5 - a) = 0$

It should be evident that the two statements combined are sufficient to answer the question—you can plug the value of a from Statement (1) into Statement (2) to solve for the value of b, then you can plug those values into the question to solve for K.

Immediately be skeptical. C should seem too easy. After all, you didn't do anything to the question stem. So you should do some work to determine whether one of the two statements *alone* (or, in some cases, each statement alone) is sufficient to answer the question.

Let's start by rephrasing the question:

$$K = \frac{\dfrac{1}{3a} + \dfrac{1}{b}}{\dfrac{5}{ab}} = \frac{\dfrac{b}{3ab} + \dfrac{3a}{3ab}}{\dfrac{5}{ab}} = \frac{b + 3a}{3ab} \times \frac{ab}{5} = \frac{b + 3a}{15}$$

"What is the value of K?" rephrases to "What is the value of $b + 3a$?" Statement (2) rephrases and gives us the answer:

$$b - 3(5 - a) =$$
$$b - 15 + 3a = 0$$
$$b + 3a = 15$$

The correct answer is B. In these cases, the more complicated statement may be enough.

This is not a tactic to use at lower levels of the test. On 500-600 level problems, the two statements may work together in straightforward ways to produce sufficiency. The C trap may be the C answer! This is one of many reasons why the material in this book is only appropriate if you have achieved a certain level of proficiency on the math side of the GMAT.

6. Use Basic Algebraic Reasoning   *Certainty:* Moderate

IF possible … ⟶ rely on basic algebraic reasoning.

Quite often, basic intuition about algebra can lead you to the correct answer. For example, you might have the intuition on a problem that "I have two unknowns and only one equation, so I can't solve" or "this statement doesn't even mention the variable(s) that I care about." Often, you will discover that your intuition is correct.

> A sales manager at an industrial company has an opportunity to switch to a new, higher-paying job in another state. If his current annual salary is $50,000 and his current state tax rate is 5%, how much income after state tax would he make at the new job?
>
> (1) His new salary will be 10% higher than his old salary.
> (2) His annual state taxes will total $2,200 in the new state at his new job.

You may reason that in order to answer this question, we need to know how much his new salary will be, and how much his taxes will increase by. This reasoning will lead you to conclude that the answer is C. And you'll be right.

Of course, you need to be *very careful* about using this tactic. Many problems on the GMAT are designed to hoodwink your algebraic reasoning—usually to make you think that you need to know every value precisely to answer the question.

For example, suppose the question in the previous problem were changed to "Will the manager make more money at the new job, after state taxes?" The correct answer in this case would be B. The problem explicitly states that the new job is higher-paying, so we only need to check to see whether the change in state tax might lead to a lower after-tax compensation. Statement (2) tells us indirectly that his new state taxes ($2,200) will be lower than his current state taxes (5% of $50,000 = $2,500), so his after-state-tax compensation will definitely be higher in the new job. We do *not* need to find out how much higher his pre-tax salary would be to answer this question.

Because the GMAT frequently uses traps involving basic algebraic reasoning, you should only resort to using it if you are *truly stuck*.

7. Spot Cross-Multiplied Inequalities   *Certainty:* Low

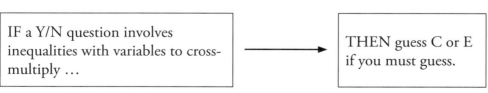

IF a Y/N question involves inequalities with variables to cross-multiply … ⟶ THEN guess C or E if you must guess.

When you are presented with an inequality problem in Data Sufficiency in which one or more variables appears in a denominator, you may need to know the sign of the variable or variables to answer the question. This might be the hidden trick.

Try-It #4-15

Is $xy < 1$?

(1) $\dfrac{2}{x} > 3y$

(2) $x > 0$

Statement (1) might imply that $xy < \dfrac{2}{3}$, but <u>only</u> if x is positive. If it is negative, we would need to flip the sign: $xy > \dfrac{2}{3}$. Thus we cannot answer the question without knowing the sign of x—information that is provided in Statement (2). The correct answer is C.

These types of questions may have an A or B trap, in that you might fail to realize that you have to set up negative and positive cases when you multiply or divide an inequality by a variable.

Watch out! In some GMAT problems, you *can* assume the sign of the variables, because the variables represent countable quantities of physical things. In those cases, you can assume that the variables are positive, and you can cross-multiply inequalities involving those variables at will.

8. Judge By Appearance   *Certainty:* Low

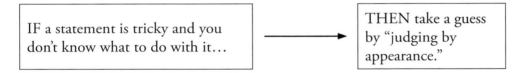

Sometimes a statement will leave you completely bewildered. In that case, the best (and only!) tactic is to guess whether it will be sufficient judging by how it looks:

- Does it simply look like it might be sufficient, even if you can't see how?
- Does it use the variables you are looking for?
- Could it likely be manipulated into a form *similar* to that of the question?

The general rule is this: if the information in a statement has a *structure* and *complexity* similar to the question, and has the right ingredients (variables, coefficients, etc.), it's more likely to be sufficient than otherwise. This won't crack every case by any means, but you'd be surprised at how much mileage you can get from this tactic.

Try-It #4-16

Does $4^a = 4^{-a} + b$?

(1) $16^a = 1 + \dfrac{2^{2a}}{b^{-1}}$

(2) $a = 2$

Depending on your level of comfort with exponent manipulations, you may be able to prove that Statement (1) alone is sufficient:

$$16^a = 1 + \frac{2^{2a}}{b^{-1}}$$

$$16^a = 1 + \left(2^{2a}\right)b$$

$$4^{2a} = 1 + \left(4^a\right)b$$

$$\frac{4^{2a}}{4^a} = \frac{1 + \left(4^a\right)b}{4^a}$$

$$4^a = \frac{1}{4^a} + b$$

$$4^a = 4^{-a} + b$$

However, what if you find yourself at a temporary loss on the test? Your exponent engine may shut down for a problem or two. Then what do you do?

One line of reasoning might be as follows: "Statement (2) is clearly not sufficient, since it tells me nothing about *b*. Now let's look at Statement (1). It's a very complicated expression, but it seems to have the right ingredients. It contains *a* and *b*, and uses *a* as an exponent. Also, the exponential terms in Statement (1) are powers of 2 (2, 4, 16), just like the exponential terms in *a*. I'll bet if I manipulate this equation right, it will answer the question. I choose A." And you'd be right. The GMAT never needs to know that you guessed.

Summary

That was a lot of stuff! To summarize, the following advanced strategies and guessing tactics can be used to solve Data Sufficiency problems effectively or simply increase your chances of success:

Advanced Data Sufficiency Strategies

(1) Compute to Completion – If you can't tell for certain whether the answer can be calculated in theory, keep going on the calculations *all the way*.

(2) Extract the Equation – Represent word problems with algebraic equations to avoid embedded tricks that can be difficult to find otherwise.

(3) Use the Constraints – Bring explicit and implicit constraints to the surface. These constraints will often be necessary to determine the correct answer.

(4) Beware of Inequalities – Whenever a problem involves inequality symbols, *be careful*—there are many ways in which inequalities can be used to trick you.

(5) Use the Scenario Chart – In problems with a limited number of potential outcomes, list those outcomes on paper and test them in a structured way.

(6) Test Numbers Systematically – In other Data Sufficiency problems, many possible values may exist, but underlying those values is some sort of pattern. Use *systematic number testing* when the possible values cannot be listed consecutively, and use *discrete number listing* when the values are "integer-like" (and thus can be listed consecutively).

Data Sufficiency Guessing Tactics

(1) Spot Identical Statements – If the two statements say the same thing (after rephrasing), then the answer must be D or E.

(2) Spot Clear Sufficiency – If the two statements together are clearly sufficient, then eliminate E.

(3) Spot One Statement Inside The Other – If a narrow statement is completely contained within a broader statement, then eliminate C and "broader statement only" (either A or B).

(4) Spot One Statement Adding Nothing – If one statement adds no value to the information given in the other statement, then eliminate C.

(5) Spot a C Trap – If the two statements together are *very* clearly sufficient, then C could be a trap answer, so eliminate C.

(6) Use Basic Algebraic Reasoning – Apply basic knowledge of algebra, such as considering the number of unknowns relative to the number of known equations, to guide your thought process.

(7) Spot Cross-Multiplied Inequalities – If a Yes/No question involves inequalities with variables in a denominator, then guess C or E if you must guess.

(8) Judge By Appearance – If a statement is very difficult and you're completely unsure what to do with it, then make an informed guess as to whether it *appears* to be sufficient.

APPENDIX: Selected Applications of Scenario Charts

	Trigger:	Reason:	Scenarios:	Example:
A	Even Exponents	Two solutions when you take the square root.	1. Negative root 2. Positive root	$x^2 = 9$: Case 1: $x = -3$ Case 2: $x = 3$
B	Inequalities: Multiplication or Division by a Variable	If you don't know the sign of the variable, then two possible inequalities result: one with a flipped inequality sign and one with the original sign.	1. Flipped sign 2. Original sign	$\dfrac{16}{x} > y$: Case 1: $16 < xy$ if $x < 0$ Case 2: $16 > xy$ if $x > 0$

C	Inequalities: Variables Raised to Powers	Numbers raised to powers become larger or smaller according to complicated rules:
		  a. When raised to a power greater than 1, a fraction between 0 and 1 gets smaller, but a larger number gets larger.
		  b. Even exponents make negative numbers positive, but odd exponents keep negative numbers negative.
			For each variable:
			1. greater than 1
			2. between 0 and 1
			3. between −1 and 0
			4. less than −1
			(and *possibly*)
			5. equal to 1
			6. equal to 0
			7. equal to −1
			(Some of the scenarios may be eliminated by the conditions given)
				a. Fractions vs. Integers:
				$(½)^3 < ½$
				$\lvert(-½)^3\rvert < \lvert-½\rvert$
				but
				$2^3 > 2$
				$\lvert(-2)^3\rvert > \lvert-2\rvert$
				
				b. Positive vs. Negative:
				$(-3)^1 < (-3)^2$
				but
				$(-3)^2 > (-3)^3$

D	Absolute Values	The expression within the absolute value bars could be positive or negative.	1. Expression is negative 2. Expression is positive	$\lvert x - 2\rvert = 3$: Case 1: $x - 2 = -3$ if $x - 2 < 0$ Case 2: $x - 2 = 3$ if $x - 2 > 0$
E	Zero Product	The product will be zero when any of the multiplied terms are zero	For each multiplied term: 1. Zero 2. Non-zero …as long as at least one of the terms is zero.	If $xy = 0$: Case 1: $x = 0$, or Case 2: $y = 0$, or Case 3: both $x = 0$ and $y = 0$

	Trigger:	Reason	Scenarios	Example:
F	Odd/ Even	Addition and multiplication rules allow for an output of a given parity (odd or even) to result from multiple scenarios.	For each variable: 1. Even 2. Odd There are a maximum of 2^n scenarios, where n is the number of variables.	Even results from: Case 1: Even ± Even Case 2: Odd ± Odd Case 3: Even × Even Case 4: Even × Odd Odd results from: Case 1: Even ± Odd Case 2: Odd × Odd
G	Positive/ Negative	Multiplication rules (and addition rules, in certain cases) allow for an output of a given sign to result from multiple scenarios.	For each variable: 1. Positive 2. Negative There are a maximum of 2^n scenarios, where n is the number of variables.	Pos results from: Case 1: Pos × Pos Case 2: Neg × Neg Case 3: Pos + Pos Case 4: Pos − Neg Neg results from: Case 1: Pos × Neg Case 2: Neg + Neg Case 3: Neg − Pos Uncertain when you have: Pos + Neg (depends on absolute values)
H	High/ Low	If an input variable can take on a range of values, then you should test the output at the extremes of the range.	1. High 2. Low	Gasoline costs between $3.50 and $4.00 per gallon. A trip requires 2–3 gallons of gasoline. High cost = $4.00 × 3 = $12 Low cost = $3.50 × 2 = $7
I	Remainder/ Units Digit	Many different numbers give you the same remainder when divided by some number.	Each set of inputs	7 ÷ 5 → remainder 2 *or* 12 ÷ 5 → remainder 2

In-Action Problem Set

For problems 1–3, list 5 to 8 consecutive values that satisfy each of the following constraints. Try not to skip possibilities.

1. n is a prime integer.

2. $x^2 > 0$ (Be sure to list integers as well as non-integers)

3. $\dfrac{M}{7} = N + \dfrac{3}{7}$, where M and N are positive integers. (Hint: list consecutive values for N that fit, and then list corresponding values for M.)

For problems 4–6, solve the problem by picking numbers and testing them. Be sure to note whether *Standard Number Testing* (standard set of numbers to test, both integer and non-integer) or *Discrete Number Listing* (consecutive listing of discrete numbers that fit) is the appropriate technique.

4. Is $a + a^{-1} > 2$?

    (1) $a > 0$
    (2) $a < 1$

5. What is the value of positive integer x?

    (1) $x^4 < 1{,}000$
    (2) $2^x < x^2$

6. Is $y^3 \leq |y|$?

    (1) $y < 1$
    (2) $y < 0$

For problems 7–9, use *Scenario Charts* to evaluate the possible scenarios for the problem and solve.

7. If a, b, and c are positive integers, is abc an even integer?

    (1) $a + b$ is even.
    (2) $b + c$ is odd.

8. If x, y, and z are positive integers, is $x - y - z$ positive?

    (1) $x > y$
    (2) $y > z$

9. What is the value of xyz?

    (1) $xyz - xy = 0$
    (2) Either $x = 0$ or $y = 0$ or $z = 1$.

For problems 10–15, solve the problem. Note the **strategies** used to solve the problem, and also note what **guessing tactics** could be employed to help eliminate answer choices. Even if you weren't certain as to the correct answer, which answer choices could you eliminate and why? Also, which guessing tactics would *not* work, and why?

The following Advanced Strategies and Guessing Tactics are discussed in this chapter:

Advanced Strategies	**Guessing Tactics**
(1) Compute to Completion	(1) Spot Identical Statements
(2) Extract the Equation	(2) Spot Clear Sufficiency
(3) Use the Constraints	(3) Spot One Statement Inside The Other
(4) Beware of Inequalities	(4) Spot One Statement Adding Nothing
(5) Use the Scenario Chart	(5) Spot a (C) Trap
(6) Test Numbers Systematically	(6) Use Basic Algebraic Reasoning
	(7) Spot Cross-Multiplied Inequalities
	(8) Judge By Appearance

10. Jose purchased several large and small dressers at a flea market to add to his antique furniture collection. The large dressers cost $31 apiece, while the small dressers cost $25 apiece. If Jose did not purchase any other items at the flea market, how many small dressers did he buy?

    (1) Jose purchased as many small dressers as large dressers.
    (2) In total, Jose spent $280 at the flea market.

11. Amanda and Todd purchase candy, popcorn, and pretzels at the stadium. If a package of candy costs half as much as a bag of popcorn, how much more money did Amanda and Todd spend on the candy than on the popcorn and pretzels combined?

    (1) The cost of a bag of popcorn is equal to the cost of a pretzel.
    (2) Amanda and Todd purchased 24 packages of candy, 6 pretzels, and 6 bags of popcorn.

12. What is the value of $|x + 4|$?

    (1) $x^2 + 8x + 12 = 0$
    (2) $x^2 + 6x = 0$

13. Is $\dfrac{a - k}{b - k} > \dfrac{a + k}{b + k}$?

    (1) $a > b > k$
    (2) $k > 0$

14. If j and k are positive integers, is j divisible by 6?

   (1) $j = (k + 1)(k + 2)(k + 3)$
   (2) k is an even integer.

15. What is the value of $\dfrac{5^{(a+b)^2}}{5^{(a-b)^2}}$?

   (1) $a = 0$
   (2) $b = 3$

In-Action Problem Set (Solutions)

1. $n = 2, 3, 5, 7, 11, 13, 17, 19, 23$, etc.

2. $x = 3.5, 4, 4.5, 5, -3.5, -4, -5$, etc. (Note that the list must include integers and non-integers, positive and negative values—although the items you choose do not need to match these exact values.)

3. $M = 10, 17, 24, 31, 38$, etc. and $N = 1, 2, 3, 4, 5$, etc.:

    M must have a remainder of 3 when divided by 7:
    $M = 7 + 3, 14 + 3, 21 + 3, 28 + 3, 35 + 3$, etc.
    $M = 10, 17, 24, 31, 38$, etc.
    $N = 1, 2, 3, 4, 5$, etc.

Note that successive values of M differ by 7, and the corresponding values of N are consecutive integers.

One way to generate this list is simply to pick consecutive numbers for N and then calculate values for M:

$$\frac{M}{7} = N + \frac{3}{7}$$
$$M = 7N + 3$$

$N = 1, 2, 3, 4, 5$, etc.

$M = 7(1) + 3 = 10, 7(2) + 3 = 17, 7(3) + 3 = 24, 7(4) + 3 = 31, 7(5) + 3 = 38$, etc.

4. **C:** Because there are no constraints on a, we should consider the *Standard Number Testing Set* of numbers. The inequality can be rephrased as follows:

Is $a + a^{-1} > 2$?   →   Is $a + \dfrac{1}{a} > 2$?

Statement 1: $a > 0$ (INSUFFICIENT)				Statement 2: $a < 1$ (INSUFFICIENT)		
a	$a + \dfrac{1}{a}$	> 2?		a	$a + \dfrac{1}{a}$	> 2?
$\dfrac{1}{2}$	$\dfrac{1}{2} + \dfrac{1}{1/2} = \dfrac{5}{2}$	Y		-1	$-1 + (-1) = -2$	N
1	$1 + 1 = 2$	N		$-\dfrac{1}{2}$	$-\dfrac{1}{2} + \dfrac{1}{-1/2} = -\dfrac{5}{2}$	N
$\dfrac{3}{2}$	$\dfrac{3}{2} + \dfrac{2}{3} = \dfrac{13}{6}$	Y		0	$0 + 1/0 = ???$	N/A
2	$2 + \dfrac{1}{2} = \dfrac{5}{2}$	Y		$\dfrac{1}{2}$	$\dfrac{1}{2} + \dfrac{1}{1/2} = \dfrac{5}{2}$	Y

Combining the two constraints, we have $0 < a < 1$. Within the Standard Number Testing Set, only 1/2 is within this range. Also, because the answer to the question is "No" at $a = 1$ and "Undefined" at $a = 0$, we should apply the *boundary principle*—test numbers close to the boundaries of the range.

Statements (1) & (2): $a > 0$ (SUFFICIENT)		
a	$a + \dfrac{1}{a}$	$> 2?$
$\dfrac{1}{10}$	$\dfrac{1}{10} + \dfrac{1}{1/10} = \dfrac{101}{10}$	Y
$\dfrac{1}{2}$	$\dfrac{1}{2} + \dfrac{1}{1/2} = \dfrac{5}{2}$	Y
$\dfrac{9}{10}$	$\dfrac{9}{10} + \dfrac{10}{9} = \dfrac{181}{90}$	Y

It seems that at the extreme edges, the values are greater than 2, so Statements (1) & (2) appear to be SUFFICIENT. The correct answer is C.

5.   **B:** Because we are told that x is a positive integer, we can employ **Discrete Number Listing**. We need to find a single value for x, and we need to do some work to find cases that fit the statements.

Statement 1: $x^4 < 1{,}000$ (INSUFFICIENT)		
x	x^4	< 1000
1	$1^4 = 1$	valid
2	$2^4 = 16$	valid
3	$3^4 = 81$	valid
4	$4^4 = 256$	valid
5	$5^4 = 625$	valid
6	$6^4 = 1{,}296$	invalid

Statement 2: $2^x < x^2$ (SUFFICIENT)			
x	2^x	x^2	$2^x < x^2$
1	$2^1 = 2$	$1^2 = 1$	invalid
2	$2^2 = 4$	$2^2 = 4$	invalid
3	$2^3 = 8$	$3^2 = 9$	valid
4	$2^4 = 16$	$4^2 = 16$	invalid
5	$2^5 = 32$	$5^2 = 25$	invalid
6	$2^6 = 64$	$6^2 = 36$	invalid

Listing numbers for Statement (2) indicates that 3 is the only integer for x such that $2^x < x^2$. Greater integers than 6 would only lead to a greater gap the other way. The correct answer is B.

6.   **D:** Because there are no constraints on y, we should consider the **Standard Number Testing** set of numbers, displayed here in Number Line graphic form:

	-2	$-3/2$	-1	$-1/2$	0	$1/2$	1	$3/2$	2
y^3	-8	$-27/8$	-1	$-1/8$	0	$1/8$	1	$27/8$	8
$|y|$	2	$3/2$	1	$1/2$	0	$1/2$	1	$3/2$	2
$y^3 \le |y|?$	Y	Y	Y	Y	Y	Y	Y	N	N

the new standard

Statement (1): $y < 1$. If y is less than 1, all tested values above show $y^3 \leq |y|$. SUFFICIENT.

Statement (2): $y < 0$. If y is less than 0, all tested values above show $y^3 \leq |y|$. SUFFICIENT.

Notice that we could use Guessing Tactic 3: **One Statement Contained in the Other**. $y < 0$ is more limiting than $y < 1$, so if Statement (1) is sufficient, Statement (2) must be sufficient. We can therefore eliminate answer choices A and C.

The correct answer is D.

7.   **B:** We can test the odd/even scenarios using Scenario Charts. Statement (1) tells us that $a + b$ is even, so a and b are either both odd or both even. INSUFFICIENT:

a	b	c	abc Even?
Even	Even	Even	Y
Even	Even	Odd	Y
Odd	Odd	Even	Y
Odd	Odd	Odd	N

Statement (2) tells us that $b + c$ is odd, so one of b and c is odd and the other is even. SUFFICIENT:

a	b	c	abc Even?
Even	Even	Odd	Y
Odd	Even	Odd	Y
Even	Odd	Even	Y
Odd	Odd	Even	Y

Since one of the two variables must be even, the product abc will always be even. The correct answer is B.

8.   **E:** We can test different numeric scenarios for x, y and z using Scenario Charts. Statement (1) tells us that $x > y$, but tells us nothing about z. INSUFFICIENT:

x	y	z	$x - y - z > 0$?
5	3	1	Y
5	3	10	N

Statement (2) tells us that $y > z$, but tells us nothing about x. INSUFFICIENT:

x	y	z	$x - y - z > 0$?
5	3	1	Y
2	3	1	N

Combining Statements (1) & (2), we see that many different outcomes are possible. We can pick numbers for x, y and z that give us different answers. INSUFFICIENT:

x	y	z	$x - y - z > 0$?
5	3	1	Y
5	4	2	N

The correct answer is E.

9.　**E:** We can test different numeric scenarios for x, y and z using **Scenario Charts**. Statement (1) tells us that $xyz - xy = 0$. First, let's factor the equation:

$$xyz - xy = 0$$
$$xy(z - 1) = 0$$

For this product to equal zero, either $x = 0$, or $y = 0$, or $z = 1$. We can list the scenarios and test the possible values for xyz:

x	y	z	xyz
0	*any*	*any*	0
any	0	*any*	0
any	*any*	1	xy (any value)

Thus if $x = 0$ or $y = 0$, then $xyz = 0$, but if $z = 1$, then xyz could take on any value. INSUFFICIENT.

Statement (2) tells us that either $x = 0$ or $y = 0$ or $z = 1$. This is the exact same information from Statement (1), so we can eliminate A, B and C by *Spotting Identical Statements*. Since Statement (1) also proved to be insufficient, we can eliminate D as well.

The correct answer is E.

10.　**B:** The question stem tells us that Jose purchased both large ($31 apiece) and small dressers ($25 apiece), and asks us to determine how many small dressers he purchased. Because price information is given, we will likely require some sort of information about the total <u>amount of money</u> he spent on small dressers, in order to calculate the number of small dressers he purchased.

Since this is an algebraic translations problem, we should assign variables to the unknowns in the problem:

　　L = Large dressers
　　S = Small dressers

Statement (1) tells us that Jose purchased an equal number of small dressers and large dressers. This is not sufficient, because he could have purchased any number of dressers. For example, $L = 1$ and $S = 1$ is one possibility, while $L = 10$ and $S = 10$ is another.

Statement (2) tells us that Jose spent a total of $280 at the flea market. At first glance, this doesn't seem to be enough information, because we have 2 unknowns and 1 equation:

　　$31L + 25S = 280$

However, we have to be careful. We have the *stealth constraint* that L and S must be *positive integers*, since they represent countable things (the number of large and small dressers). It's very possible that only one set of integers fulfills this constraint. Let's choose different values for L and see whether this leads to an integer solution for S:

# Large	$ Large	# Small	$ Small	$ Total	Integer?
0	0	11.2	280	280	NO
1	31	9.96	249	280	NO
2	62	8.72	218	280	NO
3	93	7.48	187	280	NO
4	124	6.24	156	280	NO
5	155	5	125	280	YES
6	186	3.76	94	280	NO
7	217	2.52	63	280	NO
8	248	1.28	32	280	NO
9	279	0.04	1	280	NO

Only $L = 5$ and $S = 5$ produces an integer result for both variables, so Statement (2) is sufficient.

Notice also that both $25S$ and 280 are divisible by 5. Therefore, for $31L + 25S$ to equal 280, $31L$ must be divisible by 5, which means that L must be divisible by 5. We only need to test multiples of 5 for L. $L = 10$ is too big, as that would be 310 spent on large dressers alone, and $L = 0$ implies that $25S = 280$, so $S = 11.2$. This gives us a non-integer for S, so L must equal 5 (and therefore S must equal 5).

Because this is an algebraic translations problem, we *Extracted the Equation* to avoid tricks embedded in the problem. By *Using the Constraints* (especially the implicit constraint that S and L must be integers), we noticed that there may be only one integer solution for Statement (2). We then tested that possibility and found that, indeed, there was only one integer solution. Also notice the use of a *Scenario Chart* to check each solution for viability.

The correct answer is B.

11. **C:** The question stem tells us that Amanda and Todd purchased candy, popcorn, and pretzels, and asks us to determine how much more money they spent on candy than on popcorn and pretzels combined. We are also told that the cost of the candy is half that of the cost of a bag of popcorn.

We need to assign variables to the unknowns in the problem. We have both quantities and prices:

C = packages of candy P_c = price of a package of candy
P = bags of popcorn P_p = price of a bag of popcorn
R = number of pretzels P_r = price of a pretzel

Algebraically, the question asks us: what is $P_c \times C - (P_p \times P + P_r \times R)$?

We are told in the question stem that $P_c = 1/2 \times P_p$.

Statement (1) tells us that $P_r = P_p$. Since we know P_c and P_r in terms of P_p, we can substitute and rephrase the question:

What is $P_c \times C - (P_p \times P + P_r \times R)$?
What is $(1/2 \times P_p) \times C - (P_p \times P + (P_p) \times R)$?
What is $P_p \times (1/2 \times C - P - R)$?

We do not know the values of P_p, C, P, and R, so Statement (1) is not sufficient.

Statement (2) tells us that $C = 24$, $P = 6$, and $R = 6$:

What is $P_c \times C - (P_p \times P + P_r \times R)$?
What is $(1/2 \times P_p) \times C - (P_p \times P + P_r \times R)$?
What is $(1/2 \times P_p) \times 24 - (P_p \times 6 + P_r \times 6)$?
What is $12P_p - 6P_p - 6P_r$?
What is $6P_p - 6P_r$?

We do not know the values of P_p or P_r, so Statement (2) is not sufficient.

Combining the two statements, we can take the rephrased question from Statement (2) and substitute using $P_p = P_r$:

What is $6P_p - 6P_r$?
What is $6P_p - 6(P_p)$?
What is 0?

Given the relative prices of the candy, popcorn, and pretzels, and the quantity of each purchased, the cost of the candy will always equal the combined cost of the popcorn and pretzels, even though we don't know the exact prices. Statements (1) and (2) combined are SUFFICIENT to answer the question. If we had not *Extracted the Equation* and *Computed to Completion*, it would have been difficult to notice this fact.

The correct answer is C.

12. **A:** Statement (1) tells us that $x^2 + 8x + 12 = 0$. Factoring:

$(x + 2)(x + 6) = 0$
$x = -2$ or -6

The question asks for the value of $|x + 4|$. At first glance, it might appear that we have 2 values for x, and thus do not know the value of $|x + 4|$. However:

$$|(-2) + 4| = |2| = 2 \qquad\qquad |(-6) + 4| = |-2| = 2$$

Therefore Statement (1) is SUFFICIENT.

Statement (2) tells us that $x^2 + 6x = 0$. Factoring:

$x(x + 6) = 0$
$x = 0$ or -6

the new standard

Testing both values for x:

$$|(0)+4|=4 \qquad\qquad |(-6)+4|=|-2|=2$$

We get two different values for x, so Statement (2) is INSUFFICIENT.

If we had not *Computed to Completion*, we might have fallen into the trap of thinking that because Statement (1) gave us two values for x, we would get two different answers to the question. That was *not* the case: we got the same answer from both values.

The correct answer is A.

13. **C:** In rephrasing this question, we should recall that we do not know the sign of $b - k$ and $b + k$. Thus, after cross-multiplying, we should set up *Flow Charts* to evaluate two different questions: one for the case in which $(b - k)$ and $(b + k)$ have the same sign and another for the case in which $(b - k)$ and $(b + k)$ have different signs:

If $(b - k)(b + k) > 0$:	If $(b - k)(b + k) < 0$:
$\dfrac{a-k}{b-k} > \dfrac{a+k}{b+k}$?	$\dfrac{a-k}{b-k} > \dfrac{a+k}{b+k}$?
$(b-k)(b+k)\left(\dfrac{a-k}{b-k}\right) > \left(\dfrac{a+k}{b+k}\right)(b-k)(b+k)$?	$(b-k)(b+k)\left(\dfrac{a-k}{b-k}\right) < \left(\dfrac{a+k}{b+k}\right)(b-k)(b+k)$?
$(b+k)(a-k) > (a+k)(b-k)$?	$(b+k)(a-k) < (a+k)(b-k)$?
$ba-bk+ka-k^2 > ab-ak+bk-k^2$?	$ba-bk+ka-k^2 < ab-ak+bk-k^2$?
$-bk+ak > -ak+bk$?	$-bk+ak < -ak+bk$?
$2ak > 2bk$?	$2ak < 2bk$?
$ak > bk$?	$ak < bk$?

Statement (1) tells us that $a > b > k$. This is not sufficient. We do not know whether $(b - k)(b + k)$ is positive, so we do not know which question to answer. Even if we did, we could get different results. For example, if a and b are positive and k is negative, then $(b - k)(b + k)$ could be positive. Thus the relevant question would be "Is $ak > bk$?" Because k is negative, $ak < bk$. By contrast, if a, b, and k are all positive, then $(b - k)(b + k)$ is positive. Thus the relevant question would be "Is $ak > bk$?" Because $a > b > k$, we would know $ak > bk$. We get two different answers depending on whether k is positive. INSUFFICIENT.

Statement (2) tells us that $k > 0$. This is not sufficient, because the statement tells us nothing about a and b. INSUFFICIENT.

Statements (1) and (2) combined are sufficient, because if $a > b > k > 0$, then $(b - k)(b + k) > 0$, so the relevant question is "Is $ak > bk$?" We know that $a > b$, and k is positive, so $ak > bk$, and the answer to the question is a definite "YES."

Notice the use of the *Scenario Chart*—specifically, *Flow Charts*—to handle the different versions of the question depending on the sign of $(b - k)(b + k)$. Additionally, we were careful to *Beware of Inequalities*—the inequalities in this problem make it easy to make a mistake in rephrasing the question in the *Flow Chart* or in evaluating the statements.

Notice also that if the algebra and thought process became too complicated, we could *Cross-Multiply Inequalities* and guess between C and E. Because the combined statements tell us that $a > b > k > 0$, we would know a lot about the relative values of the variables in the problems, and it might be reasonable to choose C as the best answer.

The correct answer is C.

14. **A:** In order to determine whether j is divisible by 6, we need to know whether j is divisible by 2 (even) and also divisible by 3.

Statement (1) is SUFFICIENT: $k + 1$, $k + 2$, and $k + 3$ are 3 consecutive integers. The product of 3 consecutive integers will always be divisible by 3, because one of the 3 integers must be a multiple of 3. Additionally, at least one of those integers must be even (it's possible that two of them are even), so the product will be even.

Statement (2) is INSUFFICIENT: knowing that k is even tells us nothing about j.

You might *Spot One Statement Adding Nothing* here. Knowing that k is even adds no information to Statement (1), because the product $(k + 1)(k + 2)(k + 3)$ is going to be even for any value of k. Therefore, C can be eliminated.

You might also *Judge by Appearance* on this problem. We need to know whether j is divisible by 2 and 3, and since Statement (1) tells us that j is the product of 3 consecutive integers, it seems as though this statement is likely to be sufficient.

You could also use *Discrete Number Listing* to test numbers for k and prove to yourself that j must be divisible by 6.

The correct answer is A.

15. **A:** We should rephrase the question before proceeding:

$$\frac{5^{(a+b)^2}}{5^{(a-b)^2}}?$$

$$\frac{5^{a^2+2ab+b^2}}{5^{a^2-2ab+b^2}}?$$

$$5^{4ab}?$$

$$ab?$$

Therefore the relevant question is "What is the value of ab?" Statement (1) tells us that $a = 0$, so $ab = 0$. SUFFICIENT. Statement (2) tells us $b = 3$, but we do not know the value of a. INSUFFICIENT.

*Manhattan*GMAT*Prep*
the new standard

In this problem, it is critical to rephrase the question to get to the kernel of the problem. The similar quadratic expressions in the exponents should also be a clue to do this rephrasing.

Also, you should *Spot Clear Sufficiency* in this problem—if we know the value of a and b, we can calculate this answer to this problem, so E can be eliminated. Because that's so obvious, we should keep in mind the *C Trap*. We should be skeptical about choosing C on such a complex problem, because one of the statements alone might be enough to answer the question.

The correct answer is A.

Chapter 5
of
ADVANCED GMAT QUANT

PATTERN
RECOGNITION

In This Chapter . . .

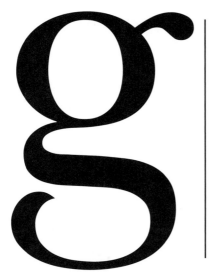

- Sequence Problems
- Units (Ones) Digit Problems
- Remainder Problems
- Other Pattern Problems

Pattern Recognition Problems

In the context of the GMAT, *pattern recognition* involves spotting a repeating cycle or other simple relationship underlying a series of numbers. If you can grasp the rule, you can predict numbers that appear later in the series. The series may be part of a defined sequence, or it may arise from a general list of possibilities. Either way, if you can spot the pattern, you can eliminate a lot of unnecessary calculation. In fact, often the only feasible way to get the answer in 2 minutes (for example, finding the 100th number in some series) is to recognize the underlying pattern. Here's a simple example.

Try-It #5-1

> Each number in a sequence is 3 more than the previous number. If the first number is 4, what is the value of the 1,000th term in the sequence?

Obviously, finding the 1,000th number the long way (by computing every intervening number) is impossible in the time allotted on the GMAT. You can solve this problem in several ways, but one powerful way is to compute the first several terms, spot the underlying *pattern*, figure out *the rule*, and then apply it.

The first 5 terms of the sequence are 4, 7, 10, 13, 16. Notice that we repeatedly add 3 to get the next value. Repeated addition is simply multiplication, so we should think to match these numbers to the multiples of 3. The first 5 multiples of 3 are 3, 6, 9, 12, 15—all 1 less than the numbers in the sequence. Thus the rule for generating the sequence is "take the corresponding multiple of 3, and add 1." Therefore, the 1,000th term of the sequence is 1 more than the 1,000th multiple of 3, which is 3,000 + 1 = 3,001. Once we spot the pattern, we can skip over vast amounts of unnecessary work.

The two most basic patterns are these:

1) The *counting numbers* (1, 2, 3, 4, …), also known as the *positive integers*. As simple as this pattern may seem, it is the basis for many other patterns. For instance, the sequence of the multiples of 7 (7, 14, 21, 28, …) can be derived from 1, 2, 3, 4, … by simply multiplying by 7. We can write this sequence as $S_n = 7n$, where n is the basic sequence of positive integers.

2) A *repeating cycle* of numbers. For instance, the sequence 4, 2, 6, 4, 2, 6, 4, 2, 6… has a repeating cycle of three terms: 4, 2, 6. Repeating cycles can be derived in various ways from the counting numbers (for example, when you raise an integer to increasing powers, the units digits of the results repeat themselves). However, it is often easier to think of repeating cycles *on their own terms*, separately from the counting numbers and related patterns.

When you are examining a string of numbers for a pattern, do the following:

1) Compute the first 5 to 8 terms and try to match them to a stock pattern that you already know. The most basic pattern is the counting numbers, but you should also have these related patterns up your sleeve:

   a. Multiples (e.g., $7 \times 1 = 7$, $7 \times 2 = 14$, $7 \times 3 = 21$, $7 \times 4 = 28$, $7 \times 5 = 35$, …, $7n$, …)
   b. Squares ($1^2 = 1$, $2^2 = 4$, $3^2 = 9$, $4^2 = 16$, $5^2 = 25$, …, n^2, …)
   c. Powers ($2^1 = 2$, $2^2 = 4$, $2^3 = 8$, $2^4 = 16$, $2^5 = 32$, …, 2^n, …)

For each of these stock sequences, notice exactly where the counting numbers come into play. For instance, in the squares series, the counting numbers are the *bases*, but in the powers series, the counting numbers are the *exponents*.

2) Look for repeating cycles. As soon as you generate a repeated term, see whether the sequence will simply repeat itself from that point onward. Repeating cycles on the GMAT typically begin repeating every four terms (or fewer), so 5 to 8 terms should easily help you identify the pattern. Of course, some cycles repeat every single term—that is, it's the same number over and over again!

3) If you are stuck, look for patterns within *differences between terms* or *sums across terms*.

   a. Look at the difference between consecutive terms. For instance, this process can help you spot linear sequences (sequences of multiples plus a constant):

Sequence:	10	17	24	31	...	$7n + 3$ ...

Differences:	7	7	7	7 (constant difference)

   b. Also look at the *cumulative sum* of all the terms up to that point. This is helpful if the terms get closer to zero or alternate in sign.

Sequence:	1/2	1/4	1/8	1/16	...	$1/2^n$	...
Cumulative Sum:	1/2	3/4	7/8	15/16	...	$(2^n - 1)/2^n$ ...	

   Notice that the cumulative sum for this sequence approaches 1 as closely as we want, always staying below.

   c. Some sums involve *matching pairs* that sum to the same number (or even cancel each other out). Be on the lookout for such matching pairs.

   What is the sum of 1, 5, 8, 10, 11, 11, 12, 14, 17, and 21?

You can of course sum these numbers in order, but look to make natural intermediate sums (subtotals) with matching pairs. In this example, spot the repeated 11's in the middle and sum them to 22. Working outward, we see that 10 and 12 sum to 22 as well. So do 8 and 14, 5 and 17, and 1 and 21. In all, we have 5 subtotals of 22, for a grand total of 110.

4) Look at characteristics of the numbers: positive/negative, odd/even, integer/non-integer, etc. Once you have extended the pattern for several terms, these characteristics will generally repeat or alternate in some predictable way.

Perhaps the most important principle to apply on Pattern Recognition problems is to *Put Pen To Paper*, as discussed in Chapter 1. Often the pattern will be completely hidden until you actually compute the first several values of the sequence or other initial results.

Several types of problems frequently involve underlying patterns. When you see these types of problems on the GMAT, be ready to analyze the pattern so you can find the rule:

1) **Sequence problems** – Nearly all sequence problems involve a pattern in the elements (or terms) of the sequence. Sequences can be defined either directly (i.e., each value in the series is a function of its *location* in the order of the sequence) or recursively (i.e., each value is a function of the *previous items* in the sequence).

2) **Units (Ones) Digit problems** – Questions involving the last digit (sometimes called the *Units* or *Ones* digit) of an integer almost always involve some sort of repeating cycle pattern that can be exploited.

3) **Remainder problems** – Remainders from the division of one integer into another will result in a pattern. For example, when divided by 5, the counting numbers will exhibit the following repeating remainder pattern: 1, 2, 3, 4, 0, 1, 2, 3, 4, 0... The units digit of an integer is a special case of a remainder: it's the remainder after division by 10.

4) **Other pattern problems** – Some pattern problems do not involve deciphering a string of numbers and discovering the rule. For instance, you may have to count a set of numbers that all fit some constraint. The point is to discover a simple rule or group of rules that let you account for all the numbers—and therefore count them—without having to generate each one. Here are some ideas:

   • Break the problem into sub-problems. For instance, a sum may be split into several smaller sums. Or you might count a larger total, then subtract items that do not fit the constraint. You even might multiply a larger total by the proportion of suitable items, if that fraction is easy to calculate.

   • Recall counting and summing methods from the Manhattan GMAT Strategy Guides:

      a. Number of Choices: The Fundamental Counting Principle (in "Combinatorics," *Word Translations*) dictates that when you have a series of successive decisions, you multiply the number of choices you have at each stage to find the number of total choices you have. For instance, if you can choose 1 appetizer out of 6 possible appetizers and 1 entrée out of 7 possible entrées, then you could have $6 \times 7 = 42$ possible meals.

      b. Number of items in a Consecutive Set of Integers (in "Consecutive Integers," *Number Properties*): The number of integers in a consecutive set of integers equals the largest minus the smallest, plus 1.

      c. Sum of a Consecutive Set of Integers: The sum of a consecutive set of integers equals the number of integers (computed above) multiplied by the average, which is simply the average of the largest integer and the smallest integer. This is also equal to the median, or "middle," number in the set.

   • As you go, always check that the extreme cases are still valid. Two or three constraints can interact in surprising ways, eliminating some of the values that would seem to work otherwise.

Sequence Problems

Any question that involves the definition of a sequence (usually involving subscripted variables, such as A_n and S_n) is very likely to involve patterns. These patterns can range from relatively straightforward linear patterns to much more complicated ones.

When you are given a sequence definition, list a few terms of the sequence, starting with any particular terms you are given, and look for a simple pattern.

Do not be intimidated by a *recursive* definition for a sequence, in which each term is defined using *earlier* terms. (By contrast, a direct definition defines each term using the *position* or *index* of the term.) To illustrate the difference, here are two ways to define the series of positive odd integers {1, 3, 5, 7, 9, etc.}:

Recursive definition	**Direct definition**
$An = A_{n-1} + 2$ where $n > 1$ and $A_1 = 1$	$An = 2n - 1$, where $n \geq 1$
Translation: "This term = The *previous term* + 2, and the first term is 1."	Translation: "This term = The *index number* × 2, minus 1. Thus the first term is $(2)(1) - 1 = 1$."

The basics of sequences are discussed in further detail in the "Formulas" material within the Manhattan GMAT *Equations, Inequalities, and VICs* Strategy Guide.

Try-It #5-2

> The sequence X_n is defined as follows: $X_n = 2X_{n-1} - 1$ whenever n is an integer greater than 1. If $X_1 = 3$, what is the value of $X_{20} - X_{19}$?

The pattern underlying this sequence could hardly be obvious, so we should simply begin computing a few of the terms in the set:

n	X_n
1	3
2	$2(3) - 1 = 5$
3	$2(5) - 1 = 9$
4	$2(9) - 1 = 17$
5	$2(17) - 1 = 33$
6	$2(33) - 1 = 65$
7	$2(65) - 1 = 129$

Having computed the first half-dozen or so terms in the sequence, we might notice that there appears to be a repeating pattern among the units digits of the elements of X_n (3, 5, 9, 7, 3, 5, 9...). However, this does not help us answer the question, which asks us about the *difference* between two consecutive elements later in the set. So we should look at the differences between consecutive elements:

n	X_n	$X_n - X_{n-1}$
1	3	–
2	$2(3) - 1 = 5$	$5 - 3 = 2$
3	$2(5) - 1 = 9$	$9 - 5 = 4$
4	$2(9) - 1 = 17$	$17 - 9 = 8$
5	$2(17) - 1 = 33$	$33 - 17 = 16$
6	$2(33) - 1 = 65$	$65 - 33 = 32$
7	$2(65) - 1 = 129$	$129 - 65 = 64$

The pattern quickly emerges: the difference between consecutive terms in the sequence appears to always be a power of 2. Specifically, $X_2 - X_1 = 2 = 2^1$, $X_3 - X_2 = 4 = 2^2$, $X_4 - X_3 = 8 = 2^3$, etc.

We now can determine the pattern for the sequence: $X_n - X_{n-1}$ equals 2^{n-1}. Therefore $X_{20} - X_{19} = 2^{20-1} = 2^{19}$. This is a *difference pattern* – a pattern or rule exists among the differences between consecutive terms in the sequence. Be careful at this last step! When you extrapolate the pattern, you might accidentally think that the number you want is 2^{20}. Always explicitly match to the index, and realize that you might be slightly shifted. In this case, the difference we want is *not* 2^n. The difference is 2^{n-1}.

Try-It #5-3

If $A_n = \dfrac{1}{n(n+1)}$ for all positive integers n, what is the sum of the first 100 elements of A_n?

Once again, we should compute the first few elements of A_n. Because we need to know the sum of the first 100 elements, we should also track the cumulative sum:

n	A_n	Sum through A_n:
1	$\dfrac{1}{1\times 2} = \dfrac{1}{2}$	$\dfrac{1}{2}$
2	$\dfrac{1}{2\times 3} = \dfrac{1}{6}$	$\dfrac{1}{2} + \dfrac{1}{6} = \dfrac{3+1}{6} = \dfrac{2}{3}$
3	$\dfrac{1}{3\times 4} = \dfrac{1}{12}$	$\dfrac{2}{3} + \dfrac{1}{12} = \dfrac{8+1}{12} = \dfrac{3}{4}$
4	$\dfrac{1}{4\times 5} = \dfrac{1}{20}$	$\dfrac{3}{4} + \dfrac{1}{20} = \dfrac{15+1}{20} = \dfrac{4}{5}$
5	$\dfrac{1}{5\times 6} = \dfrac{1}{30}$	$\dfrac{4}{5} + \dfrac{1}{30} = \dfrac{24+1}{30} = \dfrac{5}{6}$

By now the pattern should be fairly obvious: the sum of the first n terms of A_n equals $\dfrac{n}{n+1}$. Therefore, the sum of the first 100 terms is $\dfrac{100}{101}$. This is a *summing pattern*—a pattern or rule exists among the cumulative sum of the terms in the sequence.

Notice that the proof that the cumulative sum equals is $\dfrac{n}{n+1}$ completely unnecessary. The proof can be executed relatively easily, but the GMAT does not require proofs—only correct answers!

Units (Ones) Digit Problems

When you raise an integer to a power, the units digit always repeats as you increase the power.

Try-It #5-4

> What is the units digit of 4^{674}?

Let's observe what happens to the units digit of the consecutive powers of 4, starting with 4^1:

$$4^1 = 4 \quad \rightarrow \quad \text{last digit of } 4 = 4$$
$$4^2 = 4(4^1) \quad \rightarrow \quad \text{last digit of } 4(4) = \text{last digit of } 16 = 6$$
$$4^3 = 4(4^2) \quad \rightarrow \quad \text{last digit of } 4(6) = \text{last digit of } 24 = 4$$
$$4^4 = 4(4^3) \quad \rightarrow \quad \text{last digit of } 4(4) = \text{last digit of } 16 = 6$$

Because the computations $(4 \times 4 = 16)$ and $(4 \times 6 = 24)$ keep repeating, the units digit will continue to alternate [4, 6].

Thus 4^x will have a units digit of 4 whenever x is odd, and a units digit of 6 whenever x is even (assuming, of course, that x is positive). The units digit of 4^{674} is therefore 6.

Also notice that in determining the value of the units digit of a product, *all of the other digits* besides the units digit are irrelevant. Therefore, 14^{674} and $3,184^{674}$ will both also have units digits of 6. This is also true for multiplication of *any* two integers, as well as the *addition* of any integers:

$$
\begin{array}{r}
5,879 \\
\times\ 1,642 \\
\hline
11758 \\
235160 \\
3527400 \\
+\ 5879000 \\
\hline
9,653,318
\end{array}
$$

Only the units digits $(2 \times 9 = 18)$ contribute to the units digit of the result, since the other units digits in the multiplication are zeros.

$$
\begin{array}{r}
3\ 4\,5 \\
2\ 6\,2 \\
+\ 1\ 4\,9 \\
\hline
7\ 5\,6
\end{array}
$$

Only the sum of $5 + 2 + 9 = 16$ affects the units digit of the sum.

As mentioned above, every integer raised to different positive exponents has a units digit pattern:

Series	Consecutive Powers	Units digit pattern
1^x	**1**; **1**; **1**; **1**; **1**; **1**; etc.	[1]
2^x	**2**; **4**; **8**; **16**; **32**; **64**; etc.	[2, 4, 8, 6]
3^x	**3**; **9**; **27**; **81**; **243**; **729**; etc.	[3, 9, 7, 1]
4^x	**4**; **16**; **64**; **256**; **1,024**; **4,096**; etc.	[4, 6]
5^x	**5**; **25**; **125**; **625**; **3,125**; **15,625**; etc.	[5]
6^x	**6**; **36**; **216**; **1,296**; **7,776**; **46,656**; etc.	[6]
7^x	**7**; **49**; **343**; **2,401**; **16,807**; **117,649**; etc.	[7, 9, 3, 1]
8^x	**8**; **64**; **512**; **4,096**; **32,768**; **262,144**; etc.	[8, 4, 2, 6]
9^x	**9**; **81**; **729**; **6,561**; **59,049**; **531,441**; etc.	[9, 1]
10^x	**10**; **100**; **1,000**; **10,000**; **100,000**; **1,000,000**; etc.	[0]

You *do not* need to memorize this chart. Just be sure you can regenerate these patterns quickly. If you really want, you can memorize which series have a 4-term repeating cycle (2, 3, 7, and 8), which ones have a 2-term repeating cycle (9, 4), and which have a 1-term repeating cycle for the units digit (1, 5, 6, and 0). The 1-term repeating cycles are particularly convenient: in these cases, the units digit of the number raised to any positive integer power is always the same as that of the original number. For instance, 6 raised to the power of any integer ends in a 6.

Try-It #5-5

What is the units digit of 19^{40}?

As shown in the chart above, $9^1 = 9$, $9^2 = 81$, $9^3 = 729$, etc. 19 will have the same units digit pattern as 9 (that is, $19^1 = 19$, $19^2 = 361$, etc.) Therefore the pattern is a two-term repeating pattern: 9, 1, 9, 1... This pattern alternates every 2 items, just like odd and even integers. Since 40 is an even number, the units digit of 19^{40} will equal 1.

The remainder whenever an integer is divided by 10 will always be the same as the units digit of the original number.

$$\frac{84}{10} = 8\frac{4}{10} \rightarrow 8 \text{ remainder } \mathbf{4} \qquad \frac{361}{10} = 36\frac{1}{10} \rightarrow 36 \text{ remainder } \mathbf{1}$$

$$\frac{7,81\mathbf{9}}{10} = 781\frac{9}{10} \rightarrow 781 \text{ remainder } \mathbf{9}$$

What is the remainder when 19^{40} is divided by 10?

This question is equivalent to the previous example. The GMAT will occasionally disguise units digit questions by asking about the remainder after division by 10.

Remainder Problems

In general, remainders provide a means by which the GMAT can disguise an underlying pattern. For example, notice that when the positive integer n is divided by 4, the remainders follow a pattern as n increases consecutively:

1 div by 4 → remainder 1
2 div by 4 → remainder 2
3 div by 4 → remainder 3
4 div by 4 → remainder 0
5 div by 4 → remainder 1

A *repeating cycle* of [1,2,3,0] emerges for the remainders when dividing the counting numbers by 4. The number of terms in the repeat equals the divisor in this case

Surprising patterns can emerge in remainder problems as well.

Try-It #5-6

If x and y are positive integers, what is the remainder when 5^x is divided by y?

(1) $x = 3$
(2) $y = 4$

(1) INSUFFICIENT: $5^3 = 125$. If $y = 5$, then the remainder equals 0. If $y = 6$, then the remainder is 5. Therefore we cannot determine the answer just by knowing the value of x.

(2) SUFFICIENT: This statement may not appear to be sufficient, but let's test some different values for x:

x	5^x	Remainder of $\dfrac{5^x}{4}$
1	5	1
2	25	1
3	125	1
4	625	1

We could keep going, but the pattern is clear: no matter what exponent 5 is raised to, the remainder when divided by 4 will always equal 1—a fact that you probably did not expect before testing the rule for this problem. (This pattern can be proven to be the case, although doing so is beyond the scope of this discussion.)

The correct answer is B: Statement 2 ALONE is sufficient, but Statement (1) ALONE is not sufficient.

Do not fall into the easy trap of assuming that you need to know both x and y to solve this problem. Remainders can hide a wide array of underlying patterns. In this case, when $y = 4$, the answer will be the same no matter what value is chosen for x.

Other Pattern Problems

Many questions will not at first glance demonstrate an obvious pattern. For example, a word problem involving counting a collection of objects or maximizing some number may hide some sort of regularity. The point is to discover a simple rule or group of rules that let you account for all the possibilities—and therefore count or maximize them—without having to generate each possibility separately.

Try-It #5-7

> How many of the integers between 1 and 400, inclusive, are not divisible by 4 and do not contain any 4s as a digit?

This problem involves a *counting pattern*. It's clear that there are 400 integers between 1 and 400, inclusive. We must subtract the number integers that are divisible by 4 or contain a 4 as a digit. The tricky part is the overlap: some numbers, such as 64 and 124, violate both constraints.

It is easiest to first determine the number of multiples of 4. Since there are 400 integers in the set, and those 400 integers are consecutive, there must be 400/4 = 100 integers that are divisible by 4. Thus, we have 400 − 100 = 300 integers remaining.

Next, we consider the numbers that have a 4 among their digits, but haven't already been eliminated. In other words, numbers with a 4 among their digits that *are not* themselves multiples of 4.

Only one of the integers between 1 and 400, inclusive, has a 4 in the hundreds place: 400. We have already eliminated that one from our count because it is a multiple of 4.

To eliminate integers with a 4 in the tens place, of the form $x4y$, we should count only those that are not multiples of 4. These are the numbers whose last two digits are 41, 42, 43, 45, 46, 47, or 49. There are 7 such numbers in each set of "hundreds," i.e. the 300's, the 200's, the 100's and the no hundreds. That is a total of $7 \times 4 = 28$ terms. We have 300 − 28 = 272 integers remaining.

Last, we count and eliminate the integers with 4 in the units digit, of the form $xy4$, that have not already been counted for violating a constraint. These are the numbers whose last two digits are 14, 34, 54, 74, or 94 (numbers with an even integer in the tens place and 4 in the units are all divisible by 4, so have been eliminated already). There are 5 such numbers in each set of "hundreds," so that is a total of $5 \times 4 = 20$ terms. We have 272 − 20 = 252 integers remaining.

The correct answer is 400 − 100 − 28 − 20 = 252.

Try-It #5-8

> $x = 10^{10} - z$, where z is a two-digit integer. If the sum of the digits of x equals 84, how many values for z are possible?

The first thing to do in solving this problem is to subtract any two-digit number from 10^{10} and look for a pattern. Let's try subtracting 24:

$$10^{10} = 10,000,000,000$$

$$
\begin{array}{r}
10,000,000,000 \\
- \qquad\qquad 24 \\
\hline
9,999,999,976
\end{array}
$$

Notice the pattern: the first 8 digits of x are all 9's, so those digits sum to 72. This will be true no matter which two-digit integer we try for z. Therefore, the final two digits of x must sum to $84 - 72 = 12$.

What possibilities would work for these final two digits of x? 39, 48, 57, 66, 75, 84, and 93 all seem to work. We can determine the values for z that would correspond to each of these values by subtracting the values from 100:

$$100 - 39 = 61 \qquad 100 - 48 = 52 \qquad 100 - 57 = 43$$
$$100 - 66 = 34 \qquad 100 - 75 = 25 \qquad 100 - 84 = 16$$
$$100 - 93 = 7 \; (!!!)$$

What possibilities would work for these final two digits of x? 39, 48, 57, 66, 75, 84, and 93 all have digits that sum to 12. However, since z must be a two-digit integer, the last two digits of x must be ≤ 90, so 93 isn't possible. That is, in order for x to end in 93, z would have to be 7, which is not a two-digit integer. According-ing to the GMAT, a two-digit integer must have a non-zero tens digit and zeros for all higher places. Don't worry—this is the common way of thinking about two-digit integers.

Therefore, the final two digits of x can only be 39, 48, 57, 66, 75, and 84, achieved by subtracting $z = 61, 52$, 43, 34, 25, and 16, respectively. The answer to the question is that z has 6 possible values.

As the two previous problems demonstrate, unusual patterns can appear in problems on the GMAT. Some-times you must "think outside the box" to identify the wanted pattern.

Look for the examples on the next page.

Pattern Type	Example	Comments
Repeats	1, 3, −2, 1, 3, −2, 1, etc.	Often these repeating patterns can only be identified by listing out a few values in the pattern. Always figure out how long the cycle is.
Consecutive Integers	10, 11, 12, 13, 14, etc.	Can be defined as follows: $A_n = n + k$, where n and k are integers. In this example, $A_n = n + 9$, so that the first term is $1 + 9 = 10$. Note that the average term = the median term = 1/2 × (First + Last).
Consecutive Multiples	7, 14, 21, 28, etc.	Consecutive multiples of 7, for example, can be defined as follows: $A_n = 7n$, where n is a set of consecutive integers. The evens are just a special case (multiples of 2, or $2n$). Note that the average term = the median term = 1/2 × (First + Last).
Evenly spaced sets	9, 16, 23, 30, etc. (Constant difference of 7 between consecutive terms.)	When dividing this series by 7, each of the terms leaves a remainder of 2. Can be defined as a multiple plus/minus a constant: $A_n = 7n + k$, where n is a set of consecutive integers, in this example. The odds are a special case (multiples of 2, plus 1, or $2n + 1$). Note that the average term = the median term = 1/2 × (First + Last), as for consecutive multiples.
Non-uniform Spacing that itself follows a pattern	0, 1, 3, 6, 10, 15, etc. (Spacing between terms follows 1, 2, 3, 4, 5, etc. pattern.)	Another example of this type is the perfect squares: 0, 1, 4, 9, 16, 25, etc. (Spacing between squares = 1, 3, 5, 7, 9, etc. = the odd integers!)
Alternating sign	−1, 1, −2, 2, −3, 3, etc.	Can result from a $(-1)^n$ term in a direct sequence definition, or a $(-(A_{n-1}))$ term in a recursive sequence definition.

In general, listing 5 to 8 examples or terms will usually be sufficient to identify a pattern on the GMAT—you can even stop with fewer examples if you've identified the pattern by that point.

In-Action Problem Set

For the following problems, use the Pattern Recognition techniques discussed in this chapter to solve the following problems:

1. Derive the pattern for the units digit of the integer powers of 2, 3, 5, 7, and 8.

2. If x and y are integers between 0 and 9, inclusive, and the units digit of x^y is 5, what are the possible values of x and y?

3. What is the remainder when $13^{17} + 17^{13}$ is divided by 10?

For Questions #4–6, answer the following Data Sufficiency questions:

4.   What is the units digit of y?

   (1) The units digit of y^2 equals 6.
   (2) The units digit of $(y + 1)^2$ equals 5.

5.   What is the units digit of y?

   (1) The units digit of $y^2 = 1$.
   (2) The units digit of y does not equal 1.

6.   What is the units digit of y?

   (1) The units digit of $y^2 = 9$.
   (2) The units digit of $y^4 = 1$.

7. What is the remainder when x is divided by 5?

   (1) x divided by 10 has a remainder of 7.
   (2) x divided by 2 has a remainder of 1.

8. If x and y are positive integers, what is the remainder when 5^x is divided by y?

   (1) x is an even integer.
   (2) $y = 3$.

9. a, b, c, and d are positive integers. If $\dfrac{a}{b}$ has a remainder of 9 and $\dfrac{c}{d}$ has a remainder of 10, what is

the minimum possible value for bd?

10. What is the sum of the numbers in the grid below?

−2	−1	1	2	3	4
−4	−2	2	4	6	8
−6	−3	3	6	9	12
−8	−4	4	8	12	16
−10	−5	5	10	15	20
−12	−6	6	12	18	24

11. The sequence $a_1, a_2, a_3,..., a_n$ is such that $a_n = 9 + a_{n-1}$ for all $n > 1$. If $a_1 = 11$, what is the value of a_{35}?

12. The sequence S is defined as follows for all $n \geq 1$:

$$S_n = (-1)^n \frac{1}{n(n+1)}$$

The sum of the first 10 terms of S is:

(A) Between −1 and −1/2   (B) Between −1/2 and 0   (C) Between 0 and 1/2
(D) Between 1/2 and 1   (E) Greater than 1

13. In sequence Q, the first number is 3, and each subsequent number in the sequence is determined by doubling the previous number and then adding 2. How many times does the digit 8 appear in the units digit of the first 10 terms of the sequence?

14. $g(x)$ is defined as the product of all even integers k such that $0 < k \leq x$. For example, $g(14) = 2 \times 4 \times 6 \times 8 \times 10 \times 12 \times 14$. If $g(y)$ is divisible by 4^{11}, what is the smallest possible value for y?

(A) 22   (B) 24   (C) 28   (D) 32   (E) 44

15. Mitchell plans to work at a day camp over the summer. Each week, he will be paid according to the following schedule: at the end of the first week, he will receive $1. At the end of each subsequent week, he will receive $1, plus an additional amount equal to the sum of all payments he's received in previous weeks. How much money will Mitchell be paid in total during the summer, if he works for the entire duration of the 8-week-long camp?

In-Action Problem Set (Solutions)

1. **[2, 4, 8, 6]; [3, 9, 7, 1]; [5]; [7, 9, 3, 1]; [8, 4, 2, 6]:**

Pattern for 2:
$2^1 = 2$
$2^2 = 2(2^1)$ → last digit of $2(2) = 4$
$2^3 = 2(2^2)$ → last digit of $2(4) = 8$
$2^4 = 2(2^3)$ → last digit of $2(8) = $ last digit of $16 = 6$
$2^5 = 2(2^4)$ → last digit of $2(6) = $ last digit of $12 = 2$
The pattern is [2, 4, 8, 6] repeated.

Pattern for 3:
$3^1 = 3$
$3^2 = 3(3^1)$ → last digit of $3(3) = 9$
$3^3 = 3(3^2)$ → last digit of $3(9) = $ last digit of $27 = 7$
$3^4 = 3(3^3)$ → last digit of $3(7) = $ last digit of $21 = 1$
$3^5 = 3(3^4)$ → last digit of $3(1) = 3$
The pattern is [3, 9, 7, 1] repeated.

Pattern for 5:
$5^1 = 3$
$5^2 = 5(5^1)$ → last digit of $5(5) = $ last digit of $25 = 5$
The pattern is [5] repeated—in other words, for any integer x, the units digit of 5^x is 5.

Pattern for 7:
$7^1 = 7$
$7^2 = 7(7^1)$ → last digit of $7(7) = $ last digit of $49 = 9$
$7^3 = 7(7^2)$ → last digit of $7(9) = $ last digit of $63 = 3$
$7^4 = 7(7^3)$ → last digit of $7(3) = $ last digit of $21 = 1$
$7^5 = 7(7^4)$ → last digit of $7(1) = 7$
The pattern is [7, 9, 3, 1] repeated.

Pattern for 8:
$8^1 = 8$
$8^2 = 8(8^1)$ → last digit of $8(8) = $ last digit of $64 = 4$
$8^3 = 8(8^2)$ → last digit of $8(4) = $ last digit of $32 = 2$
$8^4 = 8(8^3)$ → last digit of $8(2) = $ last digit of $16 = 6$
$8^5 = 8(8^4)$ → last digit of $8(6) = $ last digit of $48 = 8$
The pattern is [8, 4, 2, 6] repeated.

2. **$x = 5$; $1 \le y \le 9$:** No integer besides 5 can be raised to a power such that the result will have a units digit of 5. Any power of 5 will have a units digit of 5 (other than zero, because $5^0 = 1$).

3. **0:** The remainder when dividing an integer by 10 always equals the units digit. We can also ignore all but the units digits, so the question can be rephrased as: *What is the units digit of $3^{17} + 7^{13}$?*

The pattern for the units digits of 3 is [3, 9, 7, 1]. Every fourth term is the same. The 17th power is 1 past the end of the repeat: 17 − 16 = 1. Thus, 3^{17} must end in 3.

The pattern for the units digits of 7 is [7, 9, 3, 1]. Every fourth term is the same. The 13th power is 1 past the end of the repeat: 13 − 12 = 1. Thus, 7^{13} must end in 7.

The sum of these units digits is 3 + 7 = 10. Thus, the units digit we want is 0.

For questions 4 through 6, we can reference the following chart:

	Units Digit Patterns for Integers ending in:									
	1	**2**	**3**	**4**	**5**	**6**	**7**	**8**	**9**	**0**
y^1	1	2	3	4	5	6	7	8	9	0
y^2	1	4	9	6	5	6	9	4	1	0
y^3	1	8	7	4	5	6	3	2	9	0
y^4	1	6	1	6	5	6	1	6	1	0

4. **B:** Using the Units Digit Patterns chart above, we notice that both 4 and 6 yield a units digit of 6 when raised to the 2nd power. Therefore Statement (1) is INSUFFICIENT. (Notice that you would only need to check even numbers for this statement, as odd numbers to any power cannot end in a 6.)

Statement (2), however, is SUFFICIENT. Only 5 yields a units digit of 5 when raised to *any* power. Since the units digit of $y + 1$ is 5, the units digit of y must be 4. The correct answer is (B): Statement 2 ALONE is sufficient, but Statement 1 ALONE is not sufficient.

5. **C:** Statement 2 is easier to evaluate—it is INSUFFICIENT because it only tells us that y does not end in a 1.

Referring to the Units Digit Patterns chart above, we can see that Statement 1 is also INSUFFICIENT— both 1 and 9 yield a units digit of 1 when raised to the 2nd power. Notice that you only need to check odd numbers for this statement, since even numbers raised to any power cannot end in a 1.

Statements 1 and 2 together are SUFFICIENT, since the units digit of y must be 9. The correct answer is (C): BOTH statements TOGETHER are sufficient, but NEITHER statement ALONE is sufficient.

6. **E:** Referring to the Units Digit Patterns chart above, we can see that Statement 1 is INSUFFICIENT— both 3 and 7 yield a units digit of 9 when raised to the 2nd power. (Notice that you would only need to check odd numbers for this statement, as even numbers to any power cannot end in a 9.)

Statement 2 is also INSUFFICIENT, as 1, 3, 7 and 9 yield a units digit of 1 when raised to the 4th power. (Once again, only odd numbers need to be checked.)

Combining these two statements, y could end in a 3 or a 7. INSUFFICIENT. The correct answer is (E): The two statements COMBINED are not sufficient.

7. **A:** Statement 2 is easier to evaluate—INSUFFICIENT. Any odd number will have a remainder of 1 when divided by 2. 3 ÷ 5 has a remainder of 3, but 5 ÷ 5 has a remainder of 0.

Statement 1, however, is SUFFICIENT. If x divided by 10 has a remainder of 7, then the units digit of x is 7. Such numbers are all 2 greater than a multiple of 5, so when x is divided by 5 the remainder is 2.

x	Remainder of $x \div 10$:	Remainder of $x \div 5$:
17	7	2
27	7	2
37	7	2
47	7	2

The correct answer is (A): Statement 1 ALONE is sufficient, but Statement 2 ALONE is not sufficient.

8. **C:** (1) INSUFFICIENT: $5^{\text{even integer}}$ means that $5^x = 25$, 625, $15{,}625$, etc. All of these numbers end in 25. If $y = 5$, then the remainder equals 0. If $y = 4$, then the remainder is 1. Therefore we cannot determine the answer just by knowing this pattern of x.

(2) INSUFFICIENT: Let's test some different values for x:

x	5^x	Remainder of $\dfrac{5^x}{3}$
1	5	2
2	25	1
3	125	2
4	625	1

The pattern is clear: when 5 is raised to an odd power, the remainder is 1, but when 5 is raised to an even power, the remainder is 2. However, with only Statement 2, we don't know whether x is even or odd.

Combining the two statements, we know the pattern for the remainder when 5^x is divided by 3, and we know which term in that pattern applies. When $5^{\text{even integer}}$ is divided by 3, the remainder is always 1. Proving this theoretically is not trivial, but we don't need to do a theoretical proof.

The correct answer is (C): BOTH statements TOGETHER are sufficient, but NEITHER statement ALONE is sufficient.

Notice that this problem is similar to Try-It #5–6, but has different results.

9. **110:** The remainder must always be smaller than the divisor. Thus b must be at least 10, and d must be at least 11. Therefore, bd must be at least 110. The purpose of this problem is to remind you of these constraints on remainders.

10. **147:** There are several patterns in the grid, depending on whether we look by row or by column. Within each row, there are positive and negative terms at the beginning that cancel each other. For example, in the first row, we have $-2 + 2 = 0$ and $-1 + 1 = 0$. The only terms in the first row that contribute to the sum are 3 and 4, in the far-right columns. The same is true for the other rows.

*Manhattan*GMAT*Prep
the new standard

Thus, the sum of the grid is equal to the sum of only the two far-right columns. The sum in the first row in those columns is $3 + 4 = 7$; the sum in the next row is $6 + 8 = 14$, etc. The sum in the final row is $18 + 24 = 42$. Because they are consecutive multiples of 7, we can use the consecutive multiples formula:

$$Sum = (\text{Lowest Term} + \text{Highest Term})\left(\frac{\text{Number of Terms}}{2}\right)$$

$$= \left(\frac{7+42}{2}\right)(6)$$

$$= \frac{(49)(6)}{2}$$

$$= 147$$

11. **317:** Each term in the sequence is 9 greater than the previous term. To make this obvious, you may want to write a few terms of the sequence: 11, 20, 29, 38, etc.

a_{35} comes 34 terms after a_1 in the sequence. In other words, a_{35} is $34 \times 9 = 306$ greater than a_1.

Thus, $a_{35} = 11 + 306 = 317$.

12. **(B) Between –1/2 and 0:** We should compute the first few elements of S_n. Because we need to know the sum of the first 10 elements, we should also track the cumulative sum:

n	S_n	Sum through S_n:
1	$(-1)^1 \dfrac{1}{1\times 2} = -\dfrac{1}{2}$	$-\dfrac{1}{2} = -0.5$
2	$(-1)^2 \dfrac{1}{2\times 3} = \dfrac{1}{6}$	$-\dfrac{1}{2}+\dfrac{1}{6} = \dfrac{-3+1}{6} = \dfrac{1}{3} \approx -0.333$
3	$(-1)^3 \dfrac{1}{3\times 4} = -\dfrac{1}{12}$	$-\dfrac{1}{3}-\dfrac{1}{12} = \dfrac{-4-1}{12} = -\dfrac{5}{12} \approx -0.41667$
4	$(-1)^4 \dfrac{1}{4\times 5} = \dfrac{1}{20}$	$-\dfrac{5}{12}+\dfrac{1}{20} = \dfrac{-25+3}{60} = -\dfrac{22}{60} \approx -0.3667$
5	$(-1)^5 \dfrac{1}{5\times 6} = -\dfrac{1}{30}$	$-\dfrac{22}{60}-\dfrac{1}{30} = \dfrac{-22-2}{60} = -\dfrac{2}{5} = -0.4$

By now (if not before!) the pattern should be fairly obvious. The sum of the first n terms of S_n converges somewhere in the range between –0.3667 and –0.4. Only (B) exhibits a range in which the sum of this series could converge.

13. **9:** After the first term in the sequence, every term has a units digit of 8:

$$Q_1 = 3$$
$$Q_2 = 2(3) + 2 = 8$$
$$Q_3 = 2(8) + 2 = 18$$
$$Q_4 = 2(18) + 2 = 38$$
$$Q_5 = 2(38) + 2 = 78$$
...

So 8 will be the units digit nine out of the first ten times.

14. **(B) 24:** This is a counting pattern problem. In order for $g(y)$ to be divisible by 4^{11}, it must be divisible by $(2^2)^{11} = 2^{22}$. Thus $g(y)$ must contain 22 twos in its prime factorization.

If $y = 10$, for example, then g(y) equals $2 \times 4 \times 6 \times 8 \times 10$. 2 has one 2 in its prime factorization; 4 has two 2s; 6 has one 2 (and a 3); 8 has three 2s; 10 has one 2 (and a 5). This amounts to a total of only eight 2s:

Number	2	4	6	8	10
Prime Factors	2	2, 2	2, 3	2, 2, 2	2, 5
Total 2s in PF	1	2	1	3	1
Cumulative 2s	1	3	4	7	8

For this question, we need 22 twos. Thus, we must keep adding even numbers to the result until we get to 22 twos in total:

Number	2	4	6	8	10	12	14	16	18	20	22	24
Prime Factors	2	2,2	2,3	2,2,2	2,5	2,2,3	2,7	2,2,2,2	2,3,3	2,2,5	2,11	2,2,2,3
Total 2s in PF	1	2	1	3	1	2	1	4	1	2	1	3
Cumulative 2s	1	3	4	7	8	10	11	15	16	18	19	22

Thus the smallest possible number for y is 24. Notice the unusual pattern in the number of twos in each even number: 1, 2, 1, 3, 1, 2, 1, 4, 1, 2, 1 ...

15. **$255 (or $2^8 - 1$):** At the end of the first week, Mitchell receives $1. At the end of the second week, he gets $1, plus $1 for the total he had been paid up to that point, for a total of $2. At the end of the third week, he gets $1, plus ($1 + $2), or $3, for the total he had been paid up to that point, so this third week total is $4. Let's put this in a table:

Week #	Paid this week($)	Cumulative Pay including this week ($)
1	1	1
2	1 + 1 = 2	1 + 2 = 3
3	1 + 3 = 4	3 + 4 = 7
4	1 + 7 = 8	7 + 8 = 15
5	1 + 15 = 16	15 + 16 = 31
6	1 + 31 = 32	31 + 32 = 63
7	1 + 63 = 64	63 + 64 = 127
8	1 + 127 = 128	127 + 128 = 255

This calculation is not so bad, however, you may notice that this payment schedule is a simple geometric sequence, 2^{n-1}, where n is the number of the week in which Mitchell is being paid. And summing that sequence is equivalent to $2^t - 1$, where t is the total number of weeks. In words, the cumulative pay is one less than the next power of 2.

The correct answer is $2^8 - 1 = \$255$.

Chapter 6
of
ADVANCED GMAT QUANT

COMMON TERMS & QUADRATIC TEMPLATES

In This Chapter . . .

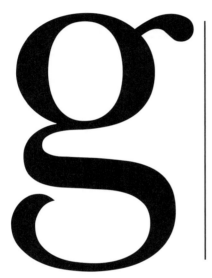

- Common Terms
- Sequence Problems
- Quadratic Templates
- Quadratic Templates In Disguise

Common Terms and Quadratic Templates

You are probably already familiar with the *mechanics* of algebraic manipulations—what is allowed and what isn't:

> You can substitute one expression for another if they are equal… You can add some number to one side of an equation as long as you do the same on the other side of the equation…You can cross-multiply to simplify fractions…and so on.

But of all the steps you *could* take, how do you decide which steps you *should* take?

Two indicators can often help you on the GMAT:
1) Common Terms
2) Quadratic Templates

Common Terms

If you spot Common Terms, you can often spot the path all the way to the solution.

Common Terms appear on the GMAT in three typical ways:

1. Algebra

Look for terms that appear in the same form more than once. Those recurring expressions might also appear in slightly modified form such as reciprocal, negative, or raised to a power:

If $\left(\dfrac{a}{b}\right) = \dfrac{3}{5}$, then $\dfrac{b + a}{a} =$	$\dfrac{b}{a}$ is the reciprocal of $\dfrac{a}{b}$.	$\dfrac{b + a}{a} = \dfrac{b}{a} + \dfrac{a}{a} = \dfrac{5}{3} + 1 = \dfrac{8}{3}$
Is $\dfrac{1}{a^2 - b^2} < b^2 - a^2$?	$b^2 - a^2$ is negative $a^2 - b^2$.	Is $\dfrac{1}{x} < -x$? where $a^2 - b^2 = x$
$\left(\dfrac{x}{3y}\right)^2 + 2\left(\dfrac{x}{3y}\right)(3y) + (3y)^2$ $\quad a \qquad\qquad b$	$\dfrac{x}{3y}$ and $3y$ appear both squared and multiplied together.	This expression is of the form: $a^2 + 2ab + b^2 = (a + b)^2$ More later in this chapter (on Quadratic Templates)

Try-It #6-1

If $y \neq 3$, simplify as much as possible: $\dfrac{2y^2(3 - y) - 3 + y}{3 - y}$

$$\frac{2y^2(3-y)-3+y}{3-y}$$

Spot the common term $(3-y)$. Note that $(-3+y)$ is $-(3-y)$, or $-1 \times (3-y)$.

Factor out the common term $(3-y)$ and cancel: $\dfrac{(3-y)\left[2y^2-1\right]}{3-y} = 2y^2 - 1$.

By the way, the condition that y could not equal 3 just prevented us from dividing by zero, something we're never allowed to do.

2. Exponents

Exponents can be manipulated when either bases or exponents are common. Also look for bases that have common factors, such as 3 and 12 (common factor of 3). You can often create a common base. For example:

$(16^x)(4^2) = 256$	4 is a factor of 4, 16, and 256.	$\left(16^x\right)\left(4^2\right) = 256$
	Similarly,	$\left(4^2\right)^x\left(4^2\right) = 4^4$
	4, 16, and 256 are all powers of 4.	$4^{2x+2} = 4^4$
		$2x + 2 = 4$
		$x = 1$

Try-It #6-2

> If $3^x + 243 = 2(3^x)$, what is the value of x?

Note the common term "3^x," and note the fact that $243 = 3^5$:

$$3^x + 243 = 2(3^x)$$
$$3^x + 243 = 3^x + 3^x$$
$$243 = 3^x$$
$$3^5 = 3^x$$
$$5 = x$$

3. Factors and Multiples

When many terms share a factor, pull that shared factor *out to the side*. These can appear in algebraic or numerical expressions.

$$x^{18} + 2x^{16} + x^{14} \;\rightarrow\; x^{14} \text{ is a factor of each term} \;\rightarrow\; x^{14}(x^4 + 2x^2 + 1) = x^{14}(x^2 + 1)^2$$

$$\frac{\dfrac{8}{15}-\dfrac{2}{5}}{\dfrac{1}{3}+\dfrac{2}{15}} \quad \rightarrow \quad \text{each fraction term is } \frac{1}{15}\times\text{integer} \quad \rightarrow \quad \frac{\dfrac{8}{15}-\dfrac{6}{15}}{\dfrac{5}{15}+\dfrac{2}{15}}=\frac{\dfrac{1}{15}(8-6)}{\dfrac{1}{15}(5+2)}=\frac{2}{7}$$

Factorials are particularly noteworthy, as they often have an abundance of shared factors. For any integer n, the factorial $n!$ is calculated as follows: $n! = n(n-1)(n-2)(n-3) \ldots 1$. Thus, all the terms in $4! = (4)(3)(2)(1)$ are also common factors of $6! = (6)(5)(4)(3)(2)(1) = (6)(5)(4!)$.

More generally, factorials are "super-multiples." Without ever computing their precise value, you can tell that they're divisible by all sorts of numbers.

If x is an integer between $7! + 2$ and $7! + 4$, inclusive… is x prime?	x is one of the following integers:	x has one of the following factors, if x is:
	$7! + 2 = (7)(6)(5)(4)(3)\mathbf{(2)}(1) + \mathbf{2}$	
	$7! + 3 = (7)(6)(5)(4)\mathbf{(3)}(2)(1) + \mathbf{3}$	$7! + 2 = \mathbf{2} \times$ Integer
	$7! + 4 = (7)(6)(5)\mathbf{(4)}(3)(2)(1) + \mathbf{4}$	$7! + 3 = \mathbf{3} \times$ Integer
		$7! + 4 = \mathbf{4} \times$ Integer
		…so x is not prime!

Sometimes a common factor is just a random number buried inside a couple of larger numbers. Find it and pull it out.

$$\frac{10.1010}{5.0505} =$$

10s in the numerator line up with 5s in the corresponding digit place of the denominator:

$$\frac{10.1010}{5.0505} = \frac{10}{5}\left(\frac{1.0101}{1.0101}\right)$$
$$= \frac{10}{5}$$
$$= 2$$

Try-It #6-3

$$\frac{\dfrac{3}{4}+\dfrac{1}{2}}{1\dfrac{1}{3}-\dfrac{11}{12}}$$

The denominators 2, 3, and 4 are all factors of 12, so you can make a common denominator of 12, pull out 1/12 and cancel it.

$$\frac{\dfrac{3}{4}+\dfrac{1}{2}}{1\dfrac{1}{3}-\dfrac{11}{12}}=\frac{\dfrac{9}{12}+\dfrac{6}{12}}{\dfrac{16}{12}-\dfrac{11}{12}}=\frac{\dfrac{1}{12}(9+6)}{\dfrac{1}{12}(16-11)}=\frac{15}{5}=3$$

Quadratic Templates

On the GMAT, quadratic expressions take three common forms, which we call Quadratic Templates. Memorize these templates, and get comfortable transforming back and forth between factored and distributed form.

	Factored ⟷	Distributed
Square of a sum	$(a + b)^2$ =	$a^2 + 2ab + b^2$
Square of a difference	$(a - b)^2$ =	$a^2 - 2ab + b^2$
Difference of two squares	$(a + b)(a - b)$ =	$a^2 - b^2$

Quick Manipulation

Expressions with both squared and non-squared common terms should make you suspect that you are looking at a Quadratic Template.

Try-It #6-4

Rewrite $\left(\dfrac{x}{3}\right)^2 + 2\left(\dfrac{x}{3}\right)(5y) + (5y)^2$ as a quadratic expression.

This problem requires us to manipulate a rather complicated expression. However, by using the common terms, we can put the problem in the more basic template form to solve.

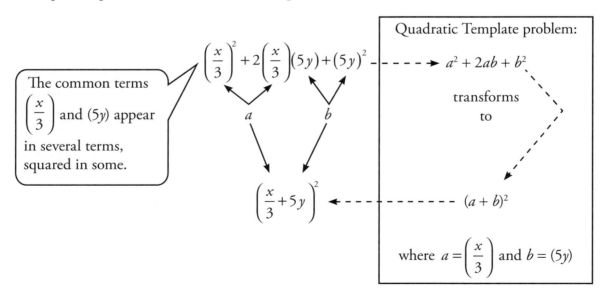

Once you are comfortable with Quadratic Templates, you can manipulate even complicated expressions quickly, as in the middle box above. Until then, you should also write down the templates and the substitution of the common terms, as in the box on the right.

The very same problem could have been presented in disguise:

Rewrite $\dfrac{x^2}{9} + \dfrac{10xy}{3} + 25y^2$ as a quadratic expression.

The common terms are slightly harder to spot in this form. In such a case, start with the squared terms, $\dfrac{x^2}{9}$

and $25y^2$. Then try to untangle their square roots, $\dfrac{x}{3}$ and $5y$, from the remaining term.

Consider all three of the common quadratic templates before deciding which one(s) are most convenient to use.

The Middle Term: 2*ab*

The "square of a sum" and "square of a difference" templates have something in common: the middle term is $\pm 2ab$. The only difference is the sign of that middle term.

Thus, when we *add* these two templates, the middle terms cancels, leaving the *end* terms:

		Factored	$\longleftrightarrow$	Distributed
"Square of a sum"		$(a + b)^2$	=	$a^2 + 2ab + b^2$
+ "Square of a difference"		$(a - b)^2$	=	$a^2 - 2ab + b^2$
Addition:		$(a + b)^2 + (a - b)^2$	=	$2a^2 + 0 + 2b^2$ $2(a^2 + b^2)$

In contrast, when we *subtract* these two templates, the end terms cancel, leaving the *middle* term:

		Factored	$\longleftrightarrow$	Distributed
"Square of a sum"		$(a + b)^2$	=	$a^2 + 2ab + b^2$
− "Square of a difference"		$(a - b)^2$	=	$a^2 - 2ab + b^2$
Subtraction:		$(a + b)^2 - (a - b)^2$	=	$0 + 4ab + 0$

This is handy for simplification, of course. Also, whenever you see the "Sum of two squares" ($a^2 + b^2$), which is not itself a Quadratic Template, remember that it can be derived from this sum of two templates.

Quadratic Templates in Disguise

Quadratic Templates can be disguised in arithmetic computations.

Try-It #6-5

$$198 \times 202 =$$

You can round each number and quickly estimate the result to be about 200^2. Or you could laboriously multiply two 3-digit numbers by hand to get an exact result. But if you need an exact result quickly, you can use a Quadratic Template. You just need to turn 198 into $(200 - 2)$ and 202 into $(200 + 2)$.

$$198 \times 202 = (200 - 2)(200 + 2) = 200^2 - 2^2 = 40,000 - 4 = 39,996 \quad \textit{How about that? Cool, right?}$$

Another place to hide a Quadratic Template is in an advanced right-triangle problem.

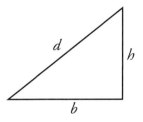

We know that Area $= \dfrac{1}{2}bh$ and $d^2 = b^2 + h^2$ (by the Pythagorean Theorem). With Quadratic Templates fresh in our minds, the common terms b^2, h^2, and bh should look familiar! Use the "square of a sum" template:

$$\left(b+h\right)^2 = b^2 + 2bh + h^2 = (b^2 + h^2) + 4\left(\frac{bh}{2}\right)$$

$$\left(b+h\right)^2 = d^2 + 4(\text{Area})$$

Likewise, we can demonstrate a similar relationship based on the "square of a difference" template.

$$\left(b-h\right)^2 = b^2 - 2bh + h^2 = (b^2 + h^2) - 4(\frac{bh}{2})$$

$$\left(b-h\right)^2 = d^2 - 4(\text{Area})$$

An advanced GMAT problem can draw on these complicated relationships. For instance, you can compute the area of a right triangle directly from the sum of the shorter sides and the hypotenuse:

$$\left(b+h\right)^2 = d^2 + 4(\text{Area})$$

$$\frac{\left(b+h\right)^2 - d^2}{4} = (\text{Area})$$

You should absolutely *not* memorize these particular formulas. Rather, be able to recognize when the GMAT is indirectly testing these generic Quadratic Templates.

In-Action Problem Set

1. $\left(5^{\frac{3}{2}}\right)^x = 5$

If $x < -1$, which of the following inequalities must be true?

2. $x^4 > x^2$

3. $x^3 + x^4 > x^3 + x^2$

4. $x^6 - x^7 > x^5 - x^6$

If $\dfrac{a}{b} = \dfrac{1}{8}$, what is the value of:

5. $\dfrac{a-b}{b}$

6. $\dfrac{b-a}{a}$

7. $\dfrac{a+b}{a}$

8. $\dfrac{a+b}{b}$

9. $\dfrac{a^2 + b^2}{ab}$

10. If n is an integer and $(-3)^{4n} = (3)^{7n-3}$, then $n =$

11. $\dfrac{(2^3)(15^4)(4^2)}{(80)(18^2)}$

12. If $\left(\dfrac{1}{5}\right)^k = 625$, what is the value of k?

Distribute the following *without* FOILing. Remember FOIL = First, Outer, Inner Last, which is a reminder of the terms to pair when you distribute the long way.

13. $\left(x + \dfrac{1}{x}\right)^2$

14. $(x^2 - y)^2$

15. $\left(z^2 + \dfrac{1}{z}\right)\left(z^2 - \dfrac{1}{z}\right)$

16. $\left(5-\sqrt{21}\right)\left(5+\sqrt{21}\right)$

17. $\left(a-\dfrac{b}{2}\right)^2$

Factor the following according to the Quadratic Templates:

18. $y^4 - 2 + \dfrac{1}{y^4}$

19. $4 + 4a + a^2$

20. $81 - x^4$

21. $x + 2\sqrt{xyz} + yz$

22. $4x^2 - 12x + 9y^2$

Simplify the following:

23. $\left(\sqrt{x}+\sqrt{y}\right)^2 + \left(\sqrt{x}-\sqrt{y}\right)^2$

24. $\left(\sqrt{x}+\sqrt{\dfrac{1}{x}}\right)^2 - \left(\sqrt{x}-\sqrt{\dfrac{1}{x}}\right)^2$

25. $\left(z^2 - \dfrac{1}{z}\right)^2 - \left(z^2 + \dfrac{1}{z}\right)^2$

26. $(111)(89)$

27. $350^2 - 320^2$

28. In the right triangle below, side a is 7 inches longer than side b. If the area of the triangle is 30 inches^2, what is the length of hypotenuse c?

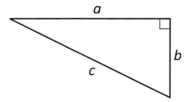

In-Action Problem Set (Solutions)

1.
$$5^{\frac{2}{3}x} = 5$$
$$\frac{2}{3}x = 1$$
$$x = \frac{3}{2}$$

2–4. Since we know $x \neq 0$, we can simply divide by the common terms, making sure to flip the inequality sign if the common term is negative.

2. $x^4 > \boxed{x^2}$ Note: is positive.
   $x^2 > 1$?   Divide both sides by x^2, leaving the sign as it is.

   TRUE

3. $x^3 + x^4 > x^3 + \boxed{x^2}$ Note: x^2 is positive.
   $x + x^2 > x + 1$ Divide both sides by x^2, leaving the sign as it is.
   $x^2 > 1$ Subtract x from both sides.

   TRUE   (Or you might have subtracted x^3 immediately.)

4. $x^6 - x^7 > \boxed{x^5} - x^6$ Note: x^5 is negative.
   $x - x^2 < 1 - x$ Divide both sides by x^5, flipping the inequality sign.
   $2x - 1 < x^2$ Group like terms.
   neg < pos?

   TRUE

5–9. We find both $\dfrac{a}{b}$ and the inverse $\dfrac{b}{a}$ below:

5. $\dfrac{a - b}{b} = \dfrac{1}{8} - 1 = -\dfrac{7}{8}$

6. $\dfrac{b - a}{a} = 8 - 1 = 7$

7. $\dfrac{a + b}{a} = 1 + 8 = 9$

8.

$$\left(\frac{a+b}{b}\right) = \frac{1}{8} + 1 = \frac{9}{8}$$

9.

$$\left(\frac{a^2+b^2}{ab}\right) = \frac{a^2}{ab} + \frac{b^2}{ab} = \left(\frac{a}{b}\right) + \left(\frac{b}{a}\right) = \frac{1}{8} + 8 = \frac{65}{8}$$

10.   Since n is an integer, $4n$ is even. Thus, because an even exponent "hides the sign" of the base. So,

$$(-3)^{4n} = (3)^{7n-3}$$
$$(3)^{4n} = (3)^{7n-3}$$
$$4n = 7n - 3$$
$$3 = 3n$$
$$1 = n$$

11.

$$\frac{\left(2^3\right)\left(15^4\right)\left(4^2\right)}{(80)\left(18^2\right)} = \frac{\left(2^3\right)\left(5^4\, 3^4\right)\left(\left(2^2\right)^2\right)}{\left(8 \times 10\right)\left(2^2 \times 9^2\right)}$$
$$= \frac{\left(5^4\right)\left(2^4\right)}{(10)\left(2^2\right)}$$
$$= \frac{\left(5^4\right)\left(2^2\right)}{(10)}$$
$$= \left(5^3\right)\left(2^1\right)$$
$$= 250$$

Note: This is just one of many ways to do the canceling.

12.

$$\left(\frac{1}{5}\right)^k = 625$$
$$\left(5^{-1}\right)^k = 5^4$$
$$5^{-k} = 5^4$$
$$-k = 4$$
$$k = -4$$

13. $x^2 + 2 + \dfrac{1}{x^2}$

14. $x^4 - 2x^2y + y^2$

15. $z^4 - \dfrac{1}{z^2}$

16. $5^2 - \left(\sqrt{21}\right)^2 = 25 - 21 = 4$

17. $a^2 - ab + \dfrac{b^2}{4}$

18. $\left(y^2 - \dfrac{1}{y^2}\right)^2$

19. $(2 + a)^2$

20. $(9 + x^2)(9 - x^2) = (9 + x^2)(3 + x)(3 - x)$

21. $\left(\sqrt{x} + \sqrt{yz}\right)^2$

22. $(2x - 3y)^2$

23. $2(x + y)$

24. $4\sqrt{x}\sqrt{\dfrac{1}{x}} = 4\sqrt{\dfrac{x}{x}} = 4$

25. $-4\left(z^2\right)\left(\dfrac{1}{z}\right) = -4z$

26. $(100 + 11)(100 - 11) = (100^2 - 11^2) = 10{,}000 - 121 = 9{,}879$

27. $(350 + 320)(350 - 320) = (670)(30) = 2{,}010$

28. $(a - b) = 7$ and $\dfrac{1}{2}ab = 30$. From the Pythagorean Theorem, we know that $a^2 + b^2 = c^2$.

Use the "square of a difference" template:

$$
\begin{aligned}
(a - b)^2 &= a^2 - 2ab + b^2 \\
&= \left(a^2 + b^2\right) - 2ab \\
&= \left(c^2\right) - 4\left(\frac{1}{2}ab\right)
\end{aligned}
$$

Plug in the values we have:

$$
\begin{aligned}
7^2 &= \left(c^2\right) - 4(30) \\
49 + 120 &= c^2 \\
169 &= c^2 \\
13 &= c
\end{aligned}
$$

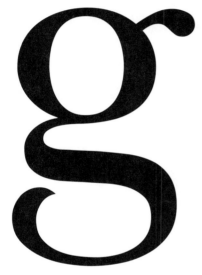

Chapter 7
of
ADVANCED GMAT QUANT

VISUAL
SOLUTIONS

In This Chapter . . .

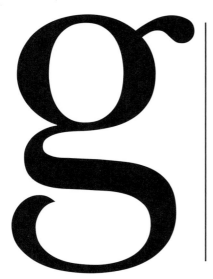

Visual Solutions

Visual interpretations—good pictures, essentially—can help you solve certain types of GMAT problems. This chapter highlights some of these types of problems and demonstrate how you can use visual techniques to solve the problems more confidently, accurately, and quickly.

Many problems discussed in this chapter can be solved with other techniques. Still, visual thinking is a powerful tool. It can expand your comprehension of a topic. It may enable you to solve particular problem types more easily or "break through" on a difficult problem. In fact, visualization is the only realistic way to approach certain problems. So it's worth trying your hand with visual approaches.

In this chapter, we will discuss the following visual techniques:

   (1) **Representing Objects With Pictures** – Many word problems and geometry problems do not provide a diagram alongside the problem. Drawing a good picture will make the problem-solving process easier and less error-prone.

   (2) **Rubber Band Geometry** – For Geometry questions involving both constraints and flexibility (especially in Data Sufficiency), drawing different "rubber band" scenarios according to those constraints and freedoms can often help us solve the problem without doing *any* computation.

   (3) **Baseline Calculations for Averages** – Visual techniques can help you compute averages (both basic and weighted) and can also foster a better understanding of those calculations.

   (4) **Number Line Techniques for Statistics Problems** – You can solve a variety of common problems involving Statistics by using a number line to visualize and manipulate the problem.

1. Representing Objects with Pictures

For word problems that describe a physical object, or for Geometry problems that do not give a diagram alongside the problem, drawing a picture is often the best approach. Sometimes it's the *only* viable approach! Even if you are good at visualizing objects in your head, you should draw the picture anyway. It's just too easy to make a mistake on many of these questions.

Try-It #7-1

A rectangular wooden dowel measures 4 inches by 1 inch by 1 inch. If the dowel is painted on all surfaces and then cut into 1/2 inch cubes, what fraction of the resulting cube faces are painted?

(A) 1/3
(B) 3/8
(C) 7/16
(D) 1/2
(E) 9/16

If you draw a picture, this problem becomes a matter of counting:

} 1/2 inch

Total Cubes = (4 inches × 2 cubes per inch) × (1 × 2) × (1 × 2) = 32 cubes
Total Cube Faces = 32 cubes × 6 faces per cube = 192 faces total

We now consider the faces that were painted on the front and back of the dowel, the top and bottom of the dowel, and the ends of the dowel. In the diagram above, we can see 16 faces on the front, 16 faces on the top, and 4 faces on the end shown. Of course, there are other sides: the back, the bottom, and the other end.

Painted Cube Faces = (16 faces × 2) + (16 faces × 2) + (4 faces × 2) = 32 + 32 + 8 = 72 painted faces

Front & Back   Top & Bottom   Ends

The fraction of faces that are painted $= \dfrac{72}{192} = \dfrac{24(3)}{24(8)} = \dfrac{3}{8}$. The correct answer is B.

Notice that there is no shortcut to solving this kind of problem, so don't waste time looking for one—just draw the diagram and count.

> **!** Even if you can easily picture 3-D shapes and objects in your head, it is still better to draw a picture on your scrapboard.
>
> Wrong answer choices are often those you might get by losing track of your progress as you process the object in your mind.

This kind of process can also help you with questions that deal with the relative size of different objects.

Try-It #7-2

> Bucket *A* has twice the capacity of bucket *B*, and bucket *A* has 1/3 the capacity of bucket *C*. Bucket *B* is full of water and bucket *C* is half full of water. When the water from bucket *B* is poured into bucket *C*, bucket *C* will be filled to what fraction of its capacity?

You could attempt to solve this problem algebraically, but the equations get messy very quickly. Instead, you should try drawing the buckets *A*, *B* and *C* in correct proportion to one another. Then think through the problem.

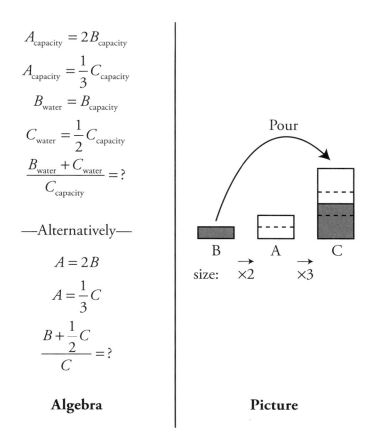

$$A_{capacity} = 2B_{capacity}$$

$$A_{capacity} = \frac{1}{3}C_{capacity}$$

$$B_{water} = B_{capacity}$$

$$C_{water} = \frac{1}{2}C_{capacity}$$

$$\frac{B_{water} + C_{water}}{C_{capacity}} = ?$$

—Alternatively—

$$A = 2B$$

$$A = \frac{1}{3}C$$

$$\frac{B + \frac{1}{2}C}{C} = ?$$

Algebra   **Picture**

The algebra and the picture say the same thing, but the picture has several advantages:

- It's much easier to comprehend at a glance.
- It's harder to mistake relative sizes (for example, accidentally thinking A is smallest).
- You can easily represent both total capacity and amount of water visually.
- It prompts you to pursue the smartest, easiest solution: <u>picking numbers</u> for the capacities of the buckets.

Based on this picture, we might pick a capacity of 1 for bucket *B*, yielding a capacity of 2 for bucket *A* and 6 for bucket *C*. Bucket *B* would contain 1 unit of water and bucket *C*, 3 units. When the contents of *B* are poured into *C*, bucket *C* would then be 4/6 = 2/3 full.

Notice that the buckets are not labeled in alphabetical order, even though that would be easy to incorrectly assume. The GMAT frequently adds little layers of disguise and complexity such as this, to induce you to make a mistake. By drawing the buckets carefully, you minimize the chance that you will fall into a trap on a problem such as this one.

2. Rubber Band Geometry

Many Geometry problems—particularly of the Data Sufficiency variety—describe objects for which only partial information is known. We call these questions *Rubber Band Geometry* problems, because they simultaneously involve constraints and flexibility. Some physical part of the diagram can stretch like a rubber band as you open or close angles.

Your job is to figure out what specifics in the problem are constrained, and what specifics are flexible.

For example, if a problem specifies that a line has a slope of 2, we know that it will be steep and upward-sloping. In fact, it will always "rise" 2 units for every unit of "run." However, we don't know where the line will appear. The line is *constrained* in its slope, but it is *flexible* in that it can be moved up or down, right or left. We can draw many different lines with a slope of 2 (these lines will all be parallel, of course).

If, however, the problem only specifies that a line must go through the point (4, 0) in the coordinate plane, then we would know that the line is "fixed" at that point. However, the slope of the line would now be flexible. We could draw many different lines with different slopes that run through that point.

If we knew both of these specifications—that the line must have a slope of 2 and must run through the point (4, 0)—then we would be able to calculate the exact line that is being described. The slope of the line and a point that the line goes through specify the line precisely—there is no remaining flexibility for either the slope or the location of the line. (Note that in this example, the line is described by the equation $y = 2x - 8$.)

Given these specifications, every other feature of this line is also known: its x-intercept, its y-intercept, whether it goes through some fixed point, which quadrants it crosses, etc. Thus, in a Data Sufficiency problem, we could answer any such questions about this line without actually calculating the answer. Remember, in Data Sufficiency, you do not need to calculate or find an answer—you merely need to know whether it can be calculated or found in principle with the given information.

Thus, for these types of problems, our goal is to figure out what combination of information "cements" the problem in place—in other words, what combination of information removes all the remaining flexibility. No flexibility means sufficiency. And by using Rubber Band Geometry thinking, you can often do this without using any calculation or algebra at all.

This line of thinking is relatively simple: for each piece of information that you're given in this type of problem, think about what is *fixed* and what is *flexible*. Try to draw multiple versions of each object (if possible), testing the boundaries of this flexibility. The following everyday objects may be useful as analogies in your thinking:

- Rubber bands – Determines a straight line segment. Can stretch between any two points.
- Drinking straws – Determines a straight line segment, but with fixed length
- Thumbtacks – Fixes a point, but can allow rotations through that point in many cases.
- Wedge – Fixes an angle.

Here are some common examples of how these objects can be used to help you think through these problems:

Constrained	Flexible	Analogous Object(s)	Mental Picture / Simplified Sketch
A line passes through a specified point	Slope of the line	Drinking straw = Line Thumbtack = Point	Line free to spin about a point.
Two lines intersect at a specified point	Slope of the lines	Drinking straw = Line Thumbtack = Point	Both lines free to spin about a point. The angle is free to change.
A line passes through two points	Nothing flexible	Drinking straw = Line Thumbtacks = Points	Two points pin down a line—no flexibility.
Specified distance between two points	Absolute or relative location of the points	Thumbtacks = Points Drinking straw = Distance between points	Fix one point temporarily. Line (straw) free to spin about one point, tracing the circle of possible locations of the other point.

Slope of a line	Location of the line, or points the line may pass through	Drinking straw = Line	Line is free to "float around" but not rotate.
Points are on a line (either in the coordinate plane or on a basic number line)	Distance between the points.	Rubber band = stretched between points	"Stretchy" distance between points.
Points on a line are a specified distance apart	Order of the points (left-to-middle-to-right)	Drinking straws = fixed lengths between points Manipulation will be determined by other stated constraints, but thinking of the points as the endpoints of rigid straws will ensure that you do not forget the distance constraint.	A (or) B Lines could be laid end-to-end, overlapping, separated, and flipped right-to-left.
Triangle with a fixed area and a fixed base (and therefore a fixed height)	Position of the third vertex along a line parallel to the base	Straw = fixed base Rubber bands = other sides of the triangle Thumbtacks = endpoints of the base	B A

This is not intended to be an exhaustive list. The idea is simply to show you a new way of thinking through some difficult Geometry problems.

Try-It #7-3

A circle in a coordinate plane has a center at point A and a diameter of 6. If points B and C also lie in the same coordinate plane, is point B inside the circle?

(1) The distance between point A and point C equals 2.

(2) The distance between point B and point C equals 2.

Is B inside the circle?

Using Rubber Band Geometry concepts, we know from the problem that the exact locations of points A, B, and C do not matter—only the relative locations of the points matter. Therefore, we can arbitrarily assign point A to a specific location (in this case, we should choose the origin of the coordinate plane), and draw a circle with a radius of 3 units around it.

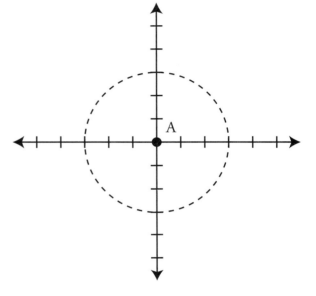

(1) The distance between A and C is 2.

Statement (1) does not tell us anything about point B, so it is not sufficient. However, it does tell us that A and C are 2 units apart, so Statement (1) enables us to place point C anywhere along the grey circle.

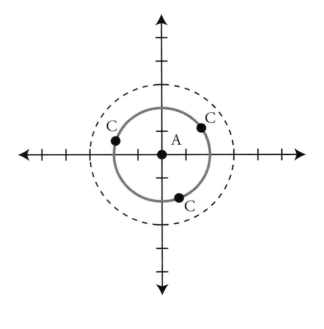

(1) The distance between B and C is 2.

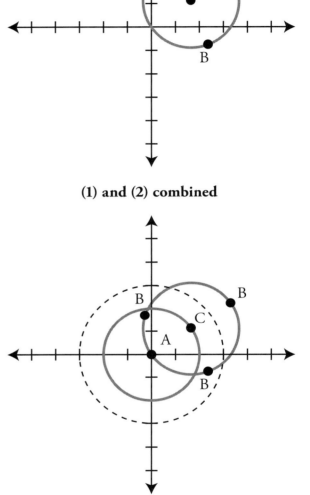

Statement (2) does not tell us anything about point B *relative* to point A, so it is not sufficient. However, it does constrain point B to be exactly 2 units away from wherever point C is. Thus we can imagine point C at the center of a circle of size 2, with point B somewhere on the circle around it.

(1) and (2) combined

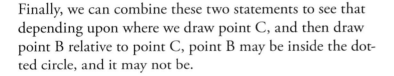

Finally, we can combine these two statements to see that depending upon where we draw point C, and then draw point B relative to point C, point B may be inside the dotted circle, and it may not be.

The correct answer is E.

Notice that we never proved the insufficiency of Statements (1) and (2) combined using algebra or any computation—but then again we didn't need to! Rather, we deduced it by drawing the information that was given to us. We reasoned visually that under the constraints, we could draw a scenario in which point B was inside the circle. We could also draw another scenario in which point B was outside of the circle. Done! We achieved a visual proof of the answer.

That's what Rubber Band Geometry is all about: testing scenarios for Geometry problems *without* the need to plug in numbers or use algebra. All we need is a visual environment that can be manipulated—one that preserves all key constraints and freedoms in the problem, and allows us to see them and test them. Rubber Band Geometry provides that environment for us.

3. Baseline Calculations for Averages

Basic Averages

Try-It #7-4

What is the average of 387, 388, and 389?

Relatively quickly, you should be able to see that the average is 388. How did you arrive at that answer?

It's very unlikely that you calculated the average the classical way:

$$\text{Average} = \frac{\text{Sum}}{\text{Number of Terms}} = \frac{387 + 388 + 389}{3} = \frac{1,164}{3} = 388$$

As part of this process you might add all three numbers together, in column format, and then divide by 3. This might take a minute or so.

Rather, you probably noticed that the numbers are very close together and evenly spaced. 387 is 1 less than 388, and 389 is 1 greater than 388. Thus the average must be 388—right in the middle.

Whether you realize it or not, you're using a relatively advanced technique to solve this problem: a **baseline calculation**. The baseline in this case is 388—the middle number. This concept can be applied to more difficult calculations of averages, making the calculation process much easier.

Try-It #7-5

A consumer finds that five bags of popcorn contain 257, 261, 273, 280, and 259 corn kernels per bag, respectively. What is the average number of corn kernels per bag of popcorn?

First, note that all of the bags have at least 257 kernels, so the average must be greater than 257. *How much greater than 257?* We will first consider how much each term differs from 257, then average those differences. We can visualize this process. Represent every number with a *column* rising above the baseline value (in this example, 257). The biggest numbers rise the highest; a number equal to the baseline has no height. The height of the column thus represents the *difference* between the number and the baseline value:

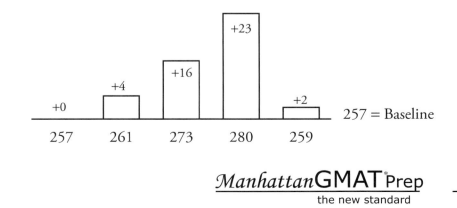

The sum of the differences is easy to compute: $0 + 4 + 16 + 23 + 2 = 45$.
The average difference is $45 \div 5 = 9$.

Therefore, the average number of kernels per bag equals baseline + average difference: $257 + 9 = 266$.

Simply put, a baseline picture is a column chart. The columns don't show the actual value of any number—rather, they show the difference between the baseline and the number.

!	The baseline can be *any* convenient number. Consider the following when choosing a baseline: • The smallest term in the set. • The largest term in the set. • The median term in the set. • A round number near the range of values.

For sets with apparent symmetry, choosing a baseline in the *middle* is a good way not only to confirm the symmetry, but also to compute the average. In this scenario, you should represent numbers lower than the baseline with columns that drop *below* the baseline. As before, the size of the column represents the difference between the number and the baseline.

Use trial and error to pick a possible average baseline, then adjust the drawing and calculations if necessary.

Try-It #7-6

> If a small business paid quarterly taxes last year of $10,079, $10,121, $10,112 and $10,088, what was the average quarterly tax payment last year?

In this case, some of the numbers are below $10,100, and others are above $10,100, so $10,100 is a natural first guess:

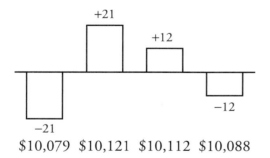

$10,079 $10,121 $10,112 $10,088

If the baseline is the average, then the sum of the differences from the baseline will be zero. Since the differences from the baseline do in fact sum to zero, $10,100 is indeed the average of this set.

This method reflects a visualization of the "Using Residuals" technique discussed in the "Combinatorics, Probability, and Statistics: Advanced" chapter of the *Word Translations Strategy Guide*.

Weighted Averages

Some sets may have many terms, but each of those terms has one of only two possible values. Rather than add each individual term together, we can simplify the calculations by using a *Weighted Average* calculation.

Try-It #7-7

The 12 students in a class take a test and score either 76 or 96. If 3 students received the lower score and the remaining students received the higher score, what was the average score for the class?

$$\text{Average} = \frac{\text{Sum}}{\text{Number of Terms}} = \frac{3(76) + 9(96)}{3+9} = \frac{228 + 864}{12} = \frac{1092}{12} = 91$$

We can simplify this calculation even further and gain a more solid grasp of the issues by applying baseline techniques. Let's choose 76 as our baseline:

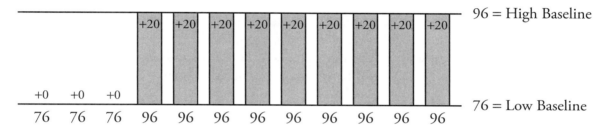

The average by which the scores exceed the low baseline of 76 is $\frac{(9)(20)}{12} = \frac{3}{4}(20) = 15$.

The average of the scores is thus baseline + average difference: $76 + 15 = 91$.

The high-scoring students effectively pull the class average up 3/4 of the way from the low baseline to the high baseline, because 3/4 of the students received that high score. In fact, our baseline visual representation of weighted average could be simplified this way:

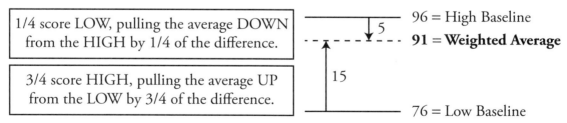

Indeed, for weighted average problems, we do not need to know the exact number of each observation – we just need to know the *relative weightings* of each. For example, this calculation would have the same result if there were 1 student who received a 76 and 3 who received a 96, or if there were 50 who received a 76 and 150 who received a 96. In each case, the weighted average score would remain the same (91).

For weighted averages, we can use visualization to advance our understanding of the math even further. Two real-life analogies can make it easier to remember how the *relative weights* of high and low values determine where the weighted average falls.

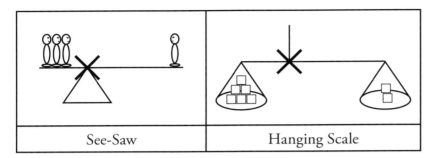

| | | See-Saw | | Hanging Scale |

With these pictures, we represent the values in a set as *horizontal* positions—left-to-right, as on a number line, not as vertical columns. (It may help to imagine the balance beam or lever marked off in equal units like a number line.) Each pin or weight corresponds to the presence of a value in a set. The X in each picture marks the *equilibrium point*—in other words, the *weighted average.*

Both visual interpretations regard weighted averages as a kind of balancing act: *the weighted average will be closer to the end of the range that has more observations.* In the pictures, there are more instances of the low (left-hand side) number in the set, so the X is relatively closer to the left-hand side. You can think of this point as the point where the weight would be "balanced" between the two sets.

Using the numbers from the previous example, you might represent these ideas visually like this:

		Low	High	Difference
Value	Test Score	76	96	20
Weighting (How many or how much at that value?)	# of students	3	9	
Fraction (or Percent) of Total		3/12 = 1/4	9/12 = 3/4	

$$3/4(20) = 15 \qquad 1/4(20) = 5$$

76   X   96

Notice that 3/4 of the observations are *high*, so the balance point is 3/4 of the way toward the *high* end of this number line segment.

When using this technique, it is important to remember that the weighted average is *closer* to (i.e., *fewer* units away from) the score that has *more* observations. In this example, there are 9 high scores out of 12, and only 3 low scores out of 12, but the weighted average is only 5 units away from the high score, while it is 15 units away from the low score. This will always be the case. It is easy to reverse this logic accidentally when solving a weighted average problem with this technique, so be very careful! Just remember: *the weighted average point will be closer to the side with* **more** *observations.*

Remember, the placement of the X (the balance point) does not depend on the *absolute* number of high or low terms. It only depends on the *proportion* of terms that are high or low. Knowing the *ratio* of high to low terms is enough to determine where the weighted average falls between the high and low. The reverse is also true: if you know where the weighted average is, you can figure out the relative proportion of high and low terms.

Try-It #7-8

> A convenience store stocks soda in 12 ounce and 24 ounce bottles. If the average capacity of all the bottles in the store is 22 ounces, then what fraction of the bottles in the store are 12 ounces?

Note that 22 is much closer to 24 than to 12. This implies that there will be many more 24-ounce bottles than 12-ounce bottles. Because the question asks about 12-ounce bottles, you could strategically eliminate any answer greater than or equal to 1/2.

This time, we can use our understanding of weighted average as a balancing act to work backwards from the weighted average to the ratio of high to low terms.

	Low	High	Difference
Bottle Size (oz.)	12	24	12
# of bottles	$1x$	$5x$	
Fraction of difference	$2/12 = 1/6$	$10/12 = 5/6$	

The total range between the high and low values (24 and 12) is 12 units. 12 is 10 units away from 22, and 24 is 2 units away from 22. Therefore, 24 will constitute $10/12 = 5/6$ of the observations, and 12 will constitute 1/6 of the observations.

We can test this solution using real numbers. Let's assume there are five 24-ounce bottles and one 12-ounce bottle. The weighted average capacity of the bottles is:

$$\frac{5\times24+1\times12}{5+1} = \frac{120+12}{6} = 22$$

Notice that we do not need to know how many bottles are in the store—just the ratio of high to low!

4. Number Line Techniques for Statistics Problems

We've seen how visualization can help solve questions involving the computation of averages. Several other common types of questions involving *Statistics* can be solved with visualization. Specifically, using a number line can help simplify the work for many of these problems.

Median Relative to Mean

Most questions involving the term **median** are really asking about the order of terms in a set. After all, we find the median by lining up the terms in a set in order of size, then selecting the *middle* term. (By contrast, the **average** or **arithmetic mean** is the sum of all of the terms divided by the number of terms. It can be visualized as the balancing point of all the terms laid out on the number line, as in the discussion of the balancing point for weighted averages in the previous section.) For Data Sufficiency questions involving median, you generally need to picture the placement of the unknown terms *relative to* the given terms in the problem.

This technique is similar to *Rubber Band Geometry* discussed earlier in this chapter, except this technique applies to problems involving sets rather than problems involving the coordinate plane. In this technique, you must place *fixed* terms in order from least to greatest (as you would on a number line), then move *variable* terms around according to the constraints. By doing so, you can visualize what impact these changes have on the answer.

Try-It #7-9

> If set S consists of the numbers n, -2, and 4, is the mean of set S greater than the median of set S?
>
> (1) $n > 2$
>
> (2) $n < 3$

The mean of set S is $\dfrac{n+(-2)+4}{3} = \dfrac{n+2}{3}$. The median depends on where n falls relative to -2 and 4: below -2, between -2 and 4, or above 4. One approach to this question is to think through the potential answers for all possible n values in the likely range (you can glance at the statements and other values in the list to get a sense of the relevant range) and draw the scenarios out on a number line. You may also want to consider a number much larger or smaller than the relevant range:

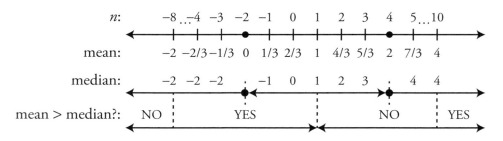

This requires a fair amount of up-front work, but evaluating the statements is fast as a result. Statement (1) tells us that $n > 2$, which is not sufficient. If $n = 4$, for example, the mean would equal 2 and the median would equal 4. By contrast, if $n = 16$, the mean would equal 6 and the median would still equal 4.

Similarly, Statement (2) tells us that $n < 3$, which is not sufficient. If $n = -2$, for example, the mean would equal 0 and the median would equal -2. By contrast, if $n = -11$, the mean would equal -3 and the median would still equal -2.

Taken together, however, any number in the range of $2 < n < 3$ would feature a median greater than the mean.

The correct answer is C.

Notice from this problem that as you move the variable terms, the mean *always* changes when the value of the variable terms change, but the median typically changes in *jumps*. The median can get stuck while the number you're changing doesn't affect *which* number is in the middle.

Changes in Standard Deviation

The GMAT will rarely (if ever) ask you to calculate the standard deviation of a set of numbers. However, the exam will expect you to have some intuition about standard deviations.

One way in which the GMAT might test your intuitive knowledge of standard deviations is by *changing numbers within a set* and asking you what the impact on standard deviation would be. The relationship is relatively simple:

- Moving terms away from the mean increases the standard deviation of the set
- Moving terms toward the mean decreases the standard deviation of the set

Try-It #7-10

The monthly sales (in thousands of $) at a certain restaurant for the past two years are given in the chart below:

Last Year	9	9.5	10	10	11	11	11	11	11	12.5	13	13
This Year	9	x	10	10	11	11	11	11	11	y	13	13

If the standard deviation of the monthly sales is greater this year than last year, which of the following are possible values for x and y?

(A) 9 and 12.5
(B) 10 and 11
(C) 10 and 12.5
(D) 11 and 11
(E) 11 and 12.5

Because the two lists of monthly sales numbers are nearly identical, we can focus exclusively on those terms that changed: 9.5 and 12.5 from last year were replaced by x and y this year. Using the baseline computation technique described earlier in the chapter, we can see that the average of the monthly sales last year was 11 (choosing 11 as the baseline, the sum of the differences below 11 is −5.5, and the sum of the differences above the baseline is +5.5). The replaced terms, 9.5 and 12.5, are equally spaced from last year's mean: −1.5 and +1.5, respectively.

Visually, here are the interesting terms from last year:

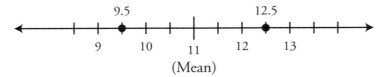

This problem does not require actual computation of the standard deviation using the new x and y values. The math would be too complex to complete in 2 minutes. Instead, we should be able to determine which x and y values increase the standard deviation visually: the pair of x and y values *that are farther from the mean* than are 9.5 and 12.5 will increase the standard deviation.

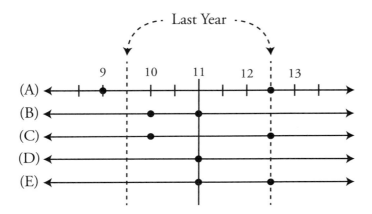

All of the sets have either one point or both points shifted in toward the mean EXCEPT (A), which has one of the points shifted away from the mean while the other is unchanged. We can determine that the deviation will greater as a result.

The correct answer is A.

Another way in which the GMAT might test you on the intuition of standard deviations is by adding numbers to a set. When new terms are added, the GMAT will often ask you to compare the old set to the new set, or to compare various options for the new set, or to do both. You must have a technique to evaluate the standard deviation of different sets *relative to one another*. Again, pictures make for great comparison tools!

Try-It #7-11

A set of 12 test scores has an average of 500 and a standard deviation of 50. Which of the following sets of additional test scores, when combined with the original set of 12 test scores, must result in a combined data set with a standard deviation less than 50?

(A) 6 test scores with average of 450 and standard deviation of 50.
(B) 6 test scores with average of 500 and standard deviation of 25.
(C) 6 test scores with average of 550 and standard deviation of 25.
(D) 12 test scores with average of 450 and standard deviation of 25.
(E) 2 test scores with average of 550 and standard deviation of 50.

It is not generally true that all of the terms in a set are within one standard deviation of the mean. However, standard deviation *is* a measure of the spread of the terms of a set, so we could represent the original set of scores this way:

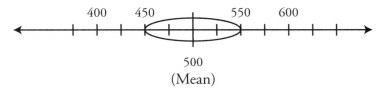

The oval spans ±1 standard deviation from the mean, where many of the scores will likely be. This simplification is acceptable as long as we represent all of the other data sets the same way, because all we want to do is compare the *relative* effects of the new test scores systematically.

For each of the answer choices, we can now overlay the representative ovals for the new data on top of the oval for the original data.

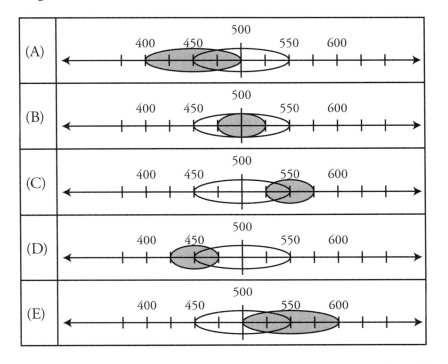

It is clear that all of the data in the answer choices, when added to the original set, will result in a likely or definite increase in the spread of the data *except* for answer choice (B), which definitely concentrates the set of scores closer to the original average of 500. Thus, adding the data in answer choice B will result in a smaller standard deviation than that found in the original data set. The correct answer is B.

We can generalize rules for adding a single term to a set as follows:

- Adding a new term *more than* 1 standard deviation from the mean generally *increases* the standard deviation of a set.
- Adding a new term *less than* 1 standard deviation from the mean generally *decreases* the standard deviation of a set.

Note that mathematically this is a slight oversimplification, but for the purpose of adding terms to a set of numbers on the GMAT, you can accept this simplification as true.

Floating Terms in a Set

On GMAT statistics problems involving elements (i.e., terms) in a set, you can usually focus your attention on a single term or two. These terms could be considered the *floating terms*—the terms that are unknown or not completely defined among a list of more clearly defined terms.

As you approach a question of this type, try to rephrase the question quickly so that you focus on the unknown, or *floating*, terms rather than on the known terms.

Try-It #7-12

> List A contains 5 positive integers, and the average (arithmetic mean) of the integers in the list is 7. If the integers 6, 7, and 8 are in list A, what is the range of list A?
>
> (1) The integer 3 is in list A.
>
> (2) The largest term in list A is greater than 3 times and less than 4 times the size of the smallest term.

The average of all five integers in the set is 7. Three of the integers in the set are given (6, 7, and 8) and they all have an average of 7. Therefore, the *floating terms* in this problem must also have an average of 7. If we assign x and y to represent these terms, we have:

$$\frac{x+y}{2} = 7$$
$$x + y = 14$$

Our rephrased question is thus, "Given that $x + y = 14$, what is either x or y?" Once we know one of the values, we can solve for the other, and thereby determine the range of the set.

(1) SUFFICIENT: If 3 is one of the unknown integers, the other must be 11. The range is thus $11 - 3 = 8$.

(2) SUFFICIENT: This statement might seem a little too vague to be sufficient, but by visually listing the possible pairs that add up to 14, we can rule out pairs that don't fit the constraint from this statement:

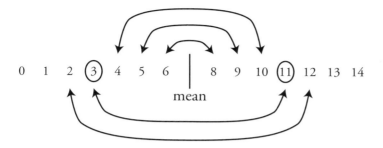

Notice that the pairings represent the constraint $x + y = 14$. Visually, this means that x and y are balanced around 7.

Among these pairs:

- 8 is 1.33 times the size of 6 (the ratio is too low).
- 9 is 1.8 times the size of 5 (the ratio is too low).
- 10 is 2.5 times the size of 4 (the ratio is too low).
- 11 is 3.66 times the size of 3 (an acceptable ratio).
- 12 is 6 times the size of 2 (the ratio is too high).

Only one pair of integers results in a ratio strictly between 3 and 4. The unknown terms must therefore be 3 and 11, and the range is $11 - 3 = 8$.

The correct answer is D.

In this problem we saw the constraint $x + y = 14$: a *fixed sum*. Another common constraint is a *fixed difference*, such as $a - b = 2$. A fixed difference can be represented visually as a fixed distance between a and b on the number line, with a to the right because it is larger. That distance could move left or right:

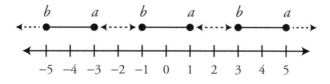

Maximizing One Term in a Set

Another visual technique for statistics involves maximizing (or minimizing) the value of a term in a set of numbers, subject to some constraints. Such problems will usually employ the word "maximum" or "minimum." For these problems, you often should maximize (or minimize) the term by minimizing (or maximizing) the *other* terms in the set. The reason is that the constraints usually involve mathematical trade-offs. For example, fixed sums and fixed averages create such trade-offs, and problems in this category often incorporate fixed sums and averages.

Try-It #7-13

Three sisters have an average (arithmetic mean) age of 25 years and a median age of 24 years. What is the minimum possible age, in years, of the oldest sister?

(A) 24
(B) 25
(C) 26
(D) 27
(E) 28

By definition, the middle sister must have the median age (24 years). The youngest sister must be less than or equal to 24 years old. Of course, the oldest sister must be at least as old as the middle sister. But the average age is 25 years, implying that the oldest sister must be *greater* than 25 years old because the other two sisters are younger than 25. On a number line, we can visualize the possibilities:

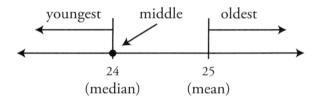

Mathematically, Average = 25 means that Sum = (3)(25) = 75 = youngest + 24 + oldest, or 51 = youngest + oldest.

The fixed sum of the ages of youngest and oldest, as well as the arrows for them pointing in opposite directions, signifies the trade-off between the ages of the oldest and youngest sisters. To *minimize* the oldest sister's age, we will *maximize* the youngest sister's age.

The maximum age of the youngest sister is 24 years, because she cannot be older than the median age:

51 = max(youngest) + min(oldest)
51 = 24 + min(oldest)
27 = min(oldest)

The correct answer is D.

Taking and Giving

Another common scenario involves taking value from one term in a set and giving it to another term. The relative value of the terms in the set will change, leading to some interesting results.

Try-It #7-14

Jake	51
Keri	63
Luke	15
Mia	38
Nora	22

The table above shows the number of points held by 5 players of a certain game. If an integer number of Keri's points were taken from her and given to Luke, and the median score of the 5 players increased, how many points were transferred from Keri to Luke?

(A) 23
(B) 24
(C) 25
(D) 26
(E) 27

The key to this problem is that by taking enough points from Keri and giving them to Luke, *the median of the set can change.*

We can understand this best by thinking about it visually. Order the scores from low to high on a number line, and represent the change in Luke's score with x:

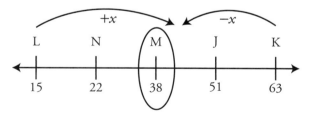

The current median is Mia's 38, circled in the diagram. In order for the median to change, Luke's score must leap-frog those of Nora and Mia, pushing Mia into the bottom two scores and making Luke's score the median. But be careful! We don't want to decrease Keri's score *so much* that Luke and Mia surpass her, leaving Mia once again in the median score position.

If $15 + x = 38$, Luke would *match* the current median score. That is $x = 23$, and Keri's new score would be $63 - 23 = 40$. However, the median score would remain 38, with both Luke and Mia having that score. Therefore, x must be greater than 23.

If $63 - x = 38$, Keri would *match* the current median score. That is $x = 25$, and Luke's new score would be $15 + 25 = 40$. The median score would again remain 38, because Keri (and Mia) would now represent the median. Therefore, x must be less than 25.

Because x must be an integer, $x = 24$. The scores after the point transfer will be:

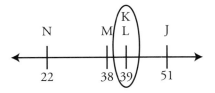

Keri and Luke would now both have the median score of 39.

The correct answer is B.

In-Action Problem Set

Use the Visual Solutions techniques discussed in this chapter to solve the following problems:

1. In the figure shown, the circumference of the circle is 10π. Which of the following is not a possible value for the area of the rectangle?

    (A) 30
    (B) 40
    (C) $20\sqrt{2}$
    (D) $30\sqrt{2}$
    (E) $40\sqrt{2}$

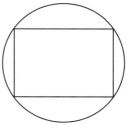

2. Lines k and ℓ intersect in the coordinate plane at point $(3, -2)$. Is the largest angle formed at the intersection between these two lines greater than $90°$?

    (1) Lines k and ℓ have positive y-axis intercepts.
    (2) The distance between the y-axis intercepts of lines k and ℓ is 5.

3. If a, b, and c are positive, is $a > \dfrac{b+c}{2}$?

    (1) On the number line, a is closer to b than it is to c.
    (2) $b > c$

4. The length of one edge of a cube equals 4. What is the distance between the center of the cube and one of its vertices?

5. A test is taken by 100 people and possible scores are the integers between 0 and 50, inclusive. Would the average score be greater than 30, if (answer Yes, No, or Uncertain):

    a) More than 70 people scored 40 or higher?
    b) 75 people scored 40 or higher?
    c) Fewer than 10 people scored 50?
    d) No more than 2 test takers scored any given score?

6. The bar graph below displays the number of temperature readings at each value from a sample, measured in degrees Fahrenheit. What was the average temperature reading?

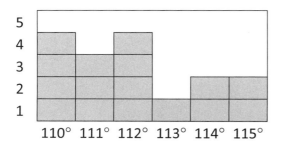

7. In a certain dance troupe, there are 55 women and 33 men. If all of the women are 62 inches tall and all of the men are 70 inches tall, what is the average height of the dancers in the troupe?

8. Three students in a science class received exam scores. The average (arithmetic mean) of their scores was 50. The lowest possible score was a 0 and the highest possible score was 100.

   a) If the highest of their scores was 80, what is the highest possible median score?
   b) If the highest of their scores was 80, what is the lowest possible median score?
   c) If the median of their scores was 60, what is the highest possible value for the lowest score?

9. Three people have $32, $72, and $98, respectively. If they pool their money then redistribute it among them, what is the maximum value for the median amount of money?

   (A) $72   (B) $85   (C) $98   (D) $101   (E) $202

10.   Set A: 1, 3, 5, 7, 9
       Set B: 6, 8, 10, 12, 14

For the sets of numbers above, which of the following is true?
I. The mean of Set B is greater than the mean of Set A.
II. The median of Set B is greater than the median of Set A.
III. The standard deviation of Set B is greater than the standard deviation of Set A.

   (A) I only   (B) I and II only   (C) I and III only
   (D) II and III only   (E) I, II, and III

In-Action Problem Set (Solutions)

1. (E): This question asks us to determine which answer choice lists an area for the inscribed rectangle that is not feasible. What makes one possible area feasible and another one infeasible?

By using a *Rubber Band Geometry* approach, we can answer the question. The inscribed rectangle can be stretched and pulled to extremes: extremely long and thin, extremely tall and narrow, and somewhere in between:

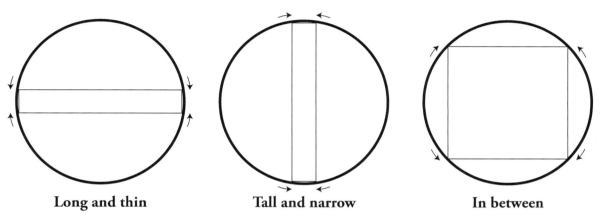

Long and thin   **Tall and narrow**   **In between**

The "long and thin" and "tall and narrow" rectangles will have a very small area, and the "in between" rectangle will have the largest possible area. In fact, the largest possible rectangle inscribed inside a circle will be a square:

In this problem, the circumference = $10\pi = 2\pi r$. Thus $r = 5$, and the diagonal of the square is $2r = 10$. The square then has a side length of $5\sqrt{2}$ and an area of $\left(5\sqrt{2}\right)^2 = 50$.

Only answer choice (E) is larger than 50. The correct answer is (E).

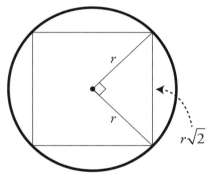

Square: maximal area

2. D: Of course, we should first draw a picture of the coordinate plane, together with the point (3, −2) and two sample lines *k* and *l*.

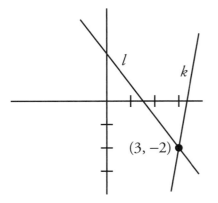

Using *Rubber Band Geometry* terms, we have a "thumbtack" at the point (3, −2). We can rotate lines *k* and *l* through any angle around this thumbtack.

The problem asks whether the largest angle formed between these lines is greater than 90°. Most of the time, when two lines intersect, they form two acute angles (less than 90°) and two obtuse angles (greater than 90°). The only case in which the two lines would *not* form any angle greater than 90° is if the two lines are perfectly perpendicular to each other: they form four 90° angles. So the question can be rephrased thus: "Are the two lines *k* and *l* perpendicular to each other?" With Rubber Band Geometry, we will try to force the lines to be perpendicular and non-perpendicular.

(1) SUFFICIENT. Both lines have positive *y*-axis intercepts. In other words, they both cross the *y*-axis above the origin (0, 0):

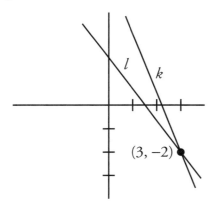

Both lines slope downward to the right (that is, they have negative slope). No matter how much we twist the lines apart, one would have to cross just above the origin, and the other would be nearly vertical—but they will form acute and obtuse angles. There is no way to make the lines perpendicular to each other. In other words, the answer to the question is a definite No, making this statement sufficient. (Another way to see this result is that any line perpendicular to a line with negative slope must have positive slope, so that their slopes can multiply together to −1, a condition of perpendicularity. However, we know that both lines must have negative slope, in order to have positive *y*-intercepts but pass through the "thumbtack" point as well.)

(2) SUFFICIENT. We are told that the distance between the *y*-intercepts of the two lines is 5. It's easy to generate a case in which the lines are not perpendicular. The real question is this: can we make the lines perpendicular?

To spread the lines as far apart as possible, we should place the distance of 5 directly opposite the thumbtack, like so:

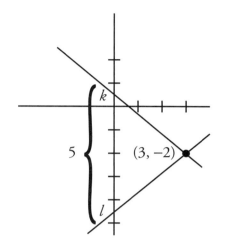

By symmetry, half of that distance of 5 will be above the thumbtack. So we can draw a right triangle:

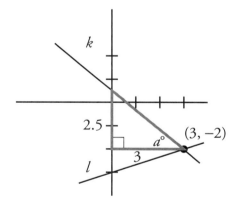

The legs of the two triangles have lengths 3 and 2.5. The angle opposite the 2.5, labeled $a°$ in the diagram, must be *less* than 45°, because it is opposite the smaller side. As a result, the angle between *k* and *l* cannot be 90°. Again, we have a definite No, which is sufficient.

The correct answer is D.

3. C: We are told only that *a*, *b*, and *c* are positive. We are asked whether *a* is greater than $\dfrac{b+c}{2}$, which is the *average* (or arithmetic mean) of *b* and *c*.

Using *Number Line Techniques for Statistics,* we can draw a picture and rephrase the question: "On the number line, is *a* positioned to the right of the midpoint between *b* and *c*?"

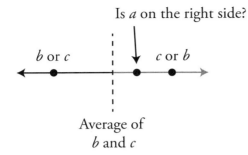

Is *a* on the right side?

b or *c*   *c* or *b*

Average of
b and *c*

(1) INSUFFICIENT. We know that *a* is closer to *b* than to *c*, but we don't know whether *b* or *c* is the larger value—the point on the right. So we don't know whether *a* is on the right side or the left side of the midpoint. All we know is that *a* is not dead-center!

(2) INSUFFICIENT. This statement tells us nothing about *a*, so it can't be sufficient.

(1) & (2) SUFFICIENT. Now we know that *b* is the point on the right, so *a* must be on the right side of the midpoint.

The correct answer is C.

4. $2\sqrt{3}$: First, we should *Represent the Object with Pictures,* as is good practice with any 3-dimensional situation.

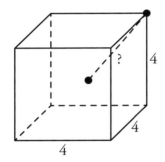

The length of any side of the cube is 4, and we are asked for the distance between the center of the cube and any of its vertices (corners). If we chop up the cube into 8 smaller cubes, we can see that the distance from the center of the $4 \times 4 \times 4$ cube to any corner is the diagonal of a $2 \times 2 \times 2$ cube.

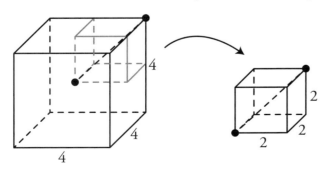

You can find the diagonal of a cube in a variety of ways. Probably the fastest (besides applying a memorized formula) is to use the "super-Pythagorean" Theorem, which extends to three dimensions:

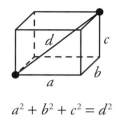

$$a^2 + b^2 + c^2 = d^2$$

In the special case when the three sides of the box are equal, as they are in a cube, then we have this equation, letting s represent any side of the cube:

$$s^2 + s^2 + s^2 = d^2$$
$$3s^2 = d^2$$
$$s\sqrt{3} = d$$

Since $s = 2$, we know that $d = 2\sqrt{3}$.

5. To visualize this *Weighted Averages* problem, we can imagine a see-saw that is 50 meters long, marked off from 0 to 50 to represent scores. One hundred people of equal weight sit on the see-saw at their respective scores. The weighted average is the position where the see-saw would balance. Thus, to answer whether the average score is greater than 30, we should take extremes according to the given conditions and see whether we can swing the balance to either side of 30 (or whether we are forced to balance on one side of 30 only).

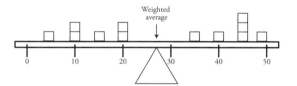

a) Uncertain: If more than 70 people scored 40 or higher, then we can easily push everyone to the right and make the average higher than 30. The question is whether we *must* have an average above 30. The answer is no. Let's push people as far to the left as we can. If 71 people have scores of exactly 40 and the other 29 people have scores of 0, then the total score is 2,840, leading to an average score is 28.4, which is less than 30.

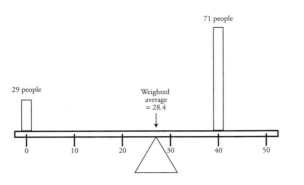

b) Uncertain: If 75 people scored 40 or higher, then again, we can easily make the overall average exceed 30. Can we make it *not* exceed 30? Yes. Again, push everyone to the left as far as possible. If 75 people have scores of exactly 40 and the other 25 people have scores of 0, then the total score is exactly 3,000, leading to an average score of exactly 30—which is not *greater than* 30.

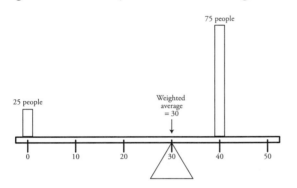

c) Uncertain: If fewer than 10 people scored 50, we can easily shift the rest of the people around to either side of 30. In fact, we could have *no one* scoring 50; we have almost complete freedom to move the population around.

d) No: If no more than 2 test takers scored any given score, then we are severely constrained. The only possible scores are the 51 integers between 0 and 50, inclusive. This means that we have a total of 102 possible slots for test-takers. Since we have 100 test-takers, almost every slot is taken.

We can push the average score to its highest possible level by taking up the 100 highest slots, leaving only the 0 scores empty. Two test-takers score a 1, two score a 2, and so on up to 50. The average score is then 25.5. Our essential move to reduce the average score is this: remove the two test-takers who scored 50 and make them score 0. Alternatively, slide everyone down 1 point. Either way, we now have two people who score 0, two who score 1, and so on up to 49. The average score is 24.5. The range of possible weighted averages is between 24.5 and 25.5, inclusive. We cannot make the average exceed 30.

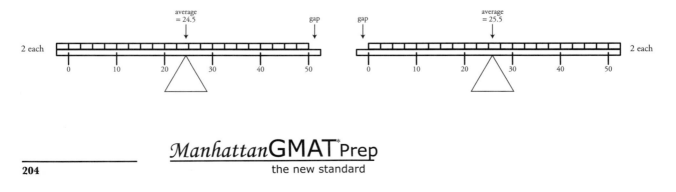

6. 112°: We can take a reasonable guess that the average is 112°. It can't be 112.5°, because there are more readings on the left, but 111° is too far: the readings from 110° through 112° center nicely around 111°, but then we have all the higher readings.

Let's try 112°. To refine our estimate and think visually with *Weighted Averages*, we cross out any readings actually at 112° or equally balanced on either side. After taking out the four readings at 112°, one each at 111° and 113°, and two each at 110° and 114°, we are left with two readings at 110°, two at 111°, and two at 115°. Now we can get tricky. We can move the readings inward by compensating amounts. For instance, we can move the two 111°'s up to 112° if we move the 115°'s down to 114°. Now that we've done so, we can see that everything left is exactly balanced at 112°. Thus 112° must have been the right average originally.

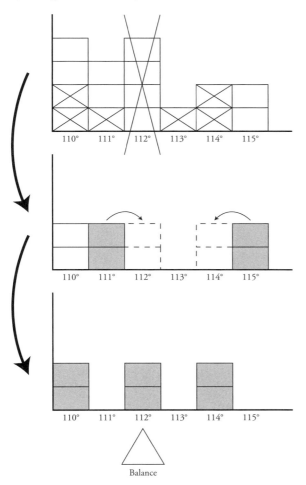

Another way to do this is to use a low *Baseline* without the drawing. Shave 110° off every reading, and you're left with four 0's, three 1's, four 2's, one 3, two 4's, and two 5's. These add up easily: 0 + 3 + 8 + 3 + 8 + 10 = 32°. Divide by the number of readings (4 + 3 + 4 + 1 + 2 + 2 = 16), and we get 2° as the average. Add back the 110° to get 112°.

Finally, if we pick a smarter *Baseline*, then the problem becomes simple as well. If the baseline is 112°, then the four 110° readings represent a total deficit of 8 degrees. The three 111° readings give us a deficit of 3 more degrees, for a total deficit of 11 degrees. The four 112° readings contribute nothing one way or the other. The one 113° gives us a net positive of 1 degree; the two 114°'s give us 2 degrees each, for 4 more degrees, bringing us to 5; and the two 115°'s give us 3 degrees each, for 6 more degrees, or a total of 11 "over" degrees canceling the deficit precisely. A drawing could help us here, or we could simply solve without a picture.

7. 65 inches: Standard solution:

$$\text{Average} = \frac{55(62 \text{ inches}) + 33(70 \text{ inches})}{(55+33)} = \frac{3,410 + 2,310}{88} \text{ inches} = \frac{5,720}{88} \text{ inches} = 65 \text{ inches}$$

Visual Solution:

		Women	Men	Difference
Value	Inches	62	70	8
Weighting	# of dancers	55	33	
Fraction (Percent) of Total		55/88 = 5/8	33/88 = 3/8	

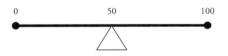

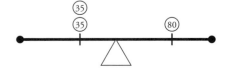

3/8(8) = 3   5/8(8) = 5

62   70

8. Using *Number Line Techniques for Statistics*, we can quickly lay out a diagram that will serve as our "playing field" for the different scenarios.

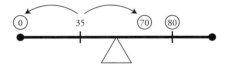

0   50   100

Since the three scores average to 50, they must sum to 150. This is good to keep in mind.

a) 70: If the highest score was 80, then the other two scores must sum to 70 and both be lower. That is, they must average to 35. Starting at 35 for both lower scores, we push one up and the other down, until the lower one hits the limit: zero. The higher of those two scores must be 70. Since that is the middle score, it is also the median.

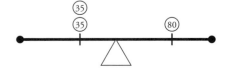

0   35   70   80

b) 35: The lowest possible median score in the previous scenario comes from keeping both lower scores together at 35.

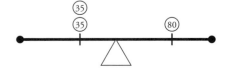

35
35   80

c) 30: The median score was 60, so the other two scores must sum to 90 and average to 45. One of those scores must bump upwards to at least 60 (otherwise 60 would be the highest score). So the other score falls to 30 to compensate. If the top score rises any more, then the lowest score falls further.

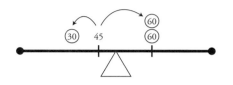

9. D: The pool of money is $32 + $72 + $98 = $202. After the redistribution, each person will have an amount between $0 and $202, inclusive. Let's call the amounts L, M, and H (low, median, high). To maximize M, we must minimize L and H.

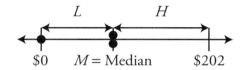

Minimum $L = $0
Minimum $H = M$

Maximum M = Total pool of money − Minimum L − Minimum H
$M = $202 − $0 − M$
$2M = 202
$M = 101

The correct answer is D.

10. B: On a number line, both sets of numbers are evenly spaced in increments of 2. The only difference between the sets is that Set B is shifted 5 to the right of Set A.

Thus,

I. TRUE. Mean of B = Mean of A + 5.
II. TRUE. Median of B = Median of A + 5
III. FALSE. Std. Dev. of B = Std. Dev. of A

The correct answer is B.

Chapter 8
of
ADVANCED GMAT QUANT

HYBRID
PROBLEMS

In This Chapter . . .

- Identify and Sequence the Parts
- Where to Start
- Minor Hybrids
- Conserving Time

Hybrid Problems

Hybrid problems blend topics together. They contain two or more qualitatively different kinds of obstacles that you must surmount on the way to the answer.

Some hybrid problems feature content areas that are fairly closely related. Here is an example (don't try it yet).

> If *a* and *b* are consecutive positive integers, and *ab* = 30*x*, is *x* an integer?
>
> (1) a^2 is divisible by 25.
> (2) 63 is a factor of b^2.

This question tests your knowledge of both *Consecutive Integers* and *Primes & Divisibility*. Both topics are discussed in the same Manhattan GMAT Strategy Guide (on *Number Properties*). The concepts used to solve problems in those areas are somewhat related.

Other hybrid problems feature content areas that share little in common; these problems must be solved in two separate steps. The following question tests both a topic within *Number Properties* and another within *Word Translations*—two general content areas that are quite distinct:

> Set S contains all integers between 6 and 20, inclusive, and Set T contains all multiples of 4 between 8 and 24, inclusive. What fraction of the integers in Set S are NOT in Set T?

This blending of subject matter makes hybrid problems more difficult. Hybrids resist simple classification. You have to *Understand* the various components (not all of which may be obvious) and then *Plan* for a complicated, multi-step approach. More than one area of your memory has to activate. There won't be a simple precursor problem that you've solved before; you'll need to draw on bits and pieces of disparate knowledge.

Finally you have to *Solve* quickly, transitioning from one step to a completely different one without delay. As a result, even a relatively simple hybrid problem can be rather tough.

The difficulty of a hybrid problem is related to the following questions:

- **How closely related are the subjects being tested?** Are the content areas covered in the same Manhattan GMAT Strategy Guide or different Strategy Guides? (The 5 Strategy Guides published by Manhattan GMAT cover *Number Properties*; *Equations, Inequalities, and VICs* (*EIVs*); *Word Translations*; *Fractions, Decimals, and Percents* (*FDPs*); and *Geometry*.) The more closely related the subjects, the easier it will be to navigate the problem.

- **How important are each of the subject areas?** Are each of the subject areas fundamental to the problem, or is one of them just a low-level disguise that can be quickly disposed of? The more important each topic is in solving the problem, the more difficult the problem will usually be.

The following example of a less difficult hybrid problem tests primarily *Probability* (*Word Translations*), but *Inequalities* (*EIVs*) and *Exponents* (*Number Properties*) play a minor role in solving the problem.

> A carnival card game gives the contestant a one in three probability of successfully choosing the right card and thereby winning the game. If a contestant plays the game repeatedly, what is the minimum number of times that he must play the game so that the probability that he never loses is less than 1%?

Problems with minor additional content areas, such as this one, are generally easier to solve than hybrids that blend topics together in an *unusual, fundamental and clever* way. The best hybrids are one of a kind. You will have to bring your A-game to solve them.

But solve them you can. That's why you're reading this chapter!

Identify and Sequence the Parts

When you encounter a hybrid problem, first pick out all the topics tested. Let's take a look at a relatively straightforward example, one we briefly saw earlier:

Try-It #8-1

> Set S contains all integers between 6 and 20, inclusive, and Set T contains all multiples of 4 between 8 and 24, inclusive. What fraction of the integers in Set S are NOT in Set T?
>
> (A) 1/2   (B) 2/3   (C) 5/7   (D) 11/15   (E) 4/5

In this problem, you are given information about integers and multiples *within various ranges*. Thus, you'll have to draw on your knowledge of *Consecutive Integers & Multiples*.

The problem also describes these integers as *sets* and asks you which elements are in one set but not the other. So you will also need to use *Overlapping Sets* techniques. Finally, we'll take a quick *Ratio* to compute a *Fraction* (we'll leave those out as separate topics). The really important topics are these:

Identify:

Now that you have identified the necessary content areas to solve the problem, you should figure out the right *order* in which to deal with those areas. Which do you tackle first, and why?

In this case, if we were starting at the logical beginning, we would first use *Consecutive Integers & Multiples* techniques to compute the number of elements in Set S and Set T. From there, we would apply *Overlapping Sets* techniques to count the elements in Set T but not in Set S.

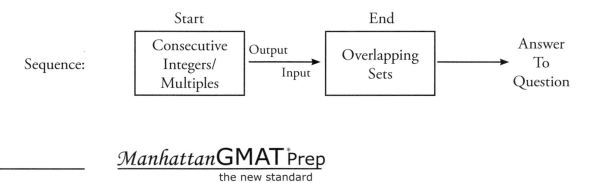

The output of Step 1 becomes the input to Step 2. In this case, the output of Step 1 will be a count of the number of integers in each set. These counts will become the input to the *Overlapping Sets* calculation in Step 2.

The good news is that we can solve this problem (and, indeed, most hybrid problems) by starting either at the beginning or at the end! Start with whichever content area you feel more comfortable with. As your work progresses, new clues will emerge that should help you figure out how to tackle other steps.

Where to Start?

Starting at the Beginning

As you contemplate the logical order of steps, you might feel less confident with the second stage than with the first. If so, go ahead and start at the beginning. Just ask yourself very clearly, "What *intermediate result* will I get once I'm finished with the first part of the problem?"

In the example problem, you can start with *Consecutive Integers & Multiples*. The output will be the number of elements in each set.

> # of elements in Set S (Consecutive Integers from 6 to 20): $20 - 6 + 1 = 15$
> # of elements in Set T (Multiples of 4 from 8 to 24): $(24 - 8) \div 4 + 1 = 5$

The *intermediate result* of applying this step is that we know the number of elements in Set S and Set T. This should help trigger our awareness of the next step: computing the number of elements that are in one set but not the other. Also note from these calculations that we can at least infer that the denominator in the correct answer will be 15, the number of elements in Set S. Even if we fail to complete the second part of the problem, we should at least pick an answer choice that has 15, or some factor of 15, as the denominator. So we can eliminate choices A and C now.)

Next, we need to calculate the number of elements in Set S that are NOT in Set T. We can plug the outputs from the first step into the *Double-Set Matrix* used to solve *Overlapping Sets* problems.

In this case, the circled cell represents the desired output—elements of Set S that are not elements in Set T.

		Element of Set S?		
		Yes	No	Total
Element of Set T?	Yes	4	1	5
	No	(11)		
	Total	15		

Using this matrix, we can compute the desired output by filling in either blank in the top row. It is easiest to note that of all of the elements of Set T, only one element (24) is NOT in Set S. Therefore, the double-set matrix can be updated, and the desired output can be computed easily.

The correct answer is D: 11 out of 15 elements, or 11/15 of the elements in Set S.

Notice that we could have directly enumerated and counted these 11 elements, but doing so is unnecessary and potentially cumbersome. Such a method would have been impractical if the sets were much larger.

Starting at the End

You might decide that it is easier to start at the end and work backwards. That's fine. Just ask yourself, "What information do I need to have as a *last step* before arriving at a solution to the question?"

In that case, the best strategy is to work through the final part of the problem as well as you can, with the hope that after that work is completed, you'll have a better sense of how to proceed on the earlier part of the problem.

In this example, we might first realize that the question involves using *Overlapping Sets* concepts. This should make us realize, "the *last step* will be to have a double-set matrix partially filled in—then I'll use the fact that the rows and columns must add up to calculate the answer." We may thus decide to write the double-set matrix first, in the hope that it triggers a thought process as to how to compute some of the values in the double-set matrix.

		Element of Set S?		
		Yes	No	Total
Element of Set T?	Yes			
	No			
	Total			

Laying out this grid might help us realize that we need to compute the number of elements in each of the sets. Any partial information about elements in one set but not the other would then enable us to solve the problem.

Perhaps we could then infer that there's only one element (24) in Set T that's not in Set S. We can then apply *Consecutive Integers & Multiples* techniques to calculate the number of elements in each set. At worst, we could use brute force to list and count the items in each set.

		Element of Set S?		
		Yes	No	Total
Element of Set T?	Yes		1	
	No			
	Total			

Plugging the number of elements in Set S and Set T enables us to solve the problem. Once again, the correct answer is D: 11/15.

Let's look at another example.

Try-It #8-2

> Set S contains 100 consecutive integers. If the range of the negative elements of Set S equals 80, what is the average (arithmetic mean) of the positive numbers in the set?

In this problem, information is given about the *range* of numbers in a set. Thus, knowing how to work with *Statistics* techniques will be important in solving the problem.

Additionally, the question talks about consecutive integers. Solving this problem will thus also require using *Consecutive Integers* techniques—namely, counting consecutive integers and computing their average. (Here, we might get into a semantic debate. General techniques for dealing with averages are covered in the Statistics chapter of the *Word Translations* Strategy Guide. However, the formula for the average of consecutive

integers, $\dfrac{First + Last}{2}$, is unique to consecutive integers and therefore considered part of the *Consecutive Integers* topic for this problem.)

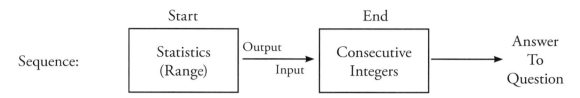

The output of Step 1 will be the highest and lowest negative numbers in the set of consecutive integers. This will act as an input to the formulas for computing the largest and smallest positive integers in the set, and subsequently the average of the positive integers in the set, in Step 2.

If we start with Step 1, we first need to determine what set of consecutive negative integers will result in a range of 80. Range is defined as the difference between the highest and lowest numbers in a set:

High − Low = Range

The high number among the negative terms is the largest negative integer, −1:

$$-1 - Low = 80$$
$$-Low = 80 + 1$$
$$Low = -81$$

Therefore the lowest number in Set A is −81. This *intermediate result* is the input to Step 2. We can plug this number into the formula for counting consecutive integers. In this case, −81 is the smallest or "First" element in the set:

$$Last - First + 1 = Count$$
$$Last - (-81) + 1 = 100$$
$$Last + 82 = 100$$
$$Last = 18$$

Therefore, the highest or "Last" number in Set A is 18.

Finally, we can calculate the average of the *positive* terms in the set using 1 as the smallest ("First Pos") positive integer and 18 as the largest ("Last Pos") positive integer:

$$Average\ of\ Pos = \dfrac{Last\ Pos + First\ Pos}{2} = \dfrac{18 + 1}{2} = \dfrac{19}{2} = 9.5$$

This is our answer.

If instead we decided to start with Step 2, we would write the formula for the average of consecutive integers first, focusing on the positive integers:

$$\text{Average of Pos} = \frac{\text{Last Pos} + \text{First Pos}}{2}$$

We could reason that the two unknowns we need to solve for are the largest positive integer ("Last Pos") and the smallest positive integer ("First Pos"), because the question asks only about the *positive* integers in the set.

Some of the integers in Set A are negative and some are positive, so clearly the smallest positive integer will be 1. Therefore, we only need to figure out what the largest integer in the set will be. This is the information needed in the *last step* of solving the problem.

In order to calculate this number, we may now realize that we need to apply the definition of range:

$$High - Low = Range$$

We know that the largest negative integer (the "High" number) is −1:

$$-1 - \text{Low} = 80$$
$$-\text{Low} = 80 + 1$$
$$\text{Low} = -81$$

Therefore the lowest number in the set is −81, which we can plug into the formula for counting Consecutive Integers, using −81 as the "First" number:

$$\text{Last} - \text{First} + 1 = \text{Count}$$
$$\text{Last} - (-81) + 1 = 100$$
$$\text{Last} + 82 = 100$$
$$\text{Last} = 18$$

Therefore, the highest number in the set is 18.

Finally, we can plug 18 into the average formula from earlier:

$$\text{Average of Pos} = \frac{\text{Last Pos} + \text{First Pos}}{2} = \frac{18 + 1}{2} = \frac{19}{2} = 9.5$$

Whether we start solving this problem from the beginning or from the end, the first work we do sheds light on everything else we need. Study how the steps hook together: the output of one step becomes the input to another. These are the "turns" you have to make in solving any hybrid problem. Often, a number that plays one role in a particular formula or calculation plays a completely different role in the next step.

Minor Hybrids

In minor hybrid problems, one of the following conditions applies:

- The content areas in the problem are closely related. For instance, they are covered in the same Manhattan GMAT Strategy Guide, such as Quadratic Equations and Inequalities *(EIVs)*, or Probability and Combinatorics *(Word Translations)*.
- One of the content areas is simply a low-level disguise or some other minor feature.

These problems are easier to solve than major hybrids. However, you will still benefit greatly from paying close attention to the turns as you move through the stages of solution.

Try-It #8-3

If a and b are consecutive positive integers, and $ab = 30x$, is x an integer?

(1) a^2 is divisible by 25.
(2) 63 is a factor of b^2.

This problem tests your skill with both *Divisibility & Primes* and *Consecutive Integers*. These topics are closely related—both are discussed in the *Number Properties* Strategy Guide. Moreover, consecutive integers concepts often lend themselves well to questions about divisibility.

First, let's rephrase the wording of this question into something easier to handle. We can isolate x by rewriting the given equation as follows:

$$x = \frac{ab}{30}$$

In order for x to be an integer, ab must be divisible by 30. To be divisible by 30, a number must have 2, 3, and 5 as prime factors. Thus the question becomes: Does ab have 2, 3, and 5 as prime factors?

Next, we can use a concept from consecutive integers: we know from the question that a and b are consecutive positive integers. Thus, either a or b is an even number, which means that the product ab is automatically divisible by 2. Since we know that 2 is a prime factor of ab, the question can be further simplified: **Does the product ab have 3 and 5 as prime factors?**

(1) INSUFFICIENT: Statement (1) tells us that 25 is a factor of a^2, meaning that 5 and 5 are prime factors of a^2. We can deduce that 5 must be a factor of a itself. Knowing that 5 is a prime factor of a tells us that 5 is a factor of ab, but we don't know anything about whether 3 is a factor.

(2) INSUFFICIENT: Statement (2) tells us that 63 is a factor of b^2 which means that 3, 3, and 7 are prime factors of b^2 ($3 \times 3 \times 7 = 63$). We can deduce from this that b has prime factors of 3 and 7. Knowing that 3 is a prime factor of b tells us that 3 is a factor of ab, but we don't know anything about whether 5 is a factor.

(1) AND (2) SUFFICIENT: If we combine both statements, we know that a is divisible by 5 and b is divisible by 3. This is sufficient information to answer our rephrased question.

The correct answer is C.

Notice that we never did figure out exactly what consecutive integers a and b were—we didn't need to. Also notice a potential trap in this problem—assuming that $a < b$ because of the way that the question is phrased. This is not a fatal assumption to make in this case, but if you realize that a and b can come in *either* order, then it's easier to create an accurate list of different scenarios for a and b.

Try-It #8-4

> A carnival card game gives the contestant a one in three probability of successfully choosing the right card and thereby winning the game. If a contestant plays the game repeatedly, what is the minimum number of times that he must play the game so that the probability that he never loses is less than 1%?

This problem tests primarily on *Probability* theory. In addition, *Exponents* are needed to represent the impact of playing multiple games on the probability of the outcomes. The probabilities are given in fractions, yet the question is asked in terms of percents, so *FDP Connections* are relevant.

Finally, the question is phrased in terms of an inequality, so *Inequalities* come into play. However, all the secondary issues can be resolved relatively easily. Therefore, we can consider this question a minor hybrid problem, in which one of the content areas (probability) is much more important than the others.

"The probability that he never loses" can be rephrased as "the probability that he always wins." This probability can be expressed as $(1/3)^n$, where 1/3 is the chance of winning on a single play and n is the number of times the contestant plays.

Let's track it in a chart:

Number of Plays	P(all wins) = $(1/3)^n$	Approx. equivalent
1	1/3	$0.33 = 33\%$
2	1/9	$0.11 = 11\%$
3	1/27	$4/100 = 0.04 = 4\%$
4	1/81	$1/80 = 1.25/100 = 1.25\%$
5	1/243	$1/250 = 0.4/100 = 0.4\% < 1\%$

We might also have noticed that only the denominator in the probabilities mattered, as the numerator was always 1. To have a probability of less than 1%, the fractional probability must be "1 over something greater than 100." In order for $3^n > 100$, n must be at least 5.

The correct answer is 5.

Conserving Time

Because hybrids contain multiple steps with twists and turns, you must complete each step quickly to finish the problem in under 2 minutes. Don't underestimate how much time it takes to mull over how the different parts fit together and to transition from one line of thinking to another.

All in all, hybrid problems can take much longer than normal problems if you are not careful. Therefore, when solving a hybrid problem, work efficiently through each step of the problem so that you minimize the risk of falling behind on time.

If it turns out that you are indeed running short on time, be ready to bail out partway. For instance, you might be able to eliminate some choices using the work you've already completed. Let's look one last time at a problem discussed earlier in this chapter:

> Set S contains all integers between 6 and 20, inclusive, and Set T contains all multiples of 4 between 8 and 24, inclusive. What fraction of the integers in Set S are NOT in Set T?
>
> (A) 1/2   (B) 2/3   (C) 5/7   (D) 11/15   (E) 4/5

If you were only able to calculate the number of elements in Set S (15) and Set T (5), you could still eliminate answer choices A and C, because the denominator of the correct fraction must be 15 (or a factor of 15).

Also think back to Chapters 2 and 4, on Strategies and Guessing Tactics. Be ready to try those tactics out on hybrids that take excessively long. Don't be too proud! A single crazy hybrid problem can't hurt your performance very much if you get it wrong quickly and move on confidently. On the other hand, if you waste a lot of time and energy on the problem and become angry or upset, then even if you get it right, you'll have won a battle to lose the war.

In-Action Problem Set

Solve the following problems and identify the topics being tested. Consider on your own: Is the question a major hybrid or a minor hybrid? If it is a minor hybrid, is that because the two topics are closely related, or because one of the topics is relatively unimportant?

Additionally, if relevant, determine the order of the topics in the solution process. Did you solve the problem by starting at the end or at the beginning?

1. The average of 6 numbers in a set is equal to 0. What is the number of positive numbers in the set minus the number of negative numbers in the set?

> (1) Each of the positive numbers in the set equals 10.
> (2) Each of the negative numbers in the set equals −5.

2. Simplify: $\dfrac{2^2 + 2^2 + 2^3 + 2^4}{\left(\sqrt{5} + \sqrt{3}\right)\left(\sqrt{5} - \sqrt{3}\right)}$.

3. If a, b, and c are positive, is $a > b$?

> (1) $\dfrac{a}{b+c} > \dfrac{b}{a+c}$
> (2) $b + c < a$

4. If c is randomly chosen from the integers 20 to 99, inclusive, what is the probability that $c^3 - c$ is divisible by 12?

5. If x and y are positive integers greater than 1 such that $x - y$ and x/y are both even integers, which of the following numbers must be non-prime integers?

> I. x
> II. $x + y$
> III. y/x

> (A) I only   (B) II only   (C) III only   (D) I and II   (E) I, II and III

6. Two fair die with sides numbered 1 to 6 are tossed. What is the probability that the sum of the exposed faces on the die is a prime number?

7. The remainder when 120 is divided by single-digit integer m is positive, as is the remainder when 120 is divided by single-digit integer n. If $m > n$, what is the remainder when 120 is divided by $m - n$?

8. A circular microchip with a radius of 2.5 centimeters is manufactured following a blueprint scaled such that a measurement of 1 centimeter on the blueprint corresponds to a measurement of 0.05 millimeters on the microchip. What is the area of the blueprint, in square centimeters? (1 centimeter = 10 millimeters)

9. Eight consecutive integers are selected from the integers 1 to 50, inclusive. What is the sum of the remainders when each of the integers is divided by *x*?

 (1) The remainder when the largest of the consecutive integers is divided by *x* is 0.
 (2) The remainder when the second largest of the consecutive integers is divided by *x* is 1.

10. The price of an automobile decreased *m* percent between 2010 and 2011 and then increased *n* percent between 2011 and 2012. Was the price of the automobile lower in 2010 than in 2012?

 (1) $m < n$
 (2) $mn < 100n - 100m$

In-Action Problem Set (Solutions)

1. E: Since the average of the 6 numbers in a set is 0, the sum of the 6 numbers is 0. We also know there could be positive numbers and negative numbers in the set. Zero is not mentioned, but this does not rule it out. In order for the sum of the numbers in the set to be 0, either all the terms are 0, or there are some positives and some negatives.

(1) INSUFFICIENT: Statement 1 tells us that the set has at least one positive number, and that each positive term is 10. We should try to prove insufficiency. For instance, the set could be {−2, −2, −2, −2, −2, 10}, and the number of positive terms minus the number of negative terms would be 1 − 5 = −4. Alternatively, the set could be {−20, −20, 10, 10, 10, 10}, and the answer would be 4 − 2 = 2.

(2) INSUFFICIENT: Statement 2 tells us that the set has at least one negative number, and that each negative term is −5. Again, we should try to prove insufficiency. The set could be {−5, 1, 1, 1, 1, 1}, and the number of positive terms minus the number of negative terms would be 5 − 1 = 4. The set could be {−5, −5, −5, 2, 5, 8}, and the answer would be 3 − 3 = 0.

(1) & (2) INSUFFICIENT: The statements together suggest that the set has twice as many −5 terms as 10 terms, in order to maintain a sum of 0. If every term is negative or positive, then the set would have to be {−5, −5, −5, −5, 10, 10} and the definitive answer would be 2 − 4 = −2. However, zero terms are possible, so the set could be {−5, −5, 0, 0, 0, 10} and an alternative answer would be 1 − 2 = −1.

2. 16: Factor a 2^2 out of the numerator, and distribute the denominator (which becomes the difference of squares).

$$\frac{2^2\left(1+1+2+2^2\right)}{\left[\left(\sqrt{5}\right)^2-\left(\sqrt{3}\right)^2\right]}=\frac{2^2\left(1+1+2+2^2\right)}{5-3}$$

$$=\frac{4(8)}{2}$$

$$=16$$

3. D: One way to rephrase the question "Is $a > b$?" is this way: "Is $a - b$ positive?"

(2) SUFFICIENT. Statement (2) is the simpler statement, so we should start there. If a, b, and c are all positive, then we know that $a > b +$ positive. Therefore, a must be *even larger* than b. We could also prove this fact by testing three basic cases.

Case	Statement 2: $b + c < a$	Is this case possible according to (2)?
$a > b$	$b +$ positive $<$ number greater than b	Possible
$a = b$	$b + c < b$	Impossible, since $c \neq 0$
$a < b$	$b + c <$ number less than b	Impossible, since c is not negative

Only the $a > b$ case is possible, so the answer is a definite Yes.

*Manhattan***GMAT***Prep
the new standard

(1) SUFFICIENT. Statement (1) can be cross-multiplied without flipping the inequality sign, since we know the denominators are positive.

$a(a + c) > b(b + c)$

$a^2 + ac > b^2 + bc$

$a^2 + ac - b^2 - bc > 0$

$a^2 - b^2 + ac - bc > 0$ (Group similar terms to make a precede b, as it does in $a - b$)

$[a^2 - b^2] + [ac - bc] > 0$ (Note the Quadratic Template)

$(a - b)(a + b) + c(a - b) > 0$

$(a - b)[(a + b) + c] > 0$ (Factor out $a - b$)

$a + b + c$ is positive, because all three additive terms are positive. So, $(a - b)(\text{positive}) > 0$. By Number Properties sign rules, $(a - b)$ must also be positive in order for the product to be greater than 0. Therefore, $a > b$.

This algebra is very tough; it is hard to see where to begin or what series of manipulations will be productive. If you did not see this, you could try the three cases to see which are allowed by Statement 1. Note: LT = less than and GT = greater than. GTb means "a number greater than b."

Case	Statement 1: $a/(b + c) > b/(a + c)$	Is this case possible according to (1)?
$a > b$	GTb/$(b + c) > b$/GT$(b + c)$	Possible. The left is greater than the right.
$a = b$	b/$(b + c) > b$/$(b + c)$	Impossible; the two expressions are equal.
$a < b$	LTb/$(b + c) > b$/LT$(b + c)$	Impossible; the left side is actually less than the right side, not greater than as (1) requires.

The correct answer is D.

4. 3/4: The words "divisible" and "probability" are used, so this question is about *Divisibility & Primes* (Manhattan GMAT *Number Properties* Strategy Guide) and *Probability* (Manhattan GMAT *Word Translations* Strategy Guide).

Probability is (favorable outcomes)/(total # of possibilities). There are $99 - 20 + 1 = 80$ possible values for c, so the unknown is how many of these c values yield a $c^3 - c$ that is divisible by 12.

The prime factorization of 12 is $2 \times 2 \times 3$. There are several ways of thinking about this: numbers are divisible by 12 if they are divisible by 3 and by 2 twice, or if they are multiples of both 4 and 3, or if half of the number is an even multiple of 3, etc.

The expression involving c can be factored.

$c^3 - c = c(c^2 - 1) = c(c - 1)(c + 1)$

These are consecutive integers. It may help to put them in increasing order: $(c - 1)c(c + 1)$. Thus, this question has a lot to do with *Consecutive Integers* (Manhattan GMAT Number Properties Strategy Guide), and not only because the integers 20 to 99 themselves are consecutive.

In any set of three consecutive integers, a multiple of 3 will be included. Thus, $(c - 1)c(c + 1)$ is always divisible by 3 for any integer c. This takes care of part of the 12. So the question simply becomes "How many of the possible $(c - 1)c(c + 1)$ values are divisible by 4?" Since the prime factors of 4 are 2's, it makes sense to think in terms of *Odds and Evens* (Manhattan GMAT *Number Properties* Strategy Guide).

$(c - 1)c(c + 1)$ could be (E)(O)(E), which is definitely divisible by 4, because the two evens would each provide at least one separate factor of 2. Thus, $c^3 - c$ is divisible by 12 whenever c is odd, which are the cases $c = 21, 23, 25, \ldots, 95, 97, 99$. That's $((99 - 21)/2) + 1 = (78/2) + 1 = 40$ possibilities.

Alternatively, $(c - 1)c(c + 1)$ could be (O)(E)(O), which will only be divisible by 4 when the even term itself is a multiple of 4. Thus, $c^3 - c$ is also divisible by 12 whenever c is a multiple of 4, which are the cases $c = 20, 24, 28, \ldots, 92, 96$. That's $((96 - 20)/4) + 1 = (76/4) + 1 = 20$ possibilities.

The probability is thus $(40 + 20)/80 = 60/80 = 3/4$.

5. D: x cannot equal y, as that would make $x/y = 1 \neq$ even. So either $x > y$ or $y > x$.

x and y are both positive, and x/y is an integer, so $x > y$.

If $x - y$ is even, either x and y are both even, or they are both odd.

Since $x/y =$ an even integer, $x = y \times$ an even integer.

Odd $\neq$ Odd $\times$ an even integer, so x and y can't be odd.

Even = Even $\times$ an even integer, so x and y must be even.

I. TRUE. x and y are both even, and x/y is an even integer. The smallest value of x is 4, when y is 2, and $x/y = 4/2 = 2$. No even number greater than 2 is prime, so x can't be prime.

II. TRUE. x and y are each positive even numbers and $x \neq y$. Thus, $x + y$ is even, and the smallest possible value of $x + y = 4 + 2 = 6$. All even numbers greater than or equal to 6 are non-prime.

III. FALSE. It could be that $x = 4$ and $y = 2$, so $y/x = 1/2$, which is technically non-prime, but is not an integer. In fact, if $x/y =$ an even integer, $y/x = 1/$an even integer = positive fraction.

The correct answer is D.

6. 5/12: Let's first think about the prime numbers less than 12, the maximum sum of the numbers on the dice. These primes are 2, 3, 5, 7, 11.

The probability of rolling 2, 3, 5, 7, or 11 = the number of ways to roll any of these sums, divided by the total number of possible rolls. The total number of possible die rolls is $6 \times 6 = 36$.

Sum of 2 can happen 1 way: 1 + 1

Sum of 3 can happen 2 ways: 1 + 2 or 2 + 1

Sum of 5 can happen 4 ways: 1 + 4, 2 + 3, 3 + 2, 4 + 1

Sum of 7 can happen 6 ways: 1 + 6, 2 + 5, 3 + 4, 4 + 3, 5 + 2, 6 + 1

Sum of 11 can happen 2 ways: 5 + 6, 6 + 5

That's a total of 1 + 2 + 4 + 6 + 2 = 15 ways to roll a prime sum.

Thus, the probability is 15/36 = 5/12.

7. 0: Since the remainder is defined as what is left over after one number is divided by another, it makes sense that the leftover amount would be positive. So why is this information provided, if the remainder is "automatically" positive? Because there is a third possibility: that the remainder is 0! So when we are told here that the remainder when 120 is divided by m is positive, we are really being told that 120/m does not have a remainder of 0. In other words, 120 is not divisible by m, or m is not a factor of 120. Similarly, n is not a factor of 120.

Another constraint on both m and n is that they are single-digit positive integers. So m and n are integers between 1 and 9, inclusive, that are *not* factors of 120. Only two such possibilities exist: 7 and 9.

Since $m > n$, $m = 9$ and $n = 7$. Thus, $m - n = 2$, and the remainder when 120 is divided by 2 is 0.

8. 250,000π: Microchip radius = (2.5 cm)(10 mm/cm) = 25 mm

Blueprint radius = 1 cm per every 0.05 mm on the microchip

$\qquad$ = 10 mm per every 0.05 mm on the microchip

$\qquad$ = (10 mm/0.05 mm on microchip)(25mm on microchip)

$\qquad$ = (10 mm/0.05)(25)

$\qquad$ = (1000 mm/5)(25)

$\qquad$ = (1000 mm)(5)

$\qquad$ = 5,000 mm

$\qquad$ = (5,000 mm)(cm/10 mm)

$\qquad$ = 500 cm

Blueprint area = $\pi \times r^2$

$\qquad$ = $\pi \times$ (500 cm)^2

$\qquad$ = 250,000π cm^2

9. C: Recall that remainders follow a repeating pattern when x is divided into consecutive integers. For example, when the integers 1 to 50 are divided by $x = 4$, the remainders form a [1, 2, 3, 0] repeating pattern,

*Manhattan*GMAT Prep
the new standard

and the sum of any consecutive 8 of these remainders would be $2 \times [1 + 2 + 3 + 0] = 12$. However, when the integers 1 to 50 are divided by $x = 3$, the remainders are a [1, 2, 0] repeating pattern, so the sum of any consecutive 8 of these remainders would depend on which term of the pattern was the starting term.

(1) INSUFFICIENT: Statement (1) simply indicates that the largest of the eight consecutive integers is divisible by x. It does not indicate the value of x, which determines the remainder pattern and, indirectly, the sum of the remainders.

(2) INSUFFICIENT: Statement 2 simply indicates that the *third* largest of the eight consecutive integers is divisible by x. It does not indicate the value of x, which determines the remainder pattern and, indirectly, the sum of the remainders.

(1) & (2) SUFFICIENT: Together, the statements indicate that Largest Term and (Largest Term − 2) are each divisible by x. Alternatively, the statements indicate a remainder pattern of [1,0] repeating. Thus, x must be 2, and the sum of the remainders is $4 \times [1 + 0] = 4$.

10. B: We can use a smart number of 100 as our starting point, to make one of the calculations more manageable.

Year	Price change (from previous year)	Price
2010	n/a	100
2011	$-m\% = -(m/100)$	$100 - m$
2012	$+n\% = +(n/100)$	$(100 - m) + (n/100)(100 - m)$

The question asks:

2010 price < 2012 price?

$100 < (100 - m) + (n/100)(100 - m)$?

$100 < 100 - m + n - mn/100$?

$0 < n - m - mn/100$?

$0 < 100n - 100m - mn$?

$mn < 100n - 100m$?

Glancing at the form of the statements can help determine the direction this rephrase should take.

(2) SUFFICIENT. Statement 2 answers this rephrase with a definite Yes.

(1) INSUFFICIENT. Statement 1 is less clear. If $n = 3$ and $m = 1$, then $(1)(3) < 300 - 100$ and the answer is Yes. If $n = 20$ and $m = 19$, then $(19)(20) > 2000-1900$ and the answer is No.

The answer is B.

## PART III

Chapter 9
of
ADVANCED GMAT QUANT

WORKOUT SETS

In This Chapter . . .

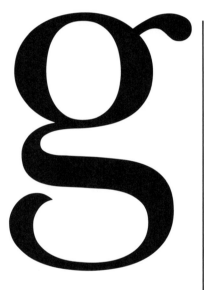

• Workout Sets 1–15

Workout Set 1

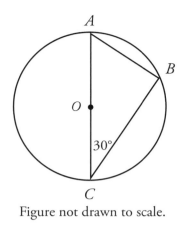

Figure not drawn to scale.

1. The circle with center O has a circumference of $6\pi\sqrt{3}$. If AC is a diameter of the circle, what is the length of line segment BC?

    (A) $\dfrac{3}{\sqrt{2}}$

    (B) 3

    (C) $3\sqrt{3}$

    (D) 9

    (E) $9\sqrt{3}$

2. A batch of widgets costs $p + 15$ dollars for a company to produce and each batch sells for $p(9 - p)$ dollars. For which of the following values of p does the company make a profit?

    (A) 3
    (B) 4
    (C) 5
    (D) 6
    (E) 7

3. If K is the sum of the reciprocals of the consecutive integers from 41 to 60 inclusive, which of the following is less than K?

    I.   1/4
    II. 1/3
    III. 1/2

    (A) None
    (B) I only
    (C) II only
    (D) I and II
    (E) I, II, and III

4. Triplets Adam, Bruce, and Charlie enter a triathlon. There are nine competitors in the triathlon. If every competitor has an equal chance of winning, and three medals will be awarded, what is the probability that at least two of the triplets will win a medal?

    (A) 3/14
    (B) 19/84
    (C) 11/42
    (D) 15/28
    (E)   3/4

5. The expression $\sqrt{2+\sqrt{2+\sqrt{2+\sqrt{2+\sqrt{2+\ldots}}}}}$ extends to an infinite number of roots. Which of the following choices most closely approximates the value of this expression?

    (A) $\sqrt{3}$
    (B) 2
    (C) $1+\sqrt{2}$
    (D) $1+\sqrt{3}$
    (E) $2\sqrt{3}$

6. Half an hour after Car A started traveling from Newtown to Oldtown, a distance of 62 miles, Car B started traveling along the same road from Oldtown to Newtown. The cars met each other on the road 15 minutes after Car B started its trip. If Car A traveled at a constant rate that was 8 miles per hour greater than Car B's constant rate, how many miles had Car B driven when they met?

    (A) 14
    (B) 12
    (C) 10
    (D) 9
    (E) 8

7. If $x = 2^b - (8^8 + 8^6)$, for which of the following b values is x closest to zero?

   (A) 20
   (B) 24
   (C) 25
   (D) 30
   (E) 42

8. If $k > 1$, which of the following must be equal to $\dfrac{2}{\sqrt{k+1} + \sqrt{k-1}}$?

   (A) 2

   (B) $2\sqrt{2k}$

   (C) $2\sqrt{k+1} + \sqrt{k-1}$

   (D) $\dfrac{\sqrt{k+1}}{\sqrt{k-1}}$

   (E) $\sqrt{k+1} - \sqrt{k-1}$

9. Bank account A contains exactly x dollars, an amount that will decrease by 10% each month for the next two months. Bank account B contains exactly y dollars, an amount that will increase by 20% each month for the next two months. If A and B contain the same amount at the end of two months, what is the ratio of $\sqrt{x}$ to $\sqrt{y}$?

   (A) $4 : 3$
   (B) $3 : 2$
   (C) $16 : 9$
   (D) $2 : 1$
   (E) $9 : 4$

10. Let a be the sum of x consecutive positive integers. Let b be the sum of y consecutive positive integers. For which of the following values of x and y is it NOT possible that $a = b$?

    (A) $x = 2; y = 6$
    (B) $x = 3; y = 6$
    (C) $x = 6; y = 4$
    (D) $x = 6; y = 7$
    (E) $x = 7; y = 5$

Workout Set 2

11. If $a \neq b$, is $\dfrac{1}{a-b} > ab$?

    (1) $|a| > |b|$
    (2) $a < b$

12. $m = 4n + 9$, where n is a positive integer. What is the greatest common factor of m and n?

    (1) $m = 9s$, where s is a positive integer.
    (2) $n = 4t$, where t is a positive integer.

13. A museum sold 30 tickets on Saturday. Some of the tickets sold were $10 general exhibit tickets and the rest were $70 special exhibit tickets. How many general exhibit tickets did the museum sell on Saturday?

    (1) The museum's total revenue from ticket sales on Saturday was greater than $1,570 and less than $1,670.

    (2) The museum sold more than 20, but fewer than 25, special exhibit tickets on Saturday.

14. If x and y are integers, is $x^y = y^x$?

    (1) $x - y = 2$
    (2) $xy = 8$

15. If $ab^3c^4 > 0$, is $a^3bc^5 > 0$?

    (1) $b > 0$
    (2) $c > 0$

16. What is the perimeter of isosceles triangle ABC?

    (1) The length of side AB is 9.
    (2) The length of side BC is 4.

17. If x, y, and z are integers and $2^x 5^y z = 6.4 \times 10^6$, what is the value of xy?

    (1) $z = 20$
    (2) $x = 9$

18. If x and y are positive integers and $1 + x + y + xy = 21$, what is the value of x?

    (1) $y > 3$
    (2) $y = 6$

19. If j and k are positive integers such that $k > j$, what is the value of the remainder when k is divided by j?

    (1) There exists a positive integer m such that $k = jm + 5$.
    (2) $j > 5$

20. If x and y are positive integers such that $x^2 + y^3$ is a prime number less than 18, what is the value of y?

    (1) $x^2 + y^2$ is a prime number.
    (2) $x^2 - y^2$ is a prime number.

Workout Set 3

21.　Sequence S is defined as $S_n = (S_{n-1} + 1) + \dfrac{1}{(S_{n-1} + 1)}$ for all $n > 1$. If $S_1 = 100$, then which of the following must be true of Q, the sum of the first 16 terms of S?

(A) $1{,}600 \le Q \le 1{,}650$
(B) $1{,}650 \le Q \le 1{,}700$
(C) $1{,}700 \le Q \le 1{,}750$
(D) $1{,}750 \le Q \le 1{,}800$
(E) $1{,}800 \le Q \le 1{,}850$

22.　If x and y are positive integers, what is the remainder when x^y is divided by 10?

(1) $x = 26$
(2) $y^x = 1$

23.　For all positive integers n, the sequence A_n is defined by the following relationship:

$$A_n = \frac{n-1}{n!}$$

What is the sum of all the terms in the sequence from A_1 through A_{10}, inclusive?

(A) $\dfrac{9! + 1}{10!}$

(B) $\dfrac{9(9!)}{10!}$

(C) $\dfrac{10! - 1}{10!}$

(D) $\dfrac{10!}{10! + 1}$

(E) $\dfrac{10(10!)}{11!}$

24.　If x and y are positive integers and $n = 5^x + 7^{y+3}$, what is the units digit of n?

(1) $y = 2x - 16$
(2) y is divisible by 4.

25. Which of the following integers is the square of an integer?

    (A) 73,410,624
    (B) 63,398,748
    (C) 54,113,892
    (D) 42,785,337
    (E) 31,298,793

26. A certain sequence is defined by the following rule: $S_n = k(S_{n-1})$, where k is a constant. If $S_1 = 64$ and $S_{25} = 192$, what is the value of S_9?

    (A) $\sqrt{2}$

    (B) $\sqrt{3}$

    (C) $64\sqrt{3}$

    (D) $64\sqrt[3]{3}$

    (E) $64\sqrt[24]{3}$

27. n is a positive integer greater than 2. If $y = 9^0 + 9^1 + 9^2 + \ldots + 9^n$, what is the remainder when y is divided by 5?

    (1) n is divisible by 3.
    (2) n is odd.

28. In the sequence S, each term after the first is twice the previous term. If the first term of sequence S is 3, what is the sum of the 14th, 15th, and 16th terms in sequence S?

    (A) $3(2^{16})$
    (B) $9(2^{15})$
    (C) $21(2^{14})$
    (D) $9(2^{14})$
    (E) $21(2^{13})$

29. n is an integer such that $n \geq 0$. For $n > 0$, the sequence t_n is defined as $t_n = t_{n-1} + n$. If $t_0 = 3$, is t_n even?

    (1) $n + 1$ is divisible by 3
    (2) $n - 1$ is divisible by 4

30. What is the sum of the cubes of the first ten positive integers?

    (A) 10^3
    (B) 45^2
    (C) 55^2
    (D) 100^2
    (E) 100^3

Workout Set 4

31. $\dfrac{12!}{3^4(5!)2^6} =$

    (A) 2,210
    (B) 770
    (C) 480
    (D)   77
    (E)   35

32. $S_n = n^2 + 5n + 94$ and $K = S_6 - S_5 + S_4 - S_3 + S_2 - S_1$. What is the value of K?

    (A) 67
    (B) 50
    (C) 45
    (D) 41
    (E) 36

33. Is $xy + xy < xy$?

    (1) $\dfrac{x^2}{y} < 0$

    (2) $x^3 y^3 < (xy)^2$

34. If $y \neq x$, then $\dfrac{x^3 + (x^2 + x)(1 - y) - y}{x - y} = ?$

    (A) $(x - 1)^2 y$
    (B) $(x + 1)^2$
    (C) $(x^2 + x + 1)$
    (D) $(x^2 + x + 1)y$
    (E) $(x^2 + x + 1)(x - y)$

35. In the sequence g_n defined for all positive integer values of n, $g_1 = g_2 = 1$ and, for $n \geq 3$, $g_n = g_{n-1} + 2^{n-3}$. If the function $\psi(g_i)$ equals the sum of the terms $g_1, g_2, \ldots, g_i$, what is $\dfrac{\psi(g_{16})}{\psi(g_{15})}$?

    (A) g_3
    (B) g_8
    (C) $\psi(g_8)$
    (D) $\psi(g_{16}) - \psi(g_{15})$
    (E) $\dfrac{g_{16}}{2}$

the new standard

36. If $3^k + 3^k = (3^9)^{3^{3^9}} - 3^k$, then what is the value of k?

(A) $\dfrac{11}{3}$

(B) $\dfrac{11}{2}$

(C) 242

(D) 3^{10}

(E) $3^{11} - 1$

37. If a, b, c, and d are positive integers, what is the value of $(a + b)(c + d)$?

(1) $4a! = b!$
(2) $5c! = d!$

38. If k is an integer and $\dfrac{33!}{22!}$ is divisible by 6^k, what is the maximum possible value of k?

(A) 3
(B) 4
(C) 5
(D) 6
(E) 7

39. The sequence S is defined as $s_n = (n + 1)!$ for all integers $n \geq 1$. For example, $s_3 = 4! = (4)(3)(2)(1)$. Which of the following is equivalent to the difference between s_{100} and s_{99}?

(A) 101!
(B) 100!
(C) $99^2(98!)$
(D) $100^2(99!)$
(E) $(100!)^2$

40. If $p = \dfrac{9^7 - 9^5}{7^5 + 7^3}$ and $q = \dfrac{9^5}{7^3}$, what is the value of $\dfrac{q}{p}$?

(A) $2\!/\!5$

(B) $1\!/\!2$

(C) $5\!/\!8$

(D) $8\!/\!5$

(E) $5\!/\!2$

Workout Set 5

41. If x and y are positive integers, what is the value of x/y?

    (1) $x^2 = 2xy - y^2$
    (2) $2xy = 8$

42. What is the remainder when $(47)(49)$ is divided by 8?

    (A) 1
    (B) 3
    (C) 4
    (D) 5
    (E) 7

43. If $a = 4x^2 + 4xy$ and $b = 4y^2 + 4xy$, which of the following is equivalent to $x + y$?

    (A) $\sqrt{a+b}$
    (B) $2\sqrt{ab}$
    (C) $\dfrac{a+b}{\sqrt{2}}$
    (D) $2\sqrt{a} - 2\sqrt{b}$
    (E) $\dfrac{\sqrt{a+b}}{2}$

44. What is the value of $\dfrac{3^{(a+b)^2}}{3^{(a-b)^2}}$?

    (1) $a + b = 7$
    (2) $ab = 12$

45. What is the value of $\left(\sqrt{24 + 5\sqrt{23}} \right)\left(\sqrt{24 - 5\sqrt{23}} \right)$?

    (A) 48
    (B) $\sqrt{24}$
    (C) $5\sqrt{2}$
    (D) 1
    (E) $24 - 5\sqrt{23}$

46. If $a^6 - b^6 = 0$, what is the value of $a^3 + b^3$?

    (1) $a^3 - b^3 = -2$
    (2) $ab < 0$

47. x and y are positive integers such that $x > y$. If $2\sqrt{x} - 2\sqrt{y} = \dfrac{(x-y)}{b}$, which of the following is equivalent to $2b$?

    (A) $\sqrt{x} - \sqrt{y}$

    (B) $\sqrt{x} + \sqrt{y}$

    (C) $\dfrac{\sqrt{x}}{\sqrt{y}}$

    (D) $2\sqrt{xy}$

    (E) $2\sqrt{x-y}$

48. If $(x + y)^2 = 16$ and $x^2 - y^2 = 16$, what is the value of $2x^2$?

    (A)   8
    (B) 16
    (C) 18
    (D) 32
    (E) 50

49. What is the value of $38^2 + 39^2 + 40^2 + 41^2 + 42^2$?

    (A) 7,950
    (B) 7,990
    (C) 8,010
    (D) 8,050
    (E) 8,070

50. If $8xy^3 + 8x^3y = \dfrac{2x^2 y^2}{2^{-3}}$, what is the value of xy?

    (1) $y > x$
    (2) $x < 0$

Workout Set 6

51. In triangle *ABC*, side *AB* is 5 inches and side *BC* is 7 inches. What is the area of triangle *ABC*?

    (1) Angle *ABC* is 90°.
    (2) Triangle *ABC* is a right triangle.

52. Three of the four vertices of a rectangle in the *xy*-coordinate plane are (−5, 1), (−4, 4), and (8, 0). What is the fourth vertex?

    (A) (−4.5, 2.5)
    (B) (−4, 5)
    (C) (6, −2)
    (D) (7, −3)
    (E) (10, 1)

53. A math teacher has 30 cards, each of which is in the shape of a geometric figure. Half of the cards are rectangles, and a third of the cards are rhombuses. If 8 cards are squares, what is the maximum possible number of cards that are circles?

    (A) 9
    (B) 10
    (C) 11
    (D) 12
    (E) 13

54. A group of men and women gathered to compete in a marathon. Each competitor was weighed before the competition, and the average weight of the females was 120 pounds and the average weight of the males was greater than 120 pounds. What percentage of the competitors were women?

    (1) The average weight of the men was 150 pounds.
    (2) The average weight of the entire group was twice as far from the average weight of the women as it was from the average weight of the men.

55. What is the average of 12, 13, 14, 510, 520, 530, 1,115, 1,120, and 1,125?

    (A) 419
    (B) 551
    (C) 601
    (D) 620
    (E) 721

56. A set of 5 numbers has an average of 50. The largest element in the set is 5 greater than 3 times the smallest element in the set. If the median of the set equals the mean, what is the largest possible value in the set?

    (A) 85
    (B) 86
    (C) 88
    (D) 91
    (E) 92

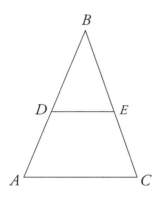

57. In the triangle above, *DE* is parallel to *AC*. What is the length of *DE*?

    (1) $AC = 14$
    (2) $BE = EC$

58. 2, 4, 5, 5, 9, *m*
    For the list of numbers above, what is the median?

    (1) The median is an integer.
    (2) $m = 8$

59. A list of 50 data points has an average (arithmetic mean) of 20 and a standard deviation of 10. Which of the following pairs of data, when added to the list, must result in a list of 52 data points with standard deviation less than 10?

    (A)   0 and 10
    (B)   0 and 20
    (C) 10 and 30
    (D) 20 and 20
    (E) 30 and 40

60. Four different children have jelly beans: Aaron has 5, Bianca has 7, Callie has 8, and Dante has 11. How many jelly beans must Dante give to Aaron to ensure that no child has more than 1 fewer jelly beans than any other child?

    (A) 2
    (B) 3
    (C) 4
    (D) 5
    (E) 6

Workout Set 7

61. A room is 480 centimeters wide and 520 centimeters long. If n identical square tiles are arranged in a grid pattern so as to cover the entire floor of the room, what is the value of n?

    (1) A whole number of tiles fit exactly along the length and width of the room, and no tiles had to be cut in order to cover the entire floor.
    (2) 12 tiles placed adjacent to one another span the width of the room.

62. A certain bakery ran a promotion: a customer can buy x donuts for the regular price of $15 total and get 3 donuts free. If the donut price per dozen during the promotion is $2 less than the normal donut price per dozen, what is x? (1 dozen = 12)

    (A) 15
    (B) 18
    (C) 21
    (D) 25
    (E) 30

63. In Smithtown, the ratio of right-handed people to left-handed people is 3 to 1 and the ratio of men to women is 3 to 2. If the number of right-handed men is maximized, then what percent of all the people in Smithtown are left-handed women?

    (A) 50%
    (B) 40%
    (C) 25%
    (D) 20%
    (E) 10%

64. The sum of the interior angle measures for any n-sided polygon equals $180(n-2)$. If Polygon A has interior angle measures that correspond to a set of consecutive integers, and if the median angle measure for Polygon A is $140°$, what is the smallest angle measure in the polygon?

    (A) 130°
    (B) 135°
    (C) 136°
    (D) 138°
    (E) 140°

65. When the positive integer x is divided by the positive integer y, the quotient is 2 and the remainder is z. When x is divided by the positive integer a, the quotient is 3 and the remainder is b. Is $z > b$?

    (1) The ratio of y to a is less than 3 to 2.
    (2) The ratio of y to a is greater than 2 to 3.

66.   If a and b are odd integers, $a \, \Delta \, b$ represents the product of all odd integers between a and b, inclusive. If y is the smallest prime factor of $(3 \, \Delta \, 47) + 2$, which of the following must be true?

(A) $y > 50$
(B) $30 \leq y \leq 50$
(C) $10 \leq y < 30$
(D) $3 \leq y < 10$
(E) $y = 2$

67.   Set S is the set of all prime integers between 0 and 20. If three numbers are chosen randomly from set S, what is the probability that the sum of these three numbers is odd?

(A) 15/56
(B) 3/8
(C) 15/28
(D) 5/8
(E) 3/4

68.   Sets A and B each consist of three terms selected from the first five prime integers. No term appears more than once within a set, but any integer may be a term in both sets. If the average of the terms in Set A is 4 and the product of the terms in Set B is divisible by 22, how many terms are shared by both sets?

(1) The product of the terms in Set B is not divisible by 5.
(2) The product of the terms in Set B is divisible by 14.

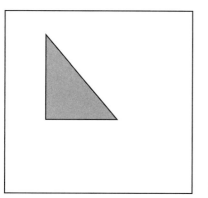

Figure not drawn to scale.

69. In the figure above, a right triangle is located entirely inside a square with side length of 6. If all three side lengths of the right triangle are integers, what fraction of the square is shaded?

(A) $\frac{1}{6}$

(B) $\frac{1}{4}$

(C) $\frac{1}{\sqrt{3}}$

(D) $\frac{\sqrt{2}}{3}$

(E) It cannot be determined.

70. All the terms in Set S are integers. Five terms in S are even, and four terms are multiples of 3. How many terms in S are even numbers that are not divisible by 3?

(1) The product of all the even terms in Set S is a multiple of 9.
(2) The integers in S are consecutive.

Workout Set 8

Energy usage (units)	11	10	8	7
Number of days	4	5	n	3

71. The table above shows daily energy usage for an office building and the number of days that amount of energy was used. If the average (arithmetic mean) daily energy usage was greater than the median daily energy usage, what is the smallest possible value for n?

    (A) 2
    (B) 3
    (C) 4
    (D) 5
    (E) 6

72. A painting crew painted 80 houses. They painted the first y houses at a rate of x houses per week. Then more painters arrived and everyone worked together to paint the remaining houses at a rate of $1.25x$ houses per week. How many weeks did it take to paint all 80 houses, in terms of x and y?

    (A) $\dfrac{320 - y}{5x}$

    (B) $\dfrac{y + 320}{5x}$

    (C) $\dfrac{5(80 - y)}{4x}$

    (D) $\dfrac{y + 400}{4x}$

    (E) $\dfrac{4y + 320}{5x}$

73. $a = x + y$ and $b = x - y$. If $a^2 = b^2$, what is the value of y?

    (1) $\sqrt{x} + \sqrt{y} > 0$
    (2) $\sqrt{x} - \sqrt{y} > 0$

74. A herd of 33 sheep is sheltered in a barn with 7 stalls, each of which is labeled with a unique letter from A to G, inclusive. Is there at least one sheep in every stall?

    (1) The ratio of the number of sheep in stall C to the number of sheep in stall E is 2 to 3.
    (2) The ratio of the number of sheep in stall E to the number of sheep in stall F is 5 to 2.

the new standard

75. If $(x \times 10^q) - (y \times 10^r) = 10^r$, where q, r, x, and y are positive integers and $q > r$, then what is the units digit of y?

    (A) 0
    (B) 1
    (C) 5
    (D) 7
    (E) 9

76. Is $\sqrt{(y-4)^2} = 4 - y$?

    (1) $|y - 3| \le 1$
    (2) $y \times |y| > 0$

77. What is the greatest prime factor of $2^{10}5^4 - 2^{13}5^2 + 2^{14}$?

    (A) 2
    (B) 3
    (C) 7
    (D) 11
    (E) 13

78. If the function $f(n)$ is defined as $f(n) = \dfrac{n}{n+1}$, for all integer values of n such that $n \ne -1$, which of the following must be true?

    I. $f(x + 1) > f(x)$
    II. $f(x) > 0$
    III. $f(x) \ne 0$

    (A) I only
    (B) II only
    (C) I and II only
    (D) I and III only
    (E) II and III only

79. If x and y are positive integers and $x + y = 3^x$, is y divisible by 6?

    (1) x is odd.
    (2) x is a multiple of 3.

80.   An (x, y) coordinate pair is to be chosen at random from the xy-plane. What is the probability that $y \geq |x|$?

      (A) 1/10
      (B) 1/8
      (C) 1/6
      (D) 1/5
      (E) 1/4

Workout Set 9

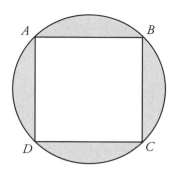

81. *ABCD* is a square inscribed in a circle with circumference $2\pi\sqrt{x}$. What is the area of the shaded region in the diagram above?

(A) $2x$
(B) $\pi x - 2x$
(C) $\pi x - x\sqrt{2}$
(D) $1 - \dfrac{2}{\pi}$
(E) $1 - \dfrac{2}{x}$

82. If $3^a + 3^{a-2} = (90)(3^b)$, what is b in terms of a?

(A) $a - 4$
(B) $a - 2$
(C) $a + 4$
(D) $3a + 2$
(E) $3a + 4$

83. What is the value of $x - y$?

1) $y = 7 - x$
2) $2\sqrt{xy} = 7$

84. When one new number is included in an existing set of 6 numbers, does the median of the set change?

(1) The mean of the original 6 numbers is 50.
(2) At least 2 of the numbers in the original set were 50.

85.   Let *abc* and *dcb* represent three-digit positive integers. If *abc* + *dcb* = 598, then which of the following
       must be equivalent to *a*?

       (A) $d - 1$
       (B) d
       (C) $3 - d$
       (D) $4 - d$
       (E) $5 - d$

86.   For non-zero integers *a*, *b*, *c* and *d*, is $\dfrac{ab}{cd}$ negative?

       (1) $ad + bc = 0$
       (2) $abcd = -4$

87.   Set *A* consists of 8 distinct prime numbers. If *x* is equal to the range of set *A* and *y* is equal to the
       median of set *A*, is the product *xy* even?

       (1) The smallest integer in the set is 5.
       (2) The largest integer in the set is 101.

88.   If $x^3 < 16x$, which of the following includes at least some of the possible solutions for *x*, but no values
       that are not solutions?

       (A) $|x| < 4$
       (B) $x < 4$
       (C) $x > 4$
       (D) $x < -4$
       (E) $x > 0$

89.   If *x* and *y* are positive integers and $5^x - 5^y = 2^{y-1}(5^{x-1})$, what is the value of *xy*?

       (A) 48
       (B) 36
       (C) 24
       (D) 18
       (E) 12

90.   Machine *A* currently takes *x* hours to complete a certain job. Machine *B* currently takes *y* hours to
       complete the same job. If $x = 4y$, by what percent will *x* have to decrease so that *A* and *B* together can
       complete the job in $\dfrac{3y}{8}$ hours?

       (A) 15%
       (B) 25%
       (C) 30%
       (D) 62.5%
       (E) 85%

*Manhattan*GMAT Prep
the new standard

Workout Set 10

91.   If $|x| \neq |y|$, $xy \neq 0$, $\dfrac{x}{x+y} = n$, and $\dfrac{x}{x-y} = m$, then $\dfrac{x}{y} =$

   (A) $\dfrac{3mn}{2}$

   (B) $\dfrac{3m}{2n}$

   (C) $\dfrac{n(m+2)}{2}$

   (D) $\dfrac{2nm}{(m-n)}$

   (E) $\dfrac{n^2 - m^2}{nm}$

92.   If a certain culture of bacteria increases by a constant factor of x every y minutes, how long will it take for the culture to increase to ten-thousand times its original size?

   (1) $\sqrt[y]{x} = 10$
   (2) In two minutes, the culture will increase to one hundred times its original size.

93.   A cylinder of height h is 3/4 of water. When all of the water is poured into an empty cylinder whose radius is 25 percent larger than that of the original cylinder, the new cylinder is 3/5 full. The height of the new cylinder is what percent of h?

   (A) 25%
   (B) 50%
   (C) 60%
   (D) 80%
   (E) 100%

94.   If a and b are distinct positive integers, what is the units digit of $2^a 8^b 4^{a+b}$?

   (1) $b = 24$ and $a < 24$
   (2) The greatest common factor of a and b is 12.

95. Employees of a certain company are each to receive a unique 7-digit identification code consisting of the digits 0, 1, 2, 3, 4, 5, and 6 such that no digit is used more than once in any given code. In valid codes, the second digit in the code is exactly twice the first digit. How many valid codes are there?

(A) 42
(B) 120
(C) 210
(D) 360
(E) 840

96. If x, y, and z are positive integers such that $x < y < z$, is x a factor of the even integer z?

(1) x and y are prime numbers whose sum is a factor of 57.
(2) y is not a factor of z.

97. w, x, y, and z are positive integers. If $\dfrac{w}{x} < \dfrac{y}{z} < 1$, what is the proper order, increasing from left to right,

of the following quantities: $\dfrac{x}{w}$, $\dfrac{z}{y}$, $\dfrac{x^2}{w^2}$, $\dfrac{xz}{wy}$, $\dfrac{x+z}{w+y}$, 1?

(A) 1, $\dfrac{z}{y}$, $\dfrac{x}{w}$, $\dfrac{x+z}{w+y}$, $\dfrac{x^2}{w^2}$, $\dfrac{xz}{wy}$

(B) 1, $\dfrac{z}{y}$, $\dfrac{x+z}{w+y}$, $\dfrac{x}{w}$, $\dfrac{xz}{wy}$, $\dfrac{x^2}{w^2}$

(C) 1, $\dfrac{z}{y}$, $\dfrac{x}{w}$, $\dfrac{x+z}{w+y}$, $\dfrac{xz}{wy}$, $\dfrac{x^2}{w^2}$

(D) 1, $\dfrac{z}{y}$, $\dfrac{x}{w}$, $\dfrac{xz}{wy}$, $\dfrac{x+z}{w+y}$, $\dfrac{x^2}{w^2}$

(E) It cannot be determined.

98. What is the value of $|a + b|$?

(1) $(a + b + c + d)(a + b - c - d) = 16$
(2) $c + d = 3$

99. Set A consists of all the integers between 10 and 21, inclusive. Set B consists of all the integers between 10 and 50, inclusive. If x is a number chosen randomly from Set A, y is a number chosen randomly from Set B, and y has no factor z such that $1 < z < y$, what is the probability that the product xy is divisible by 3?

    (A) $\dfrac{1}{4}$

    (B) $\dfrac{1}{3}$

    (C) $\dfrac{1}{2}$

    (D) $\dfrac{2}{3}$

    (E) $\dfrac{3}{4}$

100. There are x children at a birthday party, who will be seated at two different tables. At the table with the birthday cake on it, exactly y children will be seated, including the birthday girl Sally. How many different groups of children may be seated at the birthday cake table?

    (A) $\dfrac{(x-1)!}{(y-1)!(y-1)!}$

    (B) $\dfrac{x!}{y!(x-y)!}$

    (C) $\dfrac{y!}{x!(x-y)!}$

    (D) $\dfrac{(y-1)!}{(x-y)!(y-1)!}$

    (E) $\dfrac{(x-1)!}{(x-y)!(y-1)!}$

Workout Set 11

101. If $bc \neq 0$, what is the value of $\dfrac{a^2 - b^2 - c^2}{bc}$?

    (1) $|a| = 1, |b| = 2, |c| = 3$
    (2) $a + b + c = 0$

102. John and Amanda stand at opposite ends of a straight road and start running towards each other at the same moment. Their rates are randomly selected in advance so that John runs at a constant rate of 3, 4, 5, or 6 miles per hour and Amanda runs at a constant rate of 4, 5, 6, or 7 miles per hour. What is the probability that John has traveled farther than Amanda by the time they meet?

    (A) 3/16
    (B) 5/16
    (C) 3/8
    (D) 1/2
    (E) 13/16

103. If p is a positive integer, is p^2 divisible by 96?

    (1) p is a multiple of 8.
    (2) p^2 is a multiple of 12.

104. In the figure above, the trapezoid $ABCD$ is inscribed in a circle. Parallel sides AB and CD are 7 inches apart and 6 and 8 inches long, respectively. What is the radius of the circle in inches?

    (A) 4
    (B) 5
    (C) $4\sqrt{2}$
    (D) $5\sqrt{2}$
    (E) 7

105. If $9^y + 3^b = 10(3^b)$, then $2y =$

    (A) $b - 2$
    (B) $b - 1$
    (C) b
    (D) $b + 1$
    (E) $b + 2$

106. At the same time Sue began rolling a wheelbarrow from X to Y, Nancy started walking along the same road from Y to X. If Sue's traveling rate was 2 feet per second and Nancy's was 3 feet per second, and if the wheelbarrow wheel rolled without slipping, what is the radius of the wheel on Sue's wheelbarrow?

    (1) At the moment Sue and Nancy crossed paths, Sue had traveled 60 feet with the wheelbarrow.
    (2) The total number of wheel revolutions during Sue's trip from X to Y was 75.

107. For a three-digit number xyz, where x, y, and z represent the digits of the number, the function $h(xyz)$ $= 5^x2^y3^z$. If $h(abc) = 3 \times h(def)$, what is the value of $abc - def$, where the letters a through f represent digits as well?

(A) 1
(B) 2
(C) 3
(D) 9
(E) 27

108. Let x and y be positive integers, and r and s be single-digit positive integers. If $\dfrac{x}{y} = r.s\overline{s}$, where the bar above the s indicates that the decimal repeats infinitely, which of the following CANNOT be true?

(A) $y = 1.2 \times 10^a$, where a is a positive integer.
(B) $y = 1.5 \times 10^b$, where b is a positive integer.
(C) $y = 1.8 \times 10^c$, where c is a positive integer.
(D) $y = 2.5 \times 10^d$, where d is a positive integer.
(E) $y = 2.7 \times 10^e$, where e is a positive integer.

109. If $m @ n$ represents the integer remainder that results when a positive integer m is divided by a positive integer n, what is the value of positive integer x?

    (1) $81 @ x = 1$
    (2) $x @ 40 = 0$

110. The positive integers p and r have exactly three prime factors in common: two 2's and one 3. If p has exactly one additional prime factor x and r has exactly one additional prime factor y such that $x \neq y$, which of the following represents the least common multiple of p and r?

(A) $12xy$
(B) $6xy$
(C) xy
(D) 12
(E) 6

Workout Set 12

111. Which of the following equations represents a line parallel to line l in the figure above?

    (A) $2y + 3x = 0$
    (B) $2y - 3x = 0$
    (C) $2y - 3x = 6$
    (D) $3y + 2x = 6$
    (E) $3y - 2x = 9$

112. If $y = |x - 1|$ and $y = 3x + 3$, then x must be between which of the following values?

    (A) 2 and 3
    (B) 1 and 2
    (C) 0 and 1
    (D) −1 and 0
    (E) −2 and −1

113. An antiques dealer purchased three cabinets at three distinct costs last year and resold all three of those cabinets for three distinct prices this year. If the median price was received for the cabinet that had cost the median amount, and the antiques dealer made a 10% profit on that cabinet, did the dealer make more than a 10% profit margin on any one of the three cabinet sales?

    (1) One of the cabinets sold for a price less than its original cost.

    (2) The cabinet that sold for the lowest price was the one that cost the antiques dealer the most to purchase.

    ```
    |————————————————————————————————————————————————————|
            1 mile stretch of highway

      black line                                    black line
    ```

114. A road crew painted two black lines across a road as shown in the figure above, to mark the start and end of a 1-mile stretch. Between the two black lines, they will paint across the road a red line at each third of a mile, a white line at each fifth of a mile, and a blue line at each eighth of a mile. What is the smallest distance (in miles) between any of the painted lines on this stretch of highway?

    (A) 0
    (B) 1/120
    (C) 1/60
    (D) 1/40
    (E) 1/30

the new standard

115. Set S consists of n consecutive integers, where $n > 1$. What is the value of n?

    (1) The sum of the integers in Set S is divisible by 7.
    (2) The sum of the integers in Set S is 14.

116. A trapezoid is symmetrical about a vertical center line. If a circle is drawn such that it is tangent to exactly three sides of the trapezoid and is enclosed entirely within the trapezoid, what is the diameter of the circle?

    (1) The parallel sides of the trapezoid are 10 inches apart.
    (2) Of the parallel sides of the trapezoid, the shorter side is 15 inches long.

117. Three boys are ages 4, 6, and 7, respectively. Three girls are ages 5, 8, and 9, respectively. If two of the boys and two of the girls are randomly selected, and the sum of the selected children's ages is z, what is the difference between the probability that z is even and the probability that z is odd?

    (A) 1/9
    (B) 1/6
    (C) 2/9
    (D) 1/4
    (E) 1/2

118. If the three unique positive digits A, B, and C are arranged in all possible sequences (ABC, ACB, BAC, etc...), then the sum of all the resulting three-digit integers must be divisible by each of the following EXCEPT

    (A) 2
    (B) 3
    (C) 6
    (D) 11
    (E) 37

119. a and b are positive integers less than or equal to 9. If a and b are assembled into the six-digit number $ababab$, which of the following must be a factor of $ababab$?

    (A) 3
    (B) 4
    (C) 5
    (D) 6
    (E) none of the above

120. If a, b, c, and d are each integers greater than 1, is the product $abcd$ divisible by 6?

    (1) acd is even.
    (2) abd is odd.

Workout Set 13

121. If $p^2 - 13p + 40 = q$, and p is equally likely to be *any* positive integer between 1 and 10, inclusive, what is the probability that $q < 0$?

   (A) 1/10
   (B) 1/5
   (C) 2/5
   (D) 3/5
   (E) 3/10

122. If the number 200! is written in the form $p \times 10^q$, where p and q are integers, what is the maximum possible value of q?

   (A) 40
   (B) 48
   (C) 49
   (D) 55
   (E) 64

123. If x and y are integers, and $x \neq 0$, what is the value of x^y?

   (1) $|x| = 2$
   (2) $64^x 6^{2x+y} = 48^{2x}$

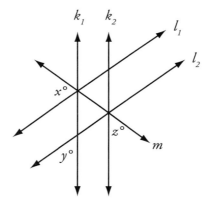

124. In the figure above, lines k_1 and k_2 are parallel to each other, lines l_1 and l_2 are parallel to each other, and line m passes through the intersection points of k_1 with l_1 and k_2 with l_2. What is the value of x?

   (1) $x = 3z - y$
   (2) $(y - z)^2 = 225$

125. If $x > 0$, what is the least possible value of $x + \dfrac{4}{x}$?

    (A) 0
    (B) 1
    (C) 2
    (D) 3
    (E) 4

126. Last year the average (arithmetic mean) cost of 5 computer models was $2,000. What is the average cost of the same 5 computer models this year?

    (1) For 3 of the 5 models, the cost this year is 12 percent lower than the cost last year.
    (2) For 2 of the 5 models, the cost this year is 10 percent higher than the cost last year.

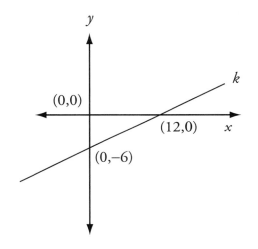

127. Which of the following equations represents a line perpendicular to line k in the figure above?

    (A) $3y + 2x = -12$
    (B) $2y + x = 0$
    (C) $2y - x = 0$
    (D) $y + 2x = 12$
    (E) $y - 2x = 12$

128. Is $x > 0$?

    (1) $|2x - 12| < 10$
    (2) $x^2 - 10x \geq -21$

129. *K*-numbers are positive integers with only 2's as their digits. For example, 2, 22, and 222 are *K*-numbers. The *K*-weight of a number *n* is the minimum number of *K*-numbers that must be added together to equal *n*. For example, the *K*-weight of 50 is 5, because $50 = 22 + 22 + 2 + 2 + 2$. What is the *K*-weight of 600?

    (A) 10
    (B) 11
    (C) 12
    (D) 13
    (E) 14

130. If the reciprocals of two consecutive positive integers are added together, what is the sum in terms of the greater integer *x*?

    (A) $\dfrac{3}{x}$

    (B) $x^2 - x$

    (C) $2x - 1$

    (D) $\dfrac{2x-1}{x^2+x}$

    (E) $\dfrac{2x-1}{x^2-x}$

Workout Set 14

131. The sequence A is defined by the following relationship: $A_n = A_{n-1} + (-1)^{n+1}(n^2)$ for all integer values of $n > 1$. If $A_1 = 1$, what is $A_{15} - A_{13}$?

    (A) 14
    (B) 29
    (C) 169
    (D) 196
    (E) 421

132. If d represents the hundredths digit and e represents the thousandths digit in the decimal $0.4de$, what is the value of this decimal rounded to the nearest tenth?

    (1) $d - e$ is a positive perfect square.
    (2) $\sqrt{d} > e^2$

133. If n is an integer and n^4 is divisible by 32, which of the following could be the remainder when n is divided by 32?

    (A) 2
    (B) 4
    (C) 5
    (D) 6
    (E) 10

134. A chain is comprised of 10 identical links, each of which independently has a 1% chance of breaking under a certain load. If the failure of any individual link means the failure of the entire chain, what is the probability that the chain will fail under the load?

    (A) $(0.01)^{10}$
    (B) $10(0.01)^{10}$
    (C) $1 - (0.10)(0.99)^{10}$
    (D) $1 - (0.99)^{10}$
    (E) $1 - (0.99)^{(10 \times 9)}$

135. If y^4 is divisible by 60, what is the minimum number of distinct factors that y must have?

    (A) 2
    (B) 6
    (C) 8
    (D) 10
    (E) 12

136. Are the positive integers x and y consecutive?

    (1) $x^2 - y^2 = 2y + 1$
    (2) $x^2 - xy - x = 0$

137. What is the value of $y - x^2 - x$?

    (1) $y = -3x$
    (2) $y = -4(x + 1)$

138. The vertical position of an object can be approximated at any given time by the function $p(t) = rt - 5t^2 + b$, where $p(t)$ is the vertical position in meters, t is the time in seconds, and r and b are constants. If $p(2) = 41$ and $p(5) = 26$, what is $p(4)$?

    (A) 24
    (B) 26
    (C) 39
    (D) 41
    (E) 45

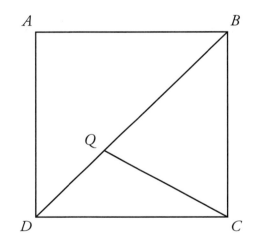

139. In the diagram above, figure $ABCD$ is a square with an area of 4.5 in². If the ratio of the length of DQ to the length of QB is 1 to 2, what is the length of QC, in inches?

    (A) $\dfrac{\sqrt{10}}{2}$

    (B) $\dfrac{\sqrt{14}}{2}$

    (C) $2\sqrt{2}$

    (D) $2\sqrt{3}$

    (E) $2\sqrt{5}$

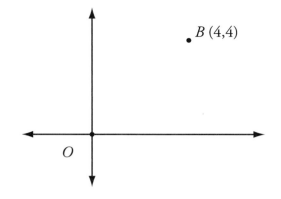

140. In the rectangular coordinate system above, if point *A* (not shown) is equidistant from points *O* and *B* and the area of triangle *OAB* is 16, which of the following are the possible coordinates of point *A*?

(A) (−2, 6)
(B) (0, 4)
(C) (2, −6)
(D) (2, 6)
(E) (4, 0)

Workout Set 15

141. If $\dfrac{(ab)^2 + 3ab - 18}{(a-1)(a+2)} = 0$, where a and b are integers, which of the following could be the value of b?

     I.   1
     II. 2
     III. 3

     (A) I only
     (B) II only
     (C) I and II only
     (D) I and III only
     (E) I, II, and III

142. Set S contains exactly four distinct positive integers. Is the mean of S equal to the median of S?

     (1) The smallest term in S is equal to the sum of the two middle terms minus the largest term in S.
     (2) When the range of S is added to the sum of all the terms in S, the resulting sum is equal to the smallest term in S plus three times the largest term in S.

143. What is the area of the quadrilateral bounded by the lines $y = \dfrac{3}{4}x + 6$, $y = \dfrac{3}{4}x - 6$, $y = -\dfrac{3}{4}x + 6$, and $y = -\dfrac{3}{4}x - 6$?

     (A) 48
     (B) 64
     (C) 96
     (D) 100
     (E) 140

144. Each digit 1 through 5 is used exactly once to create a 5-digit integer. If the 3 and the 4 cannot be adjacent digits in the integer, how many 5-digit integers are possible?

     (A) 48
     (B) 66
     (C) 72
     (D) 78
     (E) 90

145. a, b, c, and d are positive integers. If the remainder is 9 when a is divided by b, and the remainder is 5 when c is divided by d, which of the following is NOT a possible value for $b + d$?

    (A) 20
    (B) 19
    (C) 18
    (D) 16
    (E) 15

146. The ratio of cupcakes to children at a party is 27 to 7. Each child at the party eats exactly x cupcakes, where x is a positive integer, after which a total of y cupcakes remain uneaten. If y is less than the number of children at the birthday party, which of the following must be true?

    I. y is a multiple of 2.
    II. y is a multiple of 3.
    III. y is a multiple of 7.

    (A) I only
    (B) II only
    (C) III only
    (D) I and II only
    (E) I, II and III

147. What is the units digit of the positive integer x?

    (1) $\dfrac{x}{5} = y.2$, where y is a positive integer.

    (2) $\dfrac{x}{2} = z.5$, where z is a positive integer.

148. If x and y are positive integers, what is the value of $(x + y)$?

    (1) $(x + y - 1)! < 100$
    (2) $y = x^2 - x + 1$

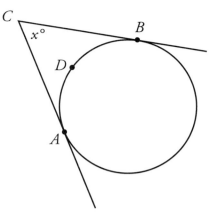

149. In the figure above, two lines are tangent to a circle at points A and B. What is x?

     (1) The area of the circle is 81π.
     (2) The length of arc ADB is 7π.

150. For all n such that n is a positive integer, the terms of a certain sequence B are given by the following rules:

     $B_n = B_{n-1} + 5$ if n is odd and greater than 1;
     $B_n = -B_{n-1}$ if n is even;
     $B_1 = 3$

     What is the sum of the first 65 terms in the sequence?

     (A) -5
     (B) 0
     (C) 3
     (D) 5
     (E) 8

Workout Set 1 Solutions

1. **D:** Some intuitive recollection of geometry rules and a picture drawn to scale can help us determine reasonable answer choices. If AC is a diameter of the circle, then triangle ABC is a right triangle, with angle $ABC = 90$ degrees. The shortest side of a triangle is across from its smallest angle, and the longest side of a triangle is across from its largest angle. Therefore, $AC > BC > AB$.

The circumference of the circle $= \pi d = 6\pi\sqrt{3}$, so $d = 6\sqrt{3} \approx 6(1.7) = 10.2$. Thus, $AC \approx 10.2$ and $BC < 10.2$. But we can clearly see from our picture drawn to scale that BC is longer than half the diameter, so we conservatively determine that $BC > 5.1$.

(A) $\dfrac{3}{\sqrt{2}} \approx \dfrac{3}{1.4} = \dfrac{30}{14} = 2\frac{1}{7}$ TOO LOW

(B) 3 TOO LOW

(C) $3\sqrt{3} \approx 3(1.7) = 5.1$ TOO LOW

(D) 9 OK

(E) $9\sqrt{3} \approx 9(1.7) = 15.3$ TOO HIGH

Alternatively, we could use rules of geometry to solve directly for the answer. Line AC passes through the center of the circle, so the inscribed triangle ABC is a right triangle with angle $ABC = 90°$. Since angle ACB is 30°, angle CAB is 60°.

The sides in a 30–60–90 triangle have the ratio $1 : \sqrt{3} : 2$, so given any side, we can compute the other two sides.

First, use the circumference to solve for AC (the diameter:

$6\pi\sqrt{3} = \pi d = \text{Circumference}$

$\dfrac{6\pi\sqrt{3}}{\pi} = d$

$6\sqrt{3} = d$

Now we can use *Ratios* (specifically, the *Unknown Multiplier*) to find BC.

	AB	**BC**	**AC**
Basic Ratio	$1x$	$\sqrt{3}x$	$2x$
Known Side			$6\sqrt{3}$
Unknown Multiplier			$x = \dfrac{6\sqrt{3}}{2} = 3\sqrt{3}$
Compute Sides	$3\sqrt{3}$	$(\sqrt{3})(3\sqrt{3}) = 9$	$2(3\sqrt{3}) = 6\sqrt{3}$

Line segment *BC* has length 9.

The correct answer is D.

2. B: Profit equals revenue minus cost. The company's profit is:

$$p(9 - p) - (p + 15) = 9p - p^2 - p - 15$$
$$= -p^2 + 8p - 15$$
$$= -(p^2 - 8p + 15)$$
$$= -(p - 5)(p - 3)$$

Profit will be zero if $p = 5$ or $p = 3$, which eliminates answers (A) and (C). For $p > 5$, both $(p - 5)$ and $(p - 3)$ are positive. In that case, the profit is negative, i.e. the company loses money. The profit is only positive if $(p - 5)$ and $(p - 3)$ have opposite signs, which occurs when $3 < p < 5$.

The correct answer is B.

3. D: The sum $(1/41 + 1/42 + 1/43 + 1/44 + \ldots + 1/57 + 1/58 + 1/59 + 1/60)$ has 20 fractional terms. It would be nearly impossible to compute if we had to find a common denominator and solve without a calculator and a lot of time. Instead, let's look at the maximum and minimum possible values for the sum.

Maximum: The largest fraction in the sum is 1/41. *K* is definitely smaller than $20 \times 1/41$, which is itself smaller than $20 \times 1/40 = 1/2$.

Minimum: The smallest fraction in the sum is 1/60. *K* is definitely larger than $20 \times 1/60 = 1/3$.

Therefore, $1/3 < K < 1/2$.

I. YES: $1/4 < 1/3 < K$
II. YES: $1/3 < K$
III. NO: $1/2 > K$

The correct answer is D.

4. B: First, let's make some observations. With 9 competitors and only 3 medals awarded, only 1/3 of the competitors will win overall. Although a simplification, it is reasonable for each competitor to see his or her chance of winning a medal as 1/3, or to expect to win 1/3 of a medal (pretending for a moment that medals can be "shared").

We are asked for the probability *at least* 2 of the triplets will win a medal. In other words, we want 2/3 to 3/3 of the triplets to win medals, or for each triplet to win 2/3 to 3/3 of a medal. Since 2/3 and 3/3 are both greater than 1/3, we are looking for the probability that the triplets will win medals at a rate greater than that expected for competitors overall. This would certainly be an unusual outcome. Thus, the probability should be less than 1/2. Eliminate D and E. We could then at least make an educated guess from among the remaining choices with at least a 1 in 3 shot at success.

To solve, we must use the probability formula and combinatorics:

$$\text{Probability} = \frac{\text{specified outcome}}{\text{all possible outcomes}} = \frac{\text{\# of ways at least 2 triplets win medal}}{\text{\# of ways 3 medals can be awarded}}$$

First, we find the total number of outcomes for the triathlon. There are nine competitors; three will win medals and six will not. We set up an anagram grid where Y represents a medal, N no medal:

competitor:	C_1	C_2	C_3	C_4	C_5	C_6	C_7	C_8	C_9
medal:	Y	Y	Y	N	N	N	N	N	N

$$\text{\# of ways 3 medals can be awarded} = \frac{9!}{3!6!} = \frac{(9)(8)(7)}{(3)(2)(1)} = (3)(4)(7) = 84$$

Now, we need to determine the number of instances when *at least two* brothers win a medal. Practically speaking, this could happen when (1) exactly three brothers win or (2) exactly two brothers win.

Let's start with *all three* triplets winning medals, where Y represents a medal:

triplet:	A	B	C		non-triplet:	C_1	C_2	C_3	C_4	C_5	C_6
medal:	Y	Y	Y		medal:	N	N	N	N	N	N

The number of ways this could happen is $\dfrac{3!}{3!} \times \dfrac{6!}{6!} = 1$. This makes sense, as there is only one instance in which all three triplets would win medals and all of the other competitors would not.

Next, let's calculate the instances when *exactly two* of the triplets win medals:

triplet:	A	B	C		non-triplet:	C_1	C_2	C_3	C_4	C_5	C_6
medal:	Y	Y	N		medal:	Y	N	N	N	N	N

Since both triplets and non-triplets win medals in this scenario, we need to consider possibilities for both sides of the grid. For the triplets, the number of ways that two could win medals is $\dfrac{3!}{2!1!} = 3$.

For the non-triplet competitors, the number of ways that one could win the remaining medal is $\dfrac{6!}{1!5!} = 6$.

We multiply these two numbers to get our total number of instances: $3 \times 6 = 18$.

The brothers win *at least two* medals in $18 + 1 = 19$ cases. The total number of cases is 84, so the probability is 19/84.

The correct answer is B.

5. B: Since the answer asks for an approximation, we should use decimal approximations for all square roots in the question and answer choices.

(A) $\sqrt{3} \approx 1.7$

(B) 2

(C) $1 + \sqrt{2} \approx 1 + 1.4 = 2.4$

(D) $1 + \sqrt{3} \approx 1 + 1.7 = 2.7$

(E) $2\sqrt{3} \approx 2(1.7) = 3.4$

Note that there is a minimum difference of 0.3 between answer choices. This implies that we must be *reasonably* careful when approximating, but will have no trouble choosing an answer if we approximate every square root to the nearest tenth.

$$\sqrt{2} \approx 1.4$$

$$\sqrt{2 + \sqrt{2}} \approx \sqrt{2 + 1.4} \approx \sqrt{3.4} \approx 1.8$$

$$\sqrt{2 + \sqrt{2 + \sqrt{2}}} \approx \sqrt{2 + 1.8} \approx \sqrt{3.8} \approx 1.9$$

$$\sqrt{2 + \sqrt{2 + \sqrt{2 + \sqrt{2}}}} \approx \sqrt{2 + 1.9} \approx \sqrt{3.9} \approx 2$$

$$\sqrt{2 + \sqrt{2 + \sqrt{2 + \sqrt{2 + \sqrt{2}}}}} \approx \sqrt{2 + 2} \approx \sqrt{4} = 2$$

At this point, we can see that the expression is converging on 2.

Alternatively, an algebraic solution is possible if we recognize that the infinite expression is nested within itself:

$$x = \sqrt{2 + \left(\sqrt{2 + \sqrt{2 + \sqrt{2 + \sqrt{2 + \ldots}}}} \right)} = \sqrt{2 + x}$$

We can solve for x as follows:

$$x = \sqrt{2 + x}$$
$$x^2 = 2 + x$$
$$x^2 - x - 2 = 0$$
$$(x - 2)(x + 1) = 0$$

This implies that $x = 2$ or $x = -1$. Since x is the square root of a real, positive number, it must be positive, and we can conclude that $x = 2$.

The correct answer is B.

6. A: Draw a diagram to illustrate the moment at which A and B pass each other moving in opposite directions:

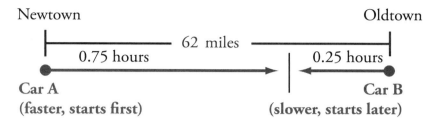

We could test the answer choices:

	B's distance (miles)	B's rate (mph) = D/T = D/0.25	A's rate (mph) = B's rate + 8	A's distance (miles) = R * T = R * 0.75	Total distance
(A)	**14**	**56**	**64**	**48**	**62**
(B)	12	48	56	42	54
(C)	10	40	48	36	46
(D)	9	36	44	33	42
(E)	8	32	40	30	38

Or we could solve algebraically, using an RTD chart. Note that we must convert 15 minutes to 1/4 (or 0.25) hours.:

	Rate	Time	Distance
Car A	$(r + 8)$ mph	0.75 hours	$(0.75)(r + 8)$ miles
Car B	r mph	0.25 hours	$0.25r$ miles
Total			62 miles

Set up and solve an equation for the total distance:

$$(0.75)(r + 8) + (0.25r) = 62$$
$$0.75r + 6 + 0.25r = 62$$
$$r = 56$$

Therefore, Car B traveled a distance of $0.25r = (0.25)(56) = 14$ miles.

The correct answer is A.

7. B: Testing the choices would be a natural way to solve this problem, since the question doesn't ask us to solve for b in general, but rather "for which of the following is x closest to zero?" However, numbers between 2^{20} and 2^{42} are too large to plug and compute. We must manipulate the terms with base 8 to see how they might balance with 2^b:

$$x = 2^b - (8^8 + 8^6)$$
$$0 \approx 2^b - (8^8 + 8^6)$$
$$2^b \approx (8^8 + 8^6)$$
$$2^b \approx (8^6)(8^2 + 1)$$
$$2^b \approx \left((2^3)^6\right)\left((2^3)^2 + 1\right)$$
$$2^b \approx (2^{18})(2^6 + 1)$$

Since 1 is very small in comparison to 2^6, we can approximate $(2^6 + 1) \approx (2^6)$. Therefore,

$$2^b \approx (2^{18})(2^6)$$
$$2^b \approx 2^{24}$$
$$b \approx 24$$

The correct answer is B.

8. E: Since there are variables in the answer choices (VIC), we should pick a number and test the choices. If $k = 2$, then $\dfrac{2}{\sqrt{k+1}+\sqrt{k-1}} = \dfrac{2}{\sqrt{3}+\sqrt{1}} \approx \dfrac{2}{1.7+1} = \dfrac{2}{2.7}$, which is less than 1. Now test the answer choices and try to match the target:

(A) 2   TOO HIGH

(B) $2\sqrt{2k} = 2\sqrt{4} = 4$ TOO HIGH

(C) $2\sqrt{k+1} + \sqrt{k-1} = 2\sqrt{3} + \sqrt{1} \approx 2(1.7) + 1 = 4.4$ TOO HIGH

(D) $\dfrac{\sqrt{k+1}}{\sqrt{k-1}} = \dfrac{\sqrt{3}}{\sqrt{1}} \approx 1.7$ TOO HIGH

(E) $\sqrt{k+1} - \sqrt{k-1} = \sqrt{3} - \sqrt{1} \approx 1.7 - 1 = 0.7$ OK

Alternatively, we could solve this problem algebraically. The expression given is of the form $\dfrac{2}{a+b}$, where $a = \sqrt{k+1}$ and $b = \sqrt{k-1}$.

We need to either simplify or cancel the denominator, as none of the answer choices have the denominator we start with, and most of the choices have no denominator at all. To be able to manipulate a denominator with radical signs, we must first try to eliminate the radical signs entirely, leaving only a^2 and b^2 in the denominator. To do so, we multiply by a fraction that is a convenient form of 1:

$$\frac{2}{(a+b)} = \frac{2}{(a+b)} \times \frac{(a-b)}{(a-b)} = \frac{2(a-b)}{a^2 - b^2}$$

Notice the "difference of two squares" special product we have created in the denominator with our choice of $(a - b)$.

$\mathcal{M}anhattan$**GMAT***Prep
the new standard
274

Substituting for a and b,

$$\frac{2}{\left(\sqrt{k+1}+\sqrt{k-1}\right)}\times\frac{\left(\sqrt{k+1}-\sqrt{k-1}\right)}{\left(\sqrt{k+1}-\sqrt{k-1}\right)}=\frac{2\left(\sqrt{k+1}-\sqrt{k-1}\right)}{(k+1)-(k-1)}=\frac{2\left(\sqrt{k+1}-\sqrt{k-1}\right)}{2}=\sqrt{k+1}-\sqrt{k-1}$$

The correct answer is E.

9. A: First, note the answer pairs (A)&(C) and (B)&(E), in which one ratio is the square of the other. This represents a likely trap in a problem that asks for the ratio of $\sqrt{x}$ to $\sqrt{y}$ rather than the more typical ratio of x to y. We can eliminate (D), as it is not paired with a trap answer and therefore probably not the correct answer. We should also suspect that the correct answer is (A) or (B), the "square root" answer choice in their respective pairs.

For problems involving successive changes in amounts — such as population-growth problems, or compound interest problems — it is helpful to make a table:

	Account A	Account B
Now	x	y
After 1 month	$\left(\dfrac{9}{10}\right)x$	$\left(\dfrac{12}{10}\right)y$
After 2 months	$\left(\dfrac{9}{10}\right)\left(\dfrac{9}{10}\right)x=\left(\dfrac{81}{100}\right)x$	$\left(\dfrac{12}{10}\right)\left(\dfrac{12}{10}\right)y=\left(\dfrac{144}{100}\right)y$

If the accounts have the same amount of money after two months, then:

$$\left(\frac{81}{100}\right)x=\left(\frac{144}{100}\right)y$$
$$81x=144y$$

This can be solved for $\dfrac{\sqrt{x}}{\sqrt{y}}$:

$$\frac{x}{y}=\frac{144}{81}$$
$$\frac{\sqrt{x}}{\sqrt{y}}=\frac{\sqrt{144}}{\sqrt{81}}=\frac{12}{9}=\frac{4}{3}$$

The correct answer is A.

10. C: Consecutive integers have two defining characteristics tested most often by the GMAT: they differ by a known, constant value (i.e. 1), and they alternate odd, even, odd, even, etc. We will use the odd/even property to evaluate these choices. This general approach is usually faster than considering specific values. It works particularly well for very general questions about whether something CANNOT or MUST be true.

(A)	$a = E + O = O$, or $a = O + E = O$	$b = 3$ pairs $(E + O) = O$, or $b = 3$ pairs $(O + E) = O$	a could equal b (both Odd)
(B)	$a = E + O + E = O$, or $a = O + E + O = E$	$b = 3$ pairs $(E + O) = O$, or $b = 3$ pairs $(O + E) = O$	a could equal b (both Odd)
(C)	$a = \textbf{3 pairs } (E + O) = O$, or $a = \textbf{3 pairs } (O + E) = O$	$b = \textbf{2 pairs } (E + O) = E$, or $b = \textbf{2 pairs } (O + E) = E$	$\boldsymbol{a \neq b}$ **(Odd ≠ Even)**
(D)	$a = 3$ pairs $(E + O) = O$, or $a = 3$ pairs $(O + E) = O$	$b = O + 3$ pairs $(E + O) = E$, or $b = E + 3$ pairs $(O + E) = O$	a could equal b (both Odd)
(E)	$a = O + 3$ pairs $(E + O) = E$, or $a = E + 3$ pairs $(O + E) = O$	$b = O + 2$ pairs $(E + O) = O$, or $b = E + 2$ pairs $(O + E) = E$	a could equal b (both Odd or both Even)

The correct answer is C.

Workout Set 2 Solutions

11. E: We can cross-multiply the inequality, as long as we are careful to consider two cases:

> If $a - b$ is negative, the question becomes "Is $1 < ab(a - b)$?" (FLIPPED inequality sign)

> If $a - b$ is positive, the question becomes "Is $1 > ab(a - b)$?" (ORIGINAL inequality sign)

This is a conditional rephrased question—importantly, one with completely opposite questions as possibilities. *Any statement that doesn't at least answer the question of whether a − b is positive or negative is unlikely to be sufficient.* The condition also makes the rephrasing less useful for plugging numbers, so we might as well test values in the original question.

(1) INSUFFICIENT: Let's set up a chart with some easy number-testing scenarios, anticipating that we may quickly see inconsistent answers to the question. Here, we can use +/−2 and +/−1:

a	b	$|a| > |b|$	Is $\dfrac{1}{a-b} > ab$?
2	1	✓	$\dfrac{1}{1} > 2$? NO

2	−1	✓	$\dfrac{1}{3} > -2$? YES
−2	1	✓	$\dfrac{1}{-3} > -2$? YES
−2	−1	✓	$\dfrac{1}{-1} > 2$? NO

(2) INSUFFICIENT: Again, let's set up a chart with easy plugging scenarios. If they are allowed by the constraint given in (2), we can re-use scenarios that we've already tried in evaluating statement (1), as long as they prove insufficiency.

a	b	$a < b$	Is $\dfrac{1}{a-b} > ab$?
−2	1	✓	$\dfrac{1}{-3} > -2$? YES
−2	−1	✓	$\dfrac{1}{-1} > 2$? NO

(1) AND (2) INSUFFICIENT: Both of the scenarios we tested for (2) were also valid for (1). In other words, even when we consider the two statements together, we must consider both of the cases in (2) above, and can get Yes or No as an answer.

The correct answer is E.

12. A: The greatest common factor or divisor of any two numbers is given by the product of the shared or overlapping primes in the two numbers. Any such question can be rephrased accordingly: "What exactly are the overlapping factors of m and n?"

(1) SUFFICIENT: We can set up a scenario chart to track the allowed values of s, m, and n:

FACTS:					QUESTION:
s = pos int	$m = 9s$	$n = \dfrac{m-9}{4}$	n = pos int		GCF of m and n?
1	9	0/4	zero ✘		
2	18	9/4	fraction ✘		
3	27	18/4	fraction ✘		
4	36	27/4	fraction ✘		

5	45	36/4 = 9	✓	9
6	54	45/4	fraction ✗	
7	63	54/4	fraction ✗	
8	72	63/4	fraction ✗	
9	81	72/4 = 18	✓	9
10	90	81/4	fraction ✗	

We quickly see a pattern: n is only a positive integer when $(s - 1)$ is a multiple of 4. Also, m and n are both multiples of 9. Here's the proof:

$$n = \frac{m-9}{4} = \frac{9s-9}{4} = 9\frac{(s-1)}{4} = 9\,(\text{int})$$

Let's continue the chart quickly, accounting for this restriction, to be confident that the apparent GCF pattern will continue:

	FACTS:			QUESTION:
s = pos int	$m = 9s$	$n = \dfrac{m-9}{4}$	n = pos int	GCF of m and n?
5	(9)(5) = 45	36/4 = 9 = (9)(1)	✓	9
9	(9)(9) = 81	72/4 = 18 = (9)(2)	✓	9
13	(9)(13) = 117	108/4 = 27 = (9)(3)	✓	9
17	(9)(17) = 153	144/4 = 36 = (9)(4)	✓	9
21	(9)(21) = 189	180/4 = 45 = (9)(5)	✓	9

We can see that m and n always share an overlapping factor of 9, but there is never any overlap between their remaining factors. The GCF is always 9.

(2) INSUFFICIENT: $n = 4t$, where t is a positive integer.

	FACTS:		QUESTION:
t = pos int	$n = 4t$	$m = 4n + 9$	GCF of m and n?
1	4	16 + 9 = 25	1
2	8	32 + 9 = 41	1
3	12	48 + 9 = 57	3
4	16	64 + 9 = 73	1
5	20	80 + 9 = 89	1
6	24	96 + 9 = 105	3
7	28	112 + 9 = 121	1

There is more than one possible GCF, so we cannot answer the question with a definite value. Of course, we can stop once we have generated more than one possible value for the GCF.

The correct answer is A.

13. A. (1) SUFFICIENT: If we call x the number of general exhibit tickets sold, then $(30 - x)$ represents the number of special exhibit tickets sold. We can set up and solve the following inequality:

$1,570 < 10x + 70(30 - x) < 1,670$
$1,570 < 10x + 2,100 - 70x < 1,670$
$1,570 < -60x + 2,100 < 1,670$
$-530 < -60x < -430$

$\dfrac{-530}{-60} > \dfrac{-60x}{-60} > \dfrac{-430}{-60}$ (flip the direction of the inequality when dividing by a negative)

$8.8 > x > 7.2$

The only integer between 7.2 and 8.8 is 8, so x must be 8. The museum sold 8 general exhibit tickets.

Alternatively, we could use the integer constraint by testing cases:
If $x = 7$, total revenue $= 10(7) + 70(23) = 70 + 1,610 = 1,680$. TOO HIGH.
If $x = 8$, total revenue $= 10(8) + 70(22) = 80 + 1,540 = 1,620$. OK.
If $x = 9$, total revenue $= 10(9) + 70(21) = 90 + 1,470 = 1,560$. TOO LOW.

Only $x = 8$ gives a total revenue in the given range.

Don't Assume that having a *range* of values automatically means a statement is insufficient to answer a value question. You must notice the *Stealth Constraint* that the number of tickets sold is an integer, and *Compute to Completion*.

(2) INSUFFICIENT: This statement tells us that the museum sold 21, 22, 23, or 24 special exhibit tickets. Since the museum sold a total of 30 tickets, this means that it sold 9, 8, 7, or 6 general exhibit tickets.

The correct answer is A.

14. C. (1) INSUFFICIENT: Use a Scenario Chart to organize number cases. If we can generate both a Yes case and a No case, we will prove insufficiency.

x	y	x^y	y^x	Does $x^y = y^x$?
2	0	$2^0 = 1$	$0^2 = 0$	N
3	1	$3^1 = 3$	$1^3 = 1$	N
4	2	$4^2 = 16$	$2^4 = 16$	Y

(2) INSUFFICIENT: Use a Scenario Chart to organize number cases. If we can generate both a Yes case and a No case, we will prove insufficiency.

x	y	x^y	y^x	Does $x^y = y^x$?
8	1	$8^1 = 8$	$1^8 = 1$	N
4	2	$4^2 = 16$	$2^4 = 16$	Y

(1) and (2) SUFFICIENT: Using a chart and testing cases would get more complicated with both constraints, so we should do some algebraic work first.

From statement (1), $x = 2 + y$. Substituting for x into statement (2):

$xy = 8$
$(2 + y)y = 8$
$2y + y^2 = 8$
$y^2 + 2y - 8 = 0$
$(y + 4)(y - 2) = 0$
$y = -4$ or $y = 2$
Therefore, $x = -2$ or $x = 4$.

Test these two cases in a chart:

x	y	x^y	y^x	Does $x^y = y^x$?
-2	-4	$(-2)^{-4} = \frac{1}{16}$	$(-4)^{-2} = \frac{1}{16}$	Y
4	2	$4^2 = 16$	$2^4 = 16$	Y

In either case, $x^y = y^x$. The correct answer is C.

15. **B:** Odd exponents do not "hide the sign" of the base. In other words, a and a^3 have the same sign, as do b and b^3, regardless of the signs of a and b. In comparing $ab^3c^4 > 0$ (the constraint) to a^3bc^5 (the question), the only unknown real difference is between c^4 and c^5. We know that c^4 must be positive (even exponent), so if we want c^5 to be positive, then c needs to be positive also. Our rephrased question is thus "Is $c > 0$?"

(1) INSUFFICIENT: No information about the sign of c.

(2) SUFFICIENT: Answers the rephrased question directly.

The correct answer is B.

16. **C:** The perimeter of a triangle is equal to the sum of the three sides.

(1) INSUFFICIENT: Knowing the length of one side of the triangle is not enough to find the sum of all three sides.

(2) INSUFFICIENT: Knowing the length of one side of the triangle is not enough to find the sum of all three sides.

(1) AND (2) SUFFICIENT: Triangle *ABC* is an isosceles triangle which means that two of the sides are equal in length. The statements give us two of the side lengths, so the third side, *AC*, must equal one of the given sides.

There is a **Stealth Constraint** in this problem: the triangle must be valid. Recall that the sum of the lengths of any two sides of a triangle must be greater than the length of the third side.

AB	*BC*	*AC*	Perimeter	Valid Triangle?
9	4	4	$9 + 4 + 4 = 17$	NO: $4 + 4 < 9$
9	4	9	$9 + 4 + 9 = 22$	YES: $4 + 9 > 9$

A "triangle" with three sides of 4, 4, and 9 is not really a triangle, as it cannot be drawn with those dimensions.

Therefore the actual sides of the triangle must be $AB = 9$, $BC = 4$, and $AC = 9$. The perimeter is 22.

The correct answer is C.

17. A: Express both sides of the equation in terms of prime numbers.

$$2^x 5^y z = 6.4 \times 10^6$$
$$= (64)(10^5)$$
$$= (2^6)(2^5 5^5)$$
$$= 2^{11} 5^5$$

The right side of the equation is composed of only 2's and 5's. The left side of the equation has *x* number of 2's and *y* number of 5's along with some factor *z*. This unknown factor *z* must be composed of only 2's and/or 5's, or it must be 1 (i.e. with no prime factors).

If $z = 1$, then $x = 11$ and $y = 5$.
If $z = 2^? 5^?$, where the exponents are not 0, then *x* and *y* will depend on the value of those exponents.

The rephrased question is thus "How many factors of 2 and 5 are in *z*?"

(1) SUFFICIENT: If $z = 20 = 2^2 5^1$, then we have the answer to our rephrased question. Incidentally, this implies that $2^x 5^y (2^2 5^1) = 2^{11} 5^5$, so $x = 9$ and $y = 4$, making $xy = 36$.

(2) INSUFFICIENT: If $x = 9$, then

$$2^x 5^y z = 2^{11} 5^5$$
$$2^9 5^y z = 2^{11} 5^5$$
$$z = \frac{2^{11} 5^5}{2^9 5^y}$$
$$z = 2^2 5^{5-y}$$

While this tells us the number of 2's among z's factors, we still do not know how many factors of 5 are in z.

The correct answer is A.

18. D: We can factor $1 + x + y + xy = 21$ to determine that $(1 + x)(1 + y) = 21$. The product of the integers $(1 + x)$ and $(1 + y)$ is 21, which has the factors 1, 3, 7, and 21. The factor pair 1 and 21 is disqualified because neither $(1 + x)$ nor $(1 + y)$ could equal 1, as that would make one of the positive integers x or y equal to zero. We therefore determine that $(1 + x)$ could equal 3 or 7, and conversely, $(1 + y)$ could equal 7 or 3 such that their product is 21.

Knowing that x will equal either 2 or 6, we can rephrase the question: "Is the value of x equal to 2 or 6?"

(1) SUFFICIENT: If $y > 3$, then it must be true that $y = 6$ and $x = 2$.

(2) SUFFICIENT: If $y = 6$, then $x = 2$.

The correct answer is D.

19. C: We are told that $k > j > 0$, and both k and j are integers. The remainder when k is divided by j may be expressed as r in this formula:

$$k = jq + r$$

In this formula,
(a) all of the variables are integers,
(b) q (the quotient) is the greatest number of j's such that $jx < k$, and
(c) $r < j$.
(If r were greater than j, then q would not be the greatest number of j's in k.)

Thus, the question may be rephrased: "If $k = jq + r$, and q is maximized such that $jq < k$ and $r < j$, what is the value of r?"

(1) INSUFFICIENT: At first glance, this may seem sufficient since it is in the form of our remainder equation. Certainly, m could equal q (the quotient) and r (the remainder) could be 5.

For example, $k = 13$ and $j = 8$ yield a remainder of 5 when k is divided by j: $13 = (8)(1) + 5$, where $m = 1$ is the greatest number of 8's such that $(8)(1) < 13$, and $r < j$ (i.e. $5 < 8$).

However, this statement does not indicate whether m is the greatest number of j's such that $jm < k$ and $r < j$, as our rephrased question requires.

For example, $k = 13$ and $j = 2$ may be expressed in this form: $13 = (2)(4) + 5$, where $m = 4$. However, 5 is not the remainder because $5 > j$, and 4 is not the greatest number of 2's in 13. When 13 is divided by 2, the quotient is 6 and the remainder is 1.

If $j \leq 5$, then 5 cannot be the remainder and m is not the quotient.
If $j > 5$, then 5 must be the remainder and m must be the quotient.

(2) INSUFFICIENT: This statement gives us a range of possible values of j. Without information about k, we cannot determine anything about the remainder when k is divided by j.

(1) AND (2) SUFFICIENT: Statement (2) tells us that $j > 5$, so we can conclude from statement (1) that 5 is the remainder and m is the quotient when k is divided by j.

The correct answer is C.

20. E: There are a limited number of primes that are less than 18: 2, 3, 5, 7, 11, 13, 17.

The sum $x^2 + y^3 \leq 17$, and the positive integers x and y each have a minimum value of 1, so $x^2 \leq 16$ and $y^3 \leq 16$. This implies that x can be 1, 2, 3, or 4 and y can be 1 or 2 (as $3^3 = 27 > 16$). Already this limits our possible (x, y) value pairs to $4 \times 2 = 8$ scenarios. Set up a chart to see whether the constraint that $x^2 + y^3$ is a prime number eliminates any of these scenarios.

x	y	$x^2 + y^3$	$x^2 + y^3$ is prime
1	1	$1 + 1 = 2$	✓
2	1	$4 + 1 = 5$	✓
3	1	$9 + 1 = 10$	✗
4	1	$16 + 1 = 17$	✓
1	2	$1 + 8 = 9$	✗
2	2	$4 + 8 = 12$	✗
3	2	$9 + 8 = 17$	✓
4	2	$16 + 8 = 24$	✗ (also, 24 > 18 ✗)

This leaves only four basic scenarios that will need to be checked against the statement constraints. Here is a cleaned up list, with invalid scenarios removed:

x	y	$x^2 + y^3$	$x^2 + y^3$ is prime
1	1	$1 + 1 = 2$	✓
2	1	$4 + 1 = 5$	✓
3	2	$9 + 8 = 17$	✓
4	1	$16 + 1 = 17$	✓

(1) INSUFFICIENT: Within a chart, determine which of the four basic scenarios also meet the constraint that $x^2 + y^2$ is a prime number, then answer the question for those that do.

x	y	$x^2 + y^2$	$x^2 + y^2$ is prime	$y = ?$
1	1	$1 + 1 = 2$	✓	1
2	1	$4 + 1 = 5$	✓	1
3	2	$9 + 4 = 13$	✓	2
4	1	$16 + 1 = 17$	✓	1

y could equal either 1 or 2.

(2) INSUFFICIENT: Within a chart, determine which of the four basic scenarios also meet the constraint that $x^2 - y^2$ is a prime number, then answer the question for those that do.

x	y	$x^2 - y^2$	$x^2 - y^2$ is prime	$y = ?$
1	1	$1 - 1 = 0$	✗	N/A
2	1	$4 - 1 = 3$	✓	1
3	2	$9 - 4 = 5$	✓	2
4	1	$16 - 1 = 15$	✗	N/A

y could equal either 1 or 2.

(1) AND (2) INSUFFICIENT: Both statements allow the second and third scenarios, so even using both statements together, we do not know whether y equals 1 or 2.

The answer is E.

Workout Set 3 Solutions

21. C: To find each successive term in S, we sum the previous term and 1, then add the reciprocal of that sum.

$$S_1 = 100$$

$$S_2 = (S_1 + 1) + \frac{1}{(S_1 + 1)}$$

$$= (100 + 1) + \frac{1}{(100 + 1)}$$

$$= 101 + \frac{1}{101}$$

$$S_3 = (S_2 + 1) + \frac{1}{(S_2 + 1)}$$

$$= \left(101 + \frac{1}{101} + 1 \right) + \frac{1}{\left(101 + \frac{1}{101} + 1 \right)}$$

$$= 102 + \frac{1}{102 + \frac{1}{101}}$$

Since each term is growing more complicated, we should stop computing exact numbers. The question and answer choices rescue us, since we are asked for a broad *range* within which the sum of the first 15 terms of S must fall. In fact, the fractional portion of each term is so small that we can safely ignore it.

$S_1 = 100$
$S_2 \approx 101$
$S_3 \approx 102$
$S_4 \approx 103$
$S_n \approx 100 + (n - 1)$

The sum of the first 16 terms of S will be approximately equal to the sum of the 16 consecutive integers 100, 101,...,115.

Now we can form matching pairs and sum:

$100 + 115 = 215$
$101 + 114 = 215$
$102 + 113 = 215$
...etc.

There are 16 terms and therefore 8 pairs in the sum:
$215 \times 8 = 1,720$

The correct answer is C.

22. A: (1) SUFFICIENT: The tendency is to deem statement (1) insufficient because we have no information about the value of y. But 26 has a units digit of 6, and remember that $6^{\text{any positive integer}}$ has a units digit of 6 (the pattern is a single-term repeat).

$6^1 = \mathbf{6}$
$6^2 = 3\mathbf{6}$
$6^3 = 21\mathbf{6}$
etc.

Thus, 26 raised to ANY positive integer power will also have a units digit of 6 and therefore a remainder of 6 when divided by 10.

(2) INSUFFICIENT: Given that $y^x = 1$, there are a few possible scenarios:

x	y	FACT (2): $y^x = 1$
0	anything nonzero	(anything nonzero)^0 = 1 ✓
anything	1	$1^{\text{anything}} = 1$ ✓
even	−1	$-1^{\text{even}} = 1$ ✓

However, the question stem tells us that x and y are POSITIVE integers, so we eliminate the first and third scenarios.

x	y	FACT (2): $y^x = 1$	FACT (QS): x and y are positive integers
0	anything nonzero	(anything nonzero)^0 = 1 ✓	✗ ($x = 0$)
any positive integer	1	$1^{\text{anything}} = 1$ ✓	✓
even	−1	$-1^{\text{even}} = 1$ ✓	✗ ($y = -1$)

The remaining scenario indicates that $y = 1$ and $x =$ any positive integer. Without more information about x, we cannot determine the remainder when x^y is divided by 10.

Since statement (1) tells us the value of x and statement (2) indirectly tells us the value of y ($y = 1$), the temptation might be to combine the information to arrive at an answer of C. This is a common trap on difficult Data Sufficiency problems. It might seem that we need both statements, when one statement alone actually provides enough information.

The correct answer is A.

23. C: Set up a table to list the first few terms of the sequence and also the cumulative sum:

n	$A_n = \dfrac{n-1}{n!}$	Cumulative sum
1	$A_1 = \dfrac{1-1}{1!} = 0$	0
2	$A_2 = \dfrac{2-1}{2!} = \dfrac{1}{2}$	$\dfrac{1}{2}$
3	$A_3 = \dfrac{3-1}{3!} = \dfrac{2}{6} = \dfrac{1}{3}$	$\dfrac{5}{6}$
4	$A_4 = \dfrac{4-1}{4!} = \dfrac{3}{24}$	$\dfrac{23}{24}$

As you build the table, compare the input column values (n) with the output column values (cumulative sum), looking for a pattern. The denominator of the cumulative sum is $n!$ and the numerator is one less than $n!$.

$$\text{Sum of terms through } A_n = \frac{n!-1}{n!}$$

Substituting, we see that the sum of terms through A_{10} is given by the following:

$$\text{Sum of terms through } A_{10} = \frac{10!-1}{10!}$$

The correct answer is C.

24. B: The units digit of n is determined solely by the units digit of the expressions 5^x and 7^{y+3}, because when two numbers are added together, the units digit of the sum is determined solely by the units digits of the added numbers.

Since x is a positive integer, and $5^{\text{any positive integer}}$ always has a units digit of 5, 5^x always ends in a 5. However, the units digit of 7^{y+3} is not certain, as the units digit pattern for the powers of 7 is a four-term repeat: [7, 9, 3, 1].

The question can thus be rephrased as "what is the units digit of 7^{y+3}?"

Note: Determining y would be one way of answering the question above, but we should not rephrase to "what is y?" Because the units digits of the powers of 7 have a repeating pattern, we might get a single answer for the units digit of 7^{y+3} *despite* having multiple values for y.

(1) INSUFFICIENT: This statement tells us neither the value of y nor the units digit of 7^{y+3}, as y depends on the value of x, which could be any positive integer. For example, if $x = 9$, then $y = 2$ and 7^{y+3} has a units digit of 7. By contrast, if $x = 10$, then $y = 4$ and 7^{y+3} has a units digit of 3.

(2) SUFFICIENT: Regardless of what multiple of 4 we pick, 7^{y+3} will have the same units digit:

y	$y+3$	Units digit of 7^{y+3}
4	7	3
8	11	3
12	15	3

Ultimately this means that n has a units digit of $5 + 3 = 8$.

The correct answer is B.

25. A: One way to approach this problem is to factor all of the answer choices. The one with matching pairs of prime factors is a perfect square. Although valid, this approach would be very time-consuming.

There is a backdoor solution: examine the units digit of the answers. Since the units digit of x^2 is simply the units digit of the square of the units digit of x, a perfect square must have the same units digit as one of 0, 1, 4, 9, 16, 25, 36, 49, 64, or 81. That is, a perfect square must have a units digit of 0, 1, 4, 5, 6, or 9. A perfect square *cannot* have a units digit of 2, 3, 7, or 8. Thus, answer choices B, C, D, and E are disqualified.

By the way, 73,410,624 is $(8,568)^2$. You would *never* be expected to figure that out on the GMAT.

The correct answer is A.

26. D: To form each new term of the sequence, we multiply the previous term by k. Given that $S_1 = 64$, we know that $S_2 = 64k$, and $S_3 = 64k^2$, and $S_n = 64k^{n-1}$. Thus $S_{25} = 64k^{24}$. Since we are told that $S_{25} = 192$, we can set up an equation to solve for k as follows:

$$64k^{24} = 192$$
$$k^{24} = 3$$
$$k = 3^{(1/24)}$$

Plugging this value for k into the expression for S_9, we have:

$$S_9 = 64k^8 = 64\left(3^{(1/24)}\right)^8 = 64\left(3^{(8/24)}\right) = 64\left(3^{1/3}\right) = 64\sqrt[3]{3}$$

The correct answer is D.

27. B: Remember the units digit pattern for 9^x, where x is an integer. The units digit of 9^x is 9 if x is odd, but the units digit is 1 if x is even: a repeating pattern of [9,1].

Now, consider the sums of the powers of 9 up to 9^n:

n	$y = 9^0 + 9^1 + 9^2 + \ldots + 9^n$	Units digit of y
1	$1+9 = 10$	0
2	$1+9+81 = 91$	1
3	$1+9+81+729 = 820$	0
4	$1+9+81+729 + \text{units digit of } 1 = \text{units digit of } 1$	1
odd	units digit: pairs of $(1+9)$	0
even	units digit: pairs of $(1+9)] + 1$	1

The alternating 1's and 9's in the units digits pair to a sum of 10, or a units digit of 0. Thus, the units digit of the sum displays another two-term repeating pattern. The units digit of y is 0 if n is odd, but 1 if n is even.

The remainder when y is divided by 5 depends only on the units digit and will be either 0 or 1 as well. So the rephrased question is "Is n odd or even?"

(1) INSUFFICIENT: If n is a multiple of 3, it may be either odd or even.

(2) SUFFICIENT: If n is odd, the units digit of y is 0, and the remainder is 0 when y is divided by 5.

The correct answer is B.

28. E: The sequence S is 3, 6, 12, 24, 48, and so on. We could write out the first 16 terms and add the 14th, 15th, and 16th together, but such an approach would be prone to error and time consuming. Additionally, we don't need to calculate the sum explicitly: the answer choices all have some power of 2 as a factor, providing a hint at the best solution method.

Let's write the sequence in terms of the powers of 2:

S: 3, 6, 12, 24, 48, and so on.
S: $3(2^0)$, $3(2^1)$, $3(2^2)$, $3(2^3)$, $3(2^4)$, and so on.

So S_n, the nth term of S, equals $3(2^{n-1})$.

Thus, the sum of the 14th, 15th, and 16th terms equals $3(2^{13}) + 3(2^{14}) + 3(2^{15})$.

All of the terms share the common factors 3 and 2^{13}, so factor those terms out:

$3(2^{13})(1 + 2^1 + 2^2)$
$3(2^{13})(1 + 2 + 4)$
$3(2^{13})(7)$
$21(2^{13})$

The correct answer is E.

29. B: Sequence problems are often best approached by charting out the first several terms of the given sequence. In this case, we need to keep track of n, t_n, and whether t_n is even or odd.

n	t_n	Is t_n even or odd?
0	3	Odd
1	$3 + 1 = 4$	Even
2	$4 + 2 = 6$	Even
3	$6 + 3 = 9$	Odd
4	$9 + 4 = 13$	Odd
5	$13 + 5 = 18$	Even
6	$18 + 6 = 24$	Even
7	$24 + 7 = 31$	Odd
8	$31 + 8 = 39$	Odd

Notice that beginning with $n = 1$, a four-term repeating cycle of [even, even, odd, odd] emerges for t_n. Thus, a statement will be sufficient only if it tells us how n relates to a multiple of 4 (i.e. $n = $ a multiple of 4 $\pm$ known constant).

(1) INSUFFICIENT: This statement does not tell us how n relates to a multiple of 4. If $n + 1$ is a multiple of 3, then $n + 1$ could be 3, 6, 9, 12, 15, etc. This means that n could be 2, 5, 8, 11, 14, etc. From the chart, if $n = 2$ or $n = 5$, then t_n is even. However, if $n = 8$ or $n = 11$, then t_n is odd.

(2) SUFFICIENT: This statement tells us exactly how n relates to a multiple of 4. If $n - 1$ is a multiple of 4, then $n - 1$ could be 4, 8, 12, 16, 20, etc. and n could be 5, 9, 13, 17, 21, etc. From the chart (and the continuation of the four-term pattern), t_n must be even.

The correct answer is B.

30. C: Set up a table to list the first few cubes and track the cumulative sum:

n	Cube	Cumulative sum
1	1	1
2	8	9
3	27	36
4	64	100

By this point, you should start to recognize that the cumulative sums are all perfect squares. Extend the table to the right to list the square roots.

*Manhattan*GMAT Prep
the new standard

n	Cube	Cumulative sum	$\sqrt{\text{Cumulative Sum}}$
1	1	1	$1 = 1$
2	8	9	$3 = 1+2$
3	27	36	$6 = 1+2+3$
4	64	100	$10 = 1+2+3+4$
5	125	225	$15 = 1+2+3+4+5$
...			
n	n^3	(Sum of integers 1 through n, inclusive)^2	Sum of integers 1 through n, inclusive.

Not only do we see a pattern emerging for the cumulative sum (always a perfect square), but also for the square root of the cumulative sum, which is always the sum of consecutive integers.

Thus, the sum of the first 10 cubes will be the square of the sum of the first 10 positive integers:

$$1^3 + 2^3 + 3^3 + 4^3 + \ldots + 10^3 = (1 + 2 + 3 + 4 + \ldots + 10)^2$$

Now, the sum of the first 10 positive integers can be computed by matching pairs:

$$1 + 2 + \ldots + 9 + 10 = 11 + 11 + 11 + 11 + 11$$
$$= 5(11)$$
$$= 55$$

So, the sum of the first 10 cubes is 55^2.

The correct answer is C.

Workout Set 4 Solutions

31. B: Since 5! and 12! share the common terms $(5)(4)(3)(2)(1)$, these terms can be canceled from both the

numerator and denominator. Thus, we can rewrite $\dfrac{12!}{3^4 (5!)2^6}$ as:

$$\frac{(12)(11)(10)(9)(8)(7)(6)}{3^4 (2^6)}$$

We need to cancel the 2's and 3's in the denominator, so we identify these common factors in the numerator.

$$\frac{(2^2 3)(11)(2 \times 5)(3^2)(2^3)(7)(2 \times 3)}{3^4 (2^6)}$$

Group the common factors of 2 and 3 in the numerator, then cancel and compute:

$$\frac{\left(2^7 3^4\right)(11)(5)(7)}{3^4\left(2^6\right)} = \left(2^1\right)(11)(5)(7)$$
$$= 770$$

The correct answer is B.

Note: If you do not have time to do all the canceling involved in this problem, you can at least rule out answer choices C (480) and E (35), because the correct answer must be a multiple of 11. The 12! in the numerator is a multiple of 11, and the denominator contains no factors of 11 that would cancel this term. You could use the same argument to eliminate non-multiples of 7; however, the divisibility rule for 7 is complicated, and on typical GMAT problems, testing by long division or inspection will be just as fast. In any event, you could eliminate answer choices C (480) and A (2,210) in this manner.

32. E: The expression for K becomes more manageable if we insert parentheses:

$$K = (S_6 - S_5) + (S_4 - S_3) + (S_2 - S_1)$$

K involves two expressions of the form $(S_{n+1} - S_n)$, so a general rule for $(S_{n+1} - S_n)$ might be helpful. We know that $S_n = n^2 + 5n + 94$, so

$S_{n+1} = (n + 1)^2 + 5(n + 1) + 94$
$S_{n+1} = (n^2 + 2n + 1) + (5n + 5) + 94$
$S_{n+1} = n^2 + 7n + 100$

In general, $(S_{n+1} - S_n) = (n^2 + 7n + 100) - (n^2 + 5n + 94) = 2n + 6$.

Applying this rule to the grouped terms in K:

$K = (S_6 - S_5) + (S_4 - S_3) + (S_2 - S_1)$
$= (2 \times 5 + 6) + (2 \times 3 + 6) + (2 \times 1 + 6)$
$= 16 + 12 + 8$
$= 36$

Alternatively, we could just plug into the S_n term definition, and identify common terms as we work:

$K = S_6 - S_5 + S_4 - S_3 + S_2 - S_1$
$= (6^2 + 5(6) + 94) - (5^2 + 5(5) + 94) + (4^2 + 5(4) + 94) - (3^2 + 5(3) + 94) + (2^2 + 5(2) + 94) - (1^2 + 5(1) + 94)$
$= (6^2 - 5^2 + 4^2 - 3^2 + 2^2 - 1^2) + 5(6 - 5 + 4 - 3 + 2 - 1)$
$= (36 - 25 + 16 - 9 + 4 - 1) + 5(3)$
$= (21) + (15)$
$= 36$

The correct answer is E.

33. E: First, rephrase the question stem by subtracting xy from both sides: "Is $xy < 0$?" The question is whether xy is negative, or "Do x and y have opposite signs?"

Be careful! Do not rephrase as follows:

Is $xy + xy < xy$?
Is $2xy < xy$?

Is $\dfrac{2xy}{xy} < \dfrac{xy}{xy}$? (Wrong! Dividing by variables is the mistake: What if $xy = 0$? What if $xy < 0$?)
Is $2 < 1$?

Not only does this rephrase make the statements moot (2 is definitely not less than 1, no matter what the statements say), but it also ignores some special cases. If $xy = 0$, then dividing by xy yields an undefined value. If $xy < 0$, we should have flipped the sign of the inequality.

This brings us back to our correct rephrasing: "Do x and y have opposite signs?"

(1) INSUFFICIENT: If $\dfrac{x^2}{y} < 0$, then x^2 and y must have opposite signs. Since x^2 must be positive, y must be negative. However, x could be either positive or negative.

(2) INSUFFICIENT: If $x^3y^3 < (xy)^2$, xy could be negative, as $x^3y^3 = \text{neg}^3 = \text{neg}$ and $(xy)^2 = \text{neg}^2 = \text{pos}$, and it is always true that neg $<$ pos.

However, $x^3y^3 < (xy)^2$ would also hold true if xy were a positive proper fraction. For example, if $xy = 1/2$, then $(1/2)^3 < (1/2)^2$. Therefore, xy could also be positive.

(1) AND (2) INSUFFICIENT: Each statement tells us that xy could be either positive or negative. The statements are equally insufficient, and neither provides any additional information to the other.

The correct answer is E.

34. C: First, distribute the numerator:

$$\frac{x^3 + (x^2 + x)(1 - y) - y}{x - y} = \frac{x^3 + x^2 + x - x^2 y - xy - y}{x - y}$$

None of the answer choices are fractions, so the $x - y$ in the denominator must be cancelled by a $x - y$ in the numerator. We group the numerator terms with x and $-y$ in mind:

$$\frac{\left(x^3+x^2+x\right)-\left(x^2 y+xy+y\right)}{x-y}=\frac{x\left(x^2+x+1\right)-y\left(x^2+x+1\right)}{x-y}$$

$$=\frac{\left(x-y\right)\left(x^2+x+1\right)}{x-y}$$

$$=\left(x^2+x+1\right)$$

Alternatively, you could pick numbers and test the answer choices. If $x = 2$ and $y = 3$, then:

$$\frac{x^3+\left(x^2+x\right)\left(1-y\right)-y}{x-y}=\frac{8+\left(4+2\right)\left(1-3\right)-3}{2-3}$$

$$=\frac{8+\left(6\right)\left(-2\right)-3}{-1}$$

$$=\frac{8-12-3}{-1}$$

$$=7$$

Plug the selected values into the choices. The choice that equals 7 is the correct answer.

(A) $(x - 1)^2 y = (2 - 1)^2(3) = 3$
(B) $(x + 1)^2 = (2 + 1)^2 = 9$
(C) $x^2 + x + 1 = 4 + 2 + 1 = 7$
(D) $(x^2 + x + 1)y = (4 + 2 + 1)(3) = 21$
(E) $(x^2 + x + 1)(x - y) = (4 + 2 + 1)(2 - 3) = -7$

The correct answer is C.

35. A: We begin by listing some values of g_n, in order to get a sense for how g_n progresses:

$g_1 = 1$
$g_2 = 1$
$g_3 = g_2 + 2^0 = 1 + 1 = 2 = 2^1$
$g_4 = g_3 + 2^1 = 2 + 2 = 4 = 2^2$
$g_5 = g_4 + 2^2 = 4 + 4 = 8 = 2^3$
$g_6 = g_5 + 2^3 = 8 + 8 = 16 = 2^4$

We can see that for $n \geq 3$, $g_n = 2^{n-2}$.

Let us now look for a pattern in the sums defined as $\psi(g_n)$:

$$\psi(g_3) = g_1 + g_2 + g_3 = 1+1+2 = 4 = 2^2$$

$$\psi(g_4) = \left(g_1 + g_2 + g_3\right) + g_4 = \psi(g_3) + g_4 = 4 + 4 = 8 = 2^3$$

$$\psi(g_5) = \left(g_1 + g_2 + g_3 + g_4\right) + g_5 = \psi(g_4) + g_5 = 8 + 8 = 16 = 2^4$$

Each value is double the previous value: $\psi(g_n) = 2 \times \psi(g_{n-1})$. This means that:

$$\frac{\psi(g_{16})}{\psi(g_{15})} = \frac{2 \times \psi(g_{15})}{\psi(g_{15})} = 2$$

Now all we need to do is scan the answer choices to find an expression that equals 2. We have already discovered that $g_3 = 2$, so we can select g_3 as the answer.

The correct answer is A.

36. E: The common term in this problem is the recurring base of 3. We will group like terms (i.e. all the terms with k on the left side, all the other powers of 3 on the right side), then simplify each power of 3 using exponent rules.

$3^k + 3^k = \left(3^9\right)^{3^{3^9}} - 3^k$

$3^k + 3^k + 3^k = \left(3^9\right)^{3^{3^9}}$

$3(3^k) = \left(3^9\right)^{3^{3^9}}$

$3^{k+1} = 3^{9 \times 3^9}$

$k + 1 = 9 \times 3^9$

$k + 1 = 3^2 \times 3^9$

$k = 3^{11} - 1$

The correct answer is E.

37. C: We could try to rephrase this question by distributing the expression, but doing so doesn't simplify things. A useful rephrase is "What are the quantities $(a + b)$ and $(c + d)$?"

(1) INSUFFICIENT: Since both $a!$ and $b! = 4a!$ are the product of consecutive integers starting at 1, it must be true that 4 immediately follows the consecutive integers $1, 2, \ldots, a - 1, a$. Therefore, $a = 3$ and $b = 4$. However, this tells us nothing about $(c + d)$.

(2) INSUFFICIENT: Since both $c!$ and $d! = 5c!$ are the product of consecutive integers starting at 1, it must be true that 5 immediately follows the consecutive integers $1, 2, \ldots, c - 1, c$. Therefore, $c = 4$ and $d = 5$. However, this tells us nothing about $(a + b)$.

(1) AND (2) SUFFICIENT: Together, the statements give us the value of all four variables.

$(a + b)(c + d) = (3 + 4)(4 + 5) = (7)(9) = 63$

The correct answer is C.

38. D: The question is asking for the largest value of k such that $\frac{33!}{22!}$ is divisible by 6^k. Since $6 = 3 \times 2$, this largest value of k will equal the number of 3×2 pairs among the prime factors of $\frac{33!}{22!}$.

To count the number of times 3 appears as a factor of $\frac{33!}{22!}$, we can rewrite the expression, pulling out any factor(s) of 3 from each term:

$(33)(32)(31)(30)(29)(28)(27)(26)(25)(24)(23)$
$= (\mathbf{3} \times 11)(32)(31)(\mathbf{3} \times 10)(29)(28)(\mathbf{3^3})(26)(25)(\mathbf{3} \times 8)(23)$

There are six factors of 3 in $\frac{33!}{22!}$.

To count the number of times 2 appears as a factor of $\frac{33!}{22!}$, we can rewrite the expression, pulling out any factor(s) of 2 from each term:

$(33)(32)(31)(30)(29)(28)(27)(26)(25)(24)(23)$
$= (33)(\mathbf{2^5})(31)(\mathbf{2} \times 15)(29)(\mathbf{2^2} \times 7)(27)(\mathbf{2} \times 13)(25)(\mathbf{2^3} \times 3)(23)$

There are twelve factors of 2 in $\frac{33!}{22!}$.

Since there are twelve 2's but only six 3's, there are only six 3×2 pairs among the prime factors of $\frac{33!}{22!}$. In general, we can focus on the largest prime in the divisor (in this case, the factor of 3 in 6^k), as it will be the limiting factor.

The correct answer is D.

39. D: $s_{100} = 101!$ and $s_{99} = 100!$

We can factor the difference as follows:

$$s_{100} - s_{99} = (101!) - (100!)$$
$$= (101)(100!) - 100!$$
$$= (100!)(101 - 1)$$
$$= (100!)(100)$$
$$= (100)(99!)(100)$$
$$= (100^2)(99!)$$

The correct answer is D.

40. C: Not only does $q = \dfrac{9^5}{7^3}$, but we can also factor $\dfrac{9^5}{7^3}$ out of p:

$$p = \frac{9^7 - 9^5}{7^5 + 7^3} = \left(\frac{9^5}{7^3}\right)\left(\frac{9^2 - 9^0}{7^2 + 7^0}\right) = \left(\frac{9^5}{7^3}\right)\left(\frac{81-1}{49+1}\right) = \left(\frac{9^5}{7^3}\right)\left(\frac{80}{50}\right) = \left(\frac{9^5}{7^3}\right)\left(\frac{8}{5}\right)$$

Thus, $p = q\left(\dfrac{8}{5}\right)$, and $\dfrac{p}{q} = \dfrac{8}{5}$. Watch out! This is one of the incorrect answers.

The question asks for $\dfrac{q}{p}$, which is $\left(\dfrac{p}{q}\right)^{-1} = \left(\dfrac{8}{5}\right)^{-1} = \dfrac{5}{8}$.

The correct answer is C.

41. If x and y are positive integers, what is the value of x/y?

(1) $x^2 = 2xy - y^2$
(2) $2xy = 8$

Workout Set 5 Solutions

41. A: (1) SUFFICIENT: If we move all terms to one side we get:

$x^2 = 2xy - y^2$
$x^2 - 2xy + y^2 = 0$

We can factor this "square of a difference" special product and simplify:

$x^2 - 2xy + y^2 = 0$
$(x - y)^2 = 0$
$x - y = 0$

Since $x = y$, the value of x/y is 1.

(2) INSUFFICIENT: Knowing that $2xy = 8$ tells us that $xy = 4$. If we consider different values for x and y, we see that the value of x/y can vary:

x (positive)	y (positive)	Fact (2): $xy = 4$	Question: $x/y =$?
2	2	$2 \times 2 = 4$ ✔	1
1	4	$1 \times 4 = 4$ ✔	1/4

Alternatively, by manipulating the equation $xy = 4$ to get x/y on one side, we see that x/y does not equal a constant:

$$xy = 4$$

$$\frac{xy}{y^2} = \frac{4}{y^2}$$

$$\frac{x}{y} = \frac{4}{y^2}$$

So x/y could take on many different values.

The correct answer is A.

42. E: One way to solve would be to multiply $(47)(49)$, then either divide the result by 8 or repeatedly subtract known multiples of 8 from the result until we are left with a remainder smaller than 8.

An alternative is to rewrite the given product as an equivalent yet easier-to-manipulate product. Note that 47 and 49 are equidistant from 48, a multiple of 8. We can write each of the original factors as terms in the form $(a + b)$ or $(a - b)$.

$$(47)(49) = (48 + 1)(48 - 1)$$

Recognizing the "difference of two squares" special product, $(a + b)(a - b) = a^2 - b^2$, we can quickly manipulate again:

$$(48 + 1)(48 - 1) = (48^2 - 1^2)$$

48 is a multiple of 8, and therefore so is 48^2. Thus, $(48^2 - 1^2)$ is 1 less than a multiple of 8. All such numbers (e.g. 7, 15, 23, 31, etc.) have a remainder of 7 when divided by 8.

The correct answer is E.

43. E: If we add a and b, we get $a + b = 4x^2 + 8xy + 4y^2 = 4(x^2 + 2xy + y^2)$.

The right side is of the "square of a sum," so we can factor and solve:

$$a + b = 4\left(x^2 + 2xy + y^2\right)$$

$$a + b = 4(x + y)^2$$

$$\frac{a + b}{4} = (x + y)^2$$

$$\sqrt{\frac{a + b}{4}} = (x + y)$$

$$\frac{\sqrt{a + b}}{2} = (x + y)$$

Note that we could safely take the square root of both sides, since we know any square is non-negative.

Alternatively, we could pick numbers and test each answer choice. For example, if $x = 2$ and $y = 3$, then the final answer $x + y = 5$.

For values to plug into the choices, we must first compute a and b:

$a = 4x^2 + 4xy = 4(2^2) + 4(2)(3) = 16 + 24 = 40$ and $b = 4y^2 + 4xy = 4(3^2) + 4(2)(3) = 36 + 24 = 60$

Next, we test each answer choice; the one that equals 5 is the correct answer.

(A) $\sqrt{a+b} = \sqrt{40+60} = 10$

(B) $2\sqrt{ab} = 2\sqrt{(40)(60)} = 2\sqrt{(400)(6)} = 40\sqrt{6}$

(C) $\dfrac{a+b}{\sqrt{2}} = \dfrac{40+60}{\sqrt{2}} = \dfrac{100}{\sqrt{2}}$

(D) $2\sqrt{a} - 2\sqrt{b} = 2\sqrt{40} - 2\sqrt{60} = 4\sqrt{10} - 4\sqrt{15}$

(E) $\dfrac{\sqrt{a+b}}{2} = \dfrac{\sqrt{40+60}}{2} = \dfrac{10}{2} = 5$

The correct answer is E.

44. B: Manipulate the question expression, noting the special products in the exponents:

$$\frac{3^{(a+b)^2}}{3^{(a-b)^2}} = \frac{3^{(a^2+2ab+b^2)}}{3^{(a^2-2ab+b^2)}}$$

$$= 3^{(a^2+2ab+b^2)-(a^2-2ab+b^2)}$$

$$= 3^{4ab}$$

The rephrased question is "What is the value of ab?" Knowing the values of a and b individually would be sufficient, of course, but the individual values are not required as long as we can determine ab.

(1) INSUFFICIENT: We cannot manipulate $a + b = 7$ to get ab, nor can we solve for a and b individually.

(2) SUFFICIENT: This statement answers the rephrased question directly.

The correct answer is B.

45. D: $\left(\sqrt{24+5\sqrt{23}}\right)\left(\sqrt{24-5\sqrt{23}}\right) = \sqrt{\left(24+5\sqrt{23}\right)\left(24-5\sqrt{23}\right)}$

Notice the special product of the form $(a + b)(a - b) = a^2 - b^2$ under the square root symbol.

$$\sqrt{\left(24+5\sqrt{23}\right)\left(24-5\sqrt{23}\right)} = \sqrt{24^2 - \left(5\sqrt{23}\right)^2} = \sqrt{24^2 - (25)(23)} = \sqrt{576-575} = 1$$

The correct answer is D.

46. D: If $a^6 - b^6 = 0$, then $a^6 = b^6$. This might seem to imply that $a = b$, but remember that even exponents hide the sign of the base, so a and b could have opposite signs. We can conclude that $|a| = |b|$.

The left side of the equation $a^6 - b^6 = 0$ is the "difference of two squares," and is equivalent to $a^6 - b^6 = (a^3 + b^3)(a^3 - b^3) = 0$, which implies that either $(a^3 + b^3) = 0$ or $(a^3 - b^3) = 0$, or both. One rephrase of this question is "Which expression is equal to zero: $(a^3 + b^3)$ or $(a^3 - b^3)$?" A related question is "Do a and b have the same sign or different sign?"

(1) SUFFICIENT: If $a^3 - b^3 = -2 \neq 0$, then it must be true that $(a^3 + b^3) = 0$.

(2) SUFFICIENT: If $ab < 0$, then a and b have opposite signs. Odd exponents do not hide the sign of the base, so a^3 and b^3 also have opposite signs. The question stem told us that $|a| = |b|$, so $(a^3 + b^3) = 0$.

The correct answer is D.

47. B: To solve this problem we can focus on solving for b as a first step:

$$2\left(\sqrt{x} - \sqrt{y}\right) = \frac{(x - y)}{b}$$
$$2b\left(\sqrt{x} - \sqrt{y}\right) = x - y$$
$$2b = \frac{(x - y)}{\left(\sqrt{x} - \sqrt{y}\right)}.$$

Note that it is OK to divide by $\sqrt{x} - \sqrt{y}$, since $x > y$, which implies that $\sqrt{x} - \sqrt{y} \neq 0$.

We have solved for $2b$, but the result does not match any of the answer choices. Most of the choices are not fractions, so we should try to cancel the denominator. Recognizing that $x - y$ is a well-disguised "difference of two squares," we can factor the numerator and denominator:

$$2b = \frac{(\sqrt{x} - \sqrt{y})(\sqrt{x} + \sqrt{y})}{(\sqrt{x} - \sqrt{y})}$$

Cancel $\left(\sqrt{x} - \sqrt{y}\right)$ in the numerator and denominator to get $2b = \sqrt{x} + \sqrt{y}$.

The correct answer is B.

48. D: Each of the expressions given is equal to 16, so we can set them equal to each other. Note that we have the "square of a sum" and the "difference of two squares" special products. We will put them both in distributed form, then simplify:

$$(x + y)^2 = x^2 - y^2$$
$$x^2 + 2xy + y^2 = x^2 - y^2$$
$$2xy + y^2 = -y^2$$
$$2xy + 2y^2 = 0$$

Since $2y(x + y) = 0$, it must be true that either $2y$ or $(x + y)$ is equal to 0. However, $(x + y)$ cannot equal 0, since we are told that $(x + y)^2 = 16$. So it must be that $2y = 0$. Thus $y = 0$.

If we plug 0 in for y in $x^2 - y^2 = 16$, we get $x^2 = 16$. Thus $2x^2 = 2(16) = 32$.

The correct answer is D.

49. C: When a problem looks like it requires large amounts of arithmetic computation, look for a shortcut. Here we can use the fact that the numbers being squared are 5 consecutive integers. If we let $x = 40$, we can represent the original expression as $(x - 2)^2 + (x - 1)^2 + x^2 + (x + 1)^2 + (x + 2)^2$.

For each of the pairs $(x - k)^2$ and $(x + k)^2$, the sum is:

$(x - k)^2 + (x + k)^2$
$(x^2 - 2kx + k^2) + (x^2 + 2kx + k^2)$
$2(x^2 + k^2)$

Thus, the sum of all 5 terms in our original expression is

$2(x^2 + 2^2) + 2(x^2 + 1^2) + x^2$
$2x^2 + 2(2^2) + 2x^2 + 2(1^2) + x^2$
$5x^2 + 8 + 2$
$5x^2 + 10$

Since $x = 40$, the sum is $5(40)^2 + 10 = 5(1,600) + 10 = 8,010$.

It's also possible to solve within 2 minutes by brute force:

$38^2 + 39^2 + 40^2 + 41^2 + 42^2 = 1,444 + 1,521 + 1,600 + 1,681 + 1,764 = 8,010$

The correct answer is C.

50. A: We begin by simplifying the equation given in the question:

$$8xy^3 + 8x^3y = \frac{2x^2y^2}{2^{-3}}$$
$$2^{-3}\left(8xy^3 + 8x^3y\right) = 2x^2y^2$$
$$\frac{1}{8}\left(8xy^3 + 8x^3y\right) = 2x^2y^2$$
$$xy^3 + x^3y = 2x^2y^2$$

At this stage, you might be tempted to divide both sides of the equation by xy, in order to arrive at the simpler equation $y^2 + x^2 = 2xy$. However, that would be a mistake—you must never divide both sides of an equation by an unknown (in this case xy), unless you are certain that the unknown cannot equal zero. (Division by zero is undefined, and can lead to nonsensical results.) So, rather than divide by xy, we subtract $2x^2y^2$ from both sides in order to group all terms on one side of the equal sign:

$$xy^3 + x^3y - 2x^2y^2 = 0$$
$$(xy)(y^2 + x^2 - 2xy) = 0$$
$$(xy)(y - x)^2 = 0$$

This last line implies that either $xy = 0$ or $y - x = 0$. In other words, either $xy = 0$ or $y = x$ and therefore $xy = x^2$, which depends on the value of x.

(1) SUFFICIENT. If $y > x$, then it is impossible that $y = x$. Therefore, we know that $xy = 0$.

(2) INSUFFICIENT. If $x < 0$, then it is possible that $xy = 0$ (i.e. if $y = 0$) or that $y = x$ (i.e. y is negative too). If $y = x =$ any negative number, then there are infinitely many solutions for xy.

The correct answer is A.

Workout Set 6 Solutions

51. A: We know the length of two sides, AB and BC. Without using the statements, we do not know any of the angles of the triangle, or the length of the third side, AC.

Draw the extreme possibilities for this triangle so we won't lose sight of them as we evaluate the statements. Triangle ABC could look like the following:

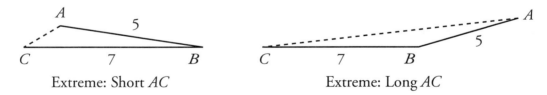

Extreme: Short AC Extreme: Long AC

To visualize all the possibilities, you might imagine that BC is horizontal and AB is on a hinge that can rotate from one extreme to the other.

(1) SUFFICIENT: Triangle ABC is a right triangle that looks like this:

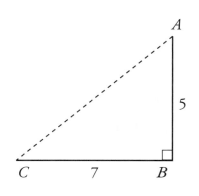

The area of the triangle is $(1/2)bh = (1/2)(5)(7) = 35/2$.

(2) INSUFFICIENT: This statement might seem equivalent to statement (1), but it is not! We do not know which angle in *ABC* is the right angle. In any right triangle, the 90° angle is the largest angle and will be directly opposite the longest side of the triangle.

If *AC* is the longest side of the triangle, then *ABC* is the right angle. The triangle looks like the one we drew for statement (1), and the area is 35/2.

But if we remember our extreme cases, we know *AC* could be relatively short, making side *BC* = 7 the longest side of the triangle. In that case, angle *CAB* would be the right angle:

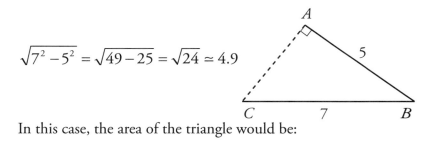

$$\sqrt{7^2 - 5^2} = \sqrt{49 - 25} = \sqrt{24} \approx 4.9$$

In this case, the area of the triangle would be:

$$(1/2)bh = (1/2)(5)(\sqrt{24}) = (1/2)(5)(2\sqrt{6}) = 5\sqrt{6}$$

The area is either 35/2 or $5\sqrt{6}$.

The correct answer is A.

52. D: Your GMAT scratchpad has a grid; use it to plot the diagram to scale.

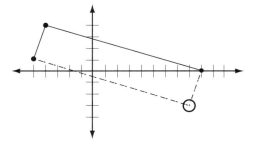

"Eyeball" solution: The corner at (−4, 4) looks like a right angle, so complete the rectangle with the dashed lines shown. The 4th point must be located approximately where the bigger dot is drawn. The closest answer choice is the point (7, −3). Alternatively, you could plot all of the answer choice points and see which one "works" with the three given points.

Alternatively, we could solve by checking the slopes of the solid lines we drew between the given points to prove those lines are perpendicular, that is, to prove we have drawn two sides of the rectangle correctly.

The slope of the long solid line = $\dfrac{4-0}{-4-8} = \dfrac{4}{-12} = -\dfrac{1}{3}$

The slope of the short solid line = $\dfrac{4-1}{-4-(-5)} = \dfrac{3}{-4+5} = 3$

The product of these slopes is $\left(-\dfrac{1}{3}\right)(3) = -1$, proving that the lines are perpendicular.

Compute the location of the 4th point, using the fact that the short sides have the same slope. The known short side connects the points (−5, 1) and (−4, 4). In other words, the bottom left corner is 1 to the left and 3 down from the top left corner. The unknown bottom right corner should therefore be 1 to the left and 3 down from the top right corner, or $x = 8 − 1 = 7$ and $y = 0 − 3 = −3$, corresponding to the point (7, −3).

The correct answer is D.

53. **E:** A square is both a rectangle (it has four 90° angles) and a rhombus (it has four sides of equal length). A circle is neither a rectangle nor a rhombus. Therefore, we can solve this problem using a double-set matrix. A few simple pictures will help us put the correct numbers in the correct boxes:

	Rectangles	Non-Rectangles	Total
Rhombuses	□	▱	
Non-Rhombuses	▭	○ ⬡ △ etc.	
Total			

The total number of cards is 30. The number of squares (i.e. figures that are both rhombuses and rectangles) is 8. The total number of rectangles is half of 30, i.e. 15. The total number of rhombuses is one-third of 30, i.e. 10. If x is the number of cards that are neither rectangles nor rhombuses, the number of circles must be less than or equal to x. Since the question asks for the maximum number of cards that could be circles, our goal is to find the value of x in the following table:

	Rectangles	Non-Rectangles	Total
Rhombuses	8		10
Non-Rhombuses		x	
Total	15		30

In order to solve for x, we need to fill in the boxes that are in the same row and/or column as x. Each row and column in the matrix must sum to the total for that row or column, so:

	Rectangles	Non-Rectangles	Total
Rhombuses	8	2	10
Non-Rhombuses	7	$x = 13$	20
Total	15	15	30

The correct answer is E.

54. B: (1) INSUFFICIENT: This only tells us the weight of the men, but nothing about the relative numbers of women and men.

(2) SUFFICIENT: This does not tell us the weight of the men or even the weighted average, but it does tell us where the weighted average falls between the two values.

	Women	Men	Difference
Weight	120	m	$m - 120$
# of people	?	?	
Fraction of people	$\dfrac{x}{3x} = \dfrac{1}{3}$	$\dfrac{2x}{3x} = \dfrac{2}{3}$	

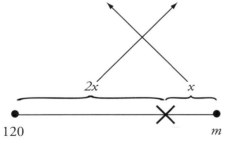

$1/3$ or approximately $33\dfrac{1}{3}\%$ of the competitors were women.

The correct answer is B.

55. B: The simple average formula (Average = Sum/Number of terms) applies to this problem. However, the chance of computational error is high on a problem with this many terms of such a large size.

A nice shortcut is possible if we group the similar terms:

Group *A*: 12, 13, 14 (equidistant terms with an average of 13, the middle term)
Group *B*: 510, 520, 530 (equidistant terms with an average of 520, the middle term)
Group *C*: 1,115, 1,120, 1,125 (equidistant terms with an average of 1,120, the middle term)

Since each group of terms consisted of three values (and thus were equally weighted in the set of nine terms), the average of all nine original terms is simply the average of the respective averages of Groups *A*, *B*, and *C*:

$$
\begin{array}{r}
13 \\
520 \\
+ 1,120 \\
\hline
1,653 \\
\end{array}
$$

Average = 1,653/3 = 551

The correct answer is B.

56. E: Two techniques will help us efficiently interpret the information given in the question. First, we draw a number line with 5 dots representing the 5 numbers in the set. Second, we label these numbers *A*, *B*, *C*, *D*, and *E*, with the understanding that $A \le B \le C \le D \le E$.

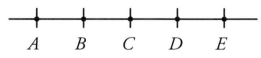

We are told that:
$A + B + C + D + E = 250$ (The set of 5 numbers has an average of 50.)
$E = 5 + 3A$ (The largest element is 5 greater than 3 times the smallest element in the set.)
$C = 50$ (The median of the set equals the mean.)

We want to maximize *E*. We should arrange our dots on the number line such that we obey the constraints, yet also note where we have some flexibility.

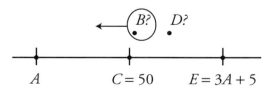

Point *D* can be anywhere on the line from Point *C* to Point *E*. Since *D* only appears in one of our formulas above ($A + B + C + D + E = 250$), we maximize *E* by minimizing *D*. Thus, $D = C = 50$.

Similarly, Point B can be anywhere on the line from Point A to Point C. We maximize E by minimizing B, so $B = A$.

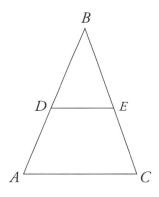

$A = B$ $C = D = 50$ $E = 3A + 5$

$$A + B + C + D + E = 250$$
$$A + (A) + 50 + 50 + (5 + 3A) = 250$$
$$105 + 5A = 250$$
$$5A = 145$$
$$A = 29$$

$E = 5 + 3A = 5 + 3(29) = 5 + 87 = 92.$

$A = B = 29$ $C = D = 50$ $E = 92$

The correct answer is E.

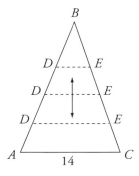

57. C: (1) INSUFFICIENT: Many elements in this triangle could vary; we don't even know the placement of B relative to AC, so the triangle itself might stretch. Even for a fixed triangle, we see that DE could slide up or down, so various lengths are possible for DE.

(2) INSUFFICIENT: We don't know the lengths of any sides of the triangle. The side that most affects the length of *DE* is *AC*, so we'll stretch that side. As we see, stretching the triangle out to the right stretches DE.

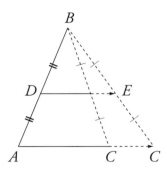

(1) AND (2) SUFFICIENT: *AC* must be 14, and *DE* must be parallel to *AC* and halfway between *AC* and *B*, in order to maintain *BE* = *EC*. Even though vertex *B* is free to move, *DE* will always be the average of the width of the triangle at *AC* (14) and the width at *B* (0). Thus, *DE* must be 7, no matter how the picture shifts.

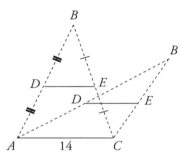

The correct answer is C.

58. D: To find the median of a set of numbers, we line them up in order of value. The question of interest to us is "Where is *m* relative to the other values?" This set has 6 values, an even number of terms, so the median is the average of the two middle terms.

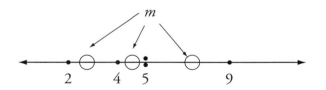

There are three scenarios:

If $m \leq 4$, then the two middle terms are 4 and 5, and the median is 4.5.

If $4 < m < 5$, then the two middle terms are *m* and 5, and the median is $\dfrac{m+5}{2}$.

If $m \geq 5$, then the two middle terms are 5 and 5, and the median is 5.

(1) SUFFICIENT: For the case where $4 < m < 5$, the median is

$\dfrac{m+5}{2} = \dfrac{\text{non-integer} + \text{odd}}{2} = \text{non-integer}$. Thus, if the median is an integer, it must be 5.

(2) If $m = 8$, then $m \geq 5$, and the median is 5.

The correct answer is D.

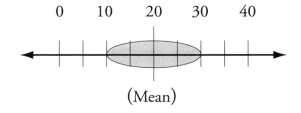

(Mean)

59. D: A handy visual simplification, the circle above spans ± 1 standard deviation from the mean. Draw dots for the answer pairs. We should be able to "see" which one results in a smaller standard deviation, or at least comparatively, which of the five affects standard deviation the *least*:

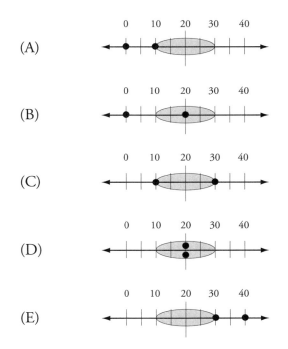

Relative to the other answer pairs, 20 and 20 are closest to the mean and within the current standard deviation of 10. Mathematically, this pair must reduce standard deviation because it increases the number of terms while leaving the sum of the squared distances of the terms from zero unchanged. By contrast, the other answer choices either leave the squared distances from the mean unchanged, or increase them.

The correct answer is D.

60. B: Conceptually, the transfer of jelly beans from Dante to Aaron reduces the range of the number of jelly beans held by individual children. Our constraint is that no children differ in their number of jelly beans by more than 1—a condition Bianca and Callie already satisfy.

We can draw the following picture (a number line) to visualize the scenario:

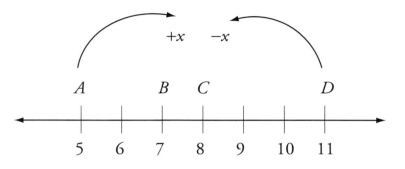

From the picture, we can infer that Aaron and Dante must end up with a number of jelly beans that is either 7 or 8. If either Aaron or Dante has a number of jelly beans *other than* 7 or 8, he will differ too much from either Bianca's or Callie's number.

$A + x = 7$ or 8
$5 + x = 7$ or 8
$x = 2$ or 3

$D - x = 7$ or 8
$11 - x = 7$ or 8
$x = 3$ or 4

The solution to both equations is $x = 3$. The resulting number of jelly beans is $A = 8$, $B = 7$, $C = 8$, and $D = 8$.

The correct answer is B.

Workout Set 7 Solutions

61. B: (1) INSUFFICIENT: There are several square tile sizes that can be placed as described. Consider these example values for s, the length of a side of the square tile:

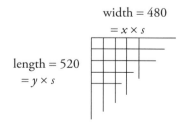

If $s = 40$, then $x = \dfrac{480}{40} = 12$ and $y = \dfrac{520}{40} = 13$, so $n = xy = (12)(13) = 156$.

If $s = 20$, then $x = \dfrac{480}{20} = 24$ and $y = \dfrac{520}{20} = 26$, so $n = xy = (24)(26) = 624$.

(2) SUFFICIENT: The width of the room is 480 centimeters, so the side of the square tile must be

$\dfrac{480}{12} = 40$ centimeters. Therefore, $n = xy = (12)(13) = 156$.

The correct answer is B.

62. A: The original price for a dozen donuts is $\dfrac{\$15}{x \text{ donuts}} \times \dfrac{12 \text{ donuts}}{\text{dozen}} = \dfrac{(15)(12)}{x} = \dfrac{180}{x}$ dollars/dozen.

The promotional price for the donuts is $\dfrac{\$15}{x + 3 \text{ donuts}} \times \dfrac{12 \text{ donuts}}{\text{dozen}} = \dfrac{180}{(x+3)}$ dollars/dozen.

The difference in price per dozen is $2, so we have the following equation:

$$\dfrac{180}{x} - \dfrac{180}{(x+3)} = 2$$

$$\dfrac{180(x+3)}{x(x+3)} - \dfrac{180x}{x(x+3)} = 2$$

$$\dfrac{180(x+3) - 180x}{x(x+3)} = 2$$

$$180(x+3) - 180x = 2x(x+3)$$

$$180(3) = 2x^2 + 6x$$

$$0 = 2x^2 + 6x - 540$$

$$0 = x^2 + 3x - 270$$

$$0 = (x+18)(x-15)$$

x must be positive, so $x = 15$. This answer checks out: If the original price was $15 for $15 donuts, that's $1 per donut or $12 for a dozen. The promotional price was $2 less per dozen, or $10 for a dozen. The promotional price was $15 for 18 donuts or 1.5 dozen, which equates to $10 for a dozen.

The correct answer is A.

63. C: We can create a double-set matrix to solve this problem:

	Right-handed	Left-handed	Total
Men			$3x$
Women			$2x$
Total	$3y$	y	$4y = 5x$

There is an unstated constraint that we can only have an integer number of people, since it is impossible to have a partial person. Thus, both x and y are integers. Moreover, the total number of people must be both a multiple of 4 and of 5 in order for the given ratios to be possible. From this constraint, there are two ways to solve.

Algebraic Solution
Since the question specifies that the number of right-handed men be as large as possible, we can assume that all the men are right-handed, and of course that means that none of the men are left-handed. Because each column in a double set matrix must total, we can also fill in the number of left-handed women (the group we are interested in):

	Right-handed	Left-handed	Total
Men	$3x$	0	$3x$
Women		y	$2x$
Total	$3y$	y	$4y = 5x$

Thus, left-handed women represent $\dfrac{y}{4y} = \dfrac{1}{4} = 25\%$ of the total population.

Smart Number Solution
Since the total number of people in Smithtown must be a multiple of 20, let's set our total to 20 and determine the subtotals of men, women, left- and right-handed based on the ratios given in the problem:

	Right-handed	Left-handed	Total
Men			12
Women			8
Total	15	5	20

To maximize the number of right-handed men, we assign all the men to the "right-handed men" cell and fill in the remaining cells:

	Right-handed	Left-handed	Total
Men	12	0	12
Women	3	5	8
Total	15	5	20

Therefore, left-handed women represent 5/20 = 1/4 = 25% of the population.

The correct answer is C.

64. **C:** If the median angle measure is 140 degrees and the interior angle measures correspond to a set of consecutive integers, then the average (arithmetic mean) angle measure must equal 140 degrees. Since the sum of the angles must equal $180(n - 2)$, the average angle must equal $\dfrac{180(n-2)}{n}$:

$$140 = \frac{180(n-2)}{n}$$
$$140n = 180n - 360$$
$$360 = 40n$$
$$n = 9.$$

Therefore, the polygon has 9 sides and 9 interior angles, and the measures of these angles are equal to a set of consecutive integers *centered at* 140. The set of 9 consecutive integers must therefore be:

$$\text{Set} = \{136, 137, 138, 139, 140, 141, 142, 143, 144\}$$

The smallest angle measure is 136°.

The correct answer is C.

65. **A:** If x/y has a quotient of 2 and a remainder of z, then x is z more than $2y$. Mathematically, $x = 2y + z$. Therefore, $z = x - 2y$.

If x/a has a quotient of 3 and a remainder of b, then x is b more than $3a$. Mathematically, $x = 3a + b$. Therefore, $b = x - 3a$.

The question asks whether $z > b$, and the statements give information about y/a. We can simplify the question by replacing z and b with their equivalents, and solving for the combination y/a:

$$z > b?$$
$$x - 2y > x - 3a?$$
$$-2y > -3a?$$
$$\frac{y}{a} < \frac{3}{2}?$$

Note that we flipped the inequality sign in the last step, because we divided by -2. We also divided by a in that last step, but we know that a is a positive integer, so no additional flip is required for that manipulation. Therefore, we can rephrase the question as "Is $\dfrac{y}{a} < \dfrac{3}{2}$?"

(1) SUFFICIENT: This directly answers the rephrased question: "Yes, $\frac{y}{a} < \frac{3}{2}$." Therefore, $z > b$.

(2) INSUFFICIENT: This tells us only that $\frac{y}{a} > \frac{2}{3}$. The answer might be "yes," if $\frac{2}{3} < \frac{y}{a} < \frac{3}{2}$.

However, the answer might be "no," if $\frac{y}{a}$ is greater than 3/2.

The correct answer is A.

66. A: The function $(3 \Delta 47)$ equals the product $(3)(5)(7)\ldots(43)(45)(47)$. This product is a very large odd number, as it is the product of only odd numbers and thus does not have 2 as a factor. Therefore, $(3 \Delta 47) + 2 = \text{Odd} + \text{Even} = \text{Odd}$, and $(3 \Delta 47) + 2$ does not have 2 as a factor either.

Every odd prime number between 3 and 47 inclusive is a factor of $(3 \Delta 47)$, since each of these primes is a component of the product. For example, $(3 \Delta 47)$ is divisible by 3, since dividing by 3 yields an integer — the product $(5)(7)(9)\ldots(43)(45)(47)$.

Now consider the sum $(3 \Delta 47) + k$, where k is an integer. The sum will only be divisible by 3 if k is also divisible by 3. In other words, when we divide $(3 \Delta 47) + k$ by 3, we are evaluating $(3 \Delta 47)/3 + k/3$. Because $(3 \Delta 47)/3$ is an integer, $k/3$ must also be an integer to yield an integer sum.

In this problem, $k = 2$, which is not divisible by any of the odd primes between 3 and 47. Since $(3 \Delta 47)$ IS divisible, but 2 is NOT divisible, we conclude that the sum $(3 \Delta 47) + 2$ is NOT divisible by any of the odd primes between 3 and 47.

So, $(3 \Delta 47) + 2$ is not divisible by any prime number less than or equal to 47. The smallest prime factor of $(3 \Delta 47) + 2$ must be greater than 47. Thus, the minimum possible prime factor is 53, since that is the smallest prime greater than 47.

The correct answer is A.

67. D: If set S is the set of all prime integers between 0 and 20 then $S = \{2, 3, 5, 7, 11, 13, 17, 19\}$.

There are 7 odd terms and 1 even term in Set S. If the even term is among those selected, the sum will be even $(E + O + O = E)$. The sum will be odd if all three terms selected are odd $(O + O + O = O)$.

The probability of selecting three odd terms is $\frac{7}{8} \times \frac{6}{7} \times \frac{5}{6} = \frac{5}{8}$.

The correct answer is D.

68. D: The first five prime integers are 2, 3, 5, 7, and 11. These are the only terms that can appear in Sets A and B. There are some other restrictions on the sets:

Set A: The average of the terms in Set A is 4, so the sum of the terms is $(4)(3) = 12$. There is only one way for three of the first five primes to sum to 12: $2 + 3 + 7$. Set A is {2, 3, 7}.

Set B: The product of the terms in Set B is divisible by 22, so 2 and 11 are terms in Set B. Set B is {2, 11, x}, where x can be 3, 5, or 7, but *not* 2 or 11 (no duplicates).

We know that Sets A and B share one term: the 2. If x is either 3 or 7, the sets will share two terms. If x is 5, the sets will only share one term.

Thus, we can rephrase the question as "Is $x = 5$?" A definite Yes or No answer leads to a definite value answer for the number of shared terms (that is, Yes = 1, No = 2).

(1) SUFFICIENT: If the product of the terms in Set B is not divisible by 5, $x \neq 5$ and the answer to our rephrased question is a definite No.

(2) SUFFICIENT: If the product of the terms in Set B is divisible by 14, then 2 and 7 are terms in B. Therefore, $x = 7$ and the answer to our rephrased question is a definite No.

The correct answer is D.

69. A: The area of the square is $(6)(6) = 36$. But what is the area of the shaded right triangle?

The constraint that all three sides of the right triangle must be integers is actually quite restrictive. The sides of the triangle must be a Pythagorean triple or a multiple thereof. The first few Pythagorean triples are 3–4–5, 5–12–13, and 8–15–17. Only 3–4–5 is compact enough to fit inside region D, since all other Pythagorean triples have a side longer than 6. We should also check whether ABC could be a *multiple* of 3–4–5. The smallest integer multiple of the 3–4–5 triple is 6–8–10, which certainly would not fit inside a 6 by 6 square.

Thus, we can conclude that ABC has sides of length 3, 4, and 5, and an area of $\frac{1}{2}(3)(4) = 6$.

The shaded area is therefore $\frac{6}{36} = \frac{1}{6}$ of the area of the square.

The correct answer is A.

70. B: We can represent the given information in a double-set matrix:

	Divisible by 3	Not Divisible by 3	Total
Odd			
Even		x	5
Total	4		

Our question is "What is *x*?"

(1) INSUFFICIENT: If the product of the even terms in *S* is divisible by 9, then those five even integers must have at least two 3's among their prime factors. Those two 3's could occur in a single even term (e.g. 18 is even and divisible by 9) or in two different even terms (e.g. 6 and 12 give a product of 72, which is divisible by 9).

	Divisible by 3	Not Divisible by 3	Total
Odd			
Even	minimum of 1	*x* = maximum of 4	5
Total	4		

Knowing that *x* ≤ 4 is not enough to determine the exact value of *x*.

(2) SUFFICIENT: If *S* consists of consecutive integers, the multiples of 3 in *S* must also be consecutive. Since multiples of 3 occur every 3rd term, and consecutive integers alternate odd-even-odd-etc., the four consecutive multiples of 3 in *S* will occur in either the pattern OEOE or EOEO. Either way, exactly two of the multiples of 3 must be even and two must be odd. Adding that information to our original matrix:

	Divisible by 3	Not Divisible by 3	Total
Odd	2		
Even	2	*x* = 3	5
Total	4		

Thus, we can conclude that *x* = 3.

Alternatively, we can test sets of consecutive integers:

{3, **4**, 5, 6, 7, **8**, 9, **10**, 11, 12} has 5 evens and 4 multiples of 3. ✔ *x* = 3
{4, 5, 6, 7, 8, 9, 10, 11, 12} has 5 evens, but not enough multiples of 3. This set does not fit the criteria. ✘
{4, 5, 6, 7, 8, 9, 10, 11, 12, 13, 14, 15} has 4 multiples of 3, but too many evens. This set does not fit either. ✘
{5, 6, 7, **8**, 9, **10**, 11, 12, 13, **14**, 15} has 5 evens and 4 multiples of 3. ✔ *x* = 3
{6, 7, **8**, 9, **10**, 11, 12, 13, **14**, 15} has 5 evens and 4 multiples of 3. ✔ *x* = 3

The correct answer is B.

Workout Set 8 Solutions

71. E: We have a formula for the arithmetic mean:

$$\text{Mean} = \frac{4(11) + 5(10) + n(8) + 3(7)}{4 + 5 + n + 3}$$

$$\text{Mean} = \frac{44 + 50 + 8n + 21}{12 + n}$$

$$\text{Mean} = \frac{115 + 8n}{12 + n}$$

In contrast, the median depends on n, but not in a linear way. To find median, we order the terms and pick the middle one, so we must try various n values (i.e., vary the number of 8's in the list). This implies the eventual need to plug n values into the mean formula above, so let's draw a picture to help eliminate some answers first.

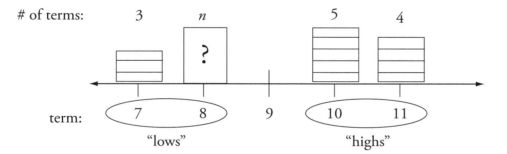

The "low" and "high" grouping is a fast way to find the relationship between median and mean for this set.

If the number of "lows" and "highs" are equal, the median is the average of the middle terms. That is, if $n = 6$, then the median = 9.

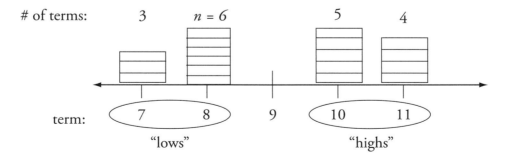

We can also see from this picture that when $n = 6$, the mean must be greater than 9. How? Pairs of 8 and 10 terms average to 9, but we have one "extra" 8. Pairs of 7 and 11 terms average to 9, but we have one "extra" 11. These "extra" terms differ from 9 by -1 and $+2$ respectively, for a total difference of $+1$. That positive difference implies that (mean > 9), or (mean > median).

To prove that $n = 5$ is too low, we could take a more conventional approach. If $n = 5$, the number of terms is $3 + 5 + 5 + 4 = 17$. The median is the 9th term in this ordered set: 7, 7, 7, 8, 8, 8, 8, 8, **10**, 10, 10, 10, 10, 11, 11, 11, 11. Thus, the median is 10, while the mean is closer to 9:

$$\text{Mean} = \frac{115 + 8n}{12 + n} = \frac{115 + 8(5)}{12 + 5} = \frac{155}{17} \approx 9$$

That is, if $n = 5$, then median > mean.
If $n = 6$, then mean > median.

The correct answer is E.

72. B: This is a combined work problem, so we will use the work formula: *rate × time = work*. The work and rates are given, but we need to calculate time, so we manipulate the formula: *time = work / rate*. This is also a *Variable In the answer Choices (VIC)* problem, so it is efficient to pick numbers and test the answer choices.

We are told that there are 80 houses, that y houses are painted at a rate of x houses per week, and that the rate increases to $1.25x$ houses per week for the remaining $80 - y$ houses. We will pick values such that x and $1.25x$ are integers (i.e., x is a multiple of 4) and y and $80 - y$ are divisible by x and $1.25x$, respectively.

	Variable	Value	Units
Total houses	80	80	houses
Houses painted at Slower Rate	y	20	houses
Houses painted at Faster Rate	$80 - y$	60	houses
Initial rate	x	4	houses/week
Increased rate	$1.25x$	5	houses/week

The total painting time is:

20 houses painted at a rate of houses/week = 5 weeks
60 houses painted at a rate of 5 houses/week = 12 weeks
Total time for 80 houses = 5 + 12 = 17 weeks

(A) $\dfrac{320 - y}{5x} = \dfrac{320 - 20}{5(4)} = \dfrac{300}{20} = 15$

(B) $\dfrac{y + 320}{5x} = \dfrac{20 + 320}{5(4)} = \dfrac{340}{20} = 17$

Manhattan **GMAT** Prep
the new standard

(C) $\dfrac{5(80-y)}{4x} = \dfrac{5(80-20)}{4(4)} = \dfrac{300}{16} = \dfrac{75}{4} = 18.75$

(D) $\dfrac{y+400}{4x} = \dfrac{20+400}{4(4)} = \dfrac{420}{16} = \dfrac{105}{4} = 26.25$

(E) $\dfrac{4y+320}{5x} = \dfrac{4(20)+320}{5(4)} = \dfrac{400}{20} = 20$

The correct answer is B.

73. B: If $a^2 = b^2$, then $(x+y)^2 = (x-y)^2$. We can distribute both sides using the "square of a sum" and "square of a difference" *special products*, then simplify:

$x^2 + 2xy + y^2 = x^2 - 2xy + y^2$
$2xy = -2xy$
$4xy = 0$
$xy = 0$

Thus, there are three basic scenarios:

x	y	$xy = 0$
0	any non-zero	✓
any non-zero	0	✓
0	0	✓

Eliminating the first scenario would give us a sufficient answer: $y = 0$.

(1) INSUFFICIENT: This statement indicates that x and y must be non-negative, in order for their square roots to be real values. The statement also eliminates the last scenario, in which $x = y = 0$. But we still cannot determine the exact value of y, which could be 0 or any positive value.

x	y	$xy = 0$	(1): $\sqrt{x} + \sqrt{y} > 0$
0	any positive	✓	✓
any positive	0	✓	✓
0	0	✓	✗

(2) SUFFICIENT: This statement indicates that x and y must be non-negative, in order for their square roots to be real values. This statement eliminates the last scenario. If x and y were both 0, $\sqrt{x} - \sqrt{y}$ would equal 0. It also eliminates the first scenario. If $\sqrt{x} - \sqrt{y} > 0$, then $\sqrt{x} > \sqrt{y}$. Therefore $x > y$. Thus we can conclude that $y = 0$.

x	y	$xy = 0$	(2): $\sqrt{x} - \sqrt{y} > 0$
0	any positive	✓	✗
any positive	0	✓	✓
0	0	✓	✗

The correct answer is B.

74. C: (1) INSUFFICIENT: Set up a table and assign sheep to stalls.

Stall:	A	B	C	D	E	F	G
# of sheep:			$2x$		$3x$		

Since a fractional sheep is not possible in this problem, x must be a positive integer. Suppose $x = 2$, so there are 4 sheep in C and 6 sheep in E. With 23 sheep remaining, it is possible for each of the other stalls to hold at least one sheep (a Yes answer). However, the 23 other sheep might all be in stall B, leaving stalls A, D, F, and G empty (a No answer).

(2) INSUFFICIENT: Set up a table and assign sheep to stalls.

Stall:	A	B	C	D	E	F	G
# of sheep:					$5y$	$2y$	

If $y = 1$, there are 5 sheep in E and 2 sheep in F. With 26 sheep remaining, it is possible for each of the other stalls to hold at least one sheep (a Yes answer). However, 13 sheep might be in both stalls A and B, leaving stalls C, D, and G empty (a No answer).

(1) & (2) SUFFICIENT: Set up a table and assign sheep to stalls.

Stall:	A	B	C	D	E	F	G
# of sheep:			$2x$		$3x = 5y$	$2y$	

Since a fractional sheep is not possible in this problem, x and y must both be positive integers that satisfy the equation $3x = 5y$. The only possibility is $x = 5$ and $y = 3$, since higher multiples would require more than 33 sheep total. Thus, 31 sheep are allocated among these stalls as follows:

Stall:	A	B	C	D	E	F	G
# of sheep:			10		15	6	

31 of the 33 sheep are in three of the 7 pens. With only two sheep unaccounted for, there is no way to place at least one sheep in each of the remaining four pens (a definite No answer).

The correct answer is C.

75. E: Group the 10^r terms on one side of the equal sign.

$$(x \times 10^q) - (y \times 10^r) = 10^r$$
$$x \times 10^q = (y \times 10^r) + (1 \times 10^r)$$
$$x \times 10^q = (y + 1) \times 10^r$$

Now, solve for y.

$$x \times 10^q = (y+1) \times 10^r$$
$$x \times \frac{10^q}{10^r} = y+1$$
$$x \times 10^{q-r} = y+1$$
$$(x \times 10^{q-r}) - 1 = y$$

Since $q > r$, the exponent on 10^{q-r} is positive. Since x is a positive integer, $x \times 10^{q-r}$ is a multiple of 10 and therefore ends 0. Any multiple of 10 minus 1 yields an integer with a units digit of 9.

The correct answer is E.

76. A: The complicated expression in the question stem leads to a disguised *Positive/Negative* problem. In general, $\sqrt{x^2} = |x|$. Think about this relationship with a real example:

$$\sqrt{3^2} = \sqrt{9} = 3 \qquad\qquad\qquad \sqrt{(-3)^2} = \sqrt{9} = 3$$

In both cases (positive or negative 3), the end result is 3. Thus in general, $\sqrt{x^2}$ will always result in a positive value, or $|x|$. We can rephrase the original question:

Is $|y - 4| = 4 - y$?   becomes   Is $|y - 4| = -(y - 4)$?

Since the absolute value of $y - 4$ must be positive or zero, we can rephrase the question further:

Is $-(y - 4) \geq 0$?   becomes   Is $(y - 4) \leq 0$?   and then   Is $y \leq 4$?

(1) SUFFICIENT: The absolute value $|y - 3|$ can be interpreted as the distance between y and 3 on a number line. Thus, y is no more than 1 unit away from 3 on the number line, so $2 \leq y \leq 4$. Thus, $y \leq 4$.

(2) INSUFFICIENT: If $y \times |y| > 0$, then $y \times |y|$ is positive. This means y and $|y|$ must have the same sign. The term $|y|$ is non-negative, so y must be positive. However, knowing that y is positive is not enough to tell us whether $y \leq 4$.

The correct answer is A.

77. C: A base of 2 is common to each term, with 10 as the smallest exponent appearing on that base. We can factor 2^{10} out from all the terms in the expression:

$2^{10}5^4 - 2^{13}5^2 + 2^{14}$
$2^{10}(5^4 - 2^3 5^2 + 2^4)$

Clearly, 2 is a prime factor, but is it the greatest? We need to examine $(5^4 - 2^3 5^2 + 2^4)$ to determine whether it has a larger prime factor. The expression is of the form $x^2 - 2xy + y^2$, where:

$x^2 = 5^4$, so $x = 5^2$
$y^2 = 2^4$, so $y = 2^2$

That is, $(5^4 - 2^3 5^2 + 2^4) = (5^2)^2 - 2(2^2)(5^2) + (2^2)^2$.

This is the "square of a difference" special product, so we can also write the expression in factored form:

$$(5^2)^2 - 2(2^2)(5^2) + (2^2)^2 = (5^2 - 2^2)^2$$
$$= (25 - 4)^2$$
$$= 21^2$$

The prime factors of 21 are 3 and 7, so the largest prime factor of the original expression is 7.

Alternatively, if we did not see the quadratic special product in $(5^4 - 2^3 5^2 + 2^4)$, we could have performed the computation and factored the result:

$(5^4 - 2^3 5^2 + 2^4)$
$(625 - (8)(25) + 16)$
$(625 - 200 + 16)$
(441)
$(3)(147)$
$(3)(3)(49)$
$(3)(3)(7)(7)$

The correct answer is C.

78. A: Set up a chart to test a representative set of possible x values, including positives, negatives, and zero:

x	$f(x)$	$f(x+1)$	$f(x+1) > f(x)$?	$f(x) > 0$?	$f(x) \neq 0$?
−4	4/3	3/2	Y	Y	Y
−3	3/2	2	Y	Y	Y
−2	2	undefined		Y	Y
−1	undefined	0			
0	0	1/2	Y	N	N

1	1/2	2/3	Y	Y	Y
2	2/3	3/4	Y	Y	Y
3	3/4	4/5	Y	Y	Y

I. ALWAYS TRUE: In all cases where $f(x)$ and $f(x + 1)$ were defined, $f(x + 1) > f(x)$.
II. USUALLY TRUE: However, $f(x)$ can equal 0 when $x = 0$.
III. USUALLY TRUE: However, $f(x)$ can equal 0 when $x = 0$.

Therefore, only statement I must be true.

The correct answer is A.

79. C: Manipulate:

$x + y = 3^x$
$y = 3^x - x$

In order for y to be divisible by 6, it must be divisible by both 2 and 3.

All of the positive powers of 3 (3^x, where x is a positive integer) are divisible by 3. Thus, y will be divisible by 3 only when x is also divisible by 3 (because multiple of 3 − multiple of 3 = multiple of 3).

Moreover, all of the positive powers of 3 (3^x, where x is a positive integer) are odd. Thus, y will be even only when x is also odd (because odd − odd = even).

Combining these number properties, we can rephrase the question as "Is x an odd multiple of 3?"

(1) INSUFFICIENT: x is odd, but we don't know whether it is a multiple of 3 (i.e. x could be 3 or 5).

(2) INSUFFICIENT: x is a multiple of 3, but we don't know whether it is odd (i.e. x could be 3 or 6).

(1) AND (2) SUFFICIENT: x is an odd multiple of 3: 3, 9, 15, etc.

The correct answer is C.

80. E: If we graph the equation $y = |x|$, we get the following:

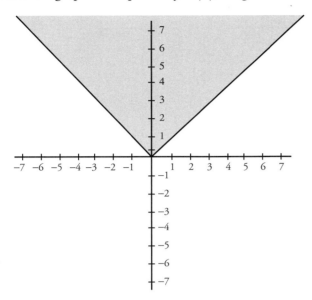

The inequality $y > |x|$ represents everything *above* the line (on either side of the y-axis)—i.e., the shaded region. Since the equation $y = |x|$ forms a 45-degree angle from the x-axis, we know that there are 90 degrees above the line (on both sides of the y-axis). This represents one-fourth of the xy-plane. Therefore, if a random pair of (x, y) coordinates is chosen from the plane, the probability is 1/4 that the point will fit the criterion $y = |x|$.

The correct answer is E.

Workout Set 9 Solutions

81. B: The circumference of the circle $= 2\pi r = 2\pi\sqrt{x}$, so $r = \sqrt{x}$.

The area of the circle $= \pi r^2 = \pi\left(\sqrt{x}\right)^2 = \pi x$.

The area of a square is side^2. The diagonal of this square is the diameter of the circle $= 2r = 2\sqrt{x}$. The diagonal of a square is always $\sqrt{2}\,(\text{side})$, so $\text{side} = \dfrac{\text{diagonal}}{\sqrt{2}}$. Therefore, $\text{side} = \dfrac{2\sqrt{x}}{\sqrt{2}} = \dfrac{2\sqrt{2}\cdot\sqrt{x}}{2} = \sqrt{2x}$ and the area of square $ABCD$ is:

$$\text{side}^2 = \left(\sqrt{2x}\right)^2 = 2x$$

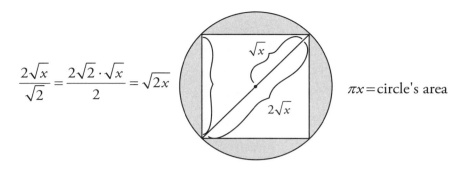

$$\frac{2\sqrt{x}}{\sqrt{2}} = \frac{2\sqrt{2} \cdot \sqrt{x}}{2} = \sqrt{2x}$$

$\pi x =$ circle's area

The shaded area is the area of the circle minus the area of the square $= \pi x - 2x$.

The correct answer is B.

82. A: Clearly some manipulation is required to determine b in terms of a, but let's spend a minute thinking strategically about what manipulations to do. It would help to isolate terms with an a, by factoring 3^a out on the left side. This will let us compare 3^a to 3^b, and thus compare a to b, once we clean up the constant terms that are left over. Also, 90 is a multiple of 9, which is a power of 3. 90 is also the sum of 81 and 9, both powers of 3 themselves. It is likely that some constant terms will cancel.

$3^a + 3^{a-2} = (90)(3^b)$	
$3^a (1 + 3^{-2}) = (90)(3^b)$	Factor out 3^a on the left side
$3^a (3^2 + 1) = (90)(3^b)(3^2)$	Multiply both sides by 3^2 to cancel the negative exponent
$3^a (10) = (90)(3^b)(3^2)$	Compute: $3^2 + 1 = 9 + 1 = 10$
$3^a = (9)(3^b)(3^2)$	Divide both sides by 10
$3^a = (3^2)(3^b)(3^2)$	Express 9 in terms of the common base: 3^2
$3^a = 3^{b+4}$	Combine terms on the right side
$a = b + 4$	Set the exponents on each side equal

Therefore, $b = a - 4$.

The correct answer is A.

83. C: (1) INSUFFICIENT: This tells us that $x + y = 7$, but nothing about the value of $x - y$.

(2) INSUFFICIENT: We cannot manipulate this statement into the form $x - y$, nor can we determine the value of x or y independently.

(1) AND (2) SUFFICIENT: First, recognize that xy must be positive in order for $\sqrt{xy}$ in statement (2) to be a real number, so x and y must have the same sign. In order for $x + y$ in statement (1) to be a positive number (i.e. 7), the sign of x and y must be positive, because negative + negative cannot be positive. So in the following steps, we know that the square roots of x and y are positive, real numbers.

From the statements, we know that $x + y = 7$ and $2\sqrt{xy} = 7$. Since both equal 7, we can set the left sides of the equations equal and simplify:

$$x + y = 2\sqrt{xy}$$
$$x + y - 2\sqrt{xy} = 0$$
$$x - 2\sqrt{xy} + y = 0$$

Recognizing the "square of a difference" *special product*, we can write this in factored form:

$$\left(\sqrt{x} - \sqrt{y}\right)^2 = 0$$

Thus, $\sqrt{x} - \sqrt{y} = 0$, so $\sqrt{x} = \sqrt{y}$. We can infer from this that $x = y$, and $x - y = 0$.

The correct answer is C.

84. **E:** This is a Yes/No question, so we will attempt to understand simple cases for both a different median and the same median.

(1) INSUFFICIENT:

No case: If the original set is 50, 50, 50, 50, 50, 50, the mean and median were 50 originally. The new term may be any value and the median will still be 50.

Yes case: If the original set is 0, 0, 0, 100, 100, 100, the mean and median were 50 originally. If the new term is 75, the median increases to 75. More generally for this set, if the new term is not equal to the original median of 50, the median will change.

(2) INSUFFICIENT:

No case: If the original set is 50, 50, 50, 50, 50, 50, the median was 50 originally. The new term may be any value and the median will still be 50.

Yes case: If the original set is 0, 0, 0, 50, 50, 50, the median was 25 originally. If the new term is 40, the median increases to 40. More generally for this set, if the new term is not equal to the original median of 25, the median will change.

(1) AND (2) INSUFFICIENT: The mean must be 50, and at least 2 terms in the original set must be 50.

No case: If the original set is 50, 50, 50, 50, 50, 50, the mean and median were 50 originally. The new term may be any value and the median will still be 50.

Yes case: If the original set is 0, 0, 0, 50, 50, 200, the mean was 50 and the median was 25 originally. If the new term is greater than 25, the median increases. If the new term is less than 25, the median decreases.

The correct answer is E.

85. D: Start with $\begin{array}{r} abc \\ +\,dcb \\ \hline 598 \end{array}$ and extract several equations by summing each digit place individually.

Note that both the ones digit and tens digit require us to sum $c + b$. Since the result is different in the ones digit (8) and the tens digit (9), we must have carried a one from the ones to the tens digit. Thus, we conclude that $c + b \neq 8$; instead, we know that $c + b = 18$.

If $c + b = 18$, then both c and b must be 9 (the largest digit). We place an 8 in the ones digit of the sum, and carry a one to the tens place. The sum in the tens digit is thus $1 + b + c = 1 + 18 = 19$, and we place a 9 in the tens digit of the sum and carry a one to the hundreds place.

In the hundreds place, the sum is thus $1 + a + d = 5$.

Now we can solve for a:

$1 + a + d = 5$
$a + d = 4$
$a = 4 - d$

The correct answer is D.

86. D: If an even number (0, 2, or 4) of the integers a, b, c and d, are negative, each pair of negatives will

cancel, because $(-1)(-1) = +1$ and $\dfrac{(-1)}{(-1)} = +1$. This would yield a positive result for $\dfrac{ab}{cd}$.

Thus, a way to rephrase the question is "Among the integers a, b, c and d, are an odd number (*one or three*) of them negative?"

(1) SUFFICIENT: This statement can be rephrased as $ad = -bc$.

a	d	b	c	$ad = -bc$	Odd number of negatives?
+	+	−	+	✓	YES
+	+	+	−	✓	YES
−	−	−	+	✓	YES
−	−	+	−	✓	YES

Though we have not listed all possibilities, we have listed enough to realize that for the signs of ad and bc to be opposite one another, either one or three of the four integers must be negative.

(2) SUFFICIENT: You might recognize that the $(-1)(-1) = +1$ property implies that $abcd$ is only negative when there are non-paired negatives among the integers. That is, an odd number (one or three) of the integers a, b, c and d must be negative. If not, you could list a few cases to see the pattern.

a	b	c	d	$abcd$ = negative	Odd number of negatives?
+	+	−	+	✓	YES
+	−	+	+	✓	YES
−	+	−	−	✓	YES
−	−	+	−	✓	YES

The correct answer is D.

87. A: The product xy will be even if x is even, y is even, or both are even.

The prime numbers include 2, 3, 5, 7, 11, 13, 17, 19, etc. The smallest possible term in Set A is 2, which is the only even prime.

x = the range of Set A = largest term − smallest term in Set A. If the smallest term in Set A is 2, then x = odd − even = odd. If the smallest term in set A is odd (i.e. not 2), then x = odd − odd = even.

The median of Set A is the average of the 2 middle terms, since the number of terms in the set is even.

Thus, $y = \dfrac{\text{odd} + \text{odd}}{2} = \dfrac{\text{even}}{2} = $ integer . However, y could be either even (e.g., when the middle terms are 11 and 13) or odd (e.g. when the middle terms are 7 and 11).

A useful rephrase of this question is "Is the smallest integer in Set A odd?"

(1) SUFFICIENT: If the smallest prime in the set is 5, x = even and therefore xy is even.

(2) INSUFFICIENT: If the largest integer in the set is 101, the range of the set can be odd or even (e.g. 101 − 3 = 98 or 101 − 2 = 99). The median of the set can also be odd or even, as discussed. Therefore, xy can be either odd or even.

The correct answer is A.

88. D: It may be tempting to simplify this way:

$x^3 < 16x$
$x^2 < 16$
$-4 < x < 4$

This solution is wrong because we divided by x *without knowing its sign*. If x were negative, we would have had to flip the sign.

Thus, we should check two cases:

x	$x^3 < 16x$ becomes:	Take square root:	Solve for x:
Positive	$x^2 < 16$ (don't flip)	$\lvert x \rvert < 4$	$0 < x < 4$
Negative	$x^2 > 16$ (flip)	$\lvert x \rvert > 4$	$x < -4$

We have two ranges of solutions for x. Let's check the answer choices to see which one agrees with at least some of these solution ranges but does not disagree with either. That is, which choice does not include any values outside of the solution ranges?

	Positive solutions only possible are: $0 < x < 4$	Negative solutions only possible are: $x < -4$	Conclusion
(A) $\lvert x \rvert < 4$	ALL AGREE ($0 < x < 4$)	ALL DISAGREE ($-4 < x < 0$)	DISAGREE
(B) $x < 4$	ALL AGREE ($0 < x < 4$)	SOME DISAGREE ($-4 < x < 0$)	DISAGREE
(C) $x > 4$	ALL DISAGREE ($x > 4$)	not applicable	DISAGREE
(D) $x < -4$	not applicable	ALL AGREE ($x < -4$)	AGREE
(E) $x > 0$	SOME DISAGREE ($x > 4$)	not applicable	DISAGREE

The correct answer is D.

89. E: Group similar bases on each side of the equal sign:

$5^x - 5^y = 2^{y-1}(5^{x-1})$
$(5^{1-x})(5^x - 5^y) = 2^{y-1}$
$(5^1 - 5^{1-x+y}) = 2^{y-1}$
$5 - 5^{1-x+y} = 2^{y-1}$

y is a positive integer, so $y - 1 \geq 0$, and the right side can equal 1, 2, 4, 8, 16, etc.

$1 - x + y$ must be an integer, but its sign will depend on the relative values of the positive integers x and y. However, if $1 - x + y < 0$, 5^{1-x+y} is fractional, and the left side of the equation will not equal one of the integers (powers of 2) possible on the right side of the equation.

The equation can thus be read:

5 less an integer that is a power of 5 equals an integer that is a power of 2. Integer powers of 5 include 1, 5, 25, 125, etc. Integer powers of 2 include 1, 2, 4, 8, etc.

By experimenting, we can see that the only possibility that works is $5 - 1 = 4$. So $1 - x + y = 0$ and $y - 1 = 2$. Therefore:

$$y = 3$$

$1 - x + y = 0$
$1 + y = x$

$$1 + 3 = x$$
$$4 = x$$

$$xy = (4)(3) = 12$$

The correct answer is E.

90. E: First, set up a table:

	Rate	Time	Work
Machine A	$\frac{1}{x}$ jobs per hour	x hours	1 job
Machine B	$\frac{1}{y}$ jobs per hour	y hours	1 job
A and B together	$\frac{1}{x} + \frac{1}{y}$ jobs per hour		

This question talks hypothetically: "If $x = 4y$, how what percent will x have to decrease…"

We can indicate that hypothetical decrease by using a factor q and substituting for this hypothetical x:

$x_{decreased} = x_{current}q = 4yq$, where $0 < q < 1$.

If machine B and this hypothetical machine A complete the whole job in $\frac{3y}{8}$ hours, then their combined rate of work is $\dfrac{1}{\dfrac{3y}{8}} = \dfrac{8}{3y}$ jobs per hour.

Therefore, we can set up the following equation: $\dfrac{1}{x_{decreased}} + \dfrac{1}{y} = \dfrac{1}{4yq} + \dfrac{1}{y} = \dfrac{8}{3y}$. We can solve for q as follows:

ManhattanGMAT Prep
the new standard

$$\frac{1}{4yq}+\frac{1}{y}=\frac{8}{3y}$$

$$\frac{1}{4q}+1=\frac{8}{3}$$

$$\frac{1}{4q}+\frac{3}{3}=\frac{8}{3}$$

$$\frac{1}{4q}=\frac{5}{3}$$

$$20q=3$$

$$q=\frac{3}{20}=\frac{15}{100}=15\%$$

Therefore, $x_{\text{decreased}}$ is 15% of x, implying that x would have to decrease by 85%.

The correct answer is E.

Note: it may be simpler to pick numbers. The answer must be independent of y, so if you pick $y = 1$ and follow the logic, you'll arrive at the same answer.

Workout Set 10 Solutions

91. D: First, a very difficult algebraic solution:

$$\frac{x}{x+y}=n \qquad\qquad \frac{x}{x-y}=m$$

$$\left(\frac{x}{x+y}\right)^{-1}=n^{-1} \quad\text{and}\quad \left(\frac{x}{x-y}\right)^{-1}=m^{-1}$$

$$\frac{x+y}{x}=\frac{1}{n} \qquad\qquad \frac{x-y}{x}=\frac{1}{m}$$

Now that the fractions have a common denominator of x, we can subtract one from the other:

$$\left(\frac{x+y}{x}\right) - \left(\frac{x-y}{x}\right) = \frac{1}{n} - \frac{1}{m}$$

$$\frac{x+y-x-(-y)}{x} = \frac{m}{nm} - \frac{n}{nm}$$

$$\frac{2y}{x} = \frac{m-n}{mn}$$

$$\frac{y}{x} = \frac{m-n}{2mn}$$

$$\frac{x}{y} = \frac{2mn}{m-n}$$

The correct answer is D.

You are not alone if the path to that solution was not obvious to you! Algebraic "false starts" are common in this type of problem. For example, an equally valid solution would have been this:

$$\frac{x}{x+y} = n \qquad\qquad \frac{x}{x-y} = m$$

$$\text{and}$$

$$x + y = \frac{x}{n} \qquad\qquad x - y = \frac{x}{m}$$

Using the squares of these expressions (both special products) and subtracting:

$$(x+y)^2 = x^2 + 2xy + y^2 = \left(\frac{x}{n}\right)^2$$

$$-\left[(x-y)^2 = x^2 - 2xy + y^2 = \left(\frac{x}{m}\right)^2\right]$$

*Manhattan*GMAT*Prep
the new standard

$$0x^2 + 4xy + 0y^2 = \left(\frac{x}{n}\right)^2 - \left(\frac{x}{m}\right)^2$$

$$4xy = \frac{(xm)^2 - (xn)^2}{(nm)^2}$$

$$4xy = \frac{x^2\left(m^2 - n^2\right)}{(nm)^2}$$

$$4y = \frac{x\left(m^2 - n^2\right)}{(nm)^2}$$

$$\frac{4(nm)^2}{\left(m^2 - n^2\right)} = \frac{x}{y}$$

This answer is mathematically valid, but not listed among the answer choices. Because of this peculiarity of algebra VICs, picking numbers and testing the answer choices is almost certainly the best approach.

If $x = 2$ and $y = 3$, then $n = \frac{2}{5}$ and $m = \frac{2}{-1} = -2$. The target number for testing the answer choices

is $\frac{x}{y} = \frac{2}{3}$.

(A) $\dfrac{3mn}{2} = negative$

(B) $\dfrac{3m}{2n} = negative$

(C) $\dfrac{n(m+2)}{2} = 0$

(D) $\dfrac{2nm}{(m-n)} = \dfrac{2\left(\frac{2}{5}\right)(-2)}{-2 - \frac{2}{5}} = \dfrac{-\frac{8}{5}}{-\frac{10}{5} - \frac{2}{5}} = \dfrac{-\frac{8}{5}}{-\frac{12}{5}} = \dfrac{8}{12} = \dfrac{2}{3}$

E) $\dfrac{n^2 - m^2}{nm} = \dfrac{\frac{4}{25} - 4}{-\frac{4}{5}} = \dfrac{\frac{4}{25} - \frac{100}{25}}{-\frac{20}{25}} = \dfrac{-96}{-20} = \dfrac{24}{5}$

The correct answer is D.

92. D: To understand what the question stem is telling us, let's pick some numbers: the bacteria culture begins with an initial quantity of $I = 100$ and increases by a factor of $x = 2$ every $y = 3$ minutes. Let's construct a table to track the growth of the bacteria:

Time (min.)	Bacteria
3	$100(2) = 100(2)^1$
6	$100(2)(2) = 100(2)^2$
9	$100(2)(2)(2) = 100(2)3$
12	$100(2)(2)(2)(2) = 100(2)^4$
...	...
$3n = t$	$100(2)^n$

n represents the number of growth periods, and $n = t/y$ where t is time in minutes. For example, the 4th growth period in our chart above ended at 12 minutes, and 4 = 12 minutes/3 minutes.

From this example, we can generalize to a formula for the quantity of bacteria, F:

$$F = I(x)^{t/y}$$

This question asks us how long it will take for the bacteria to grow to 10,000 times their original amount. In other words, "What is t when $F = 10,000I$?"

$F = 10,000I = I(x)^{t/y}$
$10,000 = (x)^{t/y}$

Thus, our final rephrased question is "What is t when $10,000 = (x)^{t/y}$?"

(1) SUFFICIENT: Note that the yth root of x is equivalent to x to the $1/y$ power. This statement tells us that $x^{1/y} = 10$. If we plug this value into the equation we can solve for t.

$10,000 = (x)^{t/y}$
$10,000 = [(x)^{1/y}]^t$
$10,000 = (10)^t$
$10^4 = 10^t$
$t = 4$

(2) SUFFICIENT: The culture grows one-hundredfold in 2 minutes. In other words, the sample grows by a factor of 10^2. Since exponential growth is characterized by a constant factor of growth (i.e. by a factor of x every y minutes), in another 2 minutes, the culture will grow by another factor of 10^2. Therefore, after a total of 4 minutes, the culture will have grown by a factor of $10^2 \times 10^2 = 10^4$, or 10,000.

The correct answer is D.

93. D: First, set up a table:

	Old cylinder	New cylinder
Radius	r	$\left(\dfrac{5}{4}\right)r$
Height	h	x = what percent of h?
Volume of container	$\pi r^2 h$	$\pi\left(\dfrac{5}{4}r\right)^2 x$
Volume of water	$\left(\dfrac{3}{4}\right)\left(\pi r^2 h\right)$ ⎯⎯ same ⎯⟶	$\left(\dfrac{3}{4}\right)\left(\pi r^2 h\right)$

If the new cylinder is 3/5 full with this volume of water, we can set up an equation:

$$Water\ volume = \left(\frac{3}{5}\right)New\ cylinder\ volume$$

$$\left(\frac{3}{4}\right)\left(\pi r^2 h\right) = \left(\frac{3}{5}\right)\left[\pi\left(\frac{5}{4}r\right)^2 x\right]$$

$$\left(\frac{3}{4}\right)\pi r^2 h = \left(\frac{3}{5}\right)\left(\frac{5}{4}\right)^2 \pi r^2 x$$

$$\left(\frac{3}{4}\right)h = \left(\frac{3}{5}\right)\left(\frac{5}{4}\right)^2 x$$

$$\left(\frac{5}{3}\right)\left(\frac{4}{5}\right)^2\left(\frac{3}{4}\right)h = x$$

$$\frac{4}{5}h = x$$

Therefore, x is 80% of h.

The correct answer is D.

94. B: This problem contains a common trap seen in many difficult DS questions. C is a tempting short-cut answer, as the combined statements would give us the values of both a and b, which we could simply plug into the expression and answer the question.

It is only by rephrasing that we can determine whether exact values for both a and b are truly required.

Manipulate the expression:

$2^a 8^b 4^{a+b} = 2^a (2^3)^b (2^2)^{a+b}$

$$= 2^a(2^{3b})(2^{2a+2b})$$
$$= 2^{3a+5b}$$

Remembering the units digit patterns for powers of 2 will help on this problem:

$2^1 = 2$
$2^2 = 4$
$2^3 = 8$
$2^4 = 16$
$2^5 = 32$
…etc.

The units digits for powers of 2 is a repeating pattern of [2, 4, 8, 6].

If we can determine the relationship of $3a + 5b$ to a multiple of 4 (i.e. where 2^{3a+5b} is in the predictable 4-term repeating pattern of units digits), we will be able to answer the question. This question can be rephrased as "What is the remainder when $3a + 5b$ is divided by 4?"

(1) INSUFFICIENT: If $b = 24$, then $5b$ is a multiple of 4. However, we know only that a is an integer less than 24. Possible remainders when $3a$ is divided by 4 are 0, 1, 2, or 3.

(2) SUFFICIENT: If the greatest common factor of a and b is 12, then 12 must be a factor of both variables. That is, both a and b are multiples of 12 and thus also multiples of 4. As a result, $3a$ and $5b$ will be multiples of 4 as well, so the remainder will be 0 when $3a + 5b$ is divided by 4.

The correct answer is B.

95. D: Valid codes must have a second digit that is exactly twice the first digit. There are three ways to do this with the available digits:

Scenario A: 12*XXXXX*
Scenario B: 24*XXXXX*
Scenario C: 36*XXXXX*

For each of these basic scenarios, there are 5! ways we can shuffle the remaining 5 numbers (represented by *X*'s above).

Thus, the total number of valid codes is $3 \times 5! = 3 \times 120 = 360$.

The correct answer is D.

96. A: If $x = 2$, then x is a factor of any even integer. Thus, this question can be rephrased "Is $x = 2$ or any other factor of z?"

(1) SUFFICIENT: We know that x and y are primes and that $x < y$. The factors of 57 are 1, 3, 19, and 57, all odd numbers. Thus $x + y =$ odd, which eliminates the possibility that x and y are both odd, implying that $x = 2$ and $y =$ an odd prime (i.e. 17).

the new standard

If $x = 2$, then x must be a factor of the even integer z.

(2) INSUFFICIENT: If y is not a factor of z, then $y \neq 2$. y cannot be 1 either, as x must be positive and $x < y$. Thus, $y \geq 3$, but we still cannot determine the shared factors (if any) of x and z.

For example, it is possible that $x = 2$, $y = 4$, and $z = 6$. In this case, x is a factor of z, and the answer is Yes.
It is also possible that $x = 3$, $y = 5$, and $z = 8$. In this case, x is not a factor of z, and the answer is No.

The correct answer is A.

97. B: It would require a lot of tricky work to solve this algebraically, so we should just pick numbers. We must pick values for the unknowns such that $\dfrac{w}{x} < \dfrac{y}{z} < 1$ holds true. For example, if we try $w = 1$, $x = 2$, $y = 3$, and $z = 4$, then $\dfrac{1}{2} < \dfrac{3}{4} < 1$ is true.

Using these values, we see that:

$$\dfrac{x}{w} = \dfrac{2}{1} = 2, \quad \dfrac{z}{y} = \dfrac{4}{3}, \quad \dfrac{x^2}{w^2} = \dfrac{2^2}{1^2} = 4, \quad \dfrac{xz}{wy} = \dfrac{(2)(4)}{(1)(3)} = \dfrac{8}{3}, \quad \text{and} \quad \dfrac{x+z}{w+y} = \dfrac{2+4}{1+3} = \dfrac{6}{4} = \dfrac{3}{2}.$$

Placed in ascending order: $1 < \dfrac{4}{3} < \dfrac{3}{2} < 2 < \dfrac{8}{3} < 4$.

Replacing the values with the expressions: $1 < \dfrac{z}{y} < \dfrac{x+z}{w+y} < \dfrac{x}{w} < \dfrac{xz}{wy} < \dfrac{x^2}{w^2}$.

The correct answer is B.

98. C: We are asked for the absolute value of $a + b$, so we will try to manipulate the statements to isolate that combination of variables, $a + b$. We will start with the easier statement, which in this case is Statement (2).

(2) INSUFFICIENT: This gives us information about c and d, and the relationship between them, but no information about a or b.

(1) INSUFFICIENT: We can manipulate the equation to group $(a + b)$ and $(c + d)$ terms:

$(a + b + c + d)(a + b - c - d) = 16$
$[(a + b) + (c + d)][(a + b) - (c + d)] = 16$

Note that this is of the form $(x + y)(x - y)$, where $x = (a + b)$ and $y = (c + d)$. We recognize this as the "difference of two squares" special product, $(x + y)(x - y) = x^2 - y^2$. Thus, we may transform this expression:

$[(a + b) + (c + d)][(a + b) - (c + d)] = 16$
$(a + b)^2 - (c + d)^2 = 16$
$(a + b)^2 = 16 + (c + d)^2$

We don't know the value of $c + d$, so we cannot determine the value of $(a + b)^2$.

(1) AND (2) SUFFICIENT: From statement (2), we know that $(a + b)^2 = 16 + (c + d)^2$. From statement (1) we know that $c + d = 3$. Substituting for $c + d$:

$(a + b)^2 = 16 + (c + d)^2$
$(a + b)^2 = 16 + 3^2$
$(a + b)^2 = 16 + 9$
$(a + b)^2 = 25$
$(a + b) = 5$ or -5
$|a + b| = 5$

The correct answer is C.

99. B: If y has no factor z such that $1 < z < y$, then y must be prime. Let's look at a few examples to see why this is true:

6 has a factor 2 such that $1 < 2 < 6$: 6 is NOT prime
15 has a factor 5 such that $1 < 5 < 15$: 15 is NOT prime
3 has NO factor between 1 and 3: 3 IS prime
7 has NO factor between 1 and 7: 7 IS prime

Because it is selected from Set B, y is a prime number between 10 and 50, inclusive. The only prime number that is divisible by 3 is 3, so y is definitely not divisible by 3.

Thus, xy is only divisible by 3 if x itself is divisible by 3. We can rephrase the question: "What is the probability that a multiple of 3 will be chosen randomly from Set A?"

There are $21 - 10 + 1 = 12$ terms in Set A. Of these, 4 terms (12, 15, 18, and 21) are divisible by 3.

Thus, the probability that x is divisible by 3 is $\dfrac{4}{12} = \dfrac{1}{3}$.

The correct answer is B.

100. E: This is a VICs problem, so we can pick numbers and test the answer choices:

$x = 8$
$y = 5$

There are 8 children at the party, and 5 will sit at the table with the cake. Sally must sit at the birthday cake table, so we must pick $5 - 1 = 4$ of the other $8 - 1 = 7$ children to sit at that table with her. How

*Manhattan*GMAT*Prep
the new standard

many different ways can we choose 4 from a group of 7? Let's set up an anagram grid, where Y means "at the cake table" and N means "at the other table."

A	B	C	D	E	F	G
Y	Y	Y	Y	N	N	N

Now we can calculate the number of possible groups:

$$\frac{7!}{4!3!} = \frac{(7)(6)(5)}{(3)(2)(1)} = 35$$

Our target answer is 35. Now we can test each answer choice by plugging in $x = 8$ and $y = 5$:

(A) $\dfrac{(x-1)!}{(y-1)!(y-1)!} = \dfrac{(8-1)!}{(5-1)!(5-1)!} = \dfrac{7!}{4!4!} = \dfrac{(7)(6)(5)}{(4)(3)(2)(1)} = \dfrac{35}{4}$ (not an integer)

(B) $\dfrac{x!}{y!(x-y)!} = \dfrac{8!}{5!(8-5)!} = \dfrac{(8)(7)(6)}{(3)(2)(1)} = 56$

(C) $\dfrac{y!}{x!(x-y)!} = \dfrac{5!}{8!(8-5)!} = \dfrac{5!}{8!3!} = \dfrac{(5)(4)}{8!}$ (not an integer)

(D) $\dfrac{(y-1)!}{(x-y)!(y-1)!} = \dfrac{1}{(8-5)!} = \dfrac{1}{3!} = \dfrac{1}{6}$ (not an integer)

(E) $\dfrac{(x-1)!}{(x-y)!(y-1)!} = \dfrac{(8-1)!}{(8-5)!(5-1)!} = \dfrac{7!}{3!4!} = \dfrac{(7)(6)(5)}{(3)(2)(1)} = 35$

Only choice E results in the target number.

As an alternative to testing all five choices, we could have set up a formula using our selected numbers, then stopped to think about where those numbers originated.

The number of possible groups was $\dfrac{7!}{4!3!}$, but remember that this formula took Sally into account.

The 7 came from $8 - 1 = x - 1$.
The 4 came from $5 - 1 = y - 1$.

The 3 came from the difference between these numbers: $7 - 4 = (x - 1) - (y - 1) = (x - y)$.

Substituting these variable expressions in place of the numbers, we get $\dfrac{7!}{4!3!} = \dfrac{(x-1)!}{(y-1)!(x-y)!}$.

The correct answer is E.

Workout Set 11 Solutions

101. B: (1) INSUFFICIENT: The absolute value signs tell us that $a = \pm 1$, $b = \pm 2$, and $c = \pm 3$. In the numerator, each variable is squared, so their signs are irrelevant:

$$a^2 - b^2 - c^2 = 1^2 - 2^2 - 3^2 = 1 - 4 - 9 = -12$$

However, while $|b||c| = (2)(3) = 6$, the denominator bc could be either 6 or -6, depending on the signs of b and c. Therefore:

$$\frac{a^2 - b^2 - c^2}{bc} = 2 \text{ or } -2$$

(2) SUFFICIENT: Given that $a + b + c = 0$, we know that $a = -(b + c)$. Substitute this value of a into the expression in the question, and simplify, using one of the quadratic *special products* along the way:

$$\frac{a^2 - b^2 - c^2}{bc} = \frac{\left[-(b+c)\right]^2 - b^2 - c^2}{bc}$$

$$= \frac{(b+c)^2 - b^2 - c^2}{bc}$$

$$= \frac{\left(b^2 + 2bc + c^2\right) - b^2 - c^2}{bc}$$

$$= \frac{2bc}{bc}$$

$$= 2$$

The correct answer is B.

102. A: If John and Amanda run at the same rate, they will meet each other exactly in the middle. John will only run farther than Amanda if John's rate is greater than Amanda's. In math terms, distance = rate × time, and since John and Amanda run for the same time, their relative distances depend solely on their relative rates. We can rephrase the question to "what is the probability that John ran faster than Amanda?"

There are four possible rates for John (3, 4, 5, and 6) and four for Amanda (4, 5, 6, and 7). In total, there are (4)(4) = 16 possible rate scenarios.

Of John's four possible rates, only two (5 and 6) are greater than some of Amanda's possible rates (4 and 5). We can easily list the 3 rate scenarios that result in a faster speed (greater distance) for John:

John ran 5 mph, and Amanda ran 4 mph.
John ran 6 mph, and Amanda ran 4 mph.
John ran 6 mph, and Amanda ran 5 mph.

Since there are 16 possible combinations of rates, the probability that John ran farther than Amanda is 3/16.

The correct answer is A.

103. C: The prime factorization of 96 is $(2)(2)(2)(2)(2)(3) = (2^5)(3^1)$. In order for p^2 to be divisible by 96, p^2 would have to have the prime factors $2^5 3^1$ in its prime box. The rephrased question is therefore "Does p^2 have *at least* five 2's and one 3 in its prime box?"

(1) INSUFFICIENT: If p is a multiple of $8 = (2)(2)(2)$, p has 2^3 in its prime box. Therefore, p^2 has $(2^3)^2 = 2^6$ in its prime box, and therefore has the required five 2's. However, it is uncertain whether p^2 has at least one 3 in its prime box.

Alternatively, we could list numbers:

$p = 0, 8, 16, 24$, etc.
$p^2 = 0, 64, 256, 576$, etc.

Divisible by 96? Yes, No, No, Yes

(2) INSUFFICIENT: If p^2 is a multiple of $12 = (2)(2)(3)$, p^2 has two 2's and one 3 in its prime box. It is uncertain whether p^2 has at least five 2's total, as there may or may not be three more 2's in the prime box.

Alternatively, we could list numbers:

$p^2 = 0, 36, 144, 96^2$, etc. (perfect squares that are multiples of 12)

Divisible by 96? Yes, No, No, Yes

(1) AND (2) SUFFICIENT: We know from (1) that p^2 has 2^6 in its prime box, and we know from (2) that p^2 has a 3 in its prime box. Therefore, it is certain that p^2 has *at least* five 2's and one 3 in its prime box.

Note that the number listing approach would be a little cumbersome for the combined statements.

The correct answer is C.

104. B: Redraw the figure as closely to scale as possible (use the grid on your scrapboard!), labeling the known dimensions and the radius in question.

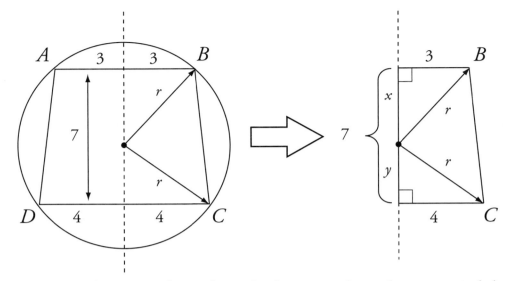

In order for the trapezoid vertices to lie on the circle, the trapezoid must be symmetrical about the dotted line, which passes through the center of the circle. By drawing this vertical and the radii to points *B* and *C* we have created two right triangles, allowing us to use the Pythagorean Theorem.

In fact, we might play an educated hunch that the triangles are 3–4–5 common right triangles. This checks out: If hypotenuse *r* is 5, then each triangle has a 3 and 4 side. The unknown vertical sides are thus 4 and 3, which sum to 7 as they must.

Algebraically, we can set up the following equations from the picture:

$x^2 + 3^2 = r^2$
$y^2 + 4^2 = r^2$
$x + y = 7$

Setting the two equations for r^2 equal:

$x^2 + 3^2 = y^2 + 4^2$
$x^2 - y^2 = 4^2 - 3^2$
$(x + y)(x - y) = 7$

Since $(x + y)(x - y) = 7$, $(x - y) = 1$.

Solve for *x* and *y*:

$(x + y) = 7$
$(x - y) = 7$
$2x = 8$
$x = 4$
$y = 7 - x = 3$

The radius of the circle is 5, because $r^2 = 3^2 + 4^2 = 25$.

The correct answer is B.

the new standard

105. E: Manipulate:

$$9^y + 3^b = 10(3^b)$$
$$(3^2)^y + 3^b = 10(3^b)$$
$$(3^2)^y = 10(3^b) - 3^b$$
$$(3^2)^y = 3^b(10 - 1)$$
$$(3^2)^y = 3^b(3^2)$$
$$(3^2)^y = 3^{b+2}$$
$$2y = b + 2$$

The correct answer is E.

106. C: For the wheelbarrow, we can set up a distance formula:

$$\text{Distance Traveled} = \left(\text{Wheel Circumference}\right)\left(\text{Number of Wheel Revolutions}\right)$$
$$\text{Distance Traveled} = \left(2\pi r\right)\left(\text{Number of Wheel Revolutions}\right)$$
$$\frac{\text{Distance Traveled}}{\left(2\pi\right)\left(\text{Number of Wheel Revolutions}\right)} = r$$

We can rephrase the question from "What is *r*?" to "What is the distance traveled and the number of wheel revolutions?"

(1) INSUFFICIENT: This provides the distance traveled, but no information about the number of wheel revolutions.

(2) INSUFFICIENT: This gives the number of wheel revolutions, but no information about the total distance from *X* to *Y*.

(1) AND (2) SUFFICIENT: If Sue traveled 60 feet at a rate of 2 feet per second, she traveled for 60/2 = 30 seconds before meeting Nancy. During those 30 seconds, Nancy had traveled at a rate of 3 feet per second, for a distance of (3)(30) = 90 feet. The total distance between *X* and *Y* is 60 + 90 = 150 feet.

We also know the total number of wheel revolutions that occurred between *X* and *Y*, so we have the answer to the rephrased question.

The correct answer is C.

107. A: We know that:

$$h(abc) = 3 \times h(def)$$

$$\frac{h(abc)}{h(def)} = 3$$

$$\frac{5^a 2^b 3^c}{5^d 2^e 3^f} = 3$$

3 has no factors of 5 or 2, so these factors must cancel out of the fraction on the left side, implying that $a = d$ and $b = e$.

That leaves $\dfrac{3^c}{3^f} = 3 = 3^{c-f}$, which implies that $c - f = 1$.

Since the only difference between abc and def is in the units digits, the difference between these three-digit numbers is equal to $c - f = 1$.

The correct answer is A.

108. D: Fractions that have only factors of 2 and 5 in the denominator equate to *terminating decimals*. Since $\dfrac{x}{y} = r.s\overline{s}$, a *non-terminating decimal*, y must have some other prime factors besides just 2 and/or 5.

(A) $y = 12, 120, 1,200$, etc. Prime factors of 12: (2)(2)(3)
(B) $y = 15, 150, 1,500$, etc. Prime factors of 15: (3)(5)
(C) $y = 18, 180, 1,800$, etc. Prime factors of 18: (2)(3)(3)
(D) $y = 25, 250, 2,500$, etc. Prime factors of 25: (5)(5). CANNOT be true—only has 5's and 2's.
(E) $y = 27, 270, 2,700$, etc. Prime factors of 27: (3)(3)(3)

The correct answer is D.

109. E: Let's be sure we understand the function given in the question stem by thinking of some examples:

$16 @ 5 = 1$, since 16 divided by 5 leaves a remainder of 1.
$21 @ 3 = 0$, since 21 divided by 3 leaves a remainder of 0.
$17 @ 3 = 2$, since 17 divided by 3 leaves a remainder of 2.

(1) INSUFFICIENT: If a remainder of 1 is left when 81 is divided by x, then x divides evenly into 80. In other words, x is a factor of 80, but not of 81. The factors of 80 are 1, 2, 4, 5, 8, 10, 16, 20, 40, and 80; of these, only the number 1 is also a factor of 80. Thus, the possible values of x are: 2, 4, 5, 8, 10, 16, 20, 40, and 80.

(2) INSUFFICIENT: If a remainder of 0 is left when 40 is divided by x, then 40 divides evenly into x. We might conclude that x must be 40. However, we must realize that x could be any multiple of 40: 40, 80, 120, 160, etc.

(1) AND (2) INSUFFICIENT: x could be either 40 or 80, according to both statements.

The correct answer is E.

110. **A:** Draw overlapping circles in which to place the shared and non-shared *prime factors* of p and r. To find the least common multiple (LCM), multiply from left to right and include all the common factors in the product:

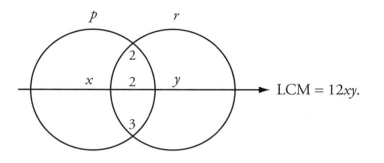

The correct answer is A.

Workout Set 12 Solutions

111. **A:** Parallel lines have the same slope. The slope of line l is $\dfrac{\text{rise}}{\text{run}} = \dfrac{\text{change in } y}{\text{change in } x} = \dfrac{0-3}{2-0} = -\dfrac{3}{2}$.

Put each choice in slope-intercept form: $y = mx + b$ form, where the slope is m.

(A) $2y = -3x$	$y = \dfrac{-3}{2}x$	Slope $= -\dfrac{3}{2}$ CORRECT
(B) $2y = 3x$	$y = \dfrac{3}{2}x$	Slope $= \dfrac{3}{2}$ INCORRECT
(C) $2y = 3x + 6$	$y = \dfrac{3}{2}x + 3$	Slope $= \dfrac{3}{2}$ INCORRECT
(D) $3y = -2x + 6$	$y = \dfrac{-2}{3}x + 2$	Slope $= -\dfrac{2}{3}$ INCORRECT
(E) $3y = 2x + 6$	$y = \dfrac{2}{3}x + 3$	Slope $= \dfrac{2}{3}$ INCORRECT

The correct answer is A.

112. **D:** We should set the two equations for y equal and algebraically solve $|x - 1| = 3x + 3$ for x. This requires two solutions: one for the case that $x - 1$ is positive, the other for the case that $x - 1$ is negative:

x − 1 is positive:
$(x - 1) = 3x + 3$
$-4 = 2x$
$-2 = x$

x − 1 is negative:
$-(x - 1) = 3x + 3$
$-x + 1 = 3x + 3$
$-2 = x$
$-\dfrac{2}{4} = -\dfrac{1}{2} = x$

INCORRECT:

$x - 1 = (-2) - 1 = -3$

CORRECT:

$x - 1 = -\dfrac{1}{2} - 1 = -\dfrac{3}{2}$

Therefore, the original assumption that _x_ − 1 is positive _does not hold._

Therefore, the original assumption that _x_ − 1 is negatives _holds._

Thus, there is only _one_ solution for _x_ and _y_, which is $y = \dfrac{3}{2}$ and $x = -\dfrac{1}{2}$.

The correct answer is D.

113. B: Let's call the cabinets _A_, _B_, and _C_, with the understanding that _A_ cost the least and _C_ the cost most for the dealer to purchase. We are told that the median cabinet, _B_, not only cost the median amount, but also was sold for the median revenue. The profit on _B_ was 10%, so for easy numbers let's say that _B_ cost $100 and was sold for $110. We can select values for _A_ and _C_ relative to these values.

(1) INSUFFICIENT: We know that cabinet _B_ was sold for a profit, so only cabinets _A_ or _C_ could have sold for less than its original cost. We'll try to come up with two scenarios: one that shows 10% was the greatest margin, and one that shows a margin greater than 10%.

In this scenario, _C_ sold for less than its cost, but _A_ has a profit margin greater than 10%.

	A	**B**	**C**
Cost	$50	$100	$150
Revenue	$75	$110	$120
Profit margin	50%	10%	−20%

In this scenario, _A_ sold for less than its cost, and the maximum profit margin is 10%.

	A	**B**	**C**
Cost	$50	$100	$150
Revenue	$25	$110	$160
Profit margin	−50%	10%	<10%

It is uncertain whether the dealer made more than 10% on any one of the three cabinet sales.

(2) SUFFICIENT: Cabinet _C_ sold for the least money, which implies that cabinet _A_ sold for the most, because cabinet _B_'s revenue was in the middle. We can relate both of these revenue possibilities to our smart number of $110 for _B_'s revenue. We have already defined cabinet _C_ as the most expensive for

the dealer to purchase, and again we can relate that cost to our smart number of $100 for *B*'s cost. Let's put the numbers into a chart:

	A	*B*	*C*
Cost	less than $100	$100	more than $100
Revenue	more than $110	$110	less than $110
Profit margin	>10%	10%	<10%

In words, this statement tells us that the dealer paid less for *A* and sold it for more (relative to *B*), so he made a greater profit on *A* than *B*. The dealer definitely made a profit greater than 10% on the sale of one of the cabinets.

The correct answer is B.

114. **D:** When comparing fractional pieces of a whole, we must find a common denominator. In this case, the 1-mile stretch is divided in thirds, fifths, and eighths. The smallest common denominator of 3, 5, and 8 is 120. If the 1-mile highway is divided into 120 equal increments, where will the red, white, and blue marks fall?

Red (thirds): 40, 80 (out of 120 increments)

White (fifths): 24, 48, 72, 96 (out of 120 increments)

Blue (sevenths): 15, 30, 45, 60, 75, 90, 105 (out of 120 increments)

The smallest distance between two marks is $75 - 72 = 3$ or $48 - 45 = 3$. This equates to 3/120, or 1/40 miles.

The correct answer is D.

115. **E:** Both statements give us information about the sum of the set, so we will rephrase with this in mind:

> Sum of Consecutive Set = (Median)(Number of Terms)
> Sum of Consecutive Set = (Median)(n)

For n = odd, the median is the middle term, an integer. For n = even, the median is the average of the two middle terms, a non-integer of the form "integer + 0.5." We can determine n if we can determine both the median of Set S and the sum of the integers in Set S.

(1) INSUFFICIENT:

> Sum of Consecutive Set = (Median)(n)
> multiple of 7 = (Median)(n)

Even if we ignore the possibility of non-integer medians, we can list some possibilities: n is a multiple of 7, the median is a multiple of 7, or both.

Check some possible median and n values:

  $n = 3$ and Median = 7: Set S is {6, 7, 8}, which has a sum of 21. OK.
  $n = 7$ and Median = 2: Set S is {−1, 0, 1, 2, 3, 4, 5}, which has a sum of 14. OK.
  $n = 7$ and Median = 7: Set S is {4, 5, 6, 7, 8, 9, 10}, which has a sum of 49. OK.

We have proven that n could equal 3 or 7, and there are probably many other possible n values.

(2) INSUFFICIENT: Since n must be an integer, we can use divisibility rules to narrow down possible median values.

$$\text{Sum of Consecutive Set} = (\text{Median})(n)$$
$$14 = (\text{Median})(n)$$
$$(2)(7) = (\text{Median})(n)$$

Check some possible median and n values:

  $n = 1$ and Median = 14: Set S is {14}, which has a sum of 14, but not enough terms. IGNORE.
  $n = 2$ and Median = 7: Set S can't have an integer median if there are only 2 terms. IGNORE.
  $n = 7$ and Median = 2: Set S is {−1, 0, 1, 2, 3, 4, 5}, which has a sum of 14. OK.
  $n = 4$ and Median = 3.5: Set S is {2, 3, 4, 5}, which has a sum of 14. OK.

n could equal 4 or 7.

(1) AND (2) INSUFFICIENT: Statement (1) does not further restrict the cases allowed by Statement (2), so together the statements are still insufficient.

The correct answer is E.

116. C: There are four basic ways this picture could look, as there are four sides of the trapezoid that could serve as the non-tangent side:

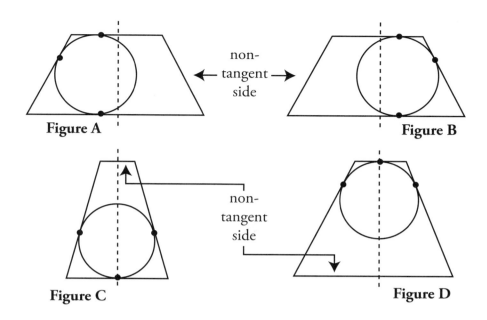

Figure A   Figure B

Figure C   Figure D

non-tangent side

non-tangent side

(1) INSUFFICIENT: If the circle is tangent to both of the parallel sides (Figure A or B), then the diameter must be 10. If the circle is tangent to only one of the parallel sides (Figure C or D), then the diameter is less than 10. Since we are left with multiple possibilities for the diameter of the circle, we do not have enough information to answer the original question.

(2) INSUFFICIENT: Just knowing the length of the shorter parallel side is not enough to determine which of the basic figures above describes the correct situation. If Figure A or B represents the correct situation, the diameter of the circle is clearly determined solely by the distance between the parallel sides; the diameter is independent of the length of the shorter parallel side, so knowing that it is 15 inches long is not useful. If Figure C or D describes the correct situation, then the diameter would depend on not only the 15-inch side but also the longer parallel side, which has an unknown length.

(1) AND (2) SUFFICIENT: If the distance between the parallel sides is 10, and the shorter parallel side has a length of 15, then Figure A or B represents the correct situation and the diameter of the circle must equal 10.

Alternatively, notice that Figure D could not represent our situation, since the circle would have to have a diameter larger than 15 inches in order to be tangent to the short parallel side and the non-parallel sides of the trapezoid. We know that the parallel sides of the trapezoid are only 10 inches apart, so the circle would be too large to be drawn entirely within the trapezoid as required. Similar logic explains why Figure C is also impossible when we consider (1) and (2) together.

The correct answer is C.

117. **A:** We could list all the ways to pick four children—two boys and two girls. We could also take the opposite approach: list all the ways to *leave out* two children—one boy and one girl. There are fewer scenarios to list with the left-out children, so let's take that approach. The sum of the ages of all six children is $(4 + 6 + 7) + (5 + 8 + 9) = 39$, an odd number. We can then list all 9 scenarios, subtracting out the ages of the left-out children.

Age of boy left out	Age of girl left out	Sum of left-out children's ages	$z = 39$ − (Sum of left-out children's ages)
4	5	9	$39 - 9 = $ EVEN
4	8	12	$39 - 12 = $ ODD
4	9	13	$39 - 13 = $ EVEN
6	5	11	$39 - 11 = $ EVEN
6	8	14	$39 - 14 = $ ODD
6	9	15	$39 - 15 = $ EVEN
7	5	12	$39 - 12 = $ ODD
7	8	15	$39 - 15 = $ EVEN
7	9	16	$39 - 16 = $ ODD

Of the 9 scenarios listed, 5 yield an even z and 4 yield an odd z. Each outcome is equally likely.

The difference between the probability that z is even and the probability that z is odd is therefore $5/9 - 4/9 = 1/9$.

The correct answer is A.

118. D: First, consider a random three digit number as an example: $375 = 100(3) + 10(7) + 1(5)$, because 3 is in the hundreds place, 7 is in the tens place, and 5 is in the ones place. More generally, $ABC = 100(A) + 10(B) + 1(C)$. For digit problems, particularly those that involve "shuffling" or permutations of digits, we must think about place value.

Since we are dealing with three unique digits, the number of possible sequences will be 3! or 6. If we write them out, we can see a pattern:

ABC
ACB
BAC
BCA
CAB
CBA

Notice that each unique digit appears exactly twice in each column, so each column individually sums to $2(A + B + C)$.

Sum of the hundreds column: $100 \times 2(A + B + C) = 200(A + B + C)$
Sum of the tens column: $100 \times 2(A + B + C) = 20(A + B + C)$
Sum of the ones column: $1 \times 2(A + B + C) = 2(A + B + C)$
Altogether, the sum of the three-digit numbers is $(200 + 20 + 2)(A + B + C) = 222(A + B + C)$.

Regardless of the values of A, B, and C, the sum of the three-digit numbers must be divisible by 222 and all of its factors: 1, 2, 3, 6, 37, 74, 111, and 222. The only answer choice that is not among these is 11.

The correct answer is D.

*Manhattan*GMAT®Prep
the new standard

119. A: This problem is most efficiently solved by testing the answer choices:

(A) 3: *ababab* is divisible by 3 because the sum of its digits is $3(a + b)$, a multiple of 3 for any integers *a* and *b*.

(B) 4: An integer is divisible by 4 if its last two digits represent a two-digit number that is itself divisible by 4. It is uncertain whether the two-digit integer *ab* is divisible by 4.

(C) 5: An integer is divisible by 5 if the last digit is 0 or 5. It is uncertain whether the positive integer *b* is 5.

(D) 6: An integer is divisible by 6 if it is even and divisible by 3. We already established that *ababab* is divisible by 3, but it is uncertain whether the last digit *b* is even, a requirement for *ababab* to be even.

Alternatively, we can tackle this problem by thinking about the place values of the unknowns. If we had a two-digit number *ab*, we could express it as $10a + 1b$. By similar logic, *ababab* can be expressed as follows:

$$ababab = 100{,}000a + 10{,}000b + 1{,}000a + 100b + 10a + b$$

If we combine like terms, we get the following:

$$ababab = 101{,}010a + 10{,}101b$$

At this point, we can spot a common term: each term is a multiple of 10,101. If we factor 10101 from each term, the expression can be written as follows:

$$ababab = 10{,}101(10a + b), \text{ where } a \text{ and } b \text{ are individual digits.}$$

Or simply:

$$ababab = 10{,}101(ab), \text{ where } ab \text{ is a two-digit number.}$$

Since we don't know the value of the two-digit number *ab*, we cannot know what its factors are. To find a known factor of *ababab*, our only option is to find a factor of 10,101.

At this point, we can recognize that 10,101 is a multiple of 3 (the sum of the digits is 3). Therefore, *ababab* must be a multiple of 3.

The correct answer is A.

120. E: Another way of saying that an integer is divisible by 6 is to say that it is a multiple of 6. Multiples of 6 <u>must</u> have all of the prime factors of 6 ($6 = 2 \times 3$) and <u>could</u> have additional prime factors. Thus, our rephrased question is "Does the product *abcd* have <u>at least</u> one 2 and one 3 as prime factors?"

(1) INSUFFICIENT: This tells us that at least one of the integers *a*, *c*, and *d* must be even. Thus we have at least one 2 as a prime factor. However, we do not know anything about the remaining factors, and cannot determine whether there is one 3 among the prime factors of *a*, *b*, *c*, and *d*.

(2) INSUFFICIENT: This tells us that *a*, *b*, and *d* are all odd, which means there is no factor of 2

among their prime factors. Without information about c, we are uncertain about whether $abcd$ has a factor of 2. Additionally, we have no information about the number of 3s among the prime factors of a, b, and d. It is possible that abd is 105, for example, and we would have the 3 required for divisibility by 6. On the other hand, abd could be 125 and we would have no 3s as factors.

(1) AND (2) INSUFFICIENT: If acd is even and if abd is odd, it must be true that c is even and that $abcd$ has at least one factor of 2. Neither of the statements gives us a conclusive answer about the number of 3s among the prime factors of a, b, c, and d, however, and combining the statements does nothing to resolve that uncertainty.

The correct answer is E.

Workout Set 13 Solutions

121. B: Factor the quadratic:

$$p^2 - 13p + 40 = q$$
$$(p - 8)(p - 5) = q$$

For $p = 5$ and $p = 8$, $q = 0$. Between $p = 5$ and $p = 8$, q has a negative sign, as $(p - 8)$ is negative and $(p - 5)$ is positive. With a total of 10 possible integer p values, only two ($p = 6$ and $p = 7$) fall in the range $5 < p < 8$, so the probability is 2/10 or 1/5.

The correct answer is B.

122. C: To maximize the value of q, we need to constrain p to NOT be a multiple of 10. In other words, q should be the count of *every* factor of 10 in 200!, and p would simply be the product of the remaining factors of 200!.

To count factors of 10 in 200!, we could start by counting the multiples of 10 between 1 and 200, inclusive. But this method would undercount the number of 10's that are factors of 200!. For example:

200! has 2 and 5 as factors, which multiply to 10, and thus another factor of 10.
200! has 6 and 15 as factors, which multiply to 90, and thus another factor of 10.
200! has 8 and 125 as factors, which multiply to 1000, and thus three more factors of 10.

Therefore, this problem is really about counting the number of 2×5 factor pairs that can be made from the factors of 200.

Let's count the number of 5s found among the factors of 200!:

	Number of multiples between 1 and 200, inclusive
Multiples of 5 (= 5^1)	200/5 = 40
Multiples of 25 (= 5^2)	200/25 = 8
Multiples of 125 (= 5^3)	125 is the only one: 1

We have counted not only the multiples of 5, but also the multiples of 25 and 125, as these higher multiples contribute *more than one* factor of 5 to the total.

There are eight multiples of 25 in our range (namely, 25, 50, 75, 100, 125, 150, 175, and 200). Each of these are also multiples of 5, so we have already counted one factor of 5 for them, and thus each of the eight multiples of 25 contributes one *additional* factor of 5. Finally, 125 contributes a total of three 5s to our count — but we already counted one factor of 5 when we counted multiples of 5, and another when we counted multiples of 25, leaving only one *additional* factor of 5 that we need to count for 125.

Thus, the prime factorization for 200! includes 40 + 8 + 1 = 49 factors of 5.

It is fairly easy to see that there are many more factors of 2 in 200!, as there are 100 even numbers between 1 and 200, not to mention the additional 2's coming from the multiples of 4, 8, 16, 32, etc. that contribute extra factors of 2.

Thus, we can only make 49 of the 2 × 5 factor pairs, and the maximum value of q is 49.

The correct answer is C.

123. B: Since $x \neq 0$, we know that x^y does not equal 0^y or 0. To determine the exact non-zero value of x^y, we need either the values of both x and y, or if y is even, the values of $|x|$ and y (an even exponent "hides the sign" of the base, so we wouldn't need to know x's sign).

(1) INSUFFICIENT: This statement tells us that x is equal to 2 or −2. However, we know nothing about y and cannot determine the value of x^y.

(2) SUFFICIENT: Simplify using exponent rules, noting the common factors of 6 and 8 on each side of the equation:

$$64^x 6^{2x+y} = 48^{2x}$$
$$(8^2)^x 6^{2x+yx} = (6 \times 8)^{2x}$$
$$8^{2x} 6^{2x} 6y = 6^{2x} 8^{2x}$$
$$6^y = 1$$
$$y = 0$$

Since $y = 0$ and $x \neq 0$ (as stated in the question stem), this information is sufficient to conclude that $x^y = x^0 = 1$.

The correct answer is B.

124. E: Redraw the diagram and label as much as possible. Using the rules about a transversal (line m) intersecting parallel lines (in this case, two sets of parallel lines), we can label at least two more angles $y°$ and $z°$:

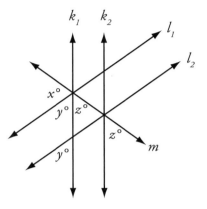

We have labeled three angles that form a straight line at the intersection of k_1, l_1, and m, so $x + y + z = 180$. Since $x = 180 - (y + z)$, the rephrased question is "What is the value of x or the value of $(y + z)$?"

(1) INSUFFICIENT: Substitute $x = 3z - y$ into $x + y + z = 180$ and simplify:

$$(3z - y) + y + z = 180$$
$$4z = 180$$
$$z = 45$$

This provides neither the value of x nor the value of $(y + z)$.

(2) INSUFFICIENT: Simplify the expression.

$$(y - z)^2 = 225$$
$$(y - z) = -15 \text{ or } 15, \text{ so } |y - z| = 15.$$

This provides neither the value of x nor the value of $(y + z)$.

(1) & (2) INSUFFICIENT: There are two solutions as indicated by the absolute value in (2):

$y - z = 15$:	OR	$y - z = -15$:
$y = 15 + z$		$y = -15 + z$
$y = 15 + 45$		$y = -15 + 45$
$y = 60$		$y = 30$

$y + z = 60 + 45 = 105$ $y + z = 30 + 45 = 75$

The correct answer is E, because even with both statements, we cannot tell whether $x = y + z = 75$ or 105.

125. E: Start by plugging x values:

x	$x + \dfrac{4}{x}$
1	$1 + 4/1 = 5$
2	$2 + 4/2 = 4$
3	$3 + 4/3 = 13/3 = 4.33$
4	$4 + 4/4 = 5$
5	$5 + 4/5 = 29/5 = 5.8$
larger x's	larger integer + smaller fraction = larger value

We can be confident from the pattern emerging that for $x > 5$, $x + \dfrac{4}{x}$ will only continue to grow as x grows. The minimum $x + \dfrac{4}{x}$ in this chart is 4, when $x = 2$, but remember we only tested integer x values. To be confident that 4 is really the minimum, we should graph these points and sketch the curve connecting them:

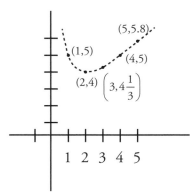

This expression will have rather regular curvature; it will not suddenly spike in one direction or another. To come anywhere near 3, this curve would have to suddenly dip between $x = 1$ and $x = 2$, or between $x = 2$ and $x = 3$. That simply doesn't fit with curvature of the rest of the function, so the least possible value of $x + \dfrac{4}{x}$ must be 4. To be sure we can test $x = 1.5$ and $x = 2.5$:

If $x = 1.5$, $x + \dfrac{4}{x} = 1.5 + \dfrac{4}{1.5} = \dfrac{3}{2} + \dfrac{8}{3} = \dfrac{9 + 16}{6} = \dfrac{25}{6} = 4\dfrac{1}{6}$.

If $x = 2.5$, $x + \dfrac{4}{x} = 2.5 + \dfrac{4}{2.5} = \dfrac{5}{2} + \dfrac{8}{5} = \dfrac{25+16}{10} = 4.1$

The correct answer is E.

126. E: Last year, the 5 computer models cost a total of $(5)(\$2,000) = \$10,000$. We cannot assume that each computer model cost exactly $2,000, as some might be more expensive than others. To determine the average cost of the 5 models this year, we would need the total cost of the 5 models this year.

(1) INSUFFICIENT: Since we do not know the actual costs of any of the computer models, there is no way for us to determine the effect of reducing 3 of them by 12 percent. Further, we do not know how the price of the other 2 models might have changed.

(2) INSUFFICIENT: Since we do not know the actual costs of any of the computers, there is no way to determine the effect of increasing 2 of them. Further, we do not know how the price of the other 3 models might have changed.

(1) AND (2) INSUFFICIENT: Now that we know 3 models decreased by 12% and the other 2 models increased by 10%, it might be tempting to assume that each cost $2,000 last year simply so that we can compute the new total cost:

Total cost this year = $(3)(0.88)(\$2,000) + (2)(1.1)(\$2,000) = \$9,680$

However, it is very dangerous to make assumptions on Data Sufficiency questions. Given that the total cost last year was $10,000, it is possible, for example, that the 3 models that decreased in price were $2,500 last year, and the 2 models that increased in price were $1,250. In that case:

Total cost this year = $(3)(0.88)(\$2,500) + (2)(1.1)(\$1,250) = \$9,350$

The correct answer is E.

127. D: The product of the slopes of two perpendicular lines is -1. The slope of line k is given by:

$$\frac{rise}{run} = \frac{change\ in\ y}{change\ in\ x} = \frac{0-(-6)}{12-0} = \frac{6}{12} = \frac{1}{2}.$$

Thus, the slope of the line perpendicular to k is -2.

Put each choice in slope-intercept form: $y = mx + b$ form, where the slope is m.

(A) $3y + 2x = -12$	$y = \dfrac{-2}{3}x - 4$	Slope $= -\dfrac{2}{3}$ INCORRECT
(B) $2y + x = 0$	$y = \dfrac{-1}{2}x$	Slope $= -\dfrac{1}{2}$ INCORRECT

(C) $2y - x = 0$	$y = \dfrac{1}{2}x$	Slope = $\dfrac{1}{2}$	INCORRECT
(D) $y + 2x = 12$	$y = -2x + 12$	Slope = -2	CORRECT
(E) $y - 2x = 12$	$y = 2x + 12$	Slope = 2	INCORRECT

The correct answer is D.

128. A: (1) SUFFICIENT: Manipulate the absolute value expression so we can represent this inequality on a number line:

$$|2x - 12| < 10$$
$$|2(x - 6)| < 10$$
$$2x|x - 6| < 10$$
$$|x - 6| < 5$$

This can be interpreted as "The distance between x and 6 is less than 5." On a number line, this is the region between 1 and 11:

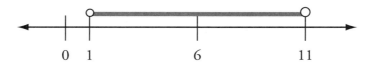

All possible values for x are positive, so the answer to the question is a definite "Yes."

(2) INSUFFICIENT: Manipulate the inequality to get 0 on one side, then factor the resulting quadratic:

$$x^2 - 10x \geq -21$$
$$x^2 - 10x + 21 \geq 0$$
$$(x - 7)(x - 3) \geq 0$$

The factored quadratic on the left side will equal 0 when $x = 3$ and 7. These are the boundary points. On a number line, we can check the regions on either side of these boundary points to determine the valid region(s) for x:

Note that when $3 < x < 7$, $(x - 7)(x - 3) = (\text{neg})(\text{pos}) = \text{neg}$.

Since both positive and negative values are possible for x, the answer is "Maybe."

The correct answer is A.

129. A: Since we are looking for the *minimum* number of *K*-numbers that sum to 600, a practical place to start is with the *largest K*-number less than 600, or 222. There are between 2 and 3 multiples of 222 in 600, so let's subtract out the two whole multiples!

$$\begin{array}{r} 600 \\ \underline{-444} \; (= 2 \times 222) \\ 156 \end{array}$$

Now, the next largest *K*-number is 22. Again subtract as many whole multiples as possible:

$$\begin{array}{r} 156 \\ \underline{-154} \; (= 7 \times 22) \\ 2 \end{array}$$

The next largest *K*-number is obviously 2:

$$\begin{array}{r} 2 \\ \underline{-2} \; (= 1 \times 2) \\ 0 \end{array}$$

Thus, $600 = 222(2) + 22(7) + 2(1)$, and the *K*-weight of 600 is $2 + 7 + 1 = 10$.

The correct answer is A.

130. E: If the greater of the two integers is x, then the two integers can be expressed as $x - 1$ and x. The sum of the reciprocals would therefore be:

$$\frac{1}{x-1} + \frac{1}{x} = \frac{x + (x-1)}{(x-1)x}$$
$$= \frac{2x-1}{x^2 - x}$$

Alternatively, we could pick numbers and test the answer choices. For example, let the larger number $x = 3$. The smaller number would therefore be $3 - 1 = 2$. The sum of the reciprocals would be:

$$\frac{1}{3} + \frac{1}{2} = \frac{2}{6} + \frac{3}{6} = {}^{5}\!/\!_{6}$$

Now we must test each answer choice by plugging $x = 3$. The choice that equals the target of 5/6 is the correct answer.

(A) $\dfrac{3}{x} = \dfrac{3}{3} = 1$

(B) $x^2 - x = 9 - 3 = 6$

(C) $2x - 1 = 6 - 1 = 5$

(D) $\dfrac{2x-1}{x^2+x} = \dfrac{5}{9+3} = \dfrac{5}{12}$

(E) $\dfrac{2x-1}{x^2-x} = \dfrac{6-1}{9-3} = \dfrac{5}{6}$

The correct answer is E. 131. The sequence A is defined by the following relationship: $A_n = A_{n-1} + (-1)^{n+1}(n^2)$ for all integer values of $n > 1$. If $A_1 = 1$, what is $A_{15} - A_{13}$?

(A) 14
(B) 29
(C) 169
(D) 196
(E) 421

Workout Set 14 Solutions

131. B: Generate the first several values of the sequence, using the given relationship. Notice that a component such as $(-1)^{n+1}$ simply switches the sign of the additive term back and forth. Use a table to keep your work organized:

n	$A_n = A_{n-1} + (-1)^{n+1}(n^2)$
1	1
2	$1 + (-1)^{2+1}(2^2) = 1 - 4 = -3$
3	$-3 + (-1)^{3+1}(3^2) = -3 + 9 = 6$
4	$6 + (-1)^{4+1}(4^2) = 6 - 16 = -10$
5	$-10 + (-1)^{5+1}(5^2) = -10 + 25 = 15$
6	$15 + (-1)^{6+1}(6^2) = -15 - 36 = -21$

We know *why* the sign of the terms alternates (the $(-1)^{n+1}$ term), and that the terms get farther from 0 as n increases, but *how much* farther from zero? It is not yet obvious how we can extrapolate to $A_{15} - A_{13}$. Ignoring the sign of the terms (taking absolute values) might help us determine the pattern:

n	$A_n = A_{n-1} + (-1)^{n+1}(n^2)$	$|A_n|$	change from previous term
1	1	1	
2	-3	3	+2
3	6	6	+3
4	-10	10	+4
5	15	15	+5
6	-21	21	+6

That is, the absolute value of each term equals the absolute value of the previous term plus n. Following this pattern, $|A_{15}|$ is 15 greater than $|A_{14}|$, and $|A_{14}|$ is 14 greater than $|A_{13}|$. Thus, $|A_{15}| - |A_{13}| = +15+14 = 29$.

Since the odd-numbered terms in the original sequence are positive, the absolute value of any odd-numbered term equals the term itself, so $|A_{15}| - |A_{13}| = A_{15} - A_{13} = 29$.

Incidentally, the sequence $|A_n|$ is known as the "triangular" numbers. The sum of the nth triangular number and its predecessor equals n^2.

The correct answer is B.

132. E: When rounding to the nearest tenth, we look at the hundredths digit, or d in this case. If $d \geq 5$, the decimal 0.4de is rounded up to 0.5. If $d \leq 4$, the decimal 0.4de is rounded down to 0.4. Thus, a rephrase of this question is "What is the value of d? Specifically, is d above or below 5?"

(1) INSUFFICIENT: Since $d - e$ is positive, $d > e$. Since d and e are digits (i.e. 0, 1, 2,..., 7, 8, 9), there is a maximum value for the difference: $d - e \leq 9$. There are only three perfect squares less than or equal to 9: $d - e = 1$, 4, or 9. We should remember the rephrased question, and try to list at least one round down case ($d \leq 4$) and one round up case ($d \geq 5$):

d	e	$d - e = $ **perfect square**	**0.4de rounded**
9	0	$9 - 0 = 9$ ✓	0.5
1	0	$1 - 0 = 1$ ✓	0.4

While there are many more scenarios that meet the constraint given in Statement (1), we have proven with just two scenarios that two answers are possible (0.5 and 0.4).

(2) INSUFFICIENT: Since d and e are positive, we can square each side of the inequality without worrying about flipping the sign, getting $d > e^4$. Since d and e are digits (i.e. 0, 1, 2,..., 7, 8, 9), $9 \geq d > e^4$, which means that e can only be 0 or 1. (Note that $2^4 = 16$, which is too large.) Again, return to the rephrased question: try to list at least one round down case ($d \leq 4$) and one round up case ($d \geq 5$).

d	e	$\sqrt{d} > e^2$	**0.4de rounded**
9	0	$3 > 0$ ✓	0.5
1	0	$\sqrt{1} > 0$ ✓	0.4

While there are many more scenarios that meet the constraint given in Statement (1), we have proven with just two scenarios that two answers are possible (0.5 and 0.4).

(1) AND (2) INSUFFICIENT: Taking both statements together, we know that e must be 0 or 1 and that $d - e$ is equal to 9, 4 or 1. Let's set up a scenario chart to track the possibilities:

d	e	$d - e$ = perfect square	$\sqrt{d} > e^2$	$0.4de$ rounded
9	0	$9 - 0 = 9$ ✔	$3 > 0$ ✔	0.5
1	0	$1 - 0 = 1$ ✔	$1 > 0$ ✔	0.4

We do not have to draw a new scenario chart, because we can use the same two cases for both statements. Thus, together, these two cases are both still valid, even when the statements are combined.

The correct answer is E.

133. B: The prime factorization of 32 is $(2)(2)(2)(2)(2) = 2^5$. Thus, $n^4 = 2^5x$, where x is some integer.

Assigning the factors of n^4 to the prime boxes of n will help us see what the factors of n could be:

n^4			
n	n	n	n
2	2	2	2
2	(2)	(2)	(2)
?	?	?	?

The prime factors in parentheses above are factors not explicitly given for n^4, but which must exist. n^4 is the 4th power of an integer, which must have "quadruples" of the prime factors of n. Since n^4 has a factor of 2^4, n must have a factor of 2. The fact that n^4 has an "extra" 2 among its factors indicates that n has an *additional* factor of 2.

If n is a multiple of $(2)(2) = 4$, then n could be 4, 8, 12, 16, 20, 24, etc. The remainder when n is divided by 32 could be 4, 8, 12, 16, 20, etc. (all multiples of 4). The only answer choice that is a multiple of 4 is 4.

The correct answer is B.

134. D: Qualitatively, many failure scenarios could occur:

- None of the links will fail,
- Exactly 1 of the links will fail,
- Exactly 2 of the links will fail,
- etc.

Given the complexity of the failure scenarios, it is easier for us to look at the opposite scenario:

probability that at least 1 link will fail = 1 − probability that all links will <u>not</u> fail

For each of the links, the probability that it will not fail is $1 - 0.01 = 0.99$. The probability that all ten will not fail is thus $(0.99)^{10}$, since the probability that all ten will not fail is simply the product of the probabilities of the individual links not failing.

Therefore, the Probability that at least 1 link will fail = $1 - (0.99)^{10}$.

The correct answer is D.

135. C: The prime factorization of 60 is $(2)(2)(3)(5) = 2^2 3^1 5^1$. Thus, $y^4 = 2^2 3^1 5^1 x$, where x is some integer.

Assigning the factors of y^4 to the prime boxes of y will help us see what the factors of y could be:

y^4			
y	y	y	y
2	2	(2)	(2)
3	(3)	(3)	(3)
5	(5)	(5)	(5)
?	?	?	?

The prime factors in parentheses above are factors not explicitly given for y^4, but which must exist. y^4 is the 4th power of an integer, which must have must have "quadruples" of the prime factors of y. Since y^4 has a factor of 2^2, y must have a factor of 2. Since y^4 has factors of 3 and 5 among its factors, y has factors of 3 and 5.

Thus y is a multiple of $(2)(3)(5) = 30$, and at the very least y has 1, 2, 3, 5, 6, 10, 15, and 30 as factors. y has at least 8 distinct factors.

The correct answer is C.

136. D: Consecutive integers differ by exactly 1. For x and y to be consecutive, either $x = y + 1$ or $x = y - 1$. We can rephrase the question as "Does x equal either $(y + 1)$ or $(y - 1)$?"

(1) SUFFICIENT: There's only one term with x but a couple with y, so it is easiest to solve for x:

$$x^2 - y^2 = 2y + 1$$
$$x^2 = y^2 + 2y + 1$$
$$x^2 = (y + 1)^2$$
$$\sqrt{x^2} = \sqrt{(y + 1)^2}$$
$$|x| = |y + 1|$$

x and y are both positive, so we can drop the absolute value signs and conclude that $x = y + 1$.

(2) SUFFICIENT: There's only one term with y but several with x, so it is easiest to solve for y:

$$x^2 - xy - x = 0$$
$$x^2 - x = xy$$
$$\frac{x^2 - x}{x} = \frac{xy}{x}$$
$$x - 1 = y$$
$$x = y + 1$$

Dividing by a variable is generally not a good practice, as you run the risk of dividing by zero; we divide by x here only because we know that it is positive and therefore not zero.

The correct answer is D.

137. C: (1) INSUFFICIENT: We can solve for the expression in question by adding $(-x^2 - x)$ to y:

$$y = -3x$$
$$y + (-x^2 - x) = -3x + (-x^2 - x)$$
$$y - x^2 - x = -x^2 - 4x$$

The answer depends on the value of x, which is not given.

(2) INSUFFICIENT: We can solve for the expression in question by adding $(-x^2 - x)$ to y:

$$y = -4(x + 1)$$
$$y + (-x^2 - x) = -4(x + 1) + (-x^2 - x)$$
$$y - x^2 - x = -4x - 4 - x^2 - x$$
$$y - x^2 - x = -x^2 - 5x - 4$$

The answer depends on the value of x, which is not given.

(1) and (2) SUFFICIENT: Each statement gave us a different expression equal to $y - x^2 - x$. Setting these equal to each other, we get:

$$-x^2 - 5x - 4 = -x^2 - 4x$$
$$-5x - 4 = -4x$$
$$5x + 4 = 4x$$
$$x = -4$$

If $x = -4$, then $y = 12$ and $y - x^2 - x = 12 - (-4)^2 - (-4) = 12 - 16 + 4 = 0$.

The correct answer is C.

138. D: The question gives a function with two unknown constants and two data points. In order to solve for $p(4)$, we need to first solve for the constants r and b by creating two equations from the two data points given:

$$p(2) = 41 = r(2) - 5(2)^2 + b$$
$$41 = 2r + b - 20$$
$$61 = 2r + b$$

$$p(5) = 26 = r(5) - 5(5)^2 + b$$
$$26 = 5r + b - 125$$
$$151 = 5r + b$$

We can now solve these equations for r and b by subtracting one from the other to cancel the b's:

$$\begin{aligned}
151 &= 5r + b \\
-(61 &= 2r + b) \\
\hline
90 &= 3r \\
30 &= r
\end{aligned}$$

Substituting back in to one of the equations, we can find b:

$$61 = 2r + b$$
$$61 = 2(30) + b$$
$$1 = b$$

Thus, we can rewrite the original function and plug in $t = 4$ to find our answer:

$$p(t) = 30t - 5t^2 + 1$$

$$\begin{aligned}
p(4) &= 30(4) - 5(4)^2 + 1 \\
&= 120 - 80 + 1 \\
&= 41
\end{aligned}$$

The correct answer is D.

139. A: If the area of the square is 4.5 and the side length is s, then

$$s^2 = \frac{9}{2}$$

$$s = \sqrt{\frac{9}{2}} = \frac{3\sqrt{2}}{2}$$

Triangle BCD is a 45–45–90 right triangle, so the ratio of its sides is $s : s : s\sqrt{2}$. Thus, DB (the hypotenuse) is $s\sqrt{2} = \left(\frac{3\sqrt{2}}{2}\right)(\sqrt{2}) = 3$. Furthermore, if DB is 3, and the ratio $DQ : QB$ is 1 : 2, it

*Manhattan*GMAT*Prep*
the new standard

must be true that $DQ = 1$ and $QB = 2$.

To be able to use Pythagorean Theorem, we must create a right triangle with QC as a side by drawing a new line. Such a right triangle will be similar to triangle BCD. Here are two solutions, the only difference being how one draws the extra line:

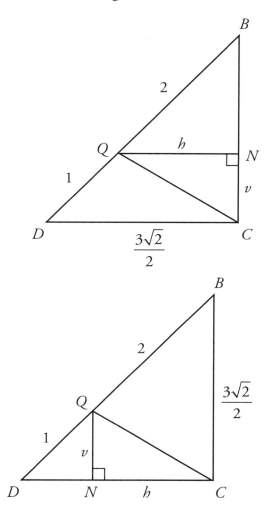

Triangle BNQ is similar to Triangle BCD

ΔBNQ	ΔBCD	Ratio
$BN = \left(\dfrac{2}{3}\right)\dfrac{3\sqrt{2}}{2}$	$BC = \dfrac{3\sqrt{2}}{2}$	$2 : 3$
$NQ = \left(\dfrac{2}{3}\right)\dfrac{3\sqrt{2}}{2}$	$CD = \dfrac{3\sqrt{2}}{2}$	$2 : 3$
$QB = 2$	$DB = 3$	$2 : 3$

$$h = \left(\frac{2}{3}\right)\frac{3\sqrt{2}}{2}$$

Triangle QND is similar to Triangle BCD

ΔQND	ΔBCD	Ratio
$QN = \left(\dfrac{1}{3}\right)\dfrac{3\sqrt{2}}{2}$	$BC = \dfrac{3\sqrt{2}}{2}$	$1 : 3$
$ND = \left(\dfrac{1}{3}\right)\dfrac{3\sqrt{2}}{2}$	$CD = \dfrac{3\sqrt{2}}{2}$	$1 : 3$
$DQ = 2$	$DB = 3$	$1 : 3$

$$v = \left(\frac{2}{3}\right)\frac{3\sqrt{2}}{2}$$

$$v = \frac{3\sqrt{2}}{2} - \left(\frac{2}{3}\right)\frac{3\sqrt{2}}{2} = \left(\frac{1}{3}\right)\frac{3\sqrt{2}}{2}$$

$$h = \frac{3\sqrt{2}}{2} - \left(\frac{1}{3}\right)\frac{3\sqrt{2}}{2} = \left(\frac{2}{3}\right)\frac{3\sqrt{2}}{2}$$

By Pythagorean Theorem:

$$QC^2 = h^2 + v^2$$

$$QC^2 = \left[\left(\frac{2}{3}\right)\frac{3\sqrt{2}}{2}\right]^2 + \left[\left(\frac{1}{3}\right)\frac{3\sqrt{2}}{2}\right]^2$$

$$QC^2 = \left(\frac{4}{9}\right)\left(\frac{9}{2}\right) + \left(\frac{1}{9}\right)\left(\frac{9}{2}\right)$$

$$QC^2 = \left(\frac{5}{9}\right)\left(\frac{9}{2}\right) = \frac{5}{2}$$

$$QC^2 = \sqrt{\frac{5}{2}} = \left(\sqrt{\frac{5}{2}}\right)\left(\sqrt{\frac{2}{2}}\right) = \frac{\sqrt{10}}{2}$$

By Pythagorean Theorem:

$$QC^2 = h^2 + v^2$$

$$QC^2 = \left[\left(\frac{2}{3}\right)\frac{3\sqrt{2}}{2}\right]^2 + \left[\left(\frac{1}{3}\right)\frac{3\sqrt{2}}{2}\right]^2$$

$$QC^2 = \left(\frac{4}{9}\right)\left(\frac{9}{2}\right) + \left(\frac{1}{9}\right)\left(\frac{9}{2}\right)$$

$$QC^2 = \left(\frac{5}{9}\right)\left(\frac{9}{2}\right) = \frac{5}{2}$$

$$QC^2 = \sqrt{\frac{5}{2}} = \left(\sqrt{\frac{5}{2}}\right)\left(\sqrt{\frac{2}{2}}\right) = \frac{\sqrt{10}}{2}$$

The correct answer is A.

140. A: First draw a "rubber band" picture:

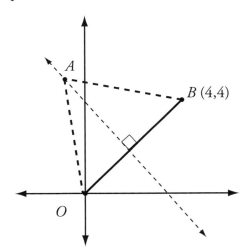

Segment OB has a slope of $+1$, which means that OB is essentially the diagonal of a 4 by 4 square in the xy-coordinate system, so $OB = 4\sqrt{2}$.

Since A must be equidistant from O and B, it must lie on the dashed line with slope -1 that passes through $(2, 2)$; that is, it must lie on the perpendicular bisector of OB. The area of triangle OAB grows as A moves away from OB. Thus, this question is indirectly asking "Exactly how far away must A be from OB to make the area of triangle $OAB = 16$?"

$$\text{Area } OAB = \frac{1}{2}bh$$

$$16 = \frac{1}{2}\left(4\sqrt{2}\right)h$$

$$16 = \left(2\sqrt{2}\right)h$$

$$\frac{16}{2\sqrt{2}} = h$$

$$\frac{16}{2\sqrt{2}}\frac{\sqrt{2}}{\sqrt{2}} = h$$

$$4\sqrt{2} = h$$

Since the dashed line for A has a slope of -1, we might again recognize $4\sqrt{2}$ as the diagonal of a 4 by 4 square in the xy-coordinate system. Thus A, must be 4 units left and up from $(2, 2)$, or 4 units right and down from $(2, 2)$.

Possible coordinates for A are thus:

$(2 - 4, 2 + 4)$ or $(2 + 4, 2 - 4)$
$(-2, 6)$ or $(6, -2)$

The correct answer is A.

Workout Set 15 Solutions

141. C: Factor the numerator:

$$\frac{\left(ab\right)^2 + 3ab - 18}{\left(a-1\right)\left(a+2\right)} = \frac{\left(ab+6\right)\left(ab-3\right)}{\left(a-1\right)\left(a+2\right)} = 0$$

Since the fraction equals 0, either $ab + 6 = 0$ or $ab - 3 = 0$. Thus $ab = -6$ or 3. If a and b are integers, and $ab = -6$ or $ab = 3$, then b must be a factor of either -6 or 3. However, to ensure a valid non-zero denominator in the constraint, $a \neq 1$ and $a \neq -2$.

I. POSSIBLE: If $b = 1$, then $a = -6$ or $a = 3$, which are both allowed.

II. POSSIBLE: If $b = 2$, then $a = -3$ or $a = \frac{3}{2}$. One of those ($a = -3$) is allowed.

III. IMPOSSIBLE: If $b = 3$, then $a = -2$ or $a = 1$, neither of which is allowed.

The correct answer is C.

142. D: Since the four integers in the set are distinct positive integers, let's give them distinct ordered variables to represent their relative sizes: a, b, c, and d are the terms of set S, such that $a < b < c < d$.

The mean of S is $\dfrac{a+b+c+d}{4}$. The median of S is the average of the two middle terms, $\dfrac{b+c}{2}$.

We can thus express the question algebraically:

$$\frac{a+b+c+d}{4} = \frac{b+c}{2} \ ?$$
$$2(a + b + c + d) = 4(b + c)?$$
$$(a + b + c + d) = 2(b + c)?$$
$$a + b + c + d = 2b + 2$$
$$a + d = b + c?$$

In words, this question has been rephrased to "Is the sum of the largest and smallest terms in S equal to the sum of the two middle terms?"

(1) SUFFICIENT: If the smallest term is equal to the sum of the two middle terms minus the largest term, we can construct the following equation:

$$a = b + c - d$$
$$a + d = b + c$$

The answer to the rephrased question is a definite "Yes."

(2) SUFFICIENT: If the sum of the range of S and all the terms in S is equal to the smallest term in S plus three times the largest term in S, we can construct the following equation:

$$(d - a) + (a + b + c + d) = a + 3d$$
$$b + c + 2d = a + 3d$$
$$b + c = a + d.$$

The answer to the rephrased question is a definite "yes."

The correct answer is D.

143. C: All of these line equations are of the form $y = mx + b$, where m is the slope and b is the y-intercept. Two of these lines have a slope of 3/4 and are thus parallel to each other. The other two lines are parallel to one another with a slope of $-3/4$. Two of the lines have a y-intercept of 6 while the other two lines have a y-intercept of -6.

Sketch the lines:

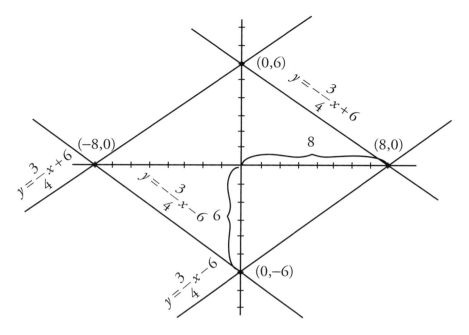

In *each* quadrant, we have a triangle with the dimensions 6–8–10, a multiple of the common 3–4–5 right triangle:

$$
\begin{aligned}
Area &= 4\left(\frac{1}{2}bh\right) \\
&= 2bh \\
&= 2(6)(8) \\
&= 96
\end{aligned}
$$

Alternatively, recognize that the quadrilateral is a rhombus (four equal sides of length 10), and use the formula for the area of a rhombus: $\dfrac{D_1 \times D_2}{2}$, where D indicates the length of the diagonals:

$$
Area = \frac{12 \times 16}{2} = 96.
$$

The correct answer is C.

144. C: In a constrained combinatorics question such as this one, it is often easier to consider the "violating" cases instead of the "ok" cases:

> # of permutations that obey the constraint = # of permutations total − # of permutations that violate the constraint

At first glance, ignore the constraint that 3 and 4 cannot be adjacent to determine the total number of 5-digit integers possible:

# of permutations total = 5! = (5)(4)(3)(2)(1) = 120.

Now let's consider the basic ways that 3 and 4 might be adjacent to each other in a 5-digit number:

3	4	x	x	x
x	3	4	x	x
x	x	3	4	x
x	x	x	3	4

For each of these 4 basic cases, there are 2 ways to order the 3 and 4 (3–4 and 4–3), as well as 3! ways the other digits (1, 2, and 5) can be arranged in the x positions. Thus,

# of permutations that violate the constraint = 4 × 2 × 3! = (4)(2)(3)(2)(1) = 48.

Therefore, the number of permutations that do not violate the constraint equals 120 − 48 = 72.

The correct answer is C.

145. E: To answer, we must recognize an important rule: *the divisor must be greater than the remainder.* Let's look at a few examples:

10 ÷ 4 = 2 remainder 2 (divisor 4 is greater than remainder 2)
23 ÷ 6 = 3 remainder 5 (divisor 6 is greater than remainder 5)

If the divisor weren't greater than the remainder, the divisor would be able to divide into the dividend *at least one more time.* Let's take an incorrect example to illustrate:

23 ÷ 6 = 2 remainder 11

In this case, we've framed the operation such that the divisor is LESS than the remainder (6 is less than 11). The error is that 6 actually goes into 23 three times. The remainder is what is left over when the divisor has been divided into the dividend *as many times as possible.*

Therefore, if a divided by b gives a remainder of 9, we can conclude that b is greater than 9: $b \geq 10$. Likewise, if c divided by d gives a remainder of 5, we can conclude that d is greater than 5: $d \geq 6$.

Therefore, we can determine a minimum for the sum: $b + d \geq 16$.

Only 15 is too small.

The correct answer is E.

146. D: $\dfrac{\text{cupcakes}}{\text{children}} = \dfrac{27}{7}$, so cupcakes $= 27a$ and children $= 7a$, where a is a positive integer.

cupcakes eaten $=$ (children)$x = 7ax$

cupcakes leftover $=$ total cupcakes $-$ cupcakes eaten
$$y = 27a - 7ax$$

$0 \le$ cupcakes leftover $<$ children
$0 \le 27a - 7ax < 7a$
$0 \le 27 - 7x < 7$
$-27 \le -7x < -20$
$27 \ge 7x > 20$

Since x is an integer, and the only multiple of 7 between 20 and 27 is 21, we know that $7x = 21$.

Therefore,
$y = 27a - 7ax$
$ = 27a - a(7x)$
$ = 27a - 21a$
$ = 6a$

I. TRUE: $6a$ is a multiple of 2.
II. TRUE: $6a$ is a multiple of 3.
III. MAYBE: $6a$ could be a multiple of 7, but only when a is a multiple of 7.

The correct answer is D.

147. C: (1) INSUFFICIENT: Manipulate the statement:

$$\frac{x}{5} = y.2$$
$$\frac{x}{5} = y + 0.2$$
$$x = 5(y + 0.2)$$
$$x = 5y + 1$$

Thus, x is 1 greater than a multiple of 5. Since all multiples of 5 end in either 0 or 5, we know that x must end in either 1 or 6.

Alternatively, we could list numbers. Since y is a positive integer, $5y$ could be 5, 10, 15, 20, etc. Thus, x could be 6, 11, 16, 21, etc. The units digit of x could be 1 or 6.

(2) INSUFFICIENT: Manipulate the statement:

$$\frac{x}{2} = z.5$$
$$\frac{x}{2} = z + 0.5$$
$$x = 2(z + 0.5)$$
$$x = 2z + 1$$

This tells us that x is odd, because $2z$ is an even number. Any odd single-digit integer is a possible units digit for x: 1, 3, 5, 7, or 9.

(1) AND (2) SUFFICIENT: Statement (1) tells us that x must end in either 1 or 6. Because Statement (2) tells us that x is odd, we know that x must end in 1, and cannot end in 6.

The correct answer is C.

148. E: (1) INSUFFICIENT: We are told that $(x + y - 1)!$ is less than 100. To see the possible values of $(x + y - 1)$, we list the factorials of the first few integers:

$1! = 1$
$2! = 2$
$3! = 6$
$4! = 24$
$5! = 120$ (too large)

So, $(x + y - 1) \leq 4$, and $(x + y) \leq 5$.

(2) INSUFFICIENT: We can add x to both sides of $y = x^2 - x + 1$ to create $(x + y)$ on one side of the equation:

$$y = x^2 - x + 1$$
$$x + y = x + x^2 - x + 1$$
$$x + y = x^2 + 1$$

The exact value of $(x + y)$ is unknown, as it depends on the value of x^2, which could be any positive integer.

(1) AND (2) INSUFFICIENT: $(x + y) \leq 5$ and $x + y = x^2 + 1$ combine to tell us that $x^2 + 1 \leq 5$. There are two integer solutions: $x = 1$ or $x = 2$.

Checking our work with the original equation from Statement (2):

If $x = 1$, then $y = 1^2 - 1 + 1 = 1$ and $x + y = 1 + 1 = 2$
If $x = 2$, then $y = 2^2 - 2 + 1 = 3$ and $x + y = 2 + 3 = 5$

The correct answer is E.

149. C: The size of the angle depends on two things:

The size of the circle   The distance of C from the circle
                                                    (inversely related to arc length ADB)

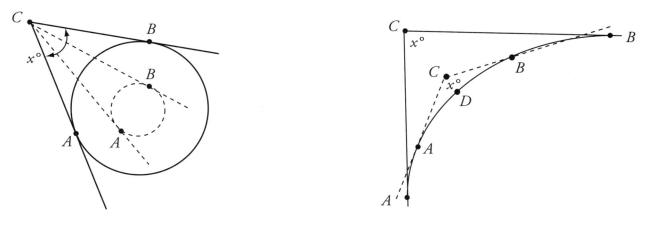

Larger circle ➤ Larger *x*   Farther *C* ➤ smaller *x*
                                                    Larger arc *ADB* ➤ smaller *x*

(1) INSUFFICIENT: From the rubber band picture on the right, we see that for a circle of fixed size, *x* can still vary with the length of arc *ADB* (i.e. *x* varies with the placement of *C*).

(2) INSUFFICIENT: We can't rely solely on the pictures above, as the arc length varies with both circle size (see left picture) and with placement of *C* relative to a circle of fixed size (see right picture). We'll draw two cases to prove that *x* can vary for a given arc *ADB*:

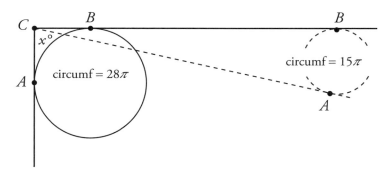

For a circle with circumference 28π, the arc *ADB* is 1/4 (= $7\pi/28\pi$) of the circle, so *x* is 90°. For a circle with circumference 15π, the arc *ADB* is nearly half of the circle (= $7\pi/15\pi$), and the lines tangent to the circle at *A* and *B* will be nearly parallel to each other, i.e. *x* is very small.

(1) AND (2) SUFFICIENT: If the area of the circle is $\pi r^2 = 81\pi$, then $r = 9$. The circumference of the circle is $2\pi r = 18$. Thus, arc *ADB* is 7/18 (= $7\pi/18\pi$) of the circumference of the circle. There is only one way to draw the lines tangent to the circle at *A* and *B*, so *x* can only be one value.

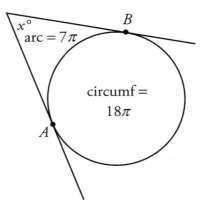

The correct answer is C.

150. C: Let's list the first few terms of the sequence according to the given rules:

$$B_1 = 3$$
$$B_2 = -B_1 = -3$$
$$B_3 = B_2 + 5 = -3 + 5 = 2$$
$$B_4 = -B_3 = -2$$
$$B_5 = B_4 + 5 = -2 + 5 = 3$$
…etc.

Note that the pattern is a four-term repeat: 3, −3, 2, −2. Also note that the sum of this repeating group is (3) + (−3) + (2) + (−2) = 0. This repeating group will occur 16 times through term number 64. Thus, the sum of the first 64 terms will be 0. This leaves the 65th term, which will have the same value as B_1: 3. Therefore, the sum of the first 65 terms is 3.

The correct answer is C.

mbaMission

Every candidate has a unique story to tell.

We have the creative experience to help you tell yours.

We are **mbaMission**, published authors with elite MBA experience who will work with you one-on-one to craft complete applications that will force the admissions committees to take notice. Benefit from straightforward guidance and personal mentorship as you define your unique attributes and reveal them to the admissions committees via a story only you can tell.

We will guide you through our "Complete Start to Finish Process":

- ☑ Candidate assessment, application strategy and program selection
- ☑ Brainstorming and selection of essay topics
- ☑ Outlining and essay structuring
- ☑ Unlimited essay editing
- ☑ Letter of recommendation advice
- ☑ Resume construction and review
- ☑ Interview preparation, mock interviews and feedback
- ☑ Post-acceptance and scholarship counseling

Monday Morning Essay Tip: Overrepresenting Your Overrepresentation

Many in the MBA application pool—particularly male investment bankers—worry that they are overrepresented. While you cannot change your work history, you can change the way you introduce yourself to admissions committees. Consider the following examples:

Example 1: "As an investment banking analyst at Bank of America, I am responsible for creating Excel models...."
Example 2: "At 5:30 pm, I could rest easy. The deadline for all other offers had passed. At that point, I knew...."

In the first example, the candidate starts off by mistakenly introducing the reader to the very over-representation that he/she should be trying to avoid emphasizing. In the second example, the banker immerses the reader in an unraveling mystery. This keeps the reader intrigued and focused on the applicant's story and actions rather than making the specific job title and responsibilities the center of the text. While each applicant's personal situation is different, every candidate can approach his/her story so as to mitigate the effects of overrepresentation.

To schedule a free consultation and read more than fifty Monday Morning Essay Tips, please visit our website:
www.mbamission.com